ORIENTAL PHILOSOPHIES
SECOND EDITION

ORIENTAL PHILOSOPHIES

SECOND EDITION

JOHN M. KOLLER
Rensselaer Polytechnic Institute

CHARLES SCRIBNER'S SONS · NEW YORK

TO JACK AND RUTH JOYCE

Copyright © 1970, 1985 Charles Scribner's Sons

Library of Congress Cataloging in Publication Data

Koller, John M.
  Oriental philosophies.

  Includes bibliographies and index.
  1. Philosophy, Oriental.   I. Title.
B121.K56   1985   181   84-20300
ISBN 0-684-18145-2
ISBN 0-02-365810-X (pbk)

1 3 5 7 9 11 13 15 17 19   F/C   20 18 16 14 12 10 8 6 4 2
1 3 5 7 9 11 13 15 17 19   F/P   20 18 16 14 12 10 8 6 4 2

PRINTED IN THE UNITED STATES OF AMERICA

Selections from *A Source Book in Chinese Philosophy*, translated and compiled by
Wing-tsit Chan (Copyright © 1963 by Princeton University Press; Princeton
Paperback, 1969), are reprinted by permission of Princeton University Press.

Contents

PART THREE: **CHINESE PHILOSOPHIES**

Preface

DURING THE FOURTEEN YEARS since the first edition of this book was published I have received numerous comments from readers suggesting changes to make in a new edition. I am delighted to have had this opportunity to revise the book, and grateful for the helpful suggestions I have received. Most of them have been incorporated into this second edition. The review questions that have been added at the end of each chapter were suggested by teachers using the book as a text in courses dealing with Oriental philosophies and Asian religions. The addition of an annotated reading list at the end of each chapter is a response to student suggestions. A new chapter, "Theistic Developments: Vishnu, Shiva, and Kali," has been added in response to many suggestions that new material be added explaining the philosophy of Hinduism. A considerable amount of new material has been added to chapter 3, explaining the main features of Vedic thought, and a fuller explanation of *yoga* has been provided in the fifth chapter. In chapter 9, I have added a section on the philosophy of Gandhi. The chapter on Zen has been rewritten to give a better sense of Zen thought and practice. In Part III, I have revised the chapters on Confucianism, Taoism, and Neo-Confucianism. And the final chapter has been expanded to include the thought of K'ang Yu-wei, Chang Tung-sun, Hsiung Shih-li, and Fung Yu-lan along with that of Mao Tse-tung.

My reasons for revising the book are the same as for writing it originally: to help readers understand the Asian mind, and to see how philosophical questions have been considered in the major Oriental traditions. My conviction that one of the most urgent tasks each of us faces is to construct a philosophy of life which reflects the wisdom of the Eastern as well as Western traditions is stronger than ever. If this new edition helps the reader in any way to construct such a personal philosophy my efforts will have been amply rewarded.

I take this opportunity to thank all who have contributed to this book. My students and my colleagues at Rensselaer Polytechnic Institute have challenged me to put forth my best effort. Comments from readers have helped me to see various issues more clearly and have led to many of the changes in this new edition. To my teachers, particularly Shri Krishna Saksena, Charles A. Moore, Kenneth Inada, and Chung-ying Cheng, I owe a great debt which I can only hope to repay through my own teaching. My greatest debt is to my wife, Patricia. Her love and encouragement over the years have sustained and nourished my life. Without her at my side I would have had neither the courage nor the strength to write and revise this book. Our children, John Thomas and Christy, have enriched our lives; I hope this book will help enrich theirs.

JOHN M. KOLLER
Troy, New York
June 26, 1984

Preface to the First Edition

THIS BOOK has been written with two basic aims in mind. First, it is intended to make possible an understanding and appreciation of Oriental thought and life. Second, it is intended to introduce the reader to certain fundamental and characteristic problems in philosophy as they are considered in the Oriental traditions. This is done in an attempt to make it possible for the reader to understand some of the answers given to the basic questions in life. The author is of the opinion that the traditions of Oriental philosophy are no less valuable and important than the traditions of Western philosophy. The assumption that a person can be introduced to philosophy only by considering the major thinkers and problems in the Western tradition is so obviously parochial that it is amazing that it continues almost completely unchallenged.

In the West philosophy is usually thought of in terms of the classical philosophers of the Western world. But in terms of understanding the nature of philosophy and philosophical problems there is no special advantage to studying philosophers who happen to have lived in the Western Hemisphere; geography is irrelevant here. Of course, there is an advantage in studying Western philosophers if the aim is not merely an understanding of the nature of philosophical activity and familiarity with certain philosophical positions, but also that of using the philosophical traditions as a means of understanding those ideas which have shaped the present condition of man in the Western Hemisphere. But by the same token, there is an advantage in studying the Oriental philosophers, for in addition to acquainting one with the nature of philosophy, one also gains understanding of the present condition of man in the Orient.

The reader who is accustomed to reading only Western philosophy will find it tempting to pigeonhole some of the material in this book as religion, or psychology, or even etiquette. He may dismiss certain areas of discussion (and the rest along with it) as "unphilosophical." But why should we force Western definitions of philosophy on the Orient? So far as I know, no one has ever demonstrated the superiority of Western concepts of philosophy over Oriental. And until this is done (if, indeed, it were possible!) Eastern thought should be studied within its own terms.

The important questions of life are no different for the Orient than for the West. Questions like, What is man? What is the nature of the universe in which man lives? In what does the good life consist? and, How can we know if the claims we make about the nature of man, the universe, and the good life are true? are basic philosophical questions, common to human beings the world over because they arise whenever and wherever man reflects upon his experience. Of course, these questions arise in different contexts and assume different forms for people living at different times and in different places, and the answers given may differ considerably. But these are the questions of man as man, arising out of the curiosity attending man's self-conscious nature and the innate urge to improve the conditions of his existence, and no human being can live without considering them. The question is not whether to answer or not answer these questions, but whether the answers will be explicit, thought-out, and well-argued, or whether they will be merely assumed, hidden, and implicit in the actions that constitute the history of a person.

On the easy assumption that an understanding of these questions as posed by philosophers and an analysis of the answers they have given will enable a person to understand and evaluate better the answers he or she gives to these questions, it seems obvious that it is important to know the forms and contexts of basic philosophical questions and answers, not just as they have appeared in the Western tradition, but as they have appeared in the whole philosophical tradition of man. This knowledge is needed to provide the imagination with the insights into man's experience which are required to provide an interpretation of experience that is worthy of the human animal. Ignoring the philosophical traditions of a majority of mankind and thereby depriving oneself of insights and knowledge needed for constructing a satisfactory philosophy of life is surely rash and unjustified.

The individual's need to construct for himself a philosophy of life is, I believe, imperative in our time. Therefore I have endeavored to make available to the lay reader some of the insights of the Oriental philosophers. To understand these ideas does not require any previous acquaintance with technical philosophy. Philosophical concepts and theories universally have their origin in, and depend for their justification and meaning upon, ordinary human experiences with which everyone is familiar. So it is possible, by tracing the relevant reflections on various aspects of experience, to show how a particular concept or theory developed, what it means, and how it can be justified. The present work not only does not assume prior acquaintance with philosophy, but should itself serve as an introduction.

These are among the reflections that have led to this attempt to provide an introduction to philosophy emphasizing the Oriental philosophical traditions. There is no doubt that in our own age we put our very existence in jeopardy by allowing ourselves to remain ignorant of at least half of the world. Never has the need been greater to come to an understanding of all the peoples of the world. Consequently, upon the assumption that to understand what a people have done and what they are likely to do it is necessary to understand their basic attitudes about life as reflected in their views of the nature of man, the good life, the nature of the universe, and the ways in which we can know reality, it is imperative that the philosophies of the Orient be studied and understood. Thus, the two functions which this book is intended to serve—to introduce the reader to an understanding of the Asian mind and to indicate the different ways in which fundamental philosophical questions have been considered in the Orient—grow out of the same basic concern, the concern to maintain and improve human existence.

ORIENTAL PHILOSOPHIES

SECOND EDITION

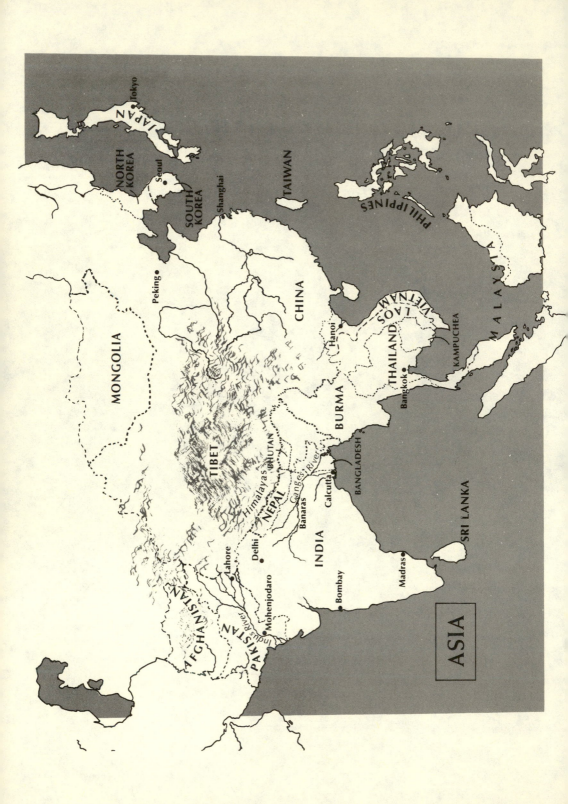

Introduction

THE STORY OF PHILOSOPHY is the story of human reflection on life. The problems of life are the source and touchstone of philosophy. If all of our practical needs were provided for and our human curiosity satisfied it is unlikely that there would be any philosophical activity in the world, for the two principal sources of philosophy are curiosity about self and the world and a desire to overcome all kinds of suffering. Practical needs and theoretical curiosity lead to philosophical activity because people are naturally self-reflective. We not only have needs and curiosity, but we are aware of ourselves having these needs and this curiosity. We see ourselves in the context of our surroundings as beings struggling to overcome suffering and trying to uncover the mysteries of existence. In this way we come to examine the kind of beings we are, the kind of world we live in, and the sources of value and knowledge that are so characteristic of our existence. It is the self-reflective activity that constitutes philosophy.

The fundamental questions of philosophy are, "Who am I?" and "How should I live?" As we reflect on our experience of life and confront the inevitability of our death, we cannot help but wonder about the meaning and value of life. Since our most important activities are aimed at preserving life and giving it value, it is natural to reflect on how we should live and who we are, developing ideas about the nature of human existence and the good life.

But how do we know these ideas are correct? Reflective thought calls each idea into question, seeking criteria against which to test its validity. In the process new ideas are generated, questioned, and either accepted or rejected. Seeking to know for sure who we are and how we should live, we not only reflect on our own experience, but we consider the ideas of others who have thought carefully about the fundamental questions of life.

Because these are the most important questions we can ask, we must challenge every proposed answer, testing it in every way we can to make sure it is reliable. Each formulation of the question and every aspect of every answer given must be examined from every side. Eventually even the criteria used to test our answers are challenged. How do we know when an answer is true? What is knowledge? How do we know that what we call knowledge is *really* knowledge?

Reflecting on what we know about our knowledge may seem very far removed from the ordinary problems of life. It is not enough that we ask a question or propose a solution; we must also attempt to justify the proposed solution as a satisfactory answer to the original question. If we discover that what we took to be knowledge was, in fact, opinion, perhaps mistaken opinion, then our whole theory which seemed to explain the meaning and value of life may have to change. And when it does, our orientation toward the good life—and our idea of the best means of achieving it—may also change. Could anything be more practical or closer to everyday life than that, even if it be abstract and subtle?

The charge is sometimes made that philosophers dwell in ivory towers, that they concentrate on logical subtleties and abstractions, ignoring the major concerns of life. There is, of course, the possibility that speculation may cease to be connected with the fundamental issues of life. When this happens philosophy loses much of its relevance; it no longer serves the ordinary person in reflecting upon his or her own existence in the world, failing to provide the materials needed for the construction of a personal philosophy of life. In the West we are accustomed, in large part, to thinking of philosophy as something apart from life, too abstract and academic for the ordinary person.

In the East the gap between the philosophers and the ordinary people is not nearly as great. Oriental philosophers keep closely in touch with life, returning to the touchstone of human experience to test their theories. The ordinary people stretch beyond their day-to-day concerns and struggle to see their existence in perspective, to understand it in philosophical terms.

This difference between East and West, which is, to be sure, a matter of degree, is due in part to the Oriental insistence on the wholeness of life and knowledge. Easterners tend to avoid cutting up and compartmentalizing life and knowledge. The result is that they do not separate the various fields of philosophy, such as theory of knowledge, theory of being, theory of art, theory of action, theory of political organization, etc. There is no clear-cut distinction between Eastern philosophy and Eastern religion, between philosophy and psychology, or philosophy and science. One consequence of this is the Oriental tendency to take philosophy seriously. Philosophy in the Orient is not an abstract academic matter with little or no relevance to daily life—it is regarded as life's most basic and most important enterprise.

In China, after Confucianism became the state philosophy, it was impossible to get a government job without knowing the works of Confucius. Chinese history tells of many kings, artists, and scholars who were philosophers. The Chinese regard thought and practice as inseparable from each other, as aspects of the same activity. The central problems of Chinese philosophy are reflected in the questions "How can I achieve harmony with all humanity?" and "How can I achieve a harmony with nature?"

These two questions turn out to be closely related, because as philosophy developed in China, there was an increasing tendency to identify nature with human nature. To the extent that this identification took place, the problem of achieving harmony with nature was the problem of being in harmony with oneself. In turn, being in harmony with oneself was regarded as the necessary basis for achieving a harmony with other people. Being in harmony with oneself and in harmony with the rest of humanity is "the highest good" in Chinese philosophy. Because the basic nature of man is seen as essentially moral, the dominant concern of much Chinese philosophy has been moral. The questions "How can I be good?" and "What is the basis of goodness?" are basic questions throughout the history of Chinese philosophy.

India is famous for the high regard it accords the seeker of wisdom and for its reverence and respect for wise persons. The accumulated practical wisdom of India takes the form of self-discipline (*yoga*) aimed at the total integration of life. In order that this discipline be available to all persons, it is channeled through the activities of worship and devotion, the activities of work, and the activities of knowledge and concentration. These paths of self-discipline are simply the philosophic wisdom of the ages being put into practice by the people. The source of this wisdom of self-discipline is to be found in that combination of deep, intense personal experience and highly abstract rational explanation which is so characteristic of the Indian mind.

Three thousand years ago, the sages of India were pondering the nature of the self, and the nature of ultimate reality. Pursuing these two questions the philosophers of the Upanishads came to the wonderful realization that in our deepest being we are one with the ultimate nature of reality. The immediate practical problem arising from this discovery was how to realize this inner Self and thereby identify with the very essence of the universe. The search for an answer prompted a variety of developments in *yoga* and religion as well as the construction of moral and social philosophies. The theoretical problems raised by this discovery centered around the difficulty of relating the multiplicity and diversity of experienced reality with the Upanishadic insight into the unity of all existence. Furthermore it was difficult to ascertain how knowledge of such an ultimate reality could be achieved. These problems—which can be formulated in terms of questions about the basis of morality, the nature and function of society, the means of valid knowledge, the principles of logic, and the relation between appearance and reality—all have a common basis in the practical question "How can we achieve the spirituality that is our true nature?"

In Buddhist Asia millions have embraced the teachings of the wisdom-seeking Gautama Siddhartha as the solution to all of life's sufferings. The central problem of Buddhism is that of overcoming suffering. The essential teachings of the Buddha revolve around the questions, What is suffering? How does it arise? How can suffering be eliminated? and, How should we live so as to achieve a suffering-less existence? These questions, however, cannot be answered without inquiring into the nature of the self that suffers and the nature of the world that constitutes a source of suffering for the self. The question, How is suffering caused? leads to a general theory of causation which shapes the theories of self and reality which constitute Buddhist metaphysics. The problems of justifying the claims made about the nature of the self and the nature of reality lead to a general theory of logic and knowledge. Thus, the eminently practical problem of overcoming suffering provokes the reflections that constitute the theoretical principles of Buddhist philosophy.

Despite the many differences between the philosophies of India, China, and Buddhist Asia, they share a common concern with living and being as well as with learning and knowing. Consequently, philosophy and the philosophers have primary importance in all Oriental cultures. In order to understand the life and the attitudes of the Oriental peoples, it is necessary to understand their philosophies. In order to understand their philosophies, it is necessary to look to the traditions in which these philosophies developed and through which they continue to nourish the cultures of Asia.

PART ONE

THE HINDU
SYSTEMS

Dancing Shiva. *Courtesy of Bob Del Bonta; photograph by Robert R. Johnston.*

CHAPTER 1

Dominant Features of Indian Philosophy

THE STORY OF Indian philosophy is long and exciting. From its beginnings in the speculations of the Vedic seers thousands of years ago to the present, Indian philosophical thought presents a richness, subtlety, and variety which constitute an awesome testimony to the human spirit. Practically every insight and shade of speculation known is found in Indian thought. This richness and complexity makes it impossible to summarize Indian philosophy with simple generalizations. Nevertheless, certain dominant features can be identified on the basis of their endurance, their popularity with philosophers, or their widespread importance in the lives of a majority of the people.

Next to its richness and comprehensiveness, the most striking feature of Indian philosophical thought is its practical character. From the very beginning, the speculations of India's sages grew out of attempts to improve life. Confronted with physical, mental, and spiritual suffering, Indian philosophers sought to understand the reasons and causes for this suffering. They attempted to improve their understanding of human nature and the universe because they wanted to uproot the causes of suffering and to achieve the best possible life. The solutions achieved—and the reasons for the conclusions underlying these solutions—constitute the philosophies of these early sages.

India's philosophies respond to both practical and speculative motivations. Practically, there was the acquaintance with ordinary forms of suffering—disease, hunger, loneliness, and the knowledge that ultimately death would overtake the sufferer. Speculatively, there was the innate human curiosity to understand and to order experience. Practical considerations motivated the search for ways to overcome the various forms of suffering. Speculative considerations led to construction of explanatory accounts of the nature of reality and of human existence. But these considerations were not undertaken separately. The understanding and knowledge derived from speculative curiosity was utilized in the attempt to overcome suffering.

The primacy of the practical considerations involved in Indian philosophies gives them substance, while the necessity of the speculative considerations determines their structure. Consequently, though the practical problems involved in determining the nature of the good life—including the social life—are always in the fore, the theoretical explanations—concerning the nature of self, reality, and knowledge—used to justify proposed solutions to the practical problems have great importance in Indian philosophies.

Two fundamentally different approaches to the problem of suffering are possible. Both approaches recognize that suffering is the result of a gap between what one is and has, and what one wants to be and wants to have. A man is poor; wanting the wealth he lacks, he suffers. A man desires deathlessness though he knows death is inevitable; fearing this inevitability, he suffers. If there were no difference between what one is and has, and what one wants to be and to have, there would be no suffering. When there is a difference, suffering is inevitable. This being the case, the solution to the problem is obvious: what is and what is desired must be made identical.

But how can this identity be achieved? One approach to the solution lies in adjusting what one is and has to what is desired. If a man is poor but desires wealth, he should endeavor to accumulate wealth. The other approach consists in adjusting one's desires to what one has. If one is poor and desires wealth, the resulting problem can be overcome by removing the desire.

It should be noted here that many shades of compromise between the two approaches are possible. If, theoretically, a pure form of each approach is possible, in practice there is always a compromise: the analyst can only observe how the emphasis falls upon one or the other. Basically it is the second approach that Indian philosophy has taken. India chose to emphasize control of desires. As a result, the philosophies of India tend to insist on self-discipline and self-control as prerequisite to happiness and the good life. Self-control rather than the satiation of desires is the basic way to eliminate suffering.

This need to regulate and control desires threw extraordinary emphasis on knowledge of the self: knowing and controlling the self could do far more than the sciences of nature to alleviate suffering. Consequently, the practice of Indian philosophy became, at best, the art of living in complete control of oneself.

The practical character of Indian philosophy is manifested in a variety of ways. The very word which is usually translated "philosophy" points to this. *Darshana* literally means vision. It is what is seen. In its technical sense it means what is seen when ultimate reality is investigated. The seers of India, seeking the solution to life's sufferings, investigated the conditions of suffering and examined the nature of human life and the world to find the causes of suffering and the means for its cessation. What they found constituted their *darshana*, their vision or philosophy.

Of course it is possible to be mistaken in one's vision; one may not see things as they really are. Consequently, the philosopher's vision must be justified by providing evidence of its truth. Historically, two methods of justifying philosophical visions are encountered. According to the first method, logical analysis is used to determine whether or not a particular view is justified. If the concepts and statements expressing the vision are inconsistent with each other the vision may be discarded as self-contradictory. For example, if according to the vision in question it is claimed that all things that are born must die, and if it is also held that man is born but will not die, then the vision contains two views which are incompatible with each other. Obviously, the vision cannot be accepted without somehow overcoming this internal inconsistency, for one cannot at the same time accept as true both the claim "all born things die," and the claim "not all born things die," for these claims are contradictory.

But suppose that several visions, each consistent within itself, are mutually incompatible. For example, one vision consistently maintains that all born things die, and the other vision consistently maintains that nothing that is born dies. What reasons are there for preferring one over another? Logic alone is not enough to determine this, for the question is not primarily one of consistency.

The second method, in recognition of the insufficiency of logic alone, is pragmatic, finding the justification of views or theories in the quality of resulting practice. Indian philosophers have always insisted that practice is the ultimate test of truth. Philosophical visions must be put into practice and life lived according to the ideals of the vision. The quality of the life lived according to those ideals is the ultimate test of any vision. The better life becomes, the closer the vision approaches complete truth.

The criteria for determining the quality of life are, in turn, derived from the basic impetus for philosophy: the drive to eliminate suffering. The vision that makes possible a life devoid of suffering is properly called a true philosophy. Degrees of philosophic truth are determined according to the degree of alleviation of suffering. Put in a positive way, views are true according to the extent they improve the quality of life.

Placing the positive emphasis for justification of a philosophy on experience rather than logic (though logic is not excluded) requires putting philosophy into practice. In India, this has meant the working-out of a way to the realization of the good life wherein suffering is eliminated. The path is part of the vision, and if the way to the realization of the goals of the vision cannot be followed the vision is itself regarded as inadequate. "Good in theory, but not in practice," is a remark that makes no sense when applied to Indian philosophies. Good in theory necessarily means good in practice.

The identification of the way to the good life with the vision of the good life itself is the integrating factor between religion and philosophy in India. When philosophy is regarded as being concerned only with the *theory* of the good life, concern with the practical means of attaining the good life is not considered philosophical. The means of life may then be regarded as falling within the religious or economic spheres, but not the philosophical. When the good life is thought to be "at a higher level" than this ordinary life, the means of achieving it are usually thought of as religious. When a materialistic view of the good life prevails, the means of achieving it are often thought to be economic. In neither case does the matter lie within the philosopher's domain—if religion and economics are practical matters and philosophy is theoretical, the consequent differences of scope, goal, and approach will sharply delineate one approach from another. But in India a philosopher's theory of the good life has to be tested by practice, and the philosopher must devise a means for achieving the good life in order to be a philosopher. No sharp distinction exists between theory and practice; philosophy and religion are not considered to be two separate activities.

The Indian insistence upon practice as a test of philosophical truth has had another effect—an emphasis on the introspective approach. To overcome suffering, a person must engage in a process of self-examination, through which the interior conditions of life can be understood. This necessitates a deep and constant self-awareness.

Since Indian philosophy is concerned primarily with the suffering of human beings, the human subject is of greater importance than the objects that come within the experience of the subject. The self that suffers is always the subject. To treat it otherwise is to regard it as a thing, a mere object. The ultimate self is described in the philosophical literature as pure subject, or subject which can never become object—"The one without a second." It is the qualitative experience of the subject that is of fundamental concern in Indian thought.

Above all, Indian philosophy is concerned with finding ways to liberate the self from bondage to fragmented and limited modes of existence—a bondage that causes suffering. According to the Upanishads, the great power (*Brahman*) that energizes the cosmos and the spiritual energy of the self (*Atman*) are ultimately the same. This vision of the identity of self with ultimate reality provides the foundation for the methods of liberation which constitute the practical core of Indian philosophy. It is a vision which sees the various distinct things and processes of the world as manifestations of a deeper reality that is undivided and unconditioned. Within this undivided wholeness are different levels of reality, distinguished by the degree to which they participate in the truth and being of ultimate reality. Because of this unity of existence, the powers needed to achieve liberation are available to every person. But a person must become aware of these powers and the means to harness them for the task of attaining liberation. Hence knowledge, especially self-knowledge, is of supreme importance.

The emphasis on the self means that relevant philosophical criteria are not primarily quantitative and public. Rather they belong to self as subject. Therefore it is impossible for one person to subscribe to one "true" philosophy and to regard the others as completely false. Truth in philosophy depends upon the human subject, and another's experience can be known only as an object. There is no knowing—according to ordinary ways of knowing, at least—the other as subject. Consequently, there is no rejecting the other's experience as inadequate or unsatisfactory. Recognition of this has led to a tolerant synthetic attitude which is commonly expressed by saying that while it may be that no vision, by itself, is absolutely true and complete, nevertheless, each vision contains some glimpse of the truth. By respecting the viewpoints and experiences assumed by the various visions, one comes closer to the absolute truth and the complete vision. Philosophical progress is not made by proceeding from falsehood to truth, but by proceeding from partial to more complete truth.

In addition to these features of Indian philosophy which stem from its practical orientation, there is a widespread tendency in Indian thought to presuppose universal moral justice. The world is seen as a great moral stage directed by justice. Everything good, bad, and indifferent is earned and deserved. The impact of this attitude is to place the responsibility for the human condition squarely upon human beings themselves. We are responsible for what we are and what we become. We ourselves have determined our past and will determine our future, according to Indian thought. In the sacred writings, the Vedas, the concept of *rita* (moral law) denoted justice as the ruler of the universe. As human duties in response to justice came to be emphasized, the concept of *dharma* as determined by the moral structure of the universe became dominant. The concept of *karma* came to refer to the relation between what one did and what one was, pointing, as it did, to the causal efficacy of human actions, standing as a principle of self-determination.

There is also rather widespread agreement in Indian philosophical thought concerning non-attachment. Suffering results from attaching oneself to what one does not have or even to what one cannot have. These attached objects then become the causes of suffering insofar as they are not attained or are lost. Therefore, if a spirit of non-attachment to the objects of suffering could be cultivated the suffering itself could be eliminated. Thus, non-attachment is recognized as an essential means to the realization of the good life.

Because of the above features of Indian thought, the people of India have usually accorded the highest respect to the philosopher, and philosophy has been regarded as the highest knowledge and wisdom.

REVIEW QUESTIONS

1. How did confrontation with physical, mental, and spiritual suffering lead to philosophical thought in India?
2. Why is knowledge, especially self-knowledge, regarded as the ultimate philosophical achievement?
3. Where does Indian thought place responsibility for the human condition?
4. What are the criteria that a successful philosophical theory must satisfy?

FURTHER READING

The Indian Mind: Essentials of Indian Philosophy and Culture, edited by Charles A. Moore (Honolulu: University of Hawaii Press, 1967), is a collection of essays by leading Indian philosophers. The topics range from social and legal thought to logic and metaphysics, but all aim at presenting what is basic to traditional Indian thought in a way that will be intelligible to the Western reader.

The Indian Way by John M. Koller (New York: Macmillan Publishing Co., 1982) is an exploration of the basic features of India's philosophical and religious thought. The seventeen chapters cover major historical developments from the Vedas up to the present time, demonstrating the continuity of basic ideas and values. My aim throughout is to show that these ideas and values are both philosophical and religious; that they have inspired the Indian heart as well as the Indian mind.

CHAPTER 2

Historical Survey of Indian Philosophy

INDIAN PHILOSOPHY has a long history. The first bits of speculation which could be called "philosophical" are from the Rig Veda, which may have been composed as early as 1500 B.C. Since those beginnings, now dimmed and obscured by time, India has acquired a vast wealth of philosophical vision, speculation, and argument. It is difficult to approach Indian philosophy chronologically, however, for Indian history is full of uncertainties with respect to names, dates, and places. In India so much emphasis has been put on the content of the thought and so little on person, place, and time that in many instances it is not known who is responsible for the particular philosophy in question. And when the author is unknown, the time and the place can be reckoned only indirectly. Because of this, time is usually reckoned in terms of centuries rather than years or decades, and authorship is attributed to schools rather than to individual persons. Nevertheless, it is possible to see changes in philosophical thinking occurring in a certain sequence. That is, it is possible to see the antecedents and successors of various philosophical problems and solutions.

The historical approach is facilitated by adopting a generally agreed upon classification of periods in the development of the philosophical traditions in India. The Vedic period stretches from about 1500 B.C. to 700 B.C. The Epic period occurred between 800 B.C. and 200 A.D. The Sutra period lasted from about 400 B.C. to 500 A.D. The Commentary period commenced about 400 A.D. and continued until about 1700 A.D. The Renaissance period, still in progress, began around 1800 A.D.

The Vedic Period: The Vedic age began when the Aryan peoples moved from Central Asia into the Indus Valley, around 1500 B.C. The cultural traditions they brought with them mingled with the traditions and customs of the people they met, and what can properly be called Indian culture began to take shape. Its growth was nourished by the climates and conditions of two earlier cultures.

The philosophical fruit of this early period is contained in the collection of writings called the Upanishads, which represent the culmination of philosophical speculation of this first period. The earlier literature, the Vedic Samhitas, Brahmanas, and Aranyakas, is for the most part, religious. Finding themselves in a new land, in many ways cut off from their familiar routines of life, these Aryan newcomers formulated questions about themselves, the world around them, and their place in it. What is speech? What is its source? What makes the wind blow? Who put the sun—giver of warmth and light—in the sky? And how is it that broad-bosomed earth brings forth these myriad life-forms? These are typical of the questions entertained in the early portions of the Vedic period—questions which at first received answers attributing all these things, both wonderful and terrible, to the gods.

Questions of how and why are the roots of philosophical speculation. At first thinkers tried to answer these questions in terms of the human person, and they attributed events in nature to superhuman persons, or gods. This tended to encourage religious thought rather than strictly philosophical speculation. Inquiring minds, however, continued to probe into the whys of nature and man, so in addition to developing the Vedic ritual and worship found in the Sama and the Yajur Vedas, they also developed the cognitive inquiry which is the spirit of philosophy. This is attested to by the literature of the Aranyakas and the Upanishads. Not only is a universal law of cause and effect called *rita* identified as the basic norm of existence, but by the time of the Upanishads that most wonderful of all discoveries already had been made—the discovery that the ultimate source and power of all existence is identical with one's ultimate self.

The literature of this period (all of it termed Veda) can be divided into the following categories: *Rig Veda, Sama Veda, Yajur Veda,* and *Atharva Veda.* Each of the first three Vedas contain hymns to the gods as well as various questions (the *Samhita* portion), arrangements of the *Samhita* portion for use in sacrifices (the *Brahmana* portion), interpretations of the rituals (*Aranyaka* portion), and speculations on the basic questions underlying religious thought and practice (the *Upanishads.*) Though all of this literature was composed prior to 700 B.C. it has exerted a very great influence on the people of India right up to our own times.

The Epic Period: The wisdom of the Vedic literature was part of a sacred and jealously guarded tradition, often unavailable to many members of the society or, where available, beyond understanding. To compensate for this there grew up a folklore recited in stories and poems which managed to transmit many of the ideals of the sacred tradition to the majority of the people. The two most notable collections of materials constituting this literature are the *Mahabharata* and the *Ramayana.*

The *Mahabharata* is an epic of considerable length (the English translation runs to thirteen volumes). It tells the story of the conquest of the land of India, and in so doing provides instruction for the various rules of life. It offers a guide to life in all its dimensions, including religion, philosophy, social science, politics, and even medicine. The single most influential part of the *Mahabharata* is the *Bhagavad Gita*, "The Song of the Great One." The *Gita* explains the nature of humanity and the universe, and from the explanation of matter and spirit are derived ways of life which will enable one to achieve the ultimately good life.

The *Ramayana*, a beautiful poem in four volumes, presents ideals for womanhood and manhood in the persons and lives of Sita, and her husband, Rama. The epic suggests an ideal order for society as a whole, and also an ideal ordering of the life of the individual.

During this period treatises on justice and righteousness—the *Dharma Shastras*—were compiled. These treatises were concerned primarily with regulating the life of the individual and the society with respect to specific codes of actions, which were presented along with their justification in the literature on *dharma*. The *Artha Shastra* of Kautilya justifies the need for and the importance of the various means of life and shows how they may be obtained. The *Manu Shastra* shows how justice and order may be secured in society by the king and the institutions of government. The *Shastra* of Yajnavalkya emphasizes justice and order in the life of the individual. The *Kama Shastra* (sometimes translated as *Kama Sutra*) of Vatsyayana deals with the attainment of pleasure. These are among the more influential of these treatises.

No doubt it was also during this time that the beginnings of the various systems of philosophy were established, for there are references in the *Mahabharata* to certain of the systems. But these systems did not receive definitive form until near the end of the Epic period.

The Sutra Period: The beginnings of several systematic philosophical explanations of the world and human nature were already established by 400 B.C. These systems represent the first purely philosophical effort in India, for not only did they attempt to explain the fundamentals of life and the world, but they did so self-consciously and self-critically, arguing for the correctness of the answers suggested on the basis of reason.

The *Sutras*, or aphorisms, of Buddhism, Jainism, and Carvaka are designated *nastika*, or unorthodox, because their authors did not accept the pronouncements of the Vedas as true and final. Neither did they endeavor to justify their analyses and solutions by showing them to be in accord with the Vedas. The aphorisms expressing the philosophies of the Schools of Nyaya, Vaishesika, Samkhya, Yoga, Mimamsa, and Vedanta, on the other hand, all accept the authority of the Vedas. These schools are all concerned to show that their analyses and solutions do indeed agree with the pronouncements of the Vedas. Consequently varying "orthodox" interpretations of the Vedas came about; each school's claim for its views was demonstrated by agreement with the "correct" interpretation of those teachings.

The major division, however, is between Carvaka and the others. Carvaka is a completely materialistic system; all the others allow for spirituality: Nyaya is concerned primarily with a logical analysis of the means of knowing; Vaishesika analyzes the kinds of things that are known; Samkhya seeks to relate the self to the external world; Yoga analyzes the nature of the self and explains how the pure Self can be realized; Mimamsa concentrates on the criteria for the self-validity of knowledge, attempting thereby to establish the truth of the Vedic pronouncements; Vedanta begins with the conclusions of the Upanishads and attempts to show that a rational analysis of knowledge and reality will support those conclusions.

Period of the Great Commentaries: As generations of seers and scholars studied and examined the *sutras* of the various schools, they occasionally wrote commentaries on them. In this way the great commentaries of Gaudapada (sixth century A.D.), Shamkara (eighth century A.D.), Bhaskara (ninth century A.D.), Yamuna (tenth century A.D.), Ramanuja (eleventh century A.D.), Nimbarka (twelfth century A.D.), Madhva (thirteenth century A.D.), and Vallabha (fifteenth century A.D.), came to be written on the Vedanta *Sutras* of Badarayana.

The Renaissance Period: As a result of outside influences, especially contact with the West, Indian philosophers began to reexamine their philosophical traditions. Beginning with the studies, translations, and commentaries of Ram Mohun Roy in the nineteenth century, this renewal of ancient traditions has flourished in the last century. Gandhi, Tagore, Ramakrishna, Aurobindo, Vivekananda, and Radhakrishnan are among the more influential of India's Renaissance thinkers.

REVIEW QUESTIONS

1. What are the main periods in the development of Indian philosophy? Briefly characterize the literature of each of these periods, and describe the main differences between periods.
2. What is the basis for the distinction between the "orthodox" and "unorthodox" systems? In what sense is the distinction between Carvaka and all the other systems fundamental?

FURTHER READING

A History of Indian Philosophy, volumes 1–5, by Surendranath Dasgupta (Cambridge: Cambridge University Press, 1922–1955), is a classic in the field. It is a work of great learning, covering most of India's philosophical thinkers in sufficient depth to give the reader a good sense of major continuities and discontinuities in the history of Indian thought.

Indian Philosophy, volumes 1–2, by Sarvepalli Radhakrishnan (London: Allen and Unwin, 1923), has been the most widely used history of Indian philosophy. The sections on the Upanishads and Vedanta are especially good, but all of the major developments through the eleventh century are covered.

CHAPTER 3

The Vedas and Upanishads

INDIAN PHILOSOPHY has its beginnings in the speculations of the Vedas, texts of wisdom that in their earliest portions date from 1500 B.C. These texts have inspired Indian philosophers throughout the ages, and commentaries on them continue to be written right up to the present time. The oldest text is the *Rig Veda*, which means "verses of wisdom." It is the single most important literary source of Indian religion and culture. Attached to Vedas, as their concluding parts, are a group of texts known as Upanishads. These texts, composed between 800 and 500 B.C., are filled with reflective and speculative thought about the nature of self and reality, providing the foundations for later philosophical thinking. In this chapter we will explore the visions of self and reality contained in this literature, focusing on the main ideas of the *Rig Veda* and key philosophical concepts of some of the earlier Upanishads.

It must be understood, however, that despite their antiquity, the Vedic texts are not the expressions of a primitive people. The thoughts expressed in the Vedas and Upanishads are both profound and subtle, the result of centuries of reflective thought about the deepest mysteries of life. They provide insights into the processes of life that constitute a timeless testament of human wisdom, enabling these texts to inspire and nurture Indian culture right up to the present time.

Indus Culture

The material culture of ancient India was also highly sophisticated. Nearly a thousand years before the Aryan sages who composed the Vedas descended into the Indus valley, it was the home of a complex urban culture known as Indus Valley civilization. Indus civilization probably began shortly after 3000 B.C. in the lower Indus river valley. By 2000 B.C. it occupied an area approximately one-third the size of India, reaching north to the Himalayas, south almost to Bombay, and from the western coast east as far as Delhi.

One of its largest cities, Mohenjo Daro, reveals something of this civilization's sophistication. Mohenjo Daro had a population of about 40,000 people in 2000 B.C. Clearly designed with attention to central planning, its paved brick streets were laid out in a rectangular grid pattern. Huge graneries provided ample food storage for the people and livestock. Its ceramic tiled underground water and drainage systems represent a marvelous engineering accomplishment. The degree of standardization achieved indicates the efficiency of their departments of planning and administration, suggesting that the people of the Indus had a highly efficient centralized social and political organization.

Fine jewelry reveals the presence of skilled craftsmen, and the great variety of beautiful toys and games suggests a culture that valued play and delighted in children. An accurate system of weights and measures, utilizing an efficient binary and decimal system of mathematical combination, reflects both the culture's mathematical accomplishments and its emphasis on trade. Trade was probably extensive, as numerous Indus seals, used to mark ownership, have been found as far away as Mesopotamia.

It is only natural to assume that the sophisticated material culture of Indus civilization was matched by an equally sophisticated system of social and religious thought. This, however, must remain merely an assumption, for no written records are available which would constitute evidence of literary, religious, or philosophical accomplishments. The material clues found in the hundreds of sites that have been identified since Sir John Marshall first discovered the Indus civilization sixty years ago, suggest that religion played a major role in this culture. Even the smaller towns and villages have large ceremonial buildings, and numerous masks, suggesting a priesthood, have been found. Female figurines emphasizing pregnancy and nourishment suggest worship of a mother goddess, and the prevalence of figures of bulls and other male animals indicate a religious preoccupation with fertility. The elaborate bathing facilities indicate a concern for religious purification. Figures in yogic postures on seals suggest that yoga may have roots in this early civilization, and support the hypothesis that later Indian culture represents a wedding of Indus and Aryan cultures.

The fact remains, however, that from 1500 B.C. on, the subcontinent gradually came to be "Aryanized," as Aryan influence spread east and south from the Indus valley. By the fourth century B.C., with the establishment of the Mauryan empire, practically the whole subcontinent was under Aryan political control. The Sanskrit language, of which the Vedas are the oldest surviving expression, became the primary vehicle of Indian thought. Although the Sanskrit tradition reflects borrowing and accommodations from non-Aryan sources, it hides more of these contributions than it reveals, being primarily Aryan in style and content. Thus, despite the grandeur of Indus civilization, it is to the Vedas that we must turn for an understanding of earliest Indian thought.

Vedic Thought

The Vedas are verses of wisdom that form the core of India's sacred liturgy. The Vedas themselves tell us that when these verses are recited, chanted, and sung, they enable all creation to share in the wisdom and energy of the divine reality. They are seen as a kind of knowing-acting capable of overcoming fragmentation and alienation in a process that unites all beings, filling life with sacred energy.

The tradition regards the Vedic wisdom as timeless and authorless. This wisdom is revealed to the hearts of great persons whose experience has reached the inner core of existence. It is timeless because it was revealed to the very first human beings even as it is revealed today to all whose experience plumbs the depths of life. It is authorless because it is not revealed by persons but by reality itself. The *Rig Veda*, as the oldest collection of these verses of wisdom, is regarded as the fountainhead of Indian spirituality. For more than three thousand years it has inspired the Indian tradition.

Most of the Vedic verses are addressed to gods and goddesses and have a central liturgical function. But this does not mean that they are merely hymns for worship or ritual incantation. Some go much deeper, presenting profound and subtle visions of reality. Indeed, the various deities addressed in these verses are not simply anthropomorphic beings, but symbols of the fundamental powers of existence. Speech, consciousness, life, water, wind, and fire—these are among the auspicious powers symbolized as deities in the Vedas. They represent the powers that create and destroy life, that control the ebb and flow of existence.

Agni, for example, one of the principal Vedic deities, is the god of fire. The word *agni* means "fire," and Agni is the symbol of fire's awesome power. Out of control, the raging flames destroy homes and forests, killing people and animals. But under control, the fire in the hearth transforms raw flesh and vegetation into food, providing energy for life. Like lightning, fire pierces heaven and earth, joining them into a cosmic unity. So awesome and mysterious is fire that Agni became lord of the great rituals of sacrificial celebrations symbolizing the renewal of existence. That nearly one-third of the *Rig Veda* hymns are addressed to Agni is testament to the importance attached to the transforming power of fire in Vedic times.

Indra, perhaps the chief god of an earlier age, is the most humanlike of the Vedic deities. As lord of the thunderbolt, Indra vanquishes enemies and protects his people. He defeats the cosmic forces of chaos and darkness, making way for creative forms of existence. But above all, the Indra that is mentioned more often than any other deity in the *Rig Veda* symbolizes the courage and strength humans need to resist their enemies and to protect family and community.

Vac, whose name means "speech," is the goddess of communication. She represents not only words, but the underlying consciousness that makes speech possible. The Vedic people understood the awesome power of speech; they knew that it transforms worlds and commands life and death. So they symbolized this power as the goddess of communication, a lovely lady adorned with bright consciousness and fair words.

Other Vedic deities are similar. They symbolize the most fundamental cosmic and human powers experienced in personal form, enabling the Vedic people to enter into relationships with them. These relationships with the personal symbolic powers of life brought the most profound dimensions of cosmic and human existence into the texture of everyday Vedic life.

Although the Vedic deities symbolize the powers of existence, they are usually not thought of as the creators of existence. Indeed, the idea of a creator separate from the universe itself is foreign to the *Rig Veda*. Both the intelligence and the material stuff of the universe are regarded as contained within existence itself and inseparable from each other. Because existence was seen to be inherently intelligent, the universe was seen as a well-ordered whole. The order present in physical regularities goes much deeper, reaching right to the heart of existence. This deep order, providing norms for the expression of existence, moral, psychic, aesthetic, religious, physical—is known as *rita.* As the essential rhythm and structuring of existence, *rita* is more fundamental than the gods, for they too are subject to demands.

Although *rita* is more fundamental than the gods and goddesses, it answers the question, "How does existence function?" not, "What is its source?" When the Vedic seers turned to the question of the origin of existence they found no words or thoughts with which to formulate an answer. If existence is said to come from prior existence, the question of origins is not answered, but simply pushed back to a prior stage. But to claim that existence issued from nonexistence flies in the face of experience and common sense, for how can something be created by nothing? In the famous creation hymn of the tenth book of the *Rig Veda* (10.129), the seer struggles mightily to discern the origins of existence. As the following translation reveals, after indicating that the limitations of "is" and "is not," of existence and nonexistence, must be left behind, he concludes that perhaps the primordial source is unknowable.

HYMN OF ORIGINS

1. In the beginning there was neither existence nor nonexistence;
   Neither the world nor the sky beyond.
   What was covered over? Where? Who gave it protection?
   Was there water, deep and unfathomable?

2. Then was neither death nor immortality,
   Nor any sign of night or day.
   THAT ONE breathed, without breath, by its own impulse;
   Other than that was nothing at all.

3. There was darkness, concealed in darkness,
   And all this was undifferentiated energy.
   THAT ONE, which had been concealed by the void,
   Through the power of heat-energy was manifested.

4. In the beginning was love,
   Which was the primal germ of the mind.
   The seers, searching in their hearts with wisdom,
   Discovered the connection between existence and nonexistence.

5. They were divided by a crosswise line.
   What was below and what was above?

There were bearers of seed and mighty forces,
Impulse from below and forward movement from above.

6. Who really knows? Who here can say?
   When it was born and from where it came—this creation?
   The Gods are later than this world's creation—
   Therefore who knows from where it came?

7. That out of which creation came,
   Whether it held it together or did not,
   He who sees it in the highest heaven,
   Only He knows—or perhaps even He does not know!

                                          (*10.129 my translation*)

These verses, taken from a relatively late portion of the *Rig Veda*, display familiarity with earlier attempts to locate the origins of existence. But here the seer is attempting to reach what is absolutely primordial, beyond all distinctions and differences. Because existence and nonexistence are opposed to each other, the seer assumes that there must be a prior reality which is the source of this pair of opposites. The very opposition between them points to their prior unity, just as, for example, if a fruit were divided into halves, these two parts would suggest a prior wholeness. It is the undivided wholeness of reality that the seer is seeking as source of all existence and nonexistence.

However, since conceptual thought is rooted in the absolute difference between *is* and *is not*, the quest for the primordial, undivided reality cannot be purely conceptual. Thus we see the poet struggle within the confining limitations of *is* and *is not*. Yet his words point beyond these limits, suggesting both the inadequacy of language and the profundity of what lies beyond that which can be said.

What was there before existence and nonexistence? asks the seer. Myths about how existence was covered over with water or how it was protected by some greater power do not go to the heart of the matter. But in his efforts to go beyond the dualities that separate death from immortality, night from day, and breath from the breather, the seer finds no room for either denials or assertions. Beyond *is* and *is not*, the inquiring mind finds only darkness; darkness concealed in darkness.

Perhaps in love, which goes beyond the mind, is to be found the primordial reality. The roots of existence are to be found in love, a power that unites opposites into a new, creative whole. Thus, in verse 4, the poet suggests that in love the forces of existence and nonexistence join together to give birth to all the things of the world. But he recognizes that this does not explain the origins of existence and nonexistence, but only their co-production of the world. So who knows this secret? Who can penetrate the fundamental mystery of life? The hymn concludes by suggesting that not even "He who sees it in the highest heaven," is capable of this knowledge. The implicit suggestion is that human beings must remain open to this mystery, participating in the processes of self-renewal through which the undivided wholeness of reality is realized in everyday life.

The discovery that there is a fundamental reality beyond the grasp of logic and language constitutes one of the great insights of the Vedas. Undivided and unnameable, That One constitutes the ground and energy of all existence. Coupled with the insight that this primordial reality functions in an essentially orderly way, according to *rita*, this discovery enabled the Vedic people to see themselves as part of a well-ordered universe. By participating in this divine order through the ritual actions of sacrificial celebration (*yajna*), they found a way to share in the continuous renewal of existence.

The Vedic vision rests on the profound philosophical insights that reality is ultimately an undivided whole, and that this whole is essentially a well-ordered process. Because they are concerned primarily with the achievement of wholeness in life through religious practice, the Vedas are generally regarded as religious, rather than philosophical, texts.

It is not a simple matter to distinguish between religion and philosophy. In the main, it can be said that philosophical thought is free—free to go in whatever direction experience leads, without the restrictions of predetermined truth. The early portions of the Vedas were philosophical to the extent that the experiences and reflections of the seers led to their conclusions about the nature of reality. But when those answers came to be regarded as absolute and final, thinkers were no longer free to continue the quest; they were limited to the framework imposed by the attitude which regarded earlier answers as definitive.

Another feature of philosophical thought is that it is self-critical, ever aware that claimed answers depend for their truth upon the justifying evidence produced. Here again, the bulk of early Vedic thought appears non-philosophical, for the question of evidence for the truth of the various claims upon which the religious practices rested did not, for the most part, arise.

The Upanishads

The concluding portions of the Vedas, known as the Upanishads, are much more philosophical than the preceding portions, for they are free from the restrictions of predetermined truth. They contain a recognition of the need to supply evidence for their claims, and they are concerned with the fundamental principles of existence. Nevertheless, even they are not philosophical in the full sense of that term, for they proceed without any formal analysis of the criteria of truth and the relation between truth and evidence. For the most part, personal experience of what is claimed is taken as sufficient evidence for the truth of the claim, but there is no attempt to show how it is that certain kinds of experience can count as evidence for claims about reality. And while there is general recognition that self-contradictory views cannot be true, it would be going too far to suggest that reason determined the truth or falsity of views, for the principles of logic and reason had not been formally worked out.

Consequently, the Upanishads tend to emphasize the content of the vision of the seer more than the means whereby the vision can be justified. The claims in the Upanishads are taken to be the reports of the experience of the seers, and not philosophical theories waiting to be justified. It is the experience of the seers that provides the evidence for the truth of the claims being made.

The key question of the Upanishads is, "What is the true nature of ultimate reality?" This question presupposes that there is a difference between what *appears* to be real and what is really real; appearance is not taken to be sufficient for its own existence, but is thought to depend on some higher reality. The search was not for the world of space and time, filled with sound, odors, colors, etc., which *appears* to us as our world, but for the *conditions* that make possible this appearing world.

The distinction is analogous to the distinction made between the colors one sees and the conditions which make possible the seeing of colors. One might say that what one sees are the various colors of the spectrum, taking the colors to be something that exist in the world. Someone else, however, might point out that colors as seen do not *really* exist, but that they *appear* to exist when certain wavelengths of light pass through specified media before striking the retina. To talk about colors is to talk about the conditioned; to talk about wavelengths and media is to talk about the sources of the conditioned which enable the conditioned to exist as appearance. Here the analogy breaks down, however, for the seers of the Upanishads were

Forest-dwelling Sages.

not seeking the specific conditions of any particular appearances, but were seeking that which conditioned or made possible existence itself.

These seers had no clear concept of what they sought; they simply knew that there must exist that by which all other things existed and which made them great. The name given to this "something" was *Brahman*, which means "that which makes great." It was a non-descriptive name for it did not name anything definite, either abstract or concrete. The search for *Brahman* is recorded in the Upanishads as the search for the ultimate external reality. At first there was an attempt to identify that "something" with religious symbols and rituals, with natural objects, such as the sun and the moon, and with certain psychological functions of human beings. All of these attempts to state what *Brahman* is in terms of something else presuppose limits on that power. But if *Brahman* is ultimate, it is impossible that it should be limited, for there could be nothing beyond it to limit it. As the seers began to realize more clearly that *Brahman* could not adequately be described by appealing to their experience of the world of appearance, they attempted to define this reality in a negative way.

According to Yajnavalka in the *Brihadaranyaka Upanishad*, *Brahman* is not conceivable, not changeable, not injurable, not graspable. According to the *Katha Upanishad*, *Brahman* is inaudible, invisible, indestructible, cannot be tasted, cannot be smelled, is without beginning or end, and greater than the great. *Brahman* is described negatively in the *Mundaka Upanishad* as follows:

> Invisible, incomprehensible, without genealogy, colorless, without eye or ear, without hands or feet, unending, pervading all and omnipresent, that is the unchangeable one whom the wise regard as the source of beings.[1]

Clearly it was felt that *Brahman* was not many and not material. But these characteristics are negative. And after regarding *Brahman* as that which makes possible time, space, and causality it was impossible to regard it as limited by them. Being prior to space, time, and causality means being beyond the characteristics of the empirical universe, and therefore beyond positive description. That which makes possible both conception itself and the conceptualized is not to be caught with the net of conceptualization. But if that is the case then the nature of *Brahman* remains elusive and mysterious.

Despite the fact that for all their concentration on *Brahman* they were unsuccessful in establishing the ultimate nature of external reality, the thinkers of the Upanishads were not completely stymied. Some of them, asking the question in a different way, were seeking the ultimate nature of the self. The question they asked was, "What am I, in my deepest existence?"

This, too, was a question about the conditions of appearance rather than about the appearances themselves. The question presupposes that the self is something more than meets the eye, for the bodily organism is not particularly elusive or mysterious. But the question of what enables the bodily organism to exist is another matter. I may appear to be a bodily organism, but is that what I really am? Is the "I" that thinks the self to be a bodily organism also a bodily organism? And is not the "I" more properly the self than the body? These are the sorts of questions that occurred to these thinkers.

There is no doubt that the distinction between what the self appears to be and what it really is was assumed by the thinkers of the Upanishads. Their search for the innermost essence of man is guided by the injunction:

---

[1] *Mundaka Upanishad*, I.1.6., my translation.

The Self (*atman*) which is free from evil, free from old age, free from death, free from grief, free from hunger and thirst, whose desire is the real, whose thoughts are true, he should be sought, him one should desire to understand. He who has found out and who understands that self, he obtains all worlds and desires.[2]

The question was, What is that wonderful and mysterious Self? Trying to answer that question, the seers of the *Taittiriya Upanishad* turned their attention to the various aspects and functions of the individual person as they searched for that ultimate Self. If the Self is thought to be the body then it is essentially food, they reasoned, for the body is simply digested food. But surely the Self is not to be identified with the body only, for it is something more; it is alive and moving. If the Self is not food, perhaps it is the life of food. But they saw that while this would serve to distinguish living from non-living matter it was not the ultimate Self of the person, for a person is more than simply living food. It sees, hears, feels, etc. Perhaps, the speculation continues, the Self should be thought of in terms of mind or perception. But this too seemed inadequate, for thinking and understanding are even more properly Self than perception. However, this too is rejected as inadequate, for there must be that which gives existence to thinking and understanding. As the Upanishad says, "Different from and within that which consists of the understanding is the Self consisting of bliss."[3]

This search for the ultimate Self was essentially a matter of going deeper and deeper into the foundations of human existence. Matter was regarded as covering for life, which in turn was a covering for the sensing self. And deeper than sensing was intellectual activity. But deeper still was the bliss of total consciousness. Consequently, the Self is not to be identified with any of the lower forms of the person exclusively, but is to be thought of as existing within the various layers of existence, giving them life while remaining distinct from them.

In the *Kena Upanishad* the search for the ultimate Self takes the form of a quest for the ultimate agent or doer of human activity. It is asked, "By whom willed and directed does the mind light on its objects? By whom commanded does life the first, move? At whose will do (people) utter this speech? And what god is it that prompts the eye and the ear?"[4]

In the very next paragraph these questions are answered by saying that

---

[2] *Chandogya Upanishad*, VII.7.1. In *The Principal Upaniṣads*, ed. by Sarvepalli Radhakrishnan (London: Allen and Unwin, 1953), p. 501. Unless otherwise noted, all quotations from the Upanishads are from this work.
[3] *Taittiriya Upanishad*, II.5.1.
[4] *Kena Upanishad*, I.1.

there is a more basic Self that directs the eye to color, the ear to sound,
the understanding to consciousness. And this Self is said to be "other than
the known and other than the unknown."[5] The question here is basically
a matter of asking what makes possible seeing, hearing, and thinking. But
the question is not about physiological processes; it it about the hearing
subject, the seeing subject, etc. That is, I may be said to be a hearing,
seeing, thinking thing; but by what do I do these things? I see the green
colors in front of me when they are present to the eye; how is it that the eye
is so directed? Must not there be an inner director, an agent directing the
functions and activities of a person? The answer in the Upanishads is a most
emphatic *yes*.

There remains, however, another question: What is that which directs all
of the human activities? The answer to that question is that it cannot be
known, for "there the eye goes not, speech goes not, nor the mind; we
know not, we understand not how one can teach this."[6] The reason it is
beyond the eye, beyond the ear, beyond the understanding, is that what is
seen, heard, and understood is always an object known by the human
subject. But the ultimate Self is the ultimate subject. Therefore it can never
be an object of knowledge, and must remain beyond the grasp of ordinary
knowledge. Nevertheless, since this Self is ultimate subject, it can be realized directly in total self-consciousness, where, so to speak, the knower
stands illumined by its own illumination. Thus, though in one sense the
ultimate Self cannot be known, in another sense, the sense of immediate
experience, it can be known intimately and completely in the experience of
total self-consciousness. In this sense it is known much more surely and
completely than any object of knowledge. This is the certitude of one's own
existence, beyond question or doubt.

Prajapati Teaches Indra

In the *Chandogya Upanishad* the search for the ultimate Self is presented in the form of a delightful story in which Prajapati (representing the
creative forces of the universe) instructs Indra (who represents the gods)
and Virocana (who represents the demons) about the Self. As students
seeking the wisdom possessed by the *guru*, or spiritual teacher, Indra and
Virocana come, bearing fuel, to Prajapati for instruction. For thirty-two

[5] *Ibid.*, I.4.
[6] *Ibid.*, I.3.

years they prepare themselves for Prajapati's teaching by practicing self-discipline. At the end of that time he tells them that the Self is what they see when they look at their reflection in a glass or a pan of water. They look and they see the physical form, clothed and adorned with jewels. Virocana, delighted with this knowlege, returns to the demon-world and teaches that the body is the Self. Such is the teaching of the demons! But Indra reflects on this teaching and sees that if the Self is the same as the body, then when the body perishes so does the Self. This cannot be the immortal Self he is seeking, so he again asks Prajapati about the Self. This time Prajapati tells him that the dreamself is the real Self. But still Indra is uneasy. For although the dreamself is not absolutely dependent upon the body, nevertheless sometimes it too is subject to pain, suffering and destruction. So again he asks what the real Self is. And this time he is told that the self that is sound asleep, beyond dreams, is the real Self. At first this satisfies Indra, but before he has reached the abode of the gods he realizes that even though the deep-sleeping self is not subject to pain and destruction, nevertheless it cannot be the real Self—in deep sleep the self is not aware of itself; one might just as well be dead, he tells Prajapati.

By this time Indra has spent a total of one hundred and one years disciplining and preparing himself for that highest knowledge (*paravidyam*) and now is ready to hear about the ultimate Self. Now Prajapati tells him that the Self being sought transcends all of the selves considered so far. It is true, there is a physical self, which some think to be the only self. And there is the self which is the subject that experiences dreams, a self recognized by some. And there is the self which experiences deep sleep, otherwise deep sleep would be the same as death. But the highest Self goes beyond all of these; it is that which makes possible the self of waking experience, of dreaming experience, and of deep sleep. Those selves are merely instruments of the highest Self, which is the very source of their existence.

The state in which one realizes the ultimate Self that gives existence to the selves of the waking, dreaming, and deep-sleeping person is sometimes called the *turiya*, or fourth state. Unlike the condition of deep sleep this state is one of total self-consciousness and illumination. In the *Brihadaranyaka Upanishad* it is said, "When one goes to sleep, he takes along the material of this all-containing world, himself tears it apart, himself builds it up and dreams by his own brightness, by his own light. Then this person becomes self-illuminated."[7]

Although ordinary knowledge, which presupposes the duality of object

---

[7] *Brihadaranyaka Upanishad*, IV.3.9.

and subject, knower and known, is impossible in this fourth state, there is no doubt of the authenticity of its existence. The same Upanishad continues:

> Indeed, while he does not there know, he is indeed knowing, though he does not know [what is usually to be known]; for there is no cessation of the knowing of a knower, because of his imperishability [as a knower]. It is not, however, a second thing, other than himself and separate, which he may know.[8]

Thus, in the Upanishads, the question, "What am I, in the deepest reaches of my existence?" is answered by saying that the very foundation of existence is self-illuminating consciousness, which can be directly experienced by a person when one goes beyond identification with the false self of the objectified world. It is tremendously significant that the ultimate Self—the *Atman*—can be known directly and immediately as a matter of direct experience. For here there can be no doubts or lingering uncertainty. This is an answer which when realized provides for the total satisfaction of the individual.

The discovery of *Atman* is also significant in another way. The seers of the Upanishads who were seeking both the ultimate external reality (*Brahman*) and the ultimate internal reality (*Atman*) came to inquire into the relations or connections between these realities. The exciting discovery they now made was that *Atman* was none other than *Brahman*. There was only one ultimate reality which could be approached either by looking outside of oneself or by looking within oneself. Thus, though the search for the nature of external reality, or *Brahman*, had appeared to end in frustration because of the impossibility of saying anything about the ultimate object, it was now realized that *Brahman* could be known by the self-certifying experience of total conscious illumination, because *Brahman* was the ultimate Subject, or *Atman*. There was no difference between the ultimate subject and the ultimate object; ultimate subjective reality and ultimate objective reality were one and the same! It is hard to imagine a more exciting discovery. Seeking to understand the ultimate nature of the world and self, it had been discovered that all things existed within *Atman*; that each person contains all things within the deepest Self. One need only know the Self to know all. And the Self can be known in the surest way possible, for it is self-

[8] *Brihadaranyaka Upanishad*, IV.3.30.

revealing in consciousness when the objects of consciousness that block out self-illumination are transcended.

The unity of *Atman* and *Brahman* is the greatest discovery made in the Upanishads. This unity above all is the mystery and sacred teaching (*upanisat*) that is so carefully guarded by the seers of the Upanishads, and that constitutes the basic message of these treatises.

The Five Householders

The quest for the nature of *Brahman* and *Atman* and the discovery of the relation between them is well illustrated by the account of the five householders who studied with Ashvapati Kaikeya.[9]

Pracinashala Aupamanyava, Satyayajna Paulusi, Indradyumna Bhallaveya, Jana Sharkaraksya, and Budila Ashvatarashvi, famous householders renowned for their learning and wisdom, got together to investigate what is Self and what is *Brahman*. They agreed that since Uddalaka Aruni was at present studying this universal Self they would go to him.

But when they came, Uddalaka reflected; "These great householders, greatly learned in sacred lore, will question me. I shall not be able to tell them all. Therefore, I shall direct them to another [teacher]." He said to them "Venerable Sirs, Ashvapati Kaikeya studies at present this Universal Self, well, let us go to him." When they arrived, they announced their purpose saying, "At present, Sir, you know the Universal Self. Tell us indeed about that."

Assuring himself that these persons were qualified to receive this sacred teaching, Ashvapati Kaikeya discovered that one of the householders regarded heaven as the universal Self. Another regarded the sun as the universal Self. A third considered space to be the universal Self. The fourth thought the Self was air, while the fifth householder regarded water as the universal Self. Uddalaka Aruni looked for the Self in the earth. Ashvapati Kaikeya told each householder that his knowledge was only partial and limited. He said to them, "Indeed you eat your food knowing this Universal Self as if it were many. He, however, who meditates on the Universal Self as of the measure of the span or as identical with the self, eats food in all worlds, in all beings, in all selves."

This teaching of Ashvapati Kaikeya is usually interpreted to mean that the universal Self is in each person and in each being without differentiation.

[9] *Chandogya Upanishad*, V.11–18.

The householders should realize the universal Self in themselves, for they are not different from that universal Self.

The *Chandogya Upanishad* also contains the famous teaching of Shandilya: "Verily, this whole world is *Brahman*. . . . Containing all works, containing all desires, containing all odors, containing all tastes, encompassing this whole world, without speech, without concern, this is the Self (*Atman*) of mine within the heart; this is *Brahman*."[10]

Because of the deep-seated ignorance that results in objectification of the world, and because of the resulting multiplicity, one is inclined to think of the ultimate reality as an other. But this is a mistake, for "in the beginning all this world was *Brahman* only. Whoever thus knows, 'I am *Brahman* (*Aham Brahman asi*)' becomes this All."[11]

Thus, the teaching received by the householders is that by knowing their deepest self they will know the universal Self; they will know all. This teaching is beautifully presented in the famous passage of the *Chandogya Upanishad* in which Uddalaka teaches his son, Shvetaketu, about the ultimate reality, telling him that he is that ultimate reality (*"tat tvam asi, Shvetaketu"*).[12] Shvetaketu had become a pupil at age twelve and for twelve years he studied the Vedas. At age twenty-four, thinking himself learned, he was arrogant and conceited. His father then said to him, "Shvetaketu, since you are now so greatly conceited, think yourself well-read and arrogant, did you ask for that instruction by which the unhearable becomes the heard, the unperceivable becomes perceived, the unknowable becomes known?" When Shvetaketu asks how such a teaching is even possible, his father responds, "just as, my dear, by one clod of clay all that is made of clay becomes known, the modification being only a name arising from speech while the truth is that it is just clay." The point of this is that the variety and plurality of objects in the world is only a disguise for the unified reality which underlies these objects. And that underlying reality is the reality of the Self.

The instruction then proceeds to the famous teaching:

That which is the subtle essence, this whole world has for its Self (*Atman*). That is the true. That is the *Atman*. That art thou [*tat tvam asi*], Shvetaketu.

The "subtle essence" referred to is *Brahman*, the source of all existence. Thus, when Shvetaketu is identified with his deepest self, or *Atman*, and

[10] *Chandogya Upanishad*, III.14.1,4.
[11] *Brihadaranyaka Upanishad*, I.4.10.
[12] *Chandogya Upanishad*, VI.

that in turn identified with *Brahman*, the mystic teaching has been imparted.

Of course, by understanding this teaching (in the sense of understanding the language in which it is presented) Shvetaketu does not thereby come to know that Self, that subtle essence. His knowledge is still of objects; the teaching itself is an object of instruction, whereas what is to be known is pure subject. Yajnavalkya brings this out when he answers Ushasta Cakrayana's request for an explanation of "the *Brahman* that is immediately present and directly perceived, that is the Self in all things," by declaring: "This is your Self that is within all things." When the question is put again, "Which is within all things?" the reply is, "You cannot see the seer of seeing, you cannot hear the hearer of hearing, you cannot think the thinker of thinking, you cannot understand the understander of understanding. He is your Self which is in all things."[13]

This is the ultimate subject which can never become an object. Consequently, it cannot be known in the way that objects in consciousness can be known, but must be realized directly in self-illuminating experiences.

The advantages brought to the search for the ultimate Reality by the nature of *Atman*-awareness as immediate and direct experience resulted in providing for the establishment of the indubitable existence of *Atman*. But this kind of knowledge carries with it also certain disadvantages. Knowledge of objects is public in a way that direct experience is not. It is open to anyone to examine the evidence for the knowledge-claims about known objects. But one's immediate experience is available only to oneself. Thus, while for the one with the experience there is nothing surer than the experience itself, for one lacking the experience there is little or no evidence for the claimed reality.

In this respect the knowledge of *Atman* is similar to the knowledge of love. Only those experiencing love know what it is. Others might make various claims about love, but they obviously lack the appropriate experience. For the person having the experience, nothing could be more sure than its existence, though a person lacking this experience might very well be skeptical of the existence of love. In a similar way, those without faith or experience might be skeptical of the existence of *Atman* and the possibility of *Atman*-realization. But those who have experienced the bliss of *Atman* know the ultimate joy—they are completely fulfilled.

---

[13] *Brihadaranyaka Upanishad*, III.4.2.

REVIEW QUESTIONS

1. What evidence is there that the people of the Indus civilization had reached a relatively high level of culture and thought even before the advent of the Aryans?
2. What is the significance of the Vedic Hymn of Origins?
3. What is the primary concern of the Upanishads?
4. How does the *Taittiriya* teaching of sheaths or layers of existence lead to the discovery of *Atman?*
5. What is the meaning of Uddalaka's teaching, "You are That" (*Tat tvam asi*)?

FURTHER READING

The Roots of Ancient India: The Archaeology of Early Indian Civilization, by Walter A. Fairservis, Jr., 2nd rev. ed. (Chicago: University of Chicago Press, 1975), is a well-rounded account of the beginnings of Indian civilization taking into account the contributions made by leading scholars in a variety of disciplines. Chapters VI–VIII (pp. 217–311) are especially helpful for understanding Indus civilization; an excellent bibliography cites literature on early Indian civilization published before 1975.

Hymns from the Ṛg Veda, translated by Jean Le Mée, with photographs by Ingbert Gruttner (New York: Alfred A. Knopf, 1975), is a wonderful book with which to begin. While it contains only a small fraction of the Ṛg Veda, the selections are judicious, the translations excellent, and the format a visual delight, giving the reader a feel for the wisdom of the verses translated. The beautiful photographs on every page are an integral part of the book.

The Rig Veda: An Anthology, translated and annotated by Wendy Doniger O'Flaherty (New York: Penguin Books, 1981), contains 108 hymns (ten percent of the total) in a modern translation.

The Vedic Experience: Mantramañjarī, by Raimundo Panikkar (Los Angeles: University of California Press, 1977), is a wonderful collection of teachings from the Vedas, Brāhmaṇas, and Upaniṣads. The introductions preceding the translations in each section give the reader a sense of the life and vigor of the Vedic experience. No other anthology comes close to matching choice of material, quality of translation, and helpfulness of commentaries found in this treasury of Vedic thought.

The Principal Upaniṣads, edited and translated by Sarvapalli Radhakrishnan (London: George Allen & Unwin, 1953), contains the Sanskrit text and excellent readable translations of all the early Upaniṣads. This work, by the late Dr.

Radhakrishnan, professor at Oxford and Madras and president of India, also has a good, although somewhat Advaitic, introductory essay. (Other translations may also be consulted. Those by R. E. Hume and Juan Mascaro are especially recommended.)

The Beginnings of Indian Philosophy, by Franklin Edgerton (Cambridge, Mass.: Harvard University Press, 1965), is the summary of a great scholar's lifetime's work on early Indian thought. An excellent thirty-page introduction is followed by careful translations from the Ṛg Veda (25 pages), Atharva Veda (53 pages), Upaniṣads (57 pages), Gītā (52 pages), and the Mahābhārata (78 pages).

CHAPTER 4

◈◈◈◈◈◈◈◈◈◈◈◈◈◈◈◈◈◈◈◈◈◈◈◈◈◈◈◈◈◈◈

Society and Philosophy

Self-Realization

BECAUSE OF the experiential nature of *Atman*-knowledge, three basic attitudes toward it were possible. The skeptics simply denied the existence of any such ultimate Subject on the grounds that they did not have any experience of it. Others were prepared to accept the existence and nature of *Atman* as a philosophical hypothesis to be established on the basis of reason. Still others, probably the great majority of people in India, were willing to accept the testimony of the sages and seers as adequate evidence for their belief in the existence and experiencability of *Atman*. For these people the major concern was to find a way to this wonderful realization.

This concern was not the privilege of a select few, but was shared by nearly all the members of society. A goodly number of the persons striving for *Atman*-realization could not, for a variety of reasons, share in the esoteric teachings and disciplines of the Upanishads, but had to rely on other means of instruction and achievement. Gradually a variety of fables, tales, poems, and codes were developed which gave the common people of India guides and ideals for the kind of life that would make possible the realization of *Atman*. This literature provides the chief vehicle for the transformation of the sacred teachings of the priests of the Vedas and the seers of the Upanishads into a way of life for the people. The early Vedic emphasis on the rituals of religion came to be combined with the philosophical teachings of the Upanishads, with their insistence of self-discipline and knowledge, in a way which tempered both the ritualism and the philosophical abstractness.

Rather than seeing the prayer, worship, and sacrifice of earlier traditions as incompatible with the Upanishadic emphasis on knowledge of *Atman* by enlargement of consciousness, this literature tended to synthesize these tendencies.

The most significant attempt at synthesis is the *Bhagavad Gita*, "The Song of the Supreme." In the *Gita*, which is a portion of the *Mahabharata*, the identification of the individual person with *Atman* and the identification of *Atman* with the ultimate reality of the universe are taken over from the Upanishads. But the *Atman* is here symbolized by God, and the divine teacher of the *Gita*, Krishna, describes himself as a finite form of the infinite, claiming to be both the god Vishnu and the *Brahman* of the Upanishads. There is no contradiction here, for Vishnu is simply a form of *Brahman*, the ultimate Self, or *Atman*.

It is easy to see that the abstract philosophical discourses of the Upanishads would not find a ready acceptance by the majority of people accustomed to dealing with life in the concrete. But when the abstract *Brahman* is given concrete form in the person of Krishna, access becomes possible. Feeling in the depths of their being the surging of the infinite struggling to free itself from the bonds of the finite and concrete, the majority of India's people welcomed the symbol of the infinite made finite in Krishna. Here was a ray of light and hope, for if the infinite could reach down into the finite, then the finite could also reach up to the infinite. The gap between the finite and the infinite—between the empirical self and the *Atman*—could be bridged. This was the promise held out by the *Gita*, a promise giving hope and inspiration to hundreds of millions of people for thousands of years. The concrete forms of religious worship were a means to the realization of that ultimate Self taught in the Upanishads.

The *Gita* not only offered hope and inspiration but also provided a guide to life leading to the fulfillment of that hope and inspiration. The two important questions taken up by the *Gita* are (1) What is the relation between the ordinary empirical self and the ultimate Self (*Atman*)? (Or, looked at from the objective point of view, what is the relation between the ordinary empirical reality and the ultimate reality (*Brahman*)?) and (2) By what means can one come to realize or experience that ultimate Self, or Reality?

It is significant that these questions are considered in the context of a moral decision. As the *Gita* opens, Arjuna, representing Everyman, finds himself unable to determine the right thing to do, a situation known to every person. The specific question concerns the decision to fight or not to fight to regain the kingdom which rightfully belongs to him. The answer given by Krishna, disguised as Arjuna's charioteer, is given in general terms so that it can be adapted to any specific moral choice. The answer, occupying all but one of the eighteen chapters constituting this work, turns on the nature of human existence and the nature of the universe, and the resulting purpose, or end, of life.

The universe is regarded as ultimately unchanging and permanent, without multiplicity or plurality. The ultimate Self is also permanent, one and the same with the ultimate reality. But because of ignorance about our true nature, we mistake ourselves for a complex changing individual, living in a world of many changing objects. Having identified ourselves with the impermanent and changing self, we seek satisfaction in the world of changing objects and desires, always without success, because the whole quest is fundamentally misguided.

But why do we make this mistake and engage in this misguided quest? Because of the dual nature of the self. On the one hand there is the empirical, or *guna*, self. This self covers and obscures the spiritual and ultimately real self—the *purusha*, or *Atman*. The *guna*-self is the psycho-physical organism which the ignorant mistake for the real self. Thus Arjuna, who was suggesting that it would be wrong to engage in this war because of the destruction and killing that would occur, is instructed by Krishna, "The dweller (the *Atman*) in the body of everyone, O Bharata (Arjuna) is eternal and can never be slain."[1] The point of this instruction is that Arjuna had failed to take into consideration that the true Self, the *Atman*, or *purusha*, is essentially independent of the psycho-physical organism; he had mistaken the psycho-physical self for the ultimate Self. Consequently, he was concerned to seek satisfaction for that lower self of the *gunas*. But this is basically wrong. Krishna says "He who thinks that this slays and he who thinks that this is slain; both of them fail to perceive the truth; this one neither slays nor is slain. . . . He [the Self] is said to be unmanifest, unthinkable, and unchanging."[2]

But if the individual person mistakenly identifies with the *guna*-self because the real Self is obscured, how can the veil of the empirical be removed so that the real Self might be seen? This is a question about the way to the realization of the *Atman*. In the *Gita* the answer rests upon the teaching that ultimately Self (*puruhsa*) and not-Self (*prakriti*) are independent. The short answer to this question is that the empirical self must be disciplined

---

[1] *Bhagavad Gita*, 2.30, trans. by Sarvepalli Radhakrishnan (New York: Harper Bros., 1948), and contained in Sarvepalli Radhakrishnan and Charles A. Moore, eds. *A Source Book in Indian Philosophy* (Princeton: Princeton University Press, 1957), pp. 101–63.
[2] *Gita*, 2.19,25.

and brought under control so that it is no longer capable of confusing a person. But even though the short answer be accurate, it is insufficient, for the starting point on the path to *Atman*-realization is always occupied by the ignorant self who necessarily looks upon the empirical as real. The real task is to present ways or paths to the ultimate knowledge which begin where the individual actually is, but progressively lead to higher and higher understanding, until gradually one is freed entirely from ignorance.

Thus, in the *Gita*, Krishna does not tell Arjuna that since activity proceeds from the world of the *gunas*, the not-Self, it should be abandoned. In fact he teaches that action is necessary, "for no one can remain even for a moment without doing work; every one is made to act helplessly by the impulses born of nature."[3] The crucial discipline is to engage in activity without becoming attached to the activity or to the results of the activity.

The *guna*-self is a combination of three different tendencies which combine in varying proportions. These tendencies, or *gunas*, are: *sattva*, which inclines one to intellectual activity; *rajas*, which inclines one to vigorous action; and *tamas*, which inclines one to devotional activity. These three *gunas*, in their varying combinations, account for the different personality types found among persons. The crucial thing, however, is that the personality type belongs to the psycho-physical self, the self of *prakriti*, and as such constitutes the binding fetters of the true Self. Even though different persons are bound by different tendencies and personality types, nevertheless, they are all bound. Now, if individual A is bound by the chains of *sattva*, it is useless to try to achieve freedom by concentrating on the bonds of *rajas*, or *tamas*. And, individual B must concentrate on achieving freedom from the bonds of *rajas* if this *guna* predominates, etc. Accordingly, the way of discipline will vary with the type of person.

The recognition that different individuals are bound by different forces led to the distinction of three basically different paths, or ways, that would take one to the realization of *Atman*. These three paths, which correspond to the *gunas*—*sattva*, *rajas*, and *tamas*—were the paths of discipline in knowledge, discipline in work, and discipline in devotion, respectively. Common to the three paths is discipline, which is a matter of progessively freeing the real Self from the *guna*-self. These are the three famous disciplines, or *yogas*, taught in the *Gita*; the *yoga* of knowledge, the *yoga* of works, and the *yoga* of devotion. Because of the nature of the *guna*-self one cannot avoid engaging in activity. But it is possible to discipline oneself, no

[3] *Gita*, 3.5.

matter what kind of activity is involved, so that one can disassociate from the activity itself, which belongs to the *guna*-world. This is the essence of the non-attachment taught in the *Gita*.

According to the *Gita*, the two basic principles underlying the teaching of these three different paths of discipline are: (1) it is possible to realize one's essential independence of the *gunas*, and (2) in order to free oneself from the *guna*-self it is necessary to cooperate with and work through that *guna*-self, progressively transcending it.

This second principle, which is primarily an answer to the question of how an individual can realize *Atman* despite the *guna*-self, underlies a variety of practices and ideals characterizing the practical social life of the individual. Obviously, if the *guna*-self is capable of ensnaring the *Atman*, then the *guna*-self must be taken seriously if the attempt to realize *Atman* is taken seriously. And if this is the case, then the life of the empirical self in society must be taken seriously, for the kind of life the individual lives will determine the progress made in the quest for *Atman*, for it is obvious that human beings cannot live independently of society. Thus, the question arises, How can the life of the individual and the institutions of society be ordered so that progress can be made toward self-realization?

Human Aims

To order the life of the individual and the institutions of society one must first be clear about the fundamental purposes of life. In India this was accomplished by considering the basic aims in life that would contribute to both the well-being of society and the fulfillment of the individual. The word for these aims is *purushartha*, which means "aim of a person." Everyone has four basic aims in life according to the Indian tradition. The first three, virtuous living (*dharma*), means of life (*artha*), and enjoyment (*kama*), were recognized already in Vedic times. The fourth, Self-liberation (*moksha*), was added more than 2,500 years ago to emphasize the importance of Self-realization. Together, these four aims have constituted the basis of Indian values since the time of the Upanishads, defining the good life.

The *purusharthas* represent the four goals in life toward which every individual should strive. Because a person is a combination of physical and spiritual existence, it is necessary to satisfy both physical and spiritual needs in order to live life fully. Thus, in order to achieve the spiritual goal of *moksha*, it is necessary to first satisfy the physical and psychological needs of the individual by attaining the necessary means of life (*artha*) and the enjoyment (*kama*) they make possible. In turn, in order to regulate the activities of *artha* and *kama*, virtue—or *dharma*—is necessary.

Essentially, the theory of human aims represents an attempt to divide the basic rules concerning possible courses of action into four categories corresponding to the four integral components of the ideal life. Thus, the rules concerning how one should act with respect to other persons are included under the heading of *dharma*. The rules concerning how one should act with respect to wealth and material goods are included under the heading of *artha*. The rules concerning how one should act with respect to possible pleasures and enjoyments of the world are included under the heading of *kama*. Finally, the rules concerning how one should act with respect to Self-realization are grouped under the heading of *moksha*.

Looked at in this way, the human aims are essentially answers to the question of how the good life is to be lived. Granted that it is the purpose of social organization to provide for the good life, the importance of considering the *purusharthas* for understanding the theory of social organization is obvious. For without understanding what the good life consists in, it would be most difficult to appreciate the means of social organization required to implement the good life in society.

Although the word *dharma* is used in a bewildering variety of ways, there is a common notion of a rule of action running through the different senses of the term. The word is derived from the root *dhri*, which means "to support" or "to maintain," and the justification of a rule is that it maintains or supports. Consequently *dharma* came to mean that which one should do because it is right. Thus, *dharma* is essentially a guide to action.

With respect to the individual, one's *dharma* may be one's moral duty. But with respect to society, *dharma* provides rules for settling disputes and possible conflicts between individuals, for only when conflicts of interest between individuals and groups are kept to a minimum can society be well maintained. Thus, *dharma* has a social sense and significance, for it represents possible rules for action in society which will enable Self-fulfillment of the individual and at the same time make a contribution to the self-fulfillment of others.

As a person does not live by righteousness and justice alone, but requires also bread and bed, it is only natural that in addition to the human aim of *dharma* there should be the aims of means of life (*artha*) and enjoyment (*kama*).

Kautilya composed a treatise on *artha* as a guide to the acquisition of the means of life in the world. In it he explains the concept of *artha* as follows:

"The sustenance of mankind is termed *artha*, the earth which contains mankind is termed *artha*; . . . "[4] The word *artha* is derived from the root *ri* which means literally, "that which one goes for." From this basic meaning which is, roughly, "aim" or "purpose," derives the meaning of "thing," "matter," or "affair," from which stem the meanings of "advantage," "wealth," "profit," and "prosperity."

The following statements from the *Mahabharata* and the *Panchatantra* will reveal the attitude taken toward *artha*. In the *Mahabharata* it is said, "What is here regarded as *dharma* depends entirely upon wealth [*artha*]. One who robs another of wealth robs him of his *dharma* as well. Poverty is a state of sinfulness. All kinds of meritorious acts flow from the possession of great wealth, as from wealth spring all religious acts, all pleasures, and heaven itself. Wealth brings about accession of wealth, as elephants capture elephants. Religious acts, pleasure, joy, courage, worth, and learning; all these proceed from wealth. From wealth one's merit increases. He that has no wealth has neither this world nor the next."[5]

The traditions of the common people as reflected in the collection of tales of wisdom known as the *Panchatantra* contain the following observations: "The smell of wealth [*artha*] is quite enough to wake a creature's sterner stuff. And wealth's enjoyment even more. Wealth gives constant vigour, confidence, and power. Poverty is a curse worse than death. Virtue without wealth is of no consequence. The lack of money is the root of all evil."[6]

Artha, as one of the four basic aims in life, refers to whatever means are necessary for human life. The emphasis is upon the means to biological and social life, but the means to spiritual life are not excluded, as it is recognized that biological and social life are conditions for spiritual life. The securing of material plenty is advocated as a goal in life subject only to the important restriction that no *artha* be pursued in violation of *dharma*.

Since accumulations of wealth or property are not valuable primarily for their own sake, however, but mainly for the satisfaction, pleasure, and enjoyment they make possible, the human aim of enjoyment, or *kama*, was included as one of the basic goals in life. The classic definition of *kama* is found in Vatsyayana's *Sutra*:

---

[4] *Kautilya Arthashastra*, 4.1, trans. by R. Shamasastry, 5th ed. (Mysore: Sri Raguveer Press, 1956).
[5] *Mahabharata, Shantiparva*, 12.8.11 (Poona: Bhandarkar Oriental Research Institute, 1927–54).
[6] *The Panchatantra*, trans. by A. W. Ryder (Chicago: University of Chicago Press, 1925), p. 210.

Kāma is the enjoyment of the appropriate objects of the five senses of hearing, feeling, seeing, tasting, and smelling, assisted by the mind, together with the soul. The ingredient in this is a peculiar contact between the organ of sense and its object, and the consciousness of pleasure that results from the contact is called *Kāma*.[7]

Discussing the relations between *dharma*, *artha*, and *kama*, Manu says, "Some declare that the good of man consists in *dharma* and *artha*; others opine that it is to be found in *artha* and *kama*; some say that *dharma* alone will give it; the rest assert that *artha* alone is the chief good of man here below. But the correct position is that the good of man consists in the harmonious coordination of the three."[8]

The basic reason for regarding enjoyment as one of the basic aims in life is that the end of all activity is some presupposed good. It is the natural inclination of all things to strive after the satisfaction of the common desires for food, drink, and sex, and therefore these desires are not to be denied and frustrated, but are to be regulated and indulged. Consequently, the enjoyments of the satisfaction of regulated desires is reason for engaging in activity and is one of the basic aims in life.

The fourth basic human aim is *moksha*. The word derives from the root "*muc*," meaning "to release," "to free." In accord with the literal meaning of the word, *moksha* means emancipation, complete freedom. This aim reflects the emphasis put on the spiritual nature of human life in India. In accord with the teachings of the Upanishads, *Atman* is regarded as the power behind the powers of the universe and the ultimate power of the Self, these being one and the same. In agreement with this conception of human nature, the ultimate perfection of a person is seen to lie in Self-realization, in identifying oneself with the ultimate source and power of reality. This realization will set one free—for this power, constituting the innermost and essential portion of one's being, cannot be bound or limited by any other power. It is the ultimate power. Therefore no power, not even the power of death, can limit one who knows that the true Self is the highest reality. A person who identifies with the lower powers is bound by the higher powers and the lower powers as well. Consequently, the goal is to realize that one is not merely body, not merely biological life, not merely social organism, etc. This realization, in the sense of completely identifying oneself with the

---

[7] *The Kama Sutra of Vatsyayana*, trans. by R. Burton and F. A. Arbuthnot (London: Panther Books, 1963).

[8] *The Laws of Manu*, 2.224, trans. by Bühler, in F. Max Müller, ed., *The Sacred Books of the East*, XXV (Oxford: Clarendon Press, 1886).

ultimate power, is the realization of *Atman*, or the true Self, and results in complete freedom, or *moksha*.

Thus, the basic presupposition of *moksha* is that each person contains the seeds of his or her own perfection. But potential perfection implies actual imperfection. The problem, therefore, is one of moving from imperfect existence to perfect existence. Because of the integral view of human nature taken in India, to regard a person as more than a social animal was not to deny his or her biological and social dimensions. Rather, it was to assert that a person is something more than a biological and social organism. Consequently, it was held that the fulfillment of the biological and social were necessary, though not sufficient, conditions for the fulfillment of a person's spiritual nature.

Social Classes

It is clear that the basic human aims require a fairly high degree of social organization, for the aims of *dharma, artha, kama,* and *moksha* cannot be realized in isolation. Society can be successfully organized only when all of the different functions requisite for its maintenance are fulfilled. This organization can occur only when personnel are provided for the different basic functions, so a basic scheme of social classification is required.

Varna is a system of social classification whereby the individuals in society are divided into four classes whose functions in society differ according to personal characteristics and social needs. The theory is that the good of society will be furthered if there are separate classes of individuals who will perform the different tasks requisite for a good life in society. Furthermore, this classification will be to the advantage of the individual in that it will prove easier to fulfill oneself and reach the true Self if one is engaging in those activities for which one is peculiarly well suited by temperament, disposition, and natural ability.

It is important to distinguish *varna*, or social class, from *caste*, or social *castes*. *Varna* refers to a system of social classification of individuals according to their qualifications, tendencies, and dispositions. This scheme of classification yields the four classes, or *varnas*, of *brahmana* (the intellectuals), *kshatriya* (military and administrators), *vaishya* (producers), and *shudra* (workers). *Caste*, on the other hand, refers properly to a system of classification according to birth. There are only four classes, or *varnas*, but there are approximately two thousand *castes* in India. The castes are distinguished from each other not by qualification of the individual, but by heredity, dietary regulations, endogamy and exogamy, occupation, and rank. The native word for caste is *jati*, which means birth. The word "caste" is modern. It is taken from *casta*, a word the Portuguese applied to the practice of classification according to birth that they found upon coming to India.

The *brahmana varna* consists of the priests and teachers, who are, generally, the maintainers of culture. Their chief tasks have been the preservation of knowledge and culture, the satisfaction of the gods, and the safeguarding of justice and morality.

The *kshatriya varna* consists of the protectors and administrators of society. They have been the guardians of the rest of society, providing for their security, and enforcing the various rules required for the necessary social functions. According to the *Gita*, "heroism, vigour, steadiness, resourcefulness, not fleeing even in battle, generosity and leadership—these are the duties of a *kshatriya*, born of his nature."[9]

The *vaishya varna* consists of the traders and producers in society. The *Gita* says that engagement in agriculture, raising cattle, and trading are the duties of a *vaishya*, born of his own nature A*guna*-self).[10] Their chief function is obviously to produce the various economic goods of life required in the society.

The *shudra varna* consists of the workers and servants in society. The *Gita* succinctly gives the duties of this class by saying, "the *dharma* [duty] of a *shudra*, born of his own nature, is action consisting of service."[11]

According to the principle of *varna*, certain rights and duties accrue to an individual by virtue of belonging to a certain class in society. Because the specific duties and rights are predetermined for each of the four classes, once an individual's class is known, so are his or her duties and rights. The rights and duties of the four *varnas* do not exhaust one's *dharma*, however, as there are certain privileges and responsibilities that belong to a person simply as a human being and a member of society, irrespective of class. Thus Bhisma, in the *Mahabharata*, says that all persons have the duties of controlling their anger, telling the truth, forgiving others, begetting offspring of their legitimate wife, pure conduct, avoidance of quarrels, the maintenance of dependents, and acting justly.[12] Non-hurting (*ahimsa*) and self-restraint are usually added to this list.

Human duties are grounded in the very order of the universe. The uni-

---

[9] *Gita*, 18.43.
[10] *Gita*, 18.44.
[11] *Ibid.*
[12] *Mahabharata, Shantiparva*, 60.7.

verse is regarded as essentially moral. Everything happens according to a rule for the benefit of the whole. Each class of beings in the universe, by functioning as designed, contributes to the order and well-being of the whole. Human beings in society are no exception to this rule and therefore, by virtue of being human and occupying a particular place in the scheme of the universe, they have certain activities to engage in to maintain the well-being of the universe in general, and the well-being of society in particular. Sin and evil result when actions necessary for the well-being of the whole are not performed. The duties common to the several *varnas* are the actions one should perform or the rules one should follow in order to avoid sin. The duties of the particular *varnas* issue from the rules to be followed to maintain the social order, which is part of the total order of creation and necessary for self-realization. The nature of the various duties is derived from a person's *guna*-nature. Krishna, in the *Gita*, says, "The duties of *brahmanas, kshatriyas, vaishyas* and *shudras* have been assigned according to the *gunas* born of nature."[13]

Life-Stages

Granted that the individual's class duties are to be performed for the good of society, it is still possible to ask how the individual's own life should be ordered to maximize his or her contribution to the social order while also making the greatest possible progress in achieving self-fulfillment and self-realization. In answer to this question the theory of life-stages, or *ashramas*, was developed. The institution of *ashrama* consists in a series of stages in life, classified according to the activities proper to each stage. The first stage is the student stage, the *brahmacarya ashrama*. The second is that of the householder in society, the *grihastha ashrama*. The third is a stage of retirement from the social world, the *vanaprastha ashrama*. After passing through these first three stages in life's journey one enters into a life of contemplation and meditation in order to completely establish oneself in perfection. This last stage is called *sannyasa ashrama*.

According to Manu, the stages in life are to be taken up successively, beginning with the student stage. He says, "Having studied the Vedas in accordance with the rule, having begot sons according to the sacred law, and having offered sacrifices according to his ability, he may direct his mind

---

[13] *Gita*, 4,13.

to final liberation. A twice-born* man who seeks final liberation without having studied the Vedas, without having begotten sons, and without having offered sacrifices sinks downward."[14]

The various duties laid down for the different *ashrama* follow from the debts contracted by birth into the world. Life in this world is regarded as an opportunity provided as a gift to us. It is an opportunity for the Self to free itself forever from the round of births and deaths. But the individual does nothing to warrant this opportunity. The gods present the gift of life in this world and therefore humankind has a debt to the gods. We also have a debt to our parents and ancestors, for without them life would not have been possible either. With a person's second birth, the birth into the world of culture and spirit, a debt to the seers and teachers who promulgate, preserve, and teach that which is worth knowing is incurred. These three debts could be satisfied by studying (debt to the seers and teachers), having children (debt to the parents and ancestors), and by offering sacrifice (debt to the gods). The three different kinds of life required to repay the debts correspond to the student, householder, and retirement stages respectively. Only upon satisfying these obligations to society and the gods could a person focus exclusively on the meditation and concentration required for full Self-realization.

This emphasis upon satisfying one's debts through various kinds of social action reveals the importance attached to life in society and social organization in India. In fact, the very principles of life-stages and social classes are justified in terms of the importance of satisfying the empirical, or the *guna*-nature of the person.

The principle of *ashrama* finds its justification in the concept of the *purusharthas*. An *ashrama* is really a stage in life's journey, the goal of the journey being complete freedom, or *moksha*. It is the aim of *moksha* that provides the overall direction for the journey through life, the various stages being the means devised for the realization of this goal. But it is recognized that the traveler along life's highway is so constituted that in order to attain the goal of *moksha*, the goals of *dharma*, *artha*, and *kama* must be attained first. Accordingly, the journey is divided into stages such that each of the

---

* "Twice-born" refers to birth into the world of Spirit in addition to the world of nature. In ancient India there were elaborate rituals marking the initiation of young people into the cultural and spiritual life of the twice-born. Initiation into the ranks of the twice-born was considered a great privilege and was, at least in theory, reserved for those judged qualified.

[14] *Manu*, 6.34–37.

basic aims can be satisfied or attained most efficiently, in a way most satis-factory to the individual.

The first life-stage, the student stage, enables the individual to learn about life in all of its various aspects. Here one learns about social and spiritual life, becoming familiar with the ideals according to which life is to be lived. It is here that one learns about social classes, life-stages, human aims, etc., and is introduced to the art of self-discipline. After the student stage, one is ready to enter the second stage of life, that of the householder. All the texts, even those concerned primarily with *moksha*, recognize the central importance of this stage of life, for the entire society is dependent upon the goods and services the householder provides. To maintain and support society the householder must uphold *dharma*, secure the economy, and support the values of the culture. Although raising children and taking care of the old and the needy are primary duties enjoined on the house-holder, this is also the period in life when wealth and pleasures are to be enjoyed.

With obligations to society fulfilled and biological and social needs satis-fied, the individual enters a period of spiritual training. Well established in *dharma*, a person now endeavors to achieve an attitude of non-attachment to all the things of this world. Through ascetic practices self-control is increased, and the spiritual strength needed to achieve *moksha* developed.

The fourth stage is characterized by complete renunciation of worldly objects and desires. Indeed, the renunciation is regarded as so complete that the renounced one (*sannyasin*) is usually regarded as having already died. Thus, upon termination of biological life, ordinary funeral rites are not performed for the *sannyasin*. Instead, special *samadhi* rites are performed in recognition that social and personal life had terminated upon entry into this stage of life. Nothing but the spiritual goal of *moksha* or complete freedom is of importance in this final stage of life.

Underlying the institutions of life-stages and social classes and the theory of human aims in which these institutions find their justification, is the perennial Indian concern to participate fully in life while at the same time fulfilling one's spiritual nature. The Indian tradition insists that these goals do not exclude each other, but that both are necessary components of a higher ideal of life. Life-stages and social classes represent ideals of organi-zation for the individual's life and for the life of the whole society that will facilitate Self-realization or *moksha*, while encouraging actualization of human potential through *dharma*, *artha*, and *kama*.

REVIEW QUESTIONS

1. What is Arjuna's dilemma in the *Bhagavad Gita*?
2. To what is the *guna*-self opposed? Why is this distinction between kinds of self important?
3. What are the basic aims in life (*purusharthas*) and how are they related to castes or *jatis*?
4. Why is life ideally divided into four life-stages or *ashramas*?
5. What are the four *varnas*? How are they distinguished from the castes?

FURTHER READING

Hindu View of Life, by Sarvapalli Radhakrishnan (New York: Macmillan Publishing Co., 1964), gives a feel for Hinduism as a practical philosophy, guiding and directing daily life. The first part places Hinduism in the wider context of world religions, while the remainder of the book provides a view of *dharma* that takes into account the underlying metaphysical and social assumptions.

The Evolution of Hindu Ethical Ideals, by S. Cromwell Crawford (Honolulu: University of Hawaii Press, 1982), is a systematic examination of the ethical philosophies of the main philosophical systems of India. A considerable amount of material in the book is drawn from primary sources.

Four Families of Karimpur, by Charlotte V. Wiser (Syracuse: Syracuse University Foreign and Comparative Studies, 1978), is a description of three generations of life and change in four village families over a fifty-year period beginning in 1925. It provides wonderful insights into how *dharma* operates in the daily social life of village India.

Hindu Social Organization: A Study in the Socio-Psychological and Ideological Foundations, Pandharinath H. Prabhu, 4th ed. (Bombay: Popular Prakashan, 1961), is an excellent study of the social practices and underlying ideals of Hinduism.

CHAPTER 5

⁂⁂⁂⁂⁂⁂⁂⁂⁂⁂⁂⁂⁂⁂⁂⁂⁂⁂⁂⁂

Self and the World: Samkhya-Yoga

THE ETHICAL, SOCIAL, POLITICAL, and religious philosophies of the epics, *Dharma shastras*, and the *Gita* presuppose certain relationships between the empirical self that is the social organism and the ultimate Self that is pure subject. This presupposition is obvious from the emphasis placed on the various prescriptions for life in society in order to realize *Atman*. Unless there were a connection between the empirical self and the *Atman*, the activities of the empirical self would be irrelevant to *Atman*-realization. The Upanishads appear to be so full of excitement over the discovery of the *Atman* that they are not, for the most part, concerned to analyze the nature of the non-*Atman* nor to analyze the relations between what is *Atman* and what is not *Atman*. It is not surprising, then, that at a later time philosophical and critical minds should inquire into these matters and attempt to show what, if any, relations existed between Self and not-Self, between the ultimate and the empirical. The underlying question is, How can one be the self of flesh and bones and desires and habits and also be the *Atman*, unchanging and identical with the ultimate reality of the universe?

Subject and Object

The oldest philosophical school to take up this question of the relation between the Self and the not-Self was the school of Samkhya. The teachings of this school suggest that it grew directly out of those portions of the

Upanishads emphasizing the reality of the non-*Atman,* or the non-*Brahman.* In the Upanishads, *Brahman* is said to have created the universe and then entered into it.[1] The world of objects cannot be unreal, for it consists of *Atman,* which is object as well as subject. In the *Brihadaranyaka Upanishad* it is said that *Atman* entered into the universe "up to the fingertips, as a knife is hidden in its sheath, or the all-sustaining fire in the fire-preserving wood."[2] Such passages indicate two basic realities; that of *Brahman* and that of the objective world of empirical selves and things.

There is no doubt that for the most part the tendency in the Upanishads is to regard *Brahman* as "more real" than the empirical or objective world. Nevertheless, as seen earlier, knowledge of *Brahman* is not an ordinary kind of knowledge, and exclusive of *Brahman* knowledge, one has no choice but to take seriously the reality of the empirical self and the objective world, for there is no other reality in evidence. Furthermore, the empirical and the objective must always be the starting point for any investigation of reality, which means that at this level at least, the reality of the empirical must be acknowledged.

It appears that Samkhya, disposed to accept the reality of the empirical, perhaps partially on the basis of certain realistic remarks in the Upanishads, felt keenly the need to analyze carefully the relationship between the empirical and the ultimate realities.

The felt need to establish the relationship between the empirical and the ultimate arose from two considerations. On the one hand, the Upanishads had taught that realization of *Atman* would bring an end to suffering. Therefore, to find ways to realize this *Atman* and put an end to pain and suffering, it was necessary to discover the relationship between the empirical and the *Atman,* and to determine the sorts of things that would lead to the experience of *Atman.* Ishvara Krishna begins his discourse on Samkhya with the statement: "From torment by three-fold misery arises the inquiry into the means of terminating it. . . ."[3]

The other consideration is a matter of the basic human urge to know and render intelligible all human experiences by the exhibition of certain relationships inhering in them.

Focusing attention on ordinary human knowledge and the ordinary world known by such knowledge, the Samkhya philosophers argue that the entire

[1] *Taittiriya Upanishad,* II.6; *Chandogya Upanishad,* VI.3.2.
[2] *Brihadaranyaka Upanishad,* I.4.7.
[3] *Samkhya-Karika,* I, ed. and trans. by S. S. Suryanaranyana Sastri (Madras: University of Madras, 1935), and reprinted in Sarvepalli Radhakrishnan and Charles A. Moore, eds., *A Source Book in Indian Philosophy* (Princeton: Princeton University Press, 1957), p. 425 ff.

world that can be experienced is fundamentally of the same nature. That is
to say, desires, feelings, intelligence, etc., are not basically different from
colors, sounds, odors, etc., all of which are fundamentally like sticks and
stones. But all of this—the world that can, in principle, be experienced—is
of the nature of object (or potential object), or not-self, as opposed to the
Self that is always experiencer, that is ultimately and finally Subject. It
would seem that the ultimate Subject is of a different nature and order than
the world, since what is ultimate Subject can never become object, and
what is object cannot be ultimate Subject. The difference between Self and
the world is fundamentally the difference between subject and object.

The starting point for any analysis of the world and the self must be the
experience of the self and the world one has available for analysis. This
experience reveals the existence of a knowing self in a changing world.
Nothing is more obvious than that we and the world around us are changing. It is with this obvious fact that the Samkhya philosophers begin, and
from which they derive the conclusion that all experience and all that is
experienced is fundamentally of the same nature, though basically different
from the ultimate experiencing subject.

Causality

The orderliness and regularity of the experienced world cannot be dismissed as the result of chance. Changes are caused. Whatever is or will be,
is or will be due to various causes. The first important consequence of this
is that human knowledge that comes to be must be caused. It is the effect of
some prior cause. But since causality is unintelligible unless the dominant
features of the effect be derived from the cause, it follows that the effect
must be essentially like the cause. Therefore, our knowledge must be essentially like the world that is known. Since knowledge is the result of ordering
experiences, the nature of experience must be basically the same as the
world. Hence the claim that experience and the experiencable are fundamentally the same.

The analysis of causality provides the main reasons for the claims made
about the world and the self by Samkhya. The theory of causality adopted
is called *satkaryavada*, which means that the effect preexists in the cause.
Now if it is admitted that nothing can occur without a cause and also that
every effect has prior existence in the cause, it follows that in an important
sense the effect does not provide any new reality, for it is simply a matter of
making explicit what already existed implicitly.

The Samkhya theory of the nature of causation is summed up by Ishvara Krishna when he says: "The effect is existent (pre-existent): (1) because what is non-existent cannot be produced; (2) because there is a definite relation of the cause with the effect; (3) because all is not possible; (4) because the efficient can do only that for which it is efficient; (5) because the effect is of the same essence as the cause."[4]

The reason for claiming that effects exist is that the reality of the effect can be denied only upon denial of the cause, as a cause is a cause only to the extent it produces its effects. Therefore if there are no real effects then there are no real causes. Furthermore, the effect is as real as the cause, for the effect is simply a transformation of the cause. If one were to deny the existence of both cause and effect one would be forced to deny the whole starting point of one's analysis, which would make all the conclusions contradictory. Consequently, the existence of effects cannot be denied.

The claim that the effect is of the same essence as the cause is crucially important to Samkhya, for it is the main support of the claim that all objective reality is ultimately of the same nature, the connection being that all of objective reality is simply the result of various transformations of some one ultimate stuff.

To see the force of the Samkhya argument here it is helpful to consider some of the objections that might be raised against this theory of causation. It might be objected that the effect is a new whole different from the constituent parts, and not simply a transformation of them. Evidence is provided for this objection by the fact that no effect can be known before it is produced. But if it were essentially the same as its cause it could be known by knowing the cause prior to the production of the effect. According to Samkhya this objection is not valid, for it makes no sense to say that a whole is different from its material cause. Take the case of a table. The pieces of wood, which are the material cause of the table when arranged in a certain way, are not different from the table. If it were different, one could perceive the table independently of its parts. But this is clearly impossible. And to argue that the effect and the cause are independent and separate because they are perceived as separate and independent is to beg the question. The Samkhya claim is that perceiving an effect is simply perceiving the cause in transformation. To go on from this to say, "and therefore seeing the effect is seeing a new entity," is not to present an objection at all, but to beg the question.

Another objection that might be raised is that if Samkhya is right in

---

[4] *Samkhya-Karika*, IX.

maintaining that causality is simply a matter of transformation and not the production of something new, then the activity of the agent, or efficient cause, would be unnecessary, for the effect was already in existence. But if the effect preexisted, then no efficient cause is required to bring the effect into existence. This objection is addressed by considering the assumption that the effect does not preexist in the cause. If the effect did not preexist in the cause, then causality would be the bringing into existence of something out of nothing. (Hence the claim, "What is nonexistent cannot be produced.") If we look at some nonexistent things, such as square circles, it will be discovered that no amount of exertion can bring them into existence. To claim that what is can be caused by what is not, is not to provide an alternative view of causation but to deny causality completely.

Furthermore, if you do not admit that the effect preexists, then you have to say that it does not exist until it is caused. This is tantamount to saying that the nonexistent effect belongs to the cause. But since the effect does not exist there is really nothing to belong to the cause, for a relation of belonging is possible only between existing things. Thus, if the effect can be said to belong to the cause it must be admitted that it preexists in the cause. But then what of the objection that in this case no cause is needed? The answer is that the agent or efficient cause simply manifests or makes explicit what was implicit and unmanifest, and does not create something new.

Another reply to the objection that cause and effect are distinct entities is that the preexistence of the effect can be seen from the fact that nothing can be gotten out of a cause which was not in the cause. For example, curd is gotten from milk because it preexisted in the milk. It cannot be gotten from water or oil because it did not preexist in them. If it were not the case that the effect preexisted in the cause it would be possible for any effect to proceed from any cause. But this is obviously not the case; for example, you cannot produce iron from water.

Now if it is the case that only certain causes can produce certain effects, then obviously some causes are potent with respect to some effects, but not with respect to others. But this shows that the effect preexists in the cause; otherwise it would make no sense to say that a cause is potent with respect to a given effect. The reason is that the potent cause of an effect has some power related to the effect, and without the preexistence of the effect there is nothing for the power to be related to, and then it makes no sense to talk about potent causes or potentiality.

Another objection that might be raised is that to talk about manifestation and transformation is to smuggle the notion of causality, in the sense of production of new events and objects, back into the picture in disguised form. This is answered by showing that the nature of transformation has nothing to do with the cessation of preexisting attributes nor with the coming-to-be of a pre-nonexistent attribute. Rather, transformation means the manifestation of an attribute or characteristic implicitly present in the substance, and alternatively, the relapse of the manifested attribute into the unmanifest condition.

To clinch the case, the Samkhya philosopher argues that the very concept of causal possibility requires the preexistence of the effect in the cause. Non-being, the nonexistent, requires no cause. So if the effect were nonexistent at any time there would be no question of locating its cause. But it does make sense to talk about the possibility of effects which do not yet exist and to try to determine what will cause these effects to come into existence. However, this makes sense only upon the assumption that the effect pre-exists in some sense, for that which is absolutely nonexistent has no possibility of coming into existence.

The foregoing are all arguments essentially designed to support the claim that causes and effects are essentially the same. Cause is here being considered in the sense of material cause—the stuff out of which something comes to be. No effect can exist in a place different from its material cause. Hence cause and effect are numerically the same. An example given of the essential sameness of cause and effect is the tortoise going in and out of its shell. The spread-out tortoise is the effect, the contracted tortoise, the cause (and vice versa). But this does not involve the production of something new. Another example is a piece of gold which can be pressed into many shapes and pieces. But changing its shape does not make the effect something totally new. The flower made of gold is basically gold, as is the tree that is made of gold; the difference involves only name and form, and not the stuff out of which they are made.

Evolution of the World

Having established that the causality that must be assumed to exist in order to make sense out of human experience is of the nature of *satkaryavada* (meaning that the effect necessarily preexists in the cause), the Samkhya philosophers proceed to argue that this implies some one ultimate principle, which as the result of its transformations is experienced in its effects as the objective world. This claim follows once one admits that the present world exists as the result of previous changes and that change is not the production of something radically new. If this is admitted, then in order to avoid ultimate infinite regress it must be admitted that there is some one ultimate material cause, which in its various transformations or manifestations constitutes the world of experience. From this it follows that the entire world of experience is of the same fundamental nature as this ultimate material cause, for everything is basically only a transformation of this first cause. In this way Samkhya comes to the conclusion that the entire experiencable world is of the nature of *prakriti*, which is the name given to the ultimate causal principle.

This conclusion brings to the fore another question, however. How does the pluralistic world of experience derive, through a series of transformations, from this basic reality called *prakriti*? Obviously, if there are no effects except those that preexisted in the cause, then all of the effects that constitute the experienced world must have preexisted in *prakriti*. Consequently, *prakriti* itself must be composed of different tendencies, or characteristics. Accordingly, *Samkhya* posits various tendencies: *sattva*, which is the tendency responsible for the self-manifestation and self-maintenance of *prakriti*; *rajas*, the tendency of motion and action; and *tamas*, the tendency of inertia. From the psychological standpoint, *sattva*, *rajas*, and *tamas* are the principles responsible for pleasure, pain, and indifference, respectively. By various combinations of these differing principles it is possible to account for the evolution of the whole world. The varying proportions of these embodied principles account for all the diversity found in the world.

But what caused the evolution of *prakriti*? If the world is looked at as evolving it is implied that there was a logical time when the principles constituting *prakriti* were in a quiet state of equilibrium. If this is the case, it is necessary to suppose another principle of reality in the world, a principle responsible for disturbing the equilibrium of the tendencies, and thereby setting in motion the evolution of *prakriti*. This second reality is called *purusha*, and it is considered to be of the nature of pure consciousness, being ultimate Subject. It is, in fact, the Samkhya version of the Upanishadic *Atman* or *Brahman*.

It is the existence of *purusha* that accounts for the evolution of *prakriti*. It is not that *purusha* actually has anything to do with *prakriti*, but simply because of the existence and presence of *purusha*, the equilibrium of *prakriti* is upset and the evolutionary process begins.

A summation of the arguments given for the existence of *purusha* is given by Ishvara Krishna as follows:

(a) Because all composite objects are for another's use, (b) because there must be absence of the three attributes and other properties, (c) because there must be control, (d) because there must be someone to experience, and (e) because there is a tendency toward "isolation" or final beatitude, therefore, the *puruṣa* must be there.[5]

Arguments (a) and (b) rest on the premises that (1) all experienced objects consist of parts, these parts being ordered in such a way as to serve the purposes of other objects or beings so that the whole of nature hangs together as an ordered whole, and (2) unless there is that which is not composed of parts for the sake of which those things composed of parts exist we are caught in an infinite regress. The conclusion is that the world of *prakriti*, which is the world of objects, exists for the sake of another, proving the existence of a principle other than *prakriti*. This principle is *purusha*.

Argument (c) assumes that material objects, the objects constituting the world of *prakriti*, could not work together, each being directed to its proper end, unless there be some principle of intelligence guiding this world. The conclusion is that *purusha* must exist in order that the world be ordered as it is.

Argument (d) claims that from the psychological point of view all the objects of the world are of the nature of pleasure, pain, or indifference. But pleasure and pain cannot exist without an experiencer. The conclusion is that the world of *prakriti* must exist for some experiencer, and therefore *purusha* as the principle of experiencer must exist.

Argument (e) claims that *purusha* must exist because of the desire for self-transcendence. In an ordered universe it couldn't happen that the universal tendency toward the infinite—toward self-realization—would be self-frustrating. Consequently, the *purusha* must be there to be realized, since it is being sought.

But aside from arguments, the existence of *purusha* is put beyond question or doubt by the experience of those who have transcended the world of *prakriti*.

That *purusha* is regarded as being independent of *prakriti* is clear from the claim that "from the repeated study of the truth, there results that wisdom, 'I do not exist [as *prakriti*], naught is mine, I am not [*prakriti*],' which leaves no residue to be known, is pure, being free from ignorance, and is absolute."[6]

---

[5] *Samkhya-Karika*, XVII.
[6] *Samkhya-Karika*, LXIV.

But if *purusha* is independent of *prakriti*, are not the questions of how they are related, and how the empirical self can realize the *purusha* within, even more enigmatic than ever? The clue to the reply is contained in the above quotation according to which it is wisdom that releases the *purusha* from *prakriti*. If the *purusha* were *really* caught up in *prakriti* and constrained by it, then to say that the *purusha* is completely different from and independent of *prakriti* would be nonsensical. But the Samkhya view is that the relation between *prakriti* and *purusha* has its basis in ignorance. In this ignorance a tragic mistake is made, and *purusha* is confused with *prakriti*.

In order to explain how an illusory connection between *purusha* and *prakriti* can cause the real evolution of *prakriti* it is necessary to see how the mere existence and presence of *purusha* affects *prakriti*. Imagine that *purusha* is a shining light and *prakriti* a pool of water reflecting the light. Without *purusha* doing anything more than shining by its own light, the reflection in *prakriti* reflects on itself. But this is not the true light of *purusha*; it is a reflection in *prakriti* and therefore essentially of the nature of *prakriti*. Now in this reflection, which is the reflection of *purusha* in *prakriti*, *purusha* is lost sight of, and *prakriti* is taken to be the ultimate reality. Due to this mistake, the illumination of the empirical self which enables a person to see, hear, feel, think, desire, etc., is not recognized to proceed from the great light that is *purusha*. Consequently, as *prakriti* continues to evolve, *purusha* is not discriminated from *prakriti* but is identified with the evolutes of *prakriti*.

The order of evolution of *prakriti* sketched in the Samkhya philosophy regards the first illumination of *prakriti* by *purusha* as *Buddhi*, or *Mahat*—the "great one." This reflection becoming aware of itself is the "I-Maker" (*ahamkara*) responsible for individuation in nature. From these evolutes proceed the mind and the organs of sensation as well as the organs of actions and the essences of the things that are sensed and acted upon. Finally the gross objects of the world evolved. In this way the origin of all of experienced reality is accounted for by Samkhya.

Yoga: The Way of Discipline

The preceding account of the nature of the empirical self and world, and their relation to the *purusha*, or ultimate Self, provides a rational basis for the techniques of discipline known as *yoga*. The practice of *yoga* is required to achieve the wisdom through which the ignorance wherein the *purusha* is confused with *prakriti* is eliminated and the essential nature of the Self as *purusha* is realized.

The basic question of *yoga* is, How can that wisdom be achieved wherein the *purusha*, pure subject, recognizes itself for what it is; simply the spectator of *prakriti*, not actually a part of it or connected to it? When this wisdom is achieved there is no longer suffering, for the *purusha* is no longer mistakenly attached to the changing and suffering *prakriti*. Now it is understood that the afflictions of *prakriti* have nothing to do with *purusha*, and cannot cause suffering.

How the relationship between *purusha* and *prakriti* results in suffering, as explained by Samkhya, can be pictured by imagining a person in a room surrounded by audio-visual devices. A film projector runs, showing someone being picked up out of the sea, wafted to the peak of a jagged cliff high over the water, and plummeted down to be dashed against the rocks below. The viewer identifies with the victim of this horrible fate. Time after time the process is repeated; each time the broken pieces are fused together again and the process commenced anew. For the person who has identified with this image there is the pain and suffering of a thousand horrible deaths. Nothing could be more wonderful than to escape this horrible fate. But when the viewer realizes that he is watching a self created out of mere film and sound, freedom from the sufferings of this illusory self is achieved. The point is that the viewer was really free from suffering all of the time, but ignorance prevented this realization. Neither the audio-visual material in itself nor the person's own nature caused the suffering. Rather, it was the mistaken identification of the one with the other that led to suffering. In an analogous way, neither *purusha* nor *prakriti* themselves are capable of suffering, but a wrong identification of *purusha* with *prakriti* leads to suffering. To overcome the suffering of the self something must be done to remove the ignorance leading to the mistaken identification of the pure Self with the not-Self.

To this end a kind of self-discipline called *yoga* is prescribed. The first four aphorisms of Patanjali's *Yoga* indicate that nature and purpose of *yoga*: "Now the exposition of *yoga*. *Yoga* is the restriction of the fluctuations of the mind-stuff (*citta*). Then the Seer [that is, the Self] abides in himself. At other times it [the Self] takes the same forms as the fluctuations [of mind-stuff]."[7]

"Mind-stuff" refers to consciousness embodied in the psycho-physical

[7] *Yoga Sutras of Patanjali*, I, 1–4, trans. by James Haughton Woods, *Harvard Oriental Series*, XVII (Cambridge: Harvard University Press, 1914).

manifestations of *prakriti*. It must be distinguished from pure consciousness or *purusha*, which is eternally distinct from *prakriti*. According to Samkhya, *purusha*, though in itself always distinct from *prakriti*, is reflected in the evolutionary manifestations of nature. Because of ignorance, these reflections embodied in *prakriti* are mistaken for the true Self, the *Purusha* or *Atman*.

We might think of *purusha* as a shining light reflected in the rippling waters of a dirty pool. Seeing only the light reflected in the pool, we think that the light itself is dirty and rippled. But when the pool is calmed and the dirt allowed to settle, the light appears clear and still. The contrast between the two images leads us to discriminate between the light itself and its reflection in the pool. In a similar way, the disciplined activities of *yoga* calm the mind and the body, stopping the movements of embodied consciousness so that *purusha*, the pure consciousness, can be seen.

Realizing pure consciousness is no easy task, however. Because of ignorance the embodied consciousness mistakes itself for the ultimate Self of *purusha*, and struggles against the disciplined efforts of *yoga* to subdue its operations. To understand the basic techniques of *yoga* we must first understand these forces through which embodied consciousness functions to maintain itself. Patanjali describes five such forces or agencies which determine the actions of the embodied self.

Forces of Bondage

First is ignorance or *avidya*. This is the lack of awareness that ultimately self is of the nature of *purusha* rather than *prakriti*. Because the self is wrongly thought to be merely a psycho-physical being, it comes to be mistakenly identified exclusively with *prakriti*. As a result, this embodied self strives to maintain its existence as a prakritic being, "forgetting" that its ultimate nature is that of pure consciousness.

The second force conditioning the activities of the embodied self is the incessant urge to create and maintain an ego. This ego-force (*asmita*) is experienced as the will to survive as a psycho-physical being. It transforms everything into "mine," and "not-mine," as the ignorant self tries desperately to maintain its prakritic existence.

The third force, *raga*, is an infatuation with things which expresses itself through grasping and attachment. To maintain its prakritic existence, the ignorant self grasps at the objects of experience, attaching itself to their ephemeral existence. Afraid to let go, the embodied self desperately hangs on to every pleasurable experience.

The fourth conditioning force, *dvesa*, is the counterpart of the third. It is the dislike of, and aversion to, everything that threatens the prakritic self. It operates through hatred and fear, seeking to avoid or destroy whatever threatens the embodied self. Together, the forces of attachment and aversion drive a person. Pushing and pulling against each other, they leave the individual in a constantly agitated state of being.

The fifth force, the will to live forever as *prakriti* (*abhinivesa*), is deeper than aversion and attachments and overrides them when they jeopardize life. This force conditions the individual to fear death, and everything associated with death. Rooted in ignorance, it supports the ego-drive of the embodied self, holding out a false promise of psycho-physical immortality.

Because these five forces condition how the embodied self acts and thinks, they must be clearly understood and counteracted. They are the basic forces that underlie the "fluctuations of the mind-stuff" that *yoga* seeks to stop. By stopping these movements and eliminating the driving forces behind them, consciousness becomes clear and can be differentiated from *prakriti*. Thus *yoga* is essentially a process of "deconditioning" the self of embodied consciousness.

Techniques of Yoga

The techniques for yogic deconditioning are divided into eight groups by Patanjali, proceeding from the more superficial and external to the inner and more profound. The earlier groups of techniques are regarded as necessary conditions for the later groups, and are incorporated into the more advanced techniques of the later stages.

Moral restraints: *Yoga* begins with a set of moral imperatives (*yama*) designed to reorient a person's will and actions. Rather than acting out of a sense of attachment or aversion, motivated by blind ego forces, a person is expected to act out of sympathetic compassion for the well-being of others. Thus, the first restraint is *ahimsa*. Although literally the word means "non-hurting," *ahimsa* is basically a positive concept. While it rules out actions that hurt other beings, and all actions based on hatred and ill-will toward other creatures, *ahimsa* is essentially the expression of compassionate love for all living creatures. Developing this universal love is recognized as an effective means for getting rid of the selfish drives of the ego.

The second moral restraint pertains to speech. Speech should contribute to the well-being of others. Intentions and words that hurt others must be avoided. This includes empty talk, mindless chatter, and lying. Since the principle is that speech should promote the good of others, any intentions or words that hurt others are considered false and are to be avoided.

Not stealing, the third moral restraint, rules out taking what belongs to another. But it goes much deeper, for it really aims at eliminating the state of mind that desires what someone else possesses. Wanting another's possessions is itself regarded as a kind of hurting of another person and must, therefore, be eliminated from the mind.

The fourth restraint, non-grasping, carries the prohibition against stealing to a more profound level. Non-grasping means eliminating all desire for possessing goods, even so-called "rightful property." This principle allows that while whatever is necessary for life may be used by anyone who needs it, the principle of ownership is itself an expression of greed driven by the blind ego drive. This is the moral basis of non-attachment, an attitude that, taken to its extreme, would not even allow one to accept a gift.

The fifth moral restraint is directed against sexual activity. To the extent that sexual activity proceeds from and nourishes the ego it constitutes a hindrance to Self-awareness that must be eliminated. Although sexual activity has its rightful place in the lives of ordinary people, for the yogin it represents a form of bondage. Thus, upon initiation, the student vows to remain celibate.

Taken together, these five moral restraints have as their goal not merely the elimination of the proscribed activity, but the elimination of the drive that gives rise to them as well. Because these drives, especially the drive to maintain ego-existence, bind one to the forms of prakritic existence that obscure the light of pure consciousness, they must be eliminated by the yogin. By replacing desire and hatred with compassionate love as the main spring of action, the yogin takes a sure first step toward liberation.

Spiritual observances: The second set of disciplinary techniques, known as *niyama*, are intended to dispose one toward a more spiritual existence. First, one must observe purity in action, thought, and word. The body must be kept scrupulously clean and all forms of social and ritual pollution must be avoided. When pollution is unavoidable, purification with sacrificial offerings must be undertaken. More important for the yogin, however, is inner purity, for if the mind is impure it is impossible for actions to be pure. Consequently, the yogin must eliminate all impure and unwholesome thoughts, striving also to eliminate the residual effects of previous thoughts and actions, for these will give rise to future thoughts.

Again, those residual impressions and active thoughts that nourish the ego are considered the worst offenders and are targeted for elimination.

The second rule is that one should be satisfied with whatever one has, unperturbed by events and circumstances. By not allowing oneself to be agitated by desires for things one does not have, a calmness conducive to spiritual activity is introduced into life. Contentment with what one has also helps foster a sense of the independence of the true Self.

The third discipline enjoined is that of asceticism. Here one undertakes a variety of activities aimed at self-denial and self-mortification. The idea behind ascetic practice is to free oneself from the pushes and pulls of likes and dislikes by generating a sense of independence of the body. The ascetic, unlike the ordinary person, is not ruled by desires, but rather is their master.

The fourth rule is to study. In the first place this rule refers to the initiate's attitude, which must be one of humility and openness to the teaching. In the second place it refers to the teachings themselves, directing one to the wisdom of the master, the Vedas, or the texts on *yoga*. Of major importance here is to understand and practice the teachings of liberation.

The fifth rule calls for devotion. This may include ritualistic devotion to one or more of the gods and goddesses, or it may refer to an attitude of service on behalf of the greater powers of the universe. It may also include an attitude of reverence to one's master. Like the previous four, this rule is intended to dispose one toward a spiritual life in which the forces of ego may be overcome.

Postures: Firm in moral and spiritual discipline, the student is now ready to practice the exercises and postures (*asanas*) designed to discipline the body and bring it under control. There are dozens of different physical postures to be learned; indeed, when variations of basic positions are included, some of the *hatha yoga* manuals refer to hundreds of positions. The importance of these various postures lies in the control over the body they provide, control making it possible to tap the deeper powers of life. Because embodied consciousness is not really distinct from the body, the bodily control the different postures makes possible increases the yogin's control over consciousness as well. This is important, because the whole point of *yoga* is to bring the psycho-physical activities under control so that they can become means of liberation rather than of bondage.

The yogic postures, which can be learned properly only from a qualified teacher, should be practiced until they become effortless. Done correctly, they will bring the body to a point where it is firm, but relaxed, ready to respond to the directions of consciousness. Initially one's entire attention is focused on the physical activities required by the postures, but as one's skill increases these activities become practically effortless, and bodily awareness can, in large part, be transcended. The body now is a proper vehicle for the life force known as *prana*.

Disciplined breathing: Controlling the breath is essential to yogic practice, for breath makes available the vital energy that sustains and nourishes life. This vital energy, the *prana*, is given to every person at birth and is nourished and purified by breath. Inhalation is thought of as providing fuel to renew this energy and exhalation removes the spent fuel. When respiration is poor the life energy is diminished because of accumulated wastes and insufficient nourishment. Since a high level of vital energy is needed to purify and free consciousness, it is important to control the breathing process in order to maximize *prana*.

In addition to increasing the amount of vital energy available, breath control is important for meditation. All of one's psycho-physical functioning is dependent upon the rhythm and flow of breath energy. In meditation it is the calm period between inhalation and exhalation that allows the deepest entry into consciousness. Inhalation fragments the conscious stream of feelings and ideas into noisy confusion. Exhalation scatters the energies of consciousness in all directions. But between inhalation and exhalation is a calm where the mind can concentrate all of its energies and contents in self-revealing vision. Consequently, learning how to retain breath for long periods of time without effort is an important aid to meditation.

Withdrawing the senses: The fifth set of yogic techniques is designed to shut off sensory inputs into consciousness. The senses are regarded as instruments that reach out into the world to make contact with sensory objects, in order to provide input for consciousness. But this input is regarded as actually a kind of noise, obscuring the pure signals of the internal and self-sufficient consciousness. To eliminate this unwanted input, the yogin practices withdrawing the senses, just as, the texts say, a tortoise withdraws its legs and head into itself, shutting out the world.

Sense withdrawal must be practiced at various levels. For not only must contact with external colors, sounds, tastes, odors, and tactile objects be stopped, but contact with the internal sensory objects generated by prior contact with external objects must also be eliminated. Eventually, all traces of sensory contact at all levels must be removed so that the mind is free to organize and direct its own activity. Ultimately the question is whether the yogin is going to allow the senses to direct the activities of the mind or whether the mind will be freed sufficiently so that it will be able to direct the senses. Since mind is a higher power than the senses, and the rule of yoga is to control the lower powers by the higher, it is clear to the yogin that the senses must be controlled and directed by the mind. With the techniques of sense withdrawal mastered, the yogin is prepared to take up the practice of concentration.

Concentration: With the practice of concentration or *dharana* one enters the meditative stage of *yoga*. With the body and senses under control, the yogin can focus on bringing the mind under control so that its activities can be stopped. We need to recall that mind is different from pure consciousness or *purusha*. Indeed, it is regarded as a kind of noisy intrusion that obscures pure consciousness. Thus, the mind must be brought under control through the practices of concentration, its movements stilled and its contents emptied in order to reveal the deeper consciousness called *purusha*.

To focus the energies of the mind the yogin may meditate on a visual image of a geometric design or a deity. Sometimes a sound is taken as the meditative object, other times a metaphysical object such as the concept of Brahman or cosmic energy (*shakti*) becomes the meditative object. But always the meditative object functions to gather together all of the mind's energies, focusing them in a single stream that turns back on itself, revealing itself to be the false consciousness of *prakriti*, rather than the pure consciousness of *purusha*.

Meditation: Because concentration employs a meditative object, it is incapable of completely overcoming the subject/object duality of consciousness. Therefore, in the seventh stage the yogi goes beyond all objects of meditation. Here consciousness confronts itself, not in the guise of any object, but as it is in its pure, self-shining, nature. The one-pointed awareness of concentration is deepened until its object becomes transparent, revealing the underlying consciousness. Here all the movements of the mind-stuff have been quieted and nothing blocks out the light of *purusha*.

Samadhi: With the movement of embodied consciousness stilled, the *purusha* is revealed by its own light. This is the perfect fulfillment in which *yoga* culminates. Since it goes beyond all object-subject duality, this state of being is beyond description. But the compound word *samadhi*, used to refer to this ultimate awareness, is suggestive. *Sam* means perfection, *a* is a reflexive indicator, pointing to the self, and *dha* is a verbal root used to indicate a putting into place. When these components are integrated in the word *samadhi*, we have a term that refers to the self's perfect placing of itself in the pure consciousness called *purusha* or *atman*. This, of course, represents the ultimate Hindu goal of *moksha*, or perfect freedom.

The explanation of the relation between the empirical and the ultimate by Samkhya, and the nature of the mistake causing bondage and suffering which is to be remedied by the discipline of *yoga*, is nicely summed up in an old and favorite Indian story. The story deals with a little tiger raised by wild goats who mistook himself for a goat and had to be instructed by a master and provided with the right kinds of experience in order to realize his true nature—that of a tiger.

The tiger's mother had died giving birth, and the infant was left all alone in the world. Fortunately, the goats were compassionate and adopted the little fellow, teaching him how to eat grass with his pointed teeth and how to bleat like they did. Time passed and the tiger assumed that he was just like the rest of the band of goats. But one day an old male tiger came upon this little band of goats. They all fled in terror, except for the tiger-goat, now about half-grown, who for some unknown reason felt no fear. As the savage jungle beast approached, the cub began to feel self-conscious and uncomfortable. To cover his self-consciousness he began to bleat a bit and nibble some grass. The old tiger roared at the little one in amazement and anger, asking him what he thought he was doing eating grass and bleating like a goat. But the little one was too embarrassed by all this to answer, and continued to nibble grass. Thoroughly outraged by this behavior, the jungle tiger grabbed him by the scruff of his neck and carried him to a nearby pool. Holding him over the water he told him to look at himself. "Is that the pot face of a tiger or the long face of a goat?" he roared.

The cub was still too frightened to answer, so the old tiger carried him to his cave, and thrust a huge chunk of juicy, red, raw meat between his jaws. As the juices trickled into his stomach the cub began to feel a new strength and a new power. No longer mistaking himself for a goat the little tiger lashed his tail from side to side and roared like the tiger he was. He had achieved Tiger-realization! He no longer took himself to be what he appeared to be in his ignorance, but realized his true nature, which had nothing to do with the world of goats.

REVIEW QUESTIONS

1. Why is causality a central topic in Samkhya philosophy?
2. Samkhya presents five arguments to show that the effect exists (preexists) in the cause. What does it mean to say that the effect exists in the cause, and what are the arguments to show that this is the case?
3. The fundamental categories of Samkhya are *prakriti* and *purusha*. What are these, and how are they related to each other?
4. What does it mean to say that *yoga* is the restriction of the fluctuations of the mind-stuff (*citta*)?

5. What are the forces that according to *yoga* constitute the bondage of the self?
6. Explain the eight groups of yogic techniques described by Patanjali for over-coming bondage.

FURTHER READING

Yoga and the Hindu Tradition, by Jean Varenne and translated by Derek Colt-man (Chicago: University of Chicago Press, 1976), is an excellent introduction to *yoga.* It is good on both the techniques of *yoga* and the underlying philosophy. In fact, the first ninety pages constitute a very good introduction to the whole panorama of Indian thought. There are nearly fifty pages devoted to explaining the eight aids to *yoga.* An account of tantric *yoga* and a translation of the *Yoga Darshana Upanishad* are also included.

The Essence of Yoga, by Georg Feuerstein (New York: Grove Press, 1976), looks at the entire Indian tradition through the lens of *yoga.* The emphasis is psycho-historical, focusing on the structures of consciousness shaping the Indian understanding of Self and world.

Yoga: Immortality and Freedom, by Mircea Eliade and translated by W. R. Trask, 2nd ed. (Princeton: Princeton University Press, 1969), is the most thorough study of *yoga* available in English. Although this is a large scholarly book, the first hundred pages present a clear, straightforward account of both the philo-sophy and the techniques of *yoga.*

Yoga Philosophy of Patanjali, by Swami Hariharananda Aranya, translated by P. N. Mukerji (Albany: State University of New York Press, 1983), is a reissue of a book published in Calcutta in 1963. It contains the aphorisms of Patanjali with Vyasa's commentary in both Sanskrit and English translation. It also con-tains a good introduction—and a valuable commentary by Swami Hariharananda Aranya.

CHAPTER 6

❧❧❧❧❧❧❧❧❧❧❧❧❧❧❧❧❧❧❧❧❧❧❧❧❧❧❧❧

Knowledge and Reality: Nyaya-Vaisheshika

WHEREAS THE Upanishads emphasized the ultimate nature of reality as an experienced unity, and the Samkhya attempted to show what reality must be like in order to make sense of both our ordinary experience and the claims of the Upanishads, the Nyaya philosophy centers on the nature of our *knowledge* of reality. The main question is not, What is reality like? but, What is our knowledge of reality like? What do we know about our knowledge? Accordingly, major portions of Nyaya philosophy are given over to consideration of the various problems of knowledge. Adopting the Nyaya analysis of the structure of human knowledge, Vaisheshika philosophy emphasized the nature of what is known, and came up with an atomistic picture of the structure of the universe.

The basic problem of knowledge is that of ascertaining whether or not what is claimed as knowledge is actually knowledge rather than just mistaken opinion. Does what is claimed as knowledge really reveal reality? Mistakes are easily made in matters of perception and inference. In the dim light the discarded rope appears to be a snake; it could cause someone to claim knowledge of a snake on the path. But if there were only a rope on the path obviously no one could have *knowledge* of a snake on the path. As examples like this are considered it becomes possible to speculate that perhaps what *appears* to us is always different from what is really there. It might be as though the eyes always present things as red, yellow, and blue, whereas all things are really orange, black, and green. The ear presents sounds differently from what they really are, and the other senses equally distort the reality with which they come in contact. Skeptical considerations of this sort push philosophers in the direction of trying to analyze what knowledge is.

In Nyaya the analysis of knowledge is taken up in terms of the knowing subject, the object to be known, the known object, and the means of coming to know the object. Analysis of claims to knowledge reveals that these four factors are involved in all knowledge, for there is no knowledge except when someone knows something. The one who knows is the subject, the something known is the object. The object is either the object to be known, or the object that is known. The whole point of coming to know things is to pass from ignorance, in which case the subject is separated from the object, to knowledge, in which case the subject, by various means, comes to be related to the object in certain ways. These relations constitute knowing the object. Consequently, anyone wishing to come to an understanding of what knowledge is must attend to (1) the knowing subject, (2) the object to be known, (3) the object as known, and (4) the means whereby the object comes to be known.

According to Nyaya, knowledge is essentially the revelation of an object, and the means of knowledge are distinguished according to the different causes responsible for the revelation of the object in knowledge. This principle of distinction yields perception, inference, analogy, and testimony as the four basic means, or sources, of knowledge. The principle for distinguishing between these sources is that a person is doing four basically different things in coming to know something in each of the different ways. We will begin our discussion of the Nyaya theory of knowledge with an analysis of these four valid means of knowledge, showing how they constitute different ways of knowing.

Perceptual Knowledge

Perceptual knowledge is defined as the true and determinate knowledge arising from the contact of the senses with their proper objects.[1] It is known, by means of perception, that these words you are reading appear on a piece of paper, because of the contact of the eye with the marks constituting the words. If one were a considerable distance from the paper and

---

[1] *The Nyaya Sutras of Gotama,* 1.4, trans. by Vidyabhusana in *The Sacred Book of the Hindus,* VIII (Allahabad: The Panini Office, 1930). Reprinted in Sarvepalli Radhakrishnan and Charles A. Moore, eds., *A Source Book in Indian Philosophy* (Princeton: Princeton University Press, 1957), pp. 358 ff.

perceived only dark spots on the paper, not knowing whether they were words, scribbles, or ants, it would not be a genuine case of perception, for the object perceived would not be determinate. If one were to mistake a rope for a snake, this would not be a case of genuine perception either, for it would not be true knowledge, since there was no snake there to be perceived.

However, even in cases of perceptual illusions or mistakes is not something actually perceived? It does not seem possible that the senses could reveal sensory objects without some external stimuli. Unless there were something with which the senses were making contact there would be nothing to be revealed. Furthermore, if it were the case that the senses could reveal something when there was no contact of any kind, it might turn out that all claimed perceptual experience was of this kind, and that in reality there was nothing in the world to be sensed. But this is self-contradictory, for the very claim itself rests on the assumption of real sensory contact.

But it still is necessary to explain how genuine perceptions of the kinds recognized as knowledge differ from and can be distinguished from perceptual mistakes. The Nyaya explanation of this point rests on a distinction between two kinds of perception. Determinate perception—perception of words on this paper—is preceded by indeterminate perception—sense contact with the marks on the paper prior to recognition and classification of them as words. To talk about a perceptual mistake in reference to the indeterminate perception doesn't make any sense, for there is nothing which is taken to be anything, and therefore it cannot be taken for something other than what it is. Indeterminate perception is simply the contact of the sense with its object. It is the most elementary sensory experience limited to precisely what is given by sense contact. But this is not classified as perceptual knowledge.

Perceptual knowledge requires determinate perception in which basic sensory experience of the indeterminate perception is revealed as some kind of thing with various qualities and relations, being, in principle, nameable. There is thus a distinction between an immediate sensory experience and perception, though the latter always includes the former. Consequently there is also a distinction between ignorance and error. Ignorance may be due to a lack of either the immediate sensory experience or to a lack of determinate perception, but error results from mistaking what is given in immediate sensory experience for something other than what it is. In terms of the example of erroneously perceiving a snake instead of a rope, the immediate sensory experience reveals a darkish-colored, elongated, and twisted color patch. But in perception this content of sensory experience is seen as a snake when it is in fact a rope and the result is the erroneous claim that a snake has been seen. From this it can be seen that true perceptual knowledge is the perception of what is perceived as it really is, and error is the perception of something other than what it really is.

But now the question may be raised as to how a particular perceptual judgment can be known to be true. Obviously it is impossible to *directly* test the correspondence between the perception and the reality being perceived, for this would mean knowing what is true knowledge by going outside of knowledge itself. But to know something outside of knowing it is impossible. If, however, the correspondence is tested within the framework of knowledge all we get is another knowledge claim about the claimed correspondence. And this can go on indefinitely without ever revealing anything about the actual correspondence between claim and reality.

Consequently Nyaya suggests that mistaken knowledge claims are detected, ultimately, in terms of the successfulness of practice. If one's perception of the finely granulated white stuff in the bowl on the table as sugar is erroneous because the bowl in reality contains salt, it will not help to take another dozen looks at it. Rather, it is necessary to take some action based on the perception and see how the action turns out. If the perception is non-erroneous a spoonful of the contents of the bowl will make the coffee a pleasant drink. If the perception is erroneous because the bowl contains salt, a spoonful in the coffee will make the contents of the cup undrinkable. Expanding this principle of verification of perceptual claims, the position is reached that whatever works—in the sense that it provides for successful activity, and eventually, human happiness and liberation—is true because it is seen to correspond to reality as attested to by the successful activity.

In this way the Nyaya philosophers define true perception in terms of correspondence to reality. But they advocate practice as the means of testing this correspondence.

Different kinds of perceptual knowledge can be distinguished according to the ways in which contact is established between the senses and their objects. Ordinary perception occurs when the eye sees color, the ear hears sound, the nose smells odors, the tongue tastes flavors, resistance is felt, or the mind comes into contact with physical states and processes. The first five kinds of perceptual knowledge yield indeterminate perception, or merely the basic sensory experience itself. The sixth kind of perceptual knowledge, which is internal, is a matter of becoming aware of the sensory experiences and perceiving them to be something or the other. It corresponds to ordinary determinate perception.

In addition, Nyaya admits extra-ordinary perception. Analysis of our knowledge reveals that not only are there basic sensory experiences and perceptions of individual things, but also that there are perceptions of natures of things. Visual experience of certain color patches is not simply perceived to be an individual thing that goes by the name of, say, Rama, but is perceived to be that *man*, Rama. Since the perception of the nature of the individual, by virtue of which the individual can be recognized as a member of a class (e.g., the class "man"), is not given in ordinary perception, it is regarded as one of the three kinds of extra-ordinary perception.

The second kind of extra-ordinary perception explains how what is proper to one sense organ can become the object of another sense. For example, it is often said that ice looks cold, or that flowers look soft, or fragrant. But coldness, softness, and fragrance are not the proper objects of sight. Consequently, these kinds of perceptual experiences are regarded as extra-ordinary.

The third kind of extra-ordinary perception refers to the perception of things in the past or future, or hidden, or infinitely small in size by one who possesses unusual powers generated by disciplined meditation, or *yoga*.

Inference

Although perception is the basic kind of knowledge, there are three other means of knowledge recognized by Nyaya. Inference is regarded as an independent means of valid knowledge that is defined as producing a knowledge that comes after other knowledge.[2] For example, from perceptual knowledge it is possible to infer something about reality that has never actually been perceived. We know that dinosaurs existed because of certain fossil remains that have been seen. Inference proceeds from what has been perceived to something that has not been perceived by means of a third "something" called a reason, which functions as a middle term in syllogistic reasoning. For example, in the syllogistic inference, "there is fire on the hill because there is smoke on the hill, and wherever there is smoke there is fire," the universal connection between smoke and fire is the reason (the third "thing") for affirming fire on the hill, even though the fire was not actually perceived.

A commonly used example of inference in its ordinary syllogistic form is as follows:

[2] *Nyaya Sutra*, I.5.

1. Yonder hill has fire.
2. Because it has smoke.
3. Whatever has smoke has fire, e.g., a stove.
4. Yonder hill has smoke such as is always accompanied by fire.
5. Therefore yonder hill has fire.

Nyaya distinguishes between reasoning to convince oneself and reasoning to convince another. When reasoning to convince oneself it is not necessary to set out the steps so elaborately as above, and either the first two or the last two steps can be eliminated. But when the inference is set down formally for the consideration of another, all five steps are insisted upon. The essential part of the inference in the above example is the coming to know that there is fire on the hill on the basis of (1) the perceived smoke and (2) the reason constituted by the invariable connection between smoke and fire.

In the above example, the first proposition represents the new knowledge claim. The second proposition gives the perceptual grounds for the new claim. The third proposition asserts the reason for making the move from a claim about smoke to one about fire. It is, so to speak, the inference ticket, enabling one to move on to the conclusion constituting the inferential knowledge claim. The fourth proposition asserts that the inference ticket is good for this trip, i.e., that the reason applies in this case. The fifth proposition repeats the claim, now not as a matter for testing, but as a valid knowledge claim, as established by the reasons provided.

Clearly, the most crucial part of the inferential process is establishing the reason (3), the invariable connection between two objects or events. Grant that it was observed on one or a hundred occasions in the past that fire was accompanied by smoke. Is this a guarantee that in the next case smoke will be accompanied by fire? After all, just because the first ten or one hundred persons who walked into the UN building were males does not mean that the next person will be male.

Nyaya philosophers regard the enumeration of individual objects or events as an important part of the establishment of universal connections between events or objects. If ten black crows are seen and no non-black crows, there is some probability that there is a universal connection between being a crow and being black. But if thousands of crows have been observed, all of them black, the probability is increased. However, even if a million crows, all black, have been observed, and the next crow observed is white, the probability that there is a universal connection between being a crow and being black is zero, even though we might want to say that the probability is very high that the millionth-and-second crow will be black.

But if this is the case it would seem that no amount of confirming instances would ever establish a necessary connection between events or objects, for it would always be possible that the very next observed case would refute the necessity of the connection. In light of this possibility, even though Nyaya places much emphasis upon presence of confirming experience and absence of unconfirming experience, the matter is not left here. After all, they argue, there is a difference between claims such as "Wherever there is smoke there is fire" on the one hand, and the claim "All crows are black," on the other. The difference is that there is nothing in the nature of a crow that requires blackness. But there is something about the nature of smoke that connects it with fire.

Nevertheless, even if there really is a difference between these cases, the question still arises as to how it is possible to determine that in some cases the connection is universal and necessary because causal, while in others the connection is mere coincidence without any causal basis. Since inference proceeds from perceptual knowledge, if there is to be knowledge of a universal and necessary connection between events or objects, it must be that this necessity is perceived, and not inferred. Accordingly, Nyaya includes in perceptual knowledge the perception of the class-nature of the individual. This is a kind of extra-ordinary perception whereby the individual is perceived not merely to be this or that particular thing or event, but as this or that particular thing *and* one of a certain *kind*, or *class*, of things, the class-nature, or essence, being perceived along with the individual characteristics of the thing or event.

Those inferences involving universal connection are of either of two kinds. Either (1) the unperceived effect can be inferred from the perceived cause, or (2) the unperceived cause can be inferred from the perceived effect. All other inferences depend upon a non-causal and non-necessary uniformity, and cannot be shown to be necessarily true.

To aid in avoiding certain common mistakes in drawing inferences, the Nyaya philosophers have listed a number of fallacies to be avoided. A fallacy is defined as that which appears to be a valid reason for inference, but which is really not a valid reason. In the inference "There is fire on the hill because there is smoke on the hill and where there is smoke there is fire," the inferred knowledge is that there is fire on the hill. The assertion "there is fire" is being made about the hill. Technically the term "fire" is called *sadhya*. The term "hill" is called *paksha*. The reason for the assertion—"There is smoke"—is called *hetu*. Unless what is taken to be a reason for connecting the *sadhya* with the *paksha* is really a reason, or *hetu,* the inference will be invalid. To insure that the given *hetu,* or reason, will really be a reason, several rules must be observed. (1) The reason, or *hetu,* must be present in the *paksha,* and in all other objects having the *sadhya* in it. (2) The reason, or *hetu,* must be absent from objects not possessing the *sadhya.* (3) The inferred proposition should not be contradicted by valid perception. (4) The reason, or *hetu,* should not make possible a conclusion contradicting the inferred proposition.

Comparison

The third means of valid knowledge recognized by Nyaya philosophers is knowledge by comparison based on similarity. For example, if you knew what a cow was, and were told that a deer was like a cow in certain respects, you might come to know that the animal you met in the woods was a deer. This is different from being told what name to apply to a certain object. If, for example, one were to see a deer for the first time and be told, "That is a deer," the knowledge would be due to testimony, not to comparison. Knowledge by means of comparison is attained when the association of the name of an unknown object is made by the knower on the basis of experiencing the similarity of the unknown object with a known object. The crucial aspect of this means of knowledge is the observation of the similarity. Nyaya thinkers hold that similarities are objective and perceivable. Accordingly, knowledge of the nature of a new object on the strength of its similarity to a known object constitutes a separate means of knowledge. While comparative knowledge involves both perception and inference, it cannot be reduced to either of them, and therefore is to be counted as a third means of knowledge.

Testimony

The fourth means of valid knowledge recognized in Nyaya is technically called *shabda.* Literally, it means the word of a person, and it refers to the knowledge achieved as a result of being told something by a reliable person. Opinion is not the same thing as knowledge, for opinion might be erroneous, but knowledge cannot be. Consequently, simply hearing the opinion of another is not a means of knowledge. But when the knowledge claims of another are heard genuine knowledge is attained if one understands the claim. The three criteria of knowledge based on the testimony of another are: (1) the person speaking must be absolutely honest and reliable; (2) the person speaking must actually *know* that which is communicated; (3) the hearer must understand exactly what is being heard.

Objects of Knowledge

Having analyzed the means of valid knowledge, the next step is to consider the objects of valid knowledge. Nyaya lists as objects of knowledge the self, the body, the senses and their objects, knowledge, mind, action, mental imperfections, pleasure and pain, suffering, and freedom from suffering.[3] These objects of knowledge all depend upon the relation between a knowing subject and a world of objects, for they have to do with the actions and impressions of a subject. If one considers objects of knowledge from the viewpoint of their own independent existence they include the categories of the Vaisheshika system. These categories are (1) substance, (2) quality, (3) motion, (4) generality, (5) particularity, (6) inherence, and (7) nonexistence.[4]

These categories are the types of objects that correspond to the different types of perceived objects. Since perceptions are due to contact with objects by an experiencing self, the differences in perceptual objects must be due to different real objects. Thus, classification of objects of knowledge yields a classification of existing things, as differences in perception are due to differences in what is perceived.

The first kind of existing thing is substance. This refers to that which exists independently of other kinds of things, but which is the *locus* of existence for the other kinds of things. Real in itself, a substance can be thought of as the substratum of qualities and actions. The category of substance includes: (1) earth, (2) water, (3) light, (4) air, (5) ether, (6) time, (7) space, (8) self, and (9) mind. Earth, water, light, air, and ether are regarded as physical elements since each of them is known by a particular external sense; earth by smell, water by taste, light by sight, air by touch, and ether by sound.

These substances can be considered in two ways. First, they can be

---

[3] *Nyaya Sutra*, I.9.
[4] *Vaisheshika Sutra*, I.4, trans. by Nandalal Sinha, *The Sacred Books of the Hindus*, VI (Allahabad: the Panini Office, 2nd ed. 1923), reprinted in *Source Book in Indian Philosophy*, pp. 387 ff. Actually, the seventh category, that of nonexistence, was added centuries later than the others.

thought of as atomic, eternal, and indivisible. Second, they are the results of combinations of atoms, in which case they are temporal, composite, and destructible, being produced by the combination of atoms. That substances in the sense of composite things, such as this jar, are made up of atoms is known on the basis of inference. If the jar is broken it is reduced to several parts. Each of these parts can again be broken, being reduced to more parts. But no matter how long this process continues it is impossible that every part should be destructible, for that would mean it is composite. But if composite things exist it is necessary that their ultimate constituents be simple, or else composite things would never be produced, according to Vaisheshika. Therefore, the ultimate constituents of gross substances must be atomic. The substance space is inferred on the grounds that sound is perceived and since sound is a quality, there must be that in which it inheres or that to which it belongs, namely, space.

Space and time are known to exist because of our perceptions of here and there, far and near, and past, present, and future. Knowledge is a quality, and therefore it must exist in a substance called the self, which is the ground of consciousness. Mind is inferred on the grounds that feeling and willing are known, but since they are not known by the external senses they must be known by the mind. In addition there is that which directs the senses and collects their contacts into experience. That in which sense contacts reside as qualities is the substance known as mind.

The second category of known objects is that of quality. It refers to the various qualifications of the substances, and includes color, odor, contact, sound, number, measure, difference, connection, separation, long or short, far or near, knowledge, happiness, sorrow, volition, hatred, effort, heaviness, fluidity, potency, merit, and demerit. This list of qualifications is a way of saying that things or substances can be, for example, red or blue, pungent or fragrant, touching or apart from, soft or loud, one or many, large or small, the same as or different from, separate or together, long or short, far or near, knowing or ignorant, happy or sorrowful, desiring to or desiring not to, loving or hating, trying or not trying, light or heavy, mobile or immobile, able or not able, and good or bad, respectively. There are many divisions of some of the qualities, but the above list is being taken as referring to the basic kinds of qualifications of substances.

The third kind of basic and irreducible reality is motion. The different kinds of motion are (1) upward, (2) downward, (3) contraction, (4) expansion, and (5) locomotion. The kinds of motion are the kinds of reality that account for the changes substances undergo.

The fourth category is that of universal essences. It accounts for sameness found in substances, qualities, or actions. Four cows, four red objects, and four upward motions are each of them the same in that they are cows, reds, or upward motions. This sameness is regarded as objective, belonging to the individual things just as truly as do qualities. The reason that the four cows can all be recognized as cows is that they share in the same essence or nature. It is this essence which enables one to form class concepts and to classify individual things into various classes.

From a continuous field of sensing and mental activity particular objects are perceived. The ability to perceive particular and distinct objects is due to the category of particularity which belongs to the objects perceived. If things did not have the character of being different from other things there would be no reason why they should be perceived as different. But since they are perceived as different there must be some foundation for this difference in reality. Hence, particularity must exist in reality.

The category of inherence reflects the fact that different things, such as substance, quality, action, etc., appear as one whole. Thus, the size of the man, his color, his nature as man, and his particularity as this man, all appear so unified that we think of one thing appearing, rather than a collection of things appearing to us. Thus, the whole inheres in its parts; the jug in the clay, the pencil in the wood, etc. The basis for the unity of different categories must, like the other categories, have a foundation in reality, as different from other kinds of things. Otherwise it would appear as one of the other kinds of things, and not as separate. Therefore, the category of inherence is recognized as an independent kind of reality.

In addition to the above kinds of knowable objects there is nonexistence. Although nonexistence may seem to be a queer kind of reality its existence cannot be questioned, according to Vaisheshika, for to question it is to suggest that it does not exist, which is to affirm the category of nonexistence. Only by assuming nonexistence does negation become possible.

In the way just outlined Nyaya and Vaisheshika come to their metaphysical view of reality. This list of the basic kinds of things that exist is a sketch of the ontological universe.

The Knower

Considering the knowing subject, rather than the objects to be known, or the objects as known, Nyaya argues that the self is a unique substance. The qualifications of this substance are knowledge, feeling, and volition. Accordingly, the self is defined as the substance in which the qualities of desire, aversion, pleasure, pain, etc., inhere, for these follow upon knowing, feeling, and volition. Now, none of these are physical qualities, since they cannot be perceived as physical qualities by any of the senses. Therefore it must be admitted that they belong to a substance other than a physical, or material, substance. Furthermore, the self must be distinct from physical objects, from sensations, from consciousness, and the mind, for the self experiences all of these. One may ask, who knows reality, who perceives, who is conscious, etc.? In every case the answer is given, "The self." Since everything else can become an object for the self, but objects—as objects—require a subject for which they are objects, it follows that the self cannot be an object, and therefore cannot be identical with anything that becomes an object, for it must be always subject.

Since the self is a unique substance and consciousness belongs to it as a quality, the self does not depend for its existence upon consciousness. In fact, according to Nyaya, ultimate liberation, or freedom, will also be freedom from consciousness. The reason for this is that consciousness is seen as consciousness of something or other. But that presupposes a duality between subject and object. And when there is duality there is possible suffering and bondage, for the subject can be bound by the object and caused to suffer. But to eliminate suffering and bondage duality must be eliminated. This can be done upon the elimination of consciousness. But if the self were essentially consciousness this would mean the extinction of the self. However, since consciousness is only a characteristic of the self, the self is not destroyed when consciousness is eliminated. All that can be said about the self in this state of liberation is that it simply exists as self.

REVIEW QUESTIONS

1. What are the four valid means of knowledge according to Nyaya?
2. Define perception. What is the distinction between determinate and indeterminate perception and why is it important?
3. Valid inference is possible because of the invariable connection between objects or events. How is this invariable connection known?
4. According to Vaisheshika, there are seven fundamental kinds or categories of existence. What are these? What categories would you add to, or eliminate from, this list? Why?
5. What is the Nyaya view of the self? What are the arguments for regarding the self as a unique substance?

FURTHER READING

The Nyaya Theory of Knowledge, 2nd ed., by Satischandra Chatterjee (Calcutta: University of Calcutta Press, 1950), is a classic account of Nyaya. It contains lucid discussions of each of the four valid means of knowledge and compares Nyaya theories to other Indian theories of knowledge. Accessible to the beginning student, this book will also be of interest to graduate students looking for a reliable exposition of the subject.

Indian Metaphysics and Epistemology: The Tradition of Nyāya—Vaiśeṣika up to Gaṅgeṣa, edited by Karl H. Potter (Princeton: Princeton University Press, 1977), is the most complete and up-to-date book on Nyaya available. The first two hundred pages introduce the reader to the important concepts, and the remaining four hundred pages contain summaries of major Nyaya works. This material is very difficult for beginners, but invaluable for serious students of Nyaya.

The Logic of Gotama, by Kisor Kumar Chakrabarti, monograph no. 5 of the Society for Asian and Comparative Philosophy (Honolulu: University of Hawaii Press, 1977), discusses the Nyaya theory of inference or deductive logic.

Epistemology, Logic and Grammar in Indian Philosophical Analysis, by Bimal K. Matilal (The Hague: Morton, 1971), is an excellent analysis of Indian theories of knowledge by an outstanding Nyaya scholar, and rewarding for the serious student. His earlier book, *The Navya-Nyāya Doctrine of Negation* (Cambridge: Harvard University Press, 1968) is by far the best analysis of negative statements in Nyaya, but is recommended only for the advanced student.

CHAPTER 7

❧❧❧❧❧❧❧❧❧❧❧❧❧❧❧❧❧❧❧❧❧❧❧❧❧❧❧❧❧❧❧❧❧

Change and Reality: Vedanta

ALL THE PHILOSOPHIES of India were greatly influenced by the teachings of the Upanishads. Even the philosophies of Jainism, Carvaka, and Buddhism, which rejected the authority of the Upanishads, were much influenced by their teachings. With the exception of these latter philosophies, all the philosophies of India took themselves to be in essential agreement with the teachings of the Upanishads. But as the canons of experience and reason were differently interpreted, there came to be a variety of interpretations of the Upanishads, some of which appeared to conflict with the literal conclusions of the Upanishads.

The Vedanta philosophers set out self-consciously to underwrite the main conclusions of the Upanishads with critical interpretations of reason and experience which did not conflict with those conclusions. As a result, the Vedanta philosophies turned out to be highly critical of some of the conclusions of the other systems. For example, the Samkhya claim that the world of the not-Self was eternally real and distinct from the Self, and the Nyaya, Vaisheshika, and Mimamsa views of the world as real and pluralistic, being made up of different kinds of atoms, came in for severe criticism, since these conclusions appeared to deviate furthest from the emphasis on the sole reality of *Atman*, or *Brahman*, in the Upanishads.

The Nyaya, Vaisheshika, Samkhya, and Mimamsa systems of philosophy are unanimous in agreeing that our perceptions have a basis in reality. That basis can be expressed by saying that what is perceived exists independently of being perceived. Genuine knowledge occurs when the knower comes to see things as they really are. Philosophically, this position is known as realism, which simply indicates that the objective world revealed by experience is real and exists independently of being known. These systems also are pluralistic in that they agree that this objective reality is constituted by a variety of ultimately different objects.

This view, pluralistic realism, is not a very startling view of the world. In fact, it is the view held by most people in the world. Philosophical proponents of this view have argued that whenever one's experiences are to be taken seriously as providing knowledge it is necessary that there be knowledge of *something*. If there is no something to be known there can be no knowledge. However, if something exists to be known, then there are objects that exist independently of perception even though they can be related to a knower in such a way that they come to be perceived and known. Therefore, it is logically necessary to admit the real existence of the world that is experienced if it is claimed that there really is knowledge. But to claim that one knows that there is no knowledge is absurd, for it is a claim that there is knowledge. And what basis other than knowledge is there for claiming that there is no knowledge of the world?

These are some of the difficulties faced by the Vedanta philosophers who felt that the realistic and pluralistic conclusions of the philosophers of the other systems were in direct opposition to the conclusions of the Upanishads. After all, the Upanishads taught the unity of reality and the identity of self with reality in passages such as the following: "All this is *Atman*."[1] "Atman being known . . . everything is known."[2] "There was only Being at the beginning, it was one without a second."[3] "All this is *Brahman*."[4] "This self is the *Brahman*."[5] "I am *Brahman*."[6]

The very fact that the unity of reality was thus taught in the Upanishads was sufficient reason for a Hindu to accept this view as true, for the Upanishads belong to the tradition of infallible literature. Nevertheless, for the critical mind it is important to show that this teaching does not conflict with reason or experience. A significant step in this direction could be taken simply by showing that opposing claims about reality were self-contradictory and implausible. Consequently the task of showing that the philosophies with conclusions at variance with the monistic teachings of the Upanishads were unsatisfactory became an important part of Vedanta

[1] *Chandogya Upanishad*, 7.25.2.
[2] *Brihadaranyaka Upanishad*, 4.5.6.
[3] *Chandogya Upanishad*, 6.2.1.
[4] *Mundaka Upanishad*, 2.2.11, and *Chandogya Upanishad*, 3.14.1.
[5] *Brihadaranyaka Upanishad*, 2.5.19.
[6] *Brihadaranyaka Upanishad*, 1.4.10.

philosophy. As a result, the critical analysis of the other philosophies came to be emphasized. But it was not sufficient simply to show that other systems were unsatisfactory. It was also necessary to show that the system of reality claimed by the Vedantic interpretation of the Upanishads was not subject to the same kinds of criticisms aimed at the other systems. In this way the Vedanta philosophies came to provide rational criticisms of the other philosophies and also to provide rational defenses of their own inter-pretations and systems.

There are three principal schools of Vedantic philosophy, differing from each other in the way they account for the relations between persons, things, and ultimate Reality (*Brahman*). The oldest of these schools, that of non-dualism, is often referred to as the Shankarite school, being named after Shankara, one of its important early philosophers who lived in the eighth century. The second school, that of qualified non-dualism, claims the eleventh-century philosopher Ramanuja as its principal figure, and is there-fore sometimes called the Ramanuja school. The third school, the dualistic Vedanta, has as its central figure the thirteenth-century philosopher named Madhva.

Shankara's Non-Dualism

Shankara's view of reality is that there is one absolute and independent reality which alone exists as real and unchanging. This reality is the *Brahman* of the Upanishads. This view rules out theories according to which the world is thought of as the product of material elements, or the transforma-tion of unconscious matter that evolves, or the product of two kinds of independent reality, such as *Brahman* and matter.

According to Shankara, *Brahman* is the reality that provides for the existence of the appearances that constitute the empirical world, but it is also beyond these appearances, not being exhausted by them. From the empirical and conceptual point of view, *Brahman* is in the world, or immanent. From the absolute point of view, *Brahman* transcends the world.

The nature and existence of *Brahman* cannot be proved from perception or reasoning, but is to be taken either on the basis of scriptural testimony (the Upanishads) or by direct and intuitive experience of the kind made possible by yogic concentration. Nevertheless, reason can be used to justify these means of knowing *Brahman*.

To reconcile the perceived plurality and objective reality of the world with the monistic conclusions of the Upanishads, Shankara regards the world as appearance rather than reality, and perception as illusion rather than knowledge.

The individual self as pure subject, or *Atman*, is not different from *Brahman*.

By way of refuting conflicting claims about the nature of reality Shankara considers first the Samkhya view and then the Vaisheshika view. According to Samkhya philosophy, the world is the result of the spontaneous evolution of unconscious matter, or *prakriti*, which is composed of the three *gunas*—*sattva*, *rajas*, and *tamas*. Samkhya includes within its view the existence of purpose in the world, for the world is such that it fits reborn selves and enables them to be liberated. But how can one suppose that the world, which is a harmonious system of related objects and ordered events as we experience it—and as claimed by Samkhya—could be the accidental result of an unconscious cause? To attribute purpose to unconscious nature is unintelligible according to Shankara's analysis, and therefore the Samkhya view is untenable.

The Vaisheshika view is that the world is caused by the combination of atoms. But again, how can unconscious atoms produce out of their combinations the order that makes possible the moral law claimed by the Vaisheshika philosophers? Even if this objection is overlooked, Vaisheshika has not explained how or why unconscious atoms should first begin to move around and join together to produce the world. If atoms were incessantly in motion and joining together because of their very nature neither the beginning of the world nor its dissolution would be explicable. Therefore the Vaisheshika view is not satisfactory according to Shankara's analysis, since it claims both production and destruction.

Thus, the explanations of Vaisheshika and Samkhya are seen to be inconsistent within the framework of their own assumptions. But their basic assumptions are not altogether satisfactory either. Nyaya, Vaisheshika, Samkhya, and Mimamsa all accept as a basic assumption the fact of real change and causation. That is, they all admit that various real changes occur in the world and that these changes are caused.

Concerning the relation between cause and effect only two views are possible. Either the effect preexists in the cause or it does not. If the effect does not preexist in the cause then the effect is totally new. This view is called *asatkaryavada* (nonexistence of the effect). If the claim is that the effect preexists in the cause—this view is called *satkaryavada*—then two consequences may follow. On the one hand, it can be admitted that change and causality is a matter of making explicit what was implicit in the cause. Or it can be claimed that there is no difference between cause and effect.

Nyaya and Vaisheshika held to *asatkaryavada,* as did some of the Mimamsa philosophers, on the grounds that effects are experienced as something totally new. Other Mimamsa philosophers and Samkhya philosophers held to *satkaryavada,* admitting change in the sense of making explicit what was implicit in the cause, but denying that effects were new realities.

Sankara, in critically examining these views of causation, finds them both logically unacceptable. Nothing can show an effect to be different from its material cause. Clay pots are clay, gold rings are gold, etc. Furthermore the clay pot cannot exist apart from the clay, nor the gold ring apart from the gold. Consequently it is incorrect to say that an effect is something new that has been produced and that it did not exist before. In terms of its material cause it has always been there. From another point of view, it is argued that it is impossible to conceive of something totally new coming into existence. All that can ever be thought is the transformation of matter, never the coming into existence of matter.

Samkhya argues that if the effect were something new we would have the coming into existence of the nonexistent. If this were possible, why not get nonexistent oil out of sand? However, even though Samkhya may be right in claiming the theory of *asatkaryavada* to be unacceptable, the Samkhya philosophers do not realize that their own interpretation of *satkaryavada* is also untenable. If the effect already preexists in the cause, how can there be a genuine change of the material into the effect? If the effect is already there, then it is impossible for the material to become the effect, for that would be the coming to be of what already is, which makes no sense. If the Samkhya philosophers reply that though matter does not come into existence, the form does—a new form is produced—they are really admitting the existence of *asatkaryavada,* admitting the effect as something that did not previously exist. But this contradicts their own arguments against *asatkaryavada.*

However, from the fact that Samkhya philosophers have contradicted themselves, it does not necessarily follow that something new does not come into existence. What follows is that either nothing new can come into existence, or that their argument is wrong and something new can come into existence. Consequently, it is still necessary for Shankara to tend to the question of whether a change of form is a real change, for it cannot be denied that changes in form are perceived.

Shankara's solution is to show that though changes in form are perceived, this does not imply a change in reality unless a form has reality of its own. But, of course, form has existence only in dependence upon matter, for there is no form except in formed matter. There is no form of a cup except the cup made of matter. Therefore, form has no independent reality. If a change in form were a change in reality, a person sitting down would be a different reality from a person standing up, since the form is different. But, of course, the same person standing up or sitting down is one and the same reality.

From another point of view, the argument is provided that if substances are distinct from their forms or qualities it would be impossible to explain the relation between the quality or form and the substance. If the form is distinct from the substance it cannot be related to the substance except in terms of a third reality which connects or relates them. But then, in order to relate this third distinct reality to the other two, another distinct reality is needed. And to relate this reality to the others, still another is needed. There would be no end to this process of multiplying entities to relate the form to the substance. But if there were no end to the process, then the form would be unrelated to the substance, making a change in reality impossible. If it is admitted that the form has no reality independent of matter then there is no change in reality.

Illusion

These arguments, if valid, lead to the conclusion that no changes are possible, for it has been shown that it is impossible for causation to bring about change. But on the other hand there is the perception of changes. Shankara's solution to the dilemma is to suggest that since the perceived changes cannot rationally be accepted as real, they be regarded as similar to the perception of an illusory object.

If the objects constituting the furniture of the world are like the illusory objects of dreaming experience, it becomes possible to reconcile the existence of *Brahman* alone as the ultimate reality with the existence of the empirical world as unreal. The snake perceived in the dream *exists* in the dream, but is not *real*. That it exists must be admitted, for otherwise there would be no dream. But that it is real cannot be admitted for its unreality is what marks this particular experience as dreaming experience. In a similar way, the objects of the empirical world exist, for they are perceived. To deny the existence of the objects of the empirical world is to deny ordinary perceptual experience. But if there is an analogy between dream objects and the objects perceived in waking experience, then perhaps the objects of waking experience could also be said to be unreal, as compared with the experience of a greater reality. After all, as long as one is dreaming it is impossible to regard the objects of the dream as unreal. It is only possible to regard the dream objects as unreal when a different level of experience is attained. From the vantage point of waking experience the dream objects can be said to be unreal. But it may also be possible that from another level of experience—the experience of *Brahman*—the objects of ordinary waking experience could be seen to be unreal.

Thus, if the objects of ordinary waking experience were like dream objects in this respect it would be possible to reconcile the existence of the perceptual and empirical world with the sole reality of *Brahman*, in a way similar to the reconciliation of the existence of dream objects with their unreality.

If it is suggested that the whole world of ordinary experience is somehow illusory, it becomes important to understand the nature of illusion in order to see what sense this suggestion makes. An example considered in Vedanta is that of the rope that is mistakenly seen as a snake. The rope is said to be a snake because of ignorance of what really is there. If it were known that there is a rope there, there would be no illusion. But ignorance in itself is not enough to produce the illusion. After all, there are many things of which one is ignorant, but one does not say that these are snakes. The ignorance that produces an illusion must have two aspects. First, it covers up the reality actually present, e.g., the rope. Second, it actually distorts what is really there, representing it as something other than what it is.

Now, if the nature of the world is like an illusory object it must be that the world is also a product of ignorance, where the basic reality is not simply obscured and hidden from view, but is actually distorted into something other than what it is. In this way, the true reality, *Brahman,* as a result of ignorance, could be mistaken for the world of ordinary empirical objects. These objects are simply the concealing distortion of *Brahman*, which alone is real. But, of course, it is only from the standpoint of the ignorant that there is any ignorance. It is only from this ignorance that the world proceeds, as it covers up the true nature of reality and causes us to see mistakenly something else in its place. Just as an illusion is produced when a magician makes one coin to appear to be many—though illusion exists only for the ignorant, not for the magician—similarly from the point of view of absolute reality there is no plurality of objects—no illusion. There is only the one true reality, just as for the magician there is only the one coin. For the wise, who succeed in seeing through the illusion of the magician, there do not appear many coins. Similarly, for the wise who experience *Brahman*, there does not appear a world of empirical objects as the ultimate reality.

It follows, if the empirical world is unreal, that there are no real changes in the world, for the changes have the same reality as the objects that are supposed to change. Consequently, the only theory of change possible is that of apparent change rather than real change. Real changes and causes are possible only if there are real objects and they really change. But if Shankara is right, there can be no real changes and causes, for there are no real objects to change. This lends support to the Vedanta claims that the Nyaya-Vaisheshika and Samkhya theories of change are incorrect.

This theory of the nature of the empirical world also enables Shankara to explain those passages in the Upanishads that speak of the world being produced out of *Brahman*. The world can be produced out of *Brahman* just as snakes are produced out of ropes and bent sticks are produced by water (by refraction). There is existence inasmuch as there are objects for experience. But there is no reality because the objects are illusory, being the result of ignorance.

This attempt on the part of Shankara to explain the world as an appearance produced by illusory perception depends for its success largely upon showing that the analogy of illusory perception applies. This is done by analyzing carefully the notion of perceptual error.

Mimamsa philosophers argue that perceptual error is impossible. Immediate perception at least must be allowed to be valid, for it is the basis of all other knowledge. In support of their claim that perceptual error is impossible, the Mimamsa philosophers analyze alleged cases of perceptual error. They argue that in the case of perceiving a snake in a rope an error is made, but it is not a perceptual error. That erroneous knowledge is not simply one piece of knowledge, but a mixture of perception and memory, along with the failure to discriminate between the two. Thus, they argue that the perception itself is correct and the memory itself is correct, but that the two are wrongly conjoined. The error lies in failing to discriminate.

To this argument the Vedanta philosophers reply that the claim, "This is a snake," does not represent three pieces of knowledge—with the mistake being made in the third kind—but represents only one piece of knowledge. That memory is involved is not denied, but the claim that memory exists independently of the perception is challenged. Unless the memory combined with the perception to produce this one bit of knowledge there would be two claims: (1) "I perceive this," and (2) "I remember a snake." But in point of fact there is only one claim, "This is a snake." And this argues for positive identification, not merely a failure to recognize the difference between the perceived and the remembered. And, of course, if the

Mimamsa reasons for their claim that no perceptual error is possible are unsatisfactory, then the claim need not be taken seriously.

The Nyaya-Vaisheshika view of error is that error is possible, but that it is really a matter of extra-ordinary perception. What happens when a snake is perceived in a rope is that this perception sets up the memory image of a snake perceived in the past so sharply that one becomes immediately aware of that image, mistaking it for the perceived object. The crucial part of this theory of error for Vedanta is the claim that error is taking something that really existed in the past for what is being perceived in the present. If this account is correct, then the notion that a perceptual illusion is possible is mistaken. The present perception of the world as an illusion makes sense only upon the assumption that a real world was perceived in the past and is being substituted now for the world presently being perceived. But this argues for the reality of the empirical world and not for the Vedantic view of the world as unreal.

The first objection to this theory of perceptual error is that it is not possible that something which existed at some other time and in some other place should be *perceived* now. What is perceived is *this*, and a memory is always of *that*, no matter how vivid. Thus, on the Nyaya account, the presence of the illusory object would be unexplainable. To suppose that a memory idea could actually transfer objects from one time and place to another is wildly implausible.

On other grounds it can be objected that the Nyaya view is unsatisfactory because what does not exist here now can appear to exist here now, and this is due to ignorance of what is here now. In the light of these objections it can be argued that a more plausible theory of error would hold that illusions are caused by the non-perception of the present object and the *construction* of another object which is substituted for the present object which is hidden by ignorance.

Of course, the illusory object must be present as an illusory object, being created by ignorance. However, it cannot be said to be real, nor can it be said to be unreal. In one sense, the snake is there: it is why one runs away and screams. It is not unreal in the way that a square circle or the child of an infertile woman is unreal. But its reality lasts only as long as the ignorance lasts. When it is discovered that there is only a rope there, the snake no longer exists, so it cannot be said to be real. The difficulty of classifying the illusory object as real or unreal is comparable to Shankara's difficulty in classifying the empirical world as real or unreal. In one sense it is real, for it is experienced. But in another sense it is unreal, for what is experienced is not what is really there but is the distortion of what is there.

Just as in claiming that dream objects and events are not ultimately real one does not deny their existence, so Shankara does not deny the existence of the empirical world, though he does deny its ultimate reality. In fact, Shankara's analysis requires a more complicated classification of the reality of objects of experience than is usually found.

On the one hand there is that which cannot exist at all, in any sense. These are the things that are logically impossible, such as square circles and children of infertile women. Then there are the objects that exist in dreams and illusory perceptions, but which are repudiated by normal waking experience. Next come the objects of ordinary waking experience, which the realist takes to be the ultimate things of the universe. These objects are or can be repudiated by experience of *Brahman*. Lastly, there is pure existence, *Atman* alone, the ultimate reality which in no way is unreal.

Thus, Shankara does not really propose an alteration of our ordinary view of the world that consists in repudiating the existence of the universe. He does not suggest that the existence of any objects of experience be denied. Rather, he extends the nature of reality by claiming that in addition to the objects existing in dreams and in waking consciousness there is an ultimate reality. Whatever reality objects have they have; no one, not even Shankara, can take that away. But to recognize that there is a higher view is to add a significant dimension to our notion of reality. It is only from this higher view that the rest of existence can be seen to be ultimately unreal. In this respect the matter is similar to waking and dreaming. Unless one wakes up it is impossible to regard dreaming objects as unreal. Within the dream they can only be regarded as real. But when one wakes up, the existence of dream objects is not denied. One simply now recognizes that dream objects were merely dream objects. They have the reality they have. Only now it is seen that there is a higher level of reality, namely, waking reality. In a similar way, one might wake up to the higher reality of enlightenment and discover that until now one has been having merely ordinary waking experience and not enlightened experience (*Atman*-realization).

Shankara's view of the nature of reality provides explanations for both the reconciliation of the perceived plurality in the world with its absolute oneness and the identity of the self with this absolute oneness. He can say, "All this is that," when the "this" refers to the empirical world, and the "that" refers to *Brahman*, because the world is merely the misperception and the misconception of *Brahman*. It is like saying that the many coins of the magician are really the one coin displayed before performing the trick. But due to our ignorance we mistake the one coin for many, and *Brahman* for the world.

In an analogous way we mistake the psycho-physical self to be the true reality, whereas in fact that self is ultimately illusory and unreal. To say, "thou art that," is to say that "thou"—the self one takes oneself to be in ignorance—is, not in its appearance, but in its very basis, that *Brahman*. For the ignorant, of course, the self is only potentially *Brahman*, and this potentiality is realized by overcoming the ignorance. From the viewpoint of *Brahman*, however, it is not possible that the self is only potentially *Brahman*. It is one thing for the ignorant to regard the snake as potentially a rope, and quite another thing to suppose that from the viewpoint of what things really are a snake is a rope.

What happens in ignorance is that the individual self, which is really a composite of self and not-self, becomes the experience of the world because of this confusion. Experience is a strange phenomenon, because it requires that in a way the self become the other, though it must also remain the self and the other must remain the other. But unless other and self become one there is no experience. This shows that for experience to be possible, there must be a combination of the self and the not-self. But from the fact that the subject always remains subject—the self having the experience—it follows that the subject, or the self, is essentially independent of the object, or the not-self. Of course, this ultimate Self cannot be *looked* at as the true self, for to look at anything (either perceptually or conceptually) requires that it be an object of experience. But since the supposition is that the self is pure subject it follows that it cannot be known in any objective way.

The question might arise as to how this ultimate Self, which is identical with *Brahman*, is related to the empirical self, which is a combination of self and other. According to Shankara, the self, or the "I," is so opposed to the not-self that they cannot really be related to each other. It is not a logically expressible relationship, for the not-self exists in ignorance, and the object of ignorance cannot be said to be either real or not real.

In this view becoming *Brahman* is a matter of the removal of ignorance which results in mistaking the appearance of the not-self for the reality of the Self. The fact of reality is the sole reality of *Brahman* and the identity of Self, or *Atman*, with *Brahman*. Ignorance veils this truth, but a practical realization of the ultimate Self will destroy the ignorance. There is no question of the theoretical knowledge of the ultimate reality. Such knowledge is ruled out by the fact that the ultimate reality is pure subject, one without a second. Knowledge of *Brahman* is practical knowledge; it is a matter of direct and immediate personal experience. Since ultimately the universe is identical with the Self, realizing *Brahman* is a matter of being completely oneself, and experiencing one's ultimate reality.

The real Self, the *Atman,* is not an appearance and is therefore not subject to the laws of appearances. The laws of causation apply to the world of appearance, not to the world of reality, or *Brahman.* There is consequently no saying that the Self is related to the appearance, for it is neither cause nor effect, these relations belonging only to the lower level of appearances. And if the *Atman* is not related to the appearances constituting the empirical world in any ways which are knowable, it becomes impossible to know *Brahman* except by an intimate experience that will be ineffable and incommunicable. This realization that one is the Self of pure consciousness, free from change and suffering, is certified by its own illumination. As Shankara asks, "How can one contest the fact of another possessing the knowledge of Brahman, vouched as it is by his heart's conviction?"[7]

In conclusion, it can be said that for Shankara the empirical world and the empirical self exist, but they are not ultimately real. The very basis of their existence is a higher reality than their appearance. This basis is pure existence, the very ground of experience and appearance. Consequently, to take the empirical world and the empirical self to be the ultimate reality is to be confused, mistaking the appearance for the reality on which the existing appearance depends. That there is something beyond the existence that is perceived empirically can be seen by the fact that empirical things come into and pass out of existence, but their possibility of existence does not itself come into being and pass out of being. Of existence itself there is no coming into being or passing out of being, since it is prior to change, and presupposed by change.

Qualified Monism

Ramanuja agrees with Shankara that ultimate reality is one rather than many. But he disagrees concerning the nature of the one. Ramanuja's view is that *Brahman* as the ultimate reality is not distinct from the empirical world, but that this world is a constituent part of *Brahman. Brahman* is a unity made up of the differences that constitute the experienced world as well as its basis.

Ramanuja argues that identity and difference are correlative, and dependent upon each other. To posit one without the other is to posit an empty nothing. Unity is the unity of different things; identity is an identity of parts.

---

[7] *Shankara Bhashya,* IV.1.15, trans. by George Thibaut in F. Max Müller, ed., *The Sacred Books of the East,* vol. XXXVIII (Oxford University Press, 1904).

When the different things or parts are denied there can be no unity or identity. The unity constituting *Brahman*, according to Ramanuja, is the union of the different selves and things making up the world. The identity is the identity of these parts in their substrata as existing.

Also, Ramanuja argues the self cannot be identified with knowledge, for knowledge requires a known and a knower. Where there is no known there is no knower, and so to regard the self as pure knower without a known is to eliminate the self. Rather, it should be said that consciousness is the substratum of the self, wherein the self can come to know the unity of reality.

Thus, Ramanuja's view is that *Brahman* is an organic unity constituted by the identity of the parts. It is not abstract, but concrete, being made up of the various objects of consciousness as well as consciousness itself. This organic unity Ramanuja calls *Brahman*, or the Lord (*Ishvara*).

His view is that things and selves are distinct from *Brahman* in the way the body of a person is distinct from the self of a person. On this view unity of reality is maintained because the person is one thing, but plurality is also maintained because a person consists of both self and body. Furthermore, on this analogy *Brahman* is superior to selves and things just as a person's self is superior to the body, the body belonging to the self as the self's qualifications. The position is stated by Ramanuja as follows: "The supreme *Brahman* is the self of all. The sentient and non-sentient entities constitute its body. The body is an entity and has being only by virtue of its being the mode of the soul of which it is the body. The body and the soul, though characterized by different attributes do not get mixed up. From all this follows the central teaching that *Brahman*, with all the non-sentient and sentient entities as its modes, is the ultimate."[8]

According to this explanation reality is one, like a person, with the many things and selves in the universe constituting the body of reality, and *Brahman* constituting the self of reality. The body is real, although real not independently, but as a mode of *Brahman's* being. Thus, individual selves and individual things are the real qualities or modes of *Brahman*.

According to the metaphysics underlying this account of the relation of *Brahman* to selves and things, substance alone is independently real, and whatever exists as a characteristic or quality of a substance exists as a mode of that substance and can be identified with the substance of which it is a mode. The teaching "All is *Brahman*" should not be taken to affirm the

---

[8] *Vedarthasamgraha of Shri Ramanujacarya*, para. 81, trans. by S. S. Raghavachar (Mysore: Sri Ramakrishna Ashrama, 1956), p. 67.

existence of *Brahman* alone without qualification, for on that interpretation there is no "All" which can be identified with *Brahman*. Rather, the "All" should be taken to refer to the various things and selves in the world, because these are the real qualifications of *Brahman*. The mode of their existence is that of the body of *Brahman*. Just as a body does not exist except as the body of a self, so things and selves do not exist except as belonging to *Brahman*.

This view is supported by a theory of meaning according to which the terms referring to the qualities of a substance refer also to the substance which the qualities qualify. For example, if we say, "The teacher is white-haired," "white-haired" refers to the color of the teacher's hair, but it also refers to the teacher whose hair is white, for having white hair qualifies the teacher. But the reference does not stop there, for being a teacher is a qualification of the person who is the teacher, and thus "white-haired teacher" refers to a qualification of a person and to the person who is so qualified. Being a person, in turn, is a qualification of matter and self, and so the term "white-haired-teaching-person" refers beyond merely the person to that of which person is a qualification. Continuing in this way, the term "white-haired" is seen to ultimately refer to the absolute reality upon which everything else is dependent for its existence. This is, of course, *Brahman*, and therefore all terms refer ultimately to *Brahman*. If *Brahman* did not exist as the ultimate reality to which all terms refer there would be nothing for terms to refer to, just as if there were no ultimate substance there would be nothing of which qualifications would be qualifications of, and then there would be no qualifications. Thus, if there are qualifications —and this cannot be denied for qualities are the primary objects of perception upon which knowledge rests—there must also be *Brahman* as the possessor of these qualities. Ramanuja puts the point this way: "This is the fundamental relationship between the Supreme and the universe of individual selves and physical entities. It is the relationship of soul and body, . . . That which, in its entirety depends upon, is controlled by and subserves another and is therefore its inseparable mode, is called the body of the latter. Such is the relation between the individual self and its body. Such being the relationship, the supreme Self, having all as its body, is denoted by all terms."[9]

In this way Ramanuja maintains the reality of both selves and *Brahman* by admitting differences within the identity that is *Brahman*. Selves are real as differentiations *within* (rather than *from*) the ultimate reality.

[9] *Vedarthasamgraha*, para. 95.

Dualistic Vedanta

A third school of Vedanta, that of Madhva, differs from the positions of the Shankara and Ramanuja schools in claiming a fundamental dualism in the world. The world as empirically experienced, and its foundation as *Brahman*, are eternally and fundamentally distinct. The self is regarded as distinct from both *Brahman* and the material things constituting the empirical world. The basic argument for this position is that perception is essentially a matter of becoming aware of the uniqueness of something. Since perception is the basis of all knowledge, and it depends upon realizing differences, to claim nonexistence of differences is to repudiate the very basis of the arguments for the nonexistence of difference. Objects are perceived as distinct from the self, and the basis of things and self is conceived to be different from either the things or the self. There is no possible evidence that these perceived differences are mistaken, as they constitute the very possibility of knowledge. Therefore these basic differences must be admitted.

Furthermore, individual selves must be distinguished from *Brahman* if they are said to be caught up in suffering and bondage. Since it is with the individual suffering self that every attempt to achieve liberation must begin, the existence of individual selves cannot be denied. But if they are admitted, they must be admitted as different from *Brahman*. It will not do to say that as *suffering* the individual is different from *Brahman*, but that as released from suffering is identical with *Brahman*, for two things that are really different cannot at *any* time be said to be the same. Being released from suffering does not change the nature of something, making it a something else. But if this is the case, and an initial difference is postulated, then individual selves and *Brahman* must remain eternally different. Madhva argues in the same way for the eternal difference between *Brahman* and matter. Along the same lines, arguing also for a real difference between selves and matter, between one self and another, and between one thing and another, he arrives at his "five differences." These are the differences between (1) *Brahman* and matter, (2) *Brahman* and selves, (3) selves and matter, (4) one self and another, and (5) one thing and another.

The epistemological basis for Madhva's claim that these five basic differences exist consists in his analysis of knowing as a simultaneous revealing of both the subject who knows and the object that is known. According to this analysis there is no denying that subject is different from object, for knowledge is always knowledge *of* something, and it is always knowledge *for* someone. Furthermore, to know one particular thing is to know it as that thing rather than another, and this is to be aware of its differences from other things. But if this is true, and the differences between subject and object and between one object and another are *known*, they must be revealed in knowledge. Thus, knowledge in its very nature reveals differences in reality. These differences cannot be called into question without calling into question the very basis and nature of knowledge. And if this is attempted within the limits of knowledge the attempt is self-defeating, for it requires rejecting that upon which a stand must be taken in order to do the rejecting.

Since knowledge reveals things to be different from each other and different from the self, and since it is acknowledged that both selves and things depend upon *Brahman* for their existence, Madhva maintains eternal difference between *Brahman*, selves, and things. Unlike Ramanuja, these differences are not accounted for in terms of the qualifications of *Brahman*, thereby maintaining the unity of reality, but are regarded as different substances. But if these are maintained to be different substances it is hard to see how things and selves—as ultimate substances—could be dependent upon a third substance, for a substance is complete in itself and independent. In fact, it is difficult to see why a third substance would be postulated as the ultimate reality. Of course, Madhva is reluctant to give up the dependency of selves upon *Brahman*, for then all traditional teachings about salvation must be given up. And if he gives up not only dependency, but also *Brahman* as the ultimate reality, he has given up the whole tradition!

These three schools of Vedanta represent the three basic ways of looking at the relations between the world and *Brahman*, and thus constitute the three basic interpretations of the Upanishads. According to Shankara, *Brahman* alone is real, the world being mere appearance. Ramanuja claims that the world is real, but is not different from *Brahman*, since *Brahman* is the unity of differences that constitute the world. Madhva argues that the world and *Brahman* are eternally distinct. Reality is of the dual nature of *Brahman* plus the world, with *Brahman* always remaining distinct and different from the world of selves and things.

REVIEW QUESTIONS

1. Shankara supports his view that Brahman alone is real by arguing against the possibility of change. What are his arguments?

2. To explain the perception of a plurality of things while maintaining that *Brahman* alone is real, Shankara analyzes the concept of illusion and applies it to all of our ordinary perceptions of the world. What does Shankara mean when he describes the world as an illusion?

3. How does Shankara's theory of perceptual error differ from the Nyaya theory? How does it differ from the Mimamsa theory?

4. How do Shankara, Ramanuja, and Madhva differ in their interpretation of the relations between selves, things, and *Brahman?*

FURTHER READING

Advaita Vedānta: A Philosophical Reconstruction, by Eliot Deutsch (Honolulu: East-West Center Press, 1966), is the best introduction to this system. Clearly written, with a minimum of technical terminology, this little book manages to make sense out of subtle and complicated concepts and arguments in a way that beginning students really appreciate.

A Source Book in Advaita Vedānta, by Eliot Deutsch and J. A. B. Van Buitenen (Honolulu: University of Hawaii Press, 1971), provides excellent translations of the important texts as well as a useful introduction to the philosophical context in which Advaita philosophers worked. The introduction is suitable for both beginning and advanced students.

A Thousand Teachings: The Upadeśasāhasrī of Śaṅkara, translated with introduction and notes by Sengaku Mayeda (University of Tokyo Press, 1979), is a valuable guide for both students and teachers. The *Upadeśasāhasrī* ("thousand teachings") is the most accessible of Shankara's works and constitutes an excellent introduction to his thought. The metrical portion (about eighty pages) is a textbook for students, while the prose portion (about forty pages) is a manual for teachers of Vedanta. Mayeda's ninety-page introduction to Shankara's thought is outstanding.

Advaita Vedānta Up to Śaṅkara and His Pupils, edited by Karl H. Potter (Princeton: Princeton University Press, 1981), contains a good introduction to Advaita and reliable summaries of the major works of Gaudapada, Shankara, and some of Shankara's pupils. This book is for the serious student.

The Six Ways of Knowing: A Critical Study of the Vedānta Theory of Knowledge, 2nd ed., by D. M. Datta (Calcutta: University of Calcutta, 1960), is a comprehensive analysis of Vedantic theories of knowledge, comparing the views of Shankara, Ramanuja, Madhva, and other thinkers. This book is for the serious student.

CHAPTER 8

✦✦✦✦✦✦✦✦✦✦✦✦✦✦✦✦✦✦✦✦✦✦✦✦✦✦

Theistic Developments: Vishnu, Shiva, and Kali

Divine Manifestations of Reality

IN THE PREVIOUS chapter we saw how Vedantic philosophers conceived of ultimate reality (*Brahman*) in abstract terms. Shankara conceived of it as absolutely non-dual, Ramanuja as non-dual, but with differences, and Madhva as two-fold. They all recognized that *Brahman*, as the ultimate reality, could not be defined in any literal way. It could be approached conceptually by describing it in terms of the most perfect qualities conceivable. But since *Brahman* is beyond conception, ultimately even these highest qualities—being, knowledge and bliss—must be denied. This is the famous *via negative*, characterized in the Indian tradition as *neti, neti*, an expression that means, literally, "not thus, not thus." *Neti, neti* clearly reveals the philosophical understanding that *Brahman* could not be comprehended in abstract, conceptual terms.

Reality can be approached in less abstract ways, however. Indian thinkers conceived of *Brahman* in personal, as well as abstract terms, making use of a great deal of sensual imagery in the process. The senses stimulate feelings and faith as well as thoughts, and India has prized this religious understanding as highly as the understanding achieved through abstract thought. This religious understanding is active, leading a person to embrace or avoid reality in its immediate, concrete forms. With this approach the knowledge, bliss, and being that describe *Brahman* abstractly take on flesh and personality as Gods and Goddesses that can be loved and feared, seen and touched.

In the *Bhagavad Gita*, Krishna, appearing as Arjuna's chariot driver, tells the young warrior prince that he is, indeed, the ultimate *Brahman*. The worshippers of Shiva know that the Shiva linga they adoringly garland with flowers is the reality that goes beyond being and non-being, that it both destroys and creates existence. But what is important for them is its concrete presence in the Shiva image, not its abstract conception. Similarly, the Bengali devotees of Kali worshipping her fearsome image know that this great goddess can help them overcome their fear of change and death.

In this chapter we will examine three concrete, personal images of the ultimate reality that have dominated Hinduism: Vishnu, Shiva, and Kali. Each of these deities represents a different dimension of reality. Vishnu is its power to sustain and nourish life; Shiva is both the destructive power that clears away the old to make room for the new, and the transcendent mystery that lies beyond creation and destruction; Kali is the divine energy that underlies the transforming power of change. As we shall see, just as there are many symbols of the ultimate, so are there many forms of each of these deities, each representing a significant function or power.

Vishnu

Vishnu nourishes and sustains life through his own greatness and generosity. He personifies the love, beauty, and goodness of reality. In Vedic times Vishnu was not a major deity, though already then he was seen as measuring out, with three world-covering strides, the space for life to dwell. It seems that with the decline of Indra and Agni, Vishnu grew in importance. In part this was accomplished through identification with other popular deities, such as Narayana, Vasudeva, and Gopal Krishna. Through this process of identification the devotional approach to Vishnu came at least partially to replace the ritualistic approach of the Vedas.

In the Hindu conception of trinity, where Brahma creates and Shiva destroys, Vishnu's function is to sustain the world. Since it is nearly universal human experience that life is nourished and sustained by love, it is natural that as the sustainer of existence, Vishnu should be seen as the embodiment of love, an embodiment most obvious in his incarnation as Krishna. But Krishna is only one of Vishnu's incarnations. His function of sustaining existence is manifested in many different ways.

Two of the most popular forms of Vishnu are Rama and Krishna. Rama, the hero of the *Ramayana* epic, is the living embodiment of goodness. He represents the ideal man, even as his wife, Sita, represents the ideal woman. Indeed, they are paradigms of human virtue, providing time-honored

The Many Forms of Vishnu. *Courtesy of Bob Del Bonta; photograph by Robert R. Johnston.*

exemplars of right action. Krishna is the most popular and beloved of all the deities, for he is the very embodiment of love and beauty. While our examination of Vishnu will focus primarily on Krishna for the rest of this chapter, we must remember that Vishnu assumed many other forms in his efforts to protect and sustain the world.

The Hindu tradition recognizes ten major incarnations of Vishnu, Supreme Lord and Sustainer of the universe (see photo). Each of these, as a form of Vishnu, is a manifestation of *Brahman*, the ultimate reality. Each also embodies Vishnu's benevolence, which is clearly manifested in their efforts to defeat evil and promote good. As Krishna tells Arjuna in the *Gita*, "Whenever righteousness declines and unrighteousness flourishes, O Son of

India, then I send forth myself. For the preservation of good, for the destruction of evil, to establish a foundation for righteousness, I come into being in age after age."[1]

In his first incarnation Vishnu appeared as Matsya, a huge fish, to save Manu during the great flood. Manu, a kind of Indian Noah, is the first man, the ancestor of all human beings. When the flood waters threatened to destroy him, and thereby the whole human race, Vishnu incarnated himself as a great fish so that he could protect the human species from the deluge.

Another time, when the gods and demons were churning the ocean to obtain the elixir of immorality they threatened to submerge the whole earth and destroy it. So Vishnu appeared in the form of a giant tortoise, Kurma, supporting the earth on his back, thereby saving it from destruction.

At yet another time, after the earth had become flooded by the oceans, Vishnu incarnated himself as a huge boar, Varaha, raising the earth above the waters. As before, Vishnu had assumed a form appropriate to the need at hand, saving the world from destruction.

Vishnu's incarnation as Narasimha, half man, half lion, was for the sake of destroying a demon threatening the world with his mischievous evil. Because the demon was convinced that he was invulnerable to attack from gods, humans, and beasts, both day and night, no fear held his evil in check. So Vishnu, knowing the secret of his vulnerability, appeared in his lion form on the demon's porch at twilight (when it was neither day nor night) and tore him to pieces.

Vamana, the dwarf incarnation of Vishnu, rescued the world from an evil demon by the name of Bali. The demons, under Bali's command, managed to gain control of the entire earth through their deceitful and cunning ways, allowing no room for the gods. Vishnu, taking form as a dwarf, begged Bali to give him only as much of the earth as he could cover in three strides. Thinking the amount this little fellow could cover with three strides insignificant, Bali agreed. But suddenly the dwarf grew to gigantic size, and with three strides covered the entire earth, winning it back for the gods.

It is not exactly clear why Paraushrama should be regarded as an incarnation of Vishnu, for he does not obviously represent Vishnu's benevolence, saving the world from disaster. What this fierce mustached *brahmana* incarnation did was to put the *kshatriyas* in their proper place, subordinate to the *brahmanas*. Perhaps from a *brahmana* perspective this prevented a major catastrophe, but it is hardly an act of godly benevolence.

[1] *Bhagavad Gita*, 4.7–8.

The next three incarnations, Rama, hero of the *Ramayana* epic, Krishna, the divine teacher of the *Gita*, and Buddha, the enlightened founder of Buddhism, clearly represent the forces of good. That even the Buddha is included as an incarnation suggests that every manifestation of goodness was seen as originating from Vishnu. It also suggests that the devotees of Vishnu were trying to absorb the other religious movements of the day.

The tenth incarnation, Kalkin on his white horse, will be the next descent of Vishnu, a descent that will occur at the end of the present age. He is a kind of savior, coming to punish the wicked and to reward the good, ushering in a new age of bliss. Whether the inspiration for this incarnation comes from the Buddhist teachings of future Buddhas, or from Zoroastrian ideas of a savior who will triumph over evil, is not clear. In any event, Kalkin has not played a significant role in Hinduism. Indeed, the influence of Krishna on the tradition is so much greater than any of these other manifestations that the rest of this examination of Vishnu will focus exclusively on his manifestation as Krishna.

Krishna

It is in the eighteen chapters of verse known as "The Song of the Lord" (*Bhagavad Gita*) that Krishna is most fully presented to the world. Here, in the guise of Arjuna's charioteer, Krishna delivers his stirring message to humankind, teaching a way of devotion to God that incorporates the ways of knowledge and action. Making sure the Arjuna understands who he really is, Krishna announces that although he is now present in human form, as a charioteer, he is truly the supreme reality, the source, ruler, power, and in-dwelling unity of all existence. As the supreme God, all things are present in him, and he is present in all things:

> All beings emerge from it [My Nature].
> Know that of all of them
> And of the whole world
> I am the origin and the dissolution.

> Nothing higher than Me exists,
> O Arjuna.
> On me this [whole universe] is strung
> Like pearls on a string.[2]

[2] *Gita*, 7.6–7.

This vision of God's presence in all things is not pantheistic, however. It does not equate God's reality with the reality of existing things, for as Krishna proclaims, "Whatever being has glory, majesty or power, know that in every case it has originated from a fraction of my glory."[3] And in the next verse he again emphasizes that though he is present in all things, his being far surpasses them, saying, "I support this whole world with a single fraction [of Myself]." In another verse Krishna proclaims that though the world depends on Him, His existence is independent of the world, saying, "My Self is the source of all beings and sustains all beings but does not rest in them."[4]

The eleventh chapter of the *Gita* eloquently demonstrates the Hindu understanding that the fullness of God's being is beyond ordinary human understanding. To see God, Arjuna must be granted a divine vision by Krishna, for which he must be given a divine eye. Even then, the vision of God in all his glory dazzles and overwhelms Arjuna, leading him to beg Krishna to assume a lesser form.

Krishna's devotees know that in his own being Vishnu surpasses all forms, remaining incomprehensible to humans. But they also know that in his goodness and by his grace he appears in forms that they can relate to in their humanness. Thus, they take the reality of his incarnations seriously, knowing that God is truly present in his various manifestations. But by the same token, they know that these various manifestations are but symbols of the supreme reality, not to be mistaken for the supreme reality itself. It is this knowledge that enables Hindus to acknowledge the existence of many deities, for all are simply different forms of the one supreme reality. But when God takes on human form appearing, for example, as Krishna, then human beings can relate to him in a direct and personal way. In his personal form Krishna invites humans to come to Him in loving devotion, surrendering themselves to his loving care.

The Krishna revealed to Arjuna in the *Gita* is perhaps so terrifying in his awesome splendor and power that it is difficult to approach him in devoted love. The gap between the Supreme Lord, as he appears to Arjuna, and human beings is too vast to be bridged by love. The human condition requires a humbler, more human form of God to love, a form like that found in the Krishna of Vrindavana.

Thus, though the Krishna of the *Gita* is of great importance to the followers of Vishnu, it is the cowherd God, Krishna of Vrindavana, who

[3] *Gita*, 10.41.
[4] *Gita*, 9.4.

fires the Hindu devotional imagination. This Krishna is revealed as an adorable little baby, a playful young boy, and a beautiful, amorous youth. In the simple pastoral setting of Vrindavana, Krishna, a humble cowherd boy, reveals the divine beauty, joy, and love of ultimate reality. Here his exuberant and carefree play is an invitation to his devotees to share the joys of existence with him.

This pastoral setting symbolizes God's approachability. The low-caste peasants who live here are the most ordinary of people, barred from Vedic scripture and ritual by caste. They do not practice asceticism or meditation. Instead they rejoice in the beauty and sacredness of the ordinary reality they find all around them. Ordinary, everyday experience is sacred; the divine presence shines forth everywhere. If the people of Vrindavana are special it is only because they recognize the sacredness of ordinary reality and open their hearts to the divine love radiating through all existence.

This Krishna is as ordinary as the Vrindavana setting. As a child he plays with the other cowherd children, and as a youth he makes love to the cowherd girls. He is approached not as lord, but as an equal with whom to share one's love and joy. Storytellers delight in describing little Krishna's wondrous beauty and grace. His playfulness and lovingness are the topic of hundreds of stories. Even his childish mischief is precious, for it symbolizes the exuberance of the divine play and the joy of existence.

This vision of God as a little child playing, freely and exuberantly, enables Hindus to emphasize the importance of spontaneity, play, and joy in human life; it affirms that life is to be celebrated. Krishna, the divine child, announces to the world that the very essence of the divine is a playful, exuberant joy. And because he is a little child, he can be approached directly and openly, without formal rituals and careful circumspection.

As an amorous youth making love to the cowherd girls, Krishna reminds his devotees that the ecstatic fulfillment of the deepest human longings in the embrace of the beloved symbolizes the loving relationship to God that is ultimate human salvation. Loving devotion, *bhakti*, enables the devotee to break out of the confining walls of self-centeredness. Through loving surrender to Krishna, the devotee's love is allowed to provide a new ground for existence that leaves behind the pettiness of selfish concerns and worldly troubles. The devotee is transported to the realm of divine ecstasy, symbolized by Krishna's love-making on the banks of the Jumna river in Vrindavana. Krishna's actions declare not only that love is the fullest and most joyous expression of life that human beings can experience, but also that God's love is the very perfection of human love. Showing the way, Krishna invites humankind to come to him through love, play, and beauty;

Krishna with the Cowherd Girls. *Courtesy of Bob Del Bonta; photograph by Robert R. Johnston.*

these are the most profound dimensions of human life and the divine attributes of God himself.

Kali

Like Vishnu and Shiva, Kali presents different faces to her devotees. As the personification of death and destruction, her appearance is hideous and terrifying. But as the divine mother, she offers her children the comfort and security of maternal love. As the personification of the terrifying dimensions of existence she helps her devotees come to grips with the violence, suffering, and death that enter into every human life. To encounter Kali in any of her fierce and gruesome manifestations is to come face to face with the instability and disorder of the world, to feel its hidden terrors. However, as the great mother she not only rescues her children from the terrors of the world, but affirms that love is more fundamental than violence, providing a way out of life's terrors.

Kali's origins are obscure. As the great goddess, the earth mother, she may well have roots in a distant past, going back at least to the Indus valley civilization of 2000 B.C. The Vedic goddesses may also have contributed to her nature, for as the energizing power of consciousness and speech, the goddess reminds us of Vac, the Vedic goddess of speech. Other traditions, since lost, may also have contributed features of this popular goddess. The Puranas and Tantric texts give Kali a mythic history accounting for her origins and explaining her features and functions. Sometimes she is seen as a particular manifestation of Durga, one of the names by which the great goddess was well known in medieval India.

According to one well-known story she came into existence as a terrible, demon-destroying force to rescue the gods and preserve the world. A race of demons had grown so strong that they were successfully challenging the supremacy of the gods, threatening to destroy the very foundations of order in the world. Unable to defeat these demons themselves and, indeed, on the very brink of defeat, the gods called upon the terrible power of their shared anger. Issuing forth from their faces as a blinding light, this force manifested itself in the form of a goddess who, in various guises, came to the gods' rescue on numerous occasions when the demons appeared certain of victory.

The most terrible and powerful form of the goddess was Kali. The texts describe her terrifying appearance in considerable detail. She is clad in a blackened tiger's skin, wearing a necklace of skulls. In one hand she carries a skull-topped staff, while in another she holds the noose of death. Her mouth gapes open revealing a bloody tongue protruding from her fanged gums. She has sunken, reddish eyes, shriveled skin, and a terrible roaring voice that fills the heavens. She is indeed the very picture of death and destruction.

Born of the gods' anger, Kali is a force greater than that possessed by the gods themselves. They depend on her for their survival. The gods represent the forces of good, but when these forces are threatened by evil, only a power great enough to destroy the forces of evil can save them. That Kali is such a great power is clear not only from the account of her origins as the

Kali Dancing on Shiva-Shava. *Courtesy of the Trustees of the Victoria and Albert Museum.*

savior of those gods, but also from the fact that she is often called, simply, Shakti, which means energy or force. Hinduism conceives of the throbbing energy of existence as female, as *shakti*, whereas the substance of things is thought of as male, passive and inert. In one of the fundamental polarities characterizing Hinduism, that of Shiva-Shakti, the male and female principles are seen cooperating in energizing and structuring the world.

Even though Kali is the embodiment of terror and anger, black with rage and covered with the blood of her victims, she is not the embodiment of evil, but rather of the power to overcome and destroy evil. Thus, despite her fearsome appearance, she is ultimately benevolent, coming to the rescue of her devotees just as she came to the rescue of the gods. Although at the proper moment she takes the form of the great destroyer, she is also the primordial, unborn being who becomes this entire existence and sustains the world. That is why some of the texts go on to describe her as the divine mother (Mata), and the beautiful Lakshmi, goddess of happiness and fortune. The implication is that the goddess takes form as the terrifying Kali, death personified, precisely in order to overcome terror and death, thereby making room for life and joy.

This duality of Kali is a common theme of the literature and art that has grown up around the goddess. For example, there are popular paintings

showing her dancing on her husband's corpse (see photo). Surrounded by
bones and skulls, jackals and vultures (symbols of death), the black Kali
does her eternal dance of destruction. As usual, the bloody tongue pro-
trudes between her gleaming fangs, and her garland of severed heads sways
to the rhythm of the dance. But the painting shows clearly that she is
much more than the power of death and destruction. Her multiple hands,
symbolizing her divine power, grasp the symbols of life as well as of death.
In her two right hands she brandishes sword and scissors, symbolizing her
power to destroy and cut the cord of life. One of her left hands offers a
bowl, symbol of nourishment, while the other displays a lotus, the symbol of
life and purity. Like the hands simultaneously offering life and death, so the
dancing feet reveal both destructive and life-giving powers. Two bodies are
shown beneath her dancing feet. The lower Shiva, a bearded, naked ascetic,
out of touch with Kali's life-giving energy, is completely lifeless (*shava*).
But the upper Shiva, young and beautiful, is stirring into life as a result of
the divine energy he has received from her dance. So the dance is simultaneously the dance of death and the dance of life.

This painting recalls a well-known story that was told to me by one of
the attendants at the Kali temple in Kalighat during my first visit to India in
1964. According to this story, the world was being threatened by a horrible
blood-seed monster who appeared totally invincible because from every
drop of blood he shed, a thousand new demon monsters, equally ferocious
and wicked, sprang forth. Frustrated by the monster's invincibility, the gods
and goddesses called upon Kali. Ever ready to do battle with the forces of
evil and destruction, the ferocious Kali swept down upon the monster and
his hordes. Leaping and whirling among them, her flashing sword cut them
down by the thousands, her thirsty tongue lapping up their blood before it
could touch the ground and generate thousands of new monsters. Having
destroyed his hordes, the blood-thirsty Kali finally swallowed the blood-seed
monster himself.

Then she started her victory dance, dancing herself into a state of frenzy,
oblivious to everything around her. She was time gone crazy, totally out of
control, threatening all creation. The earth trembled and quaked as the
tempo of her frenzied dance increased. Fearing the destruction of the very
universe, the gods appealed to her husband, Shiva, begging him to intercede
and stop this wild dance of destruction. Deaf to his pleas, Kali continued to
dance. Finally, in desperation, he threw himself under her feet. Oblivious
to her husband under her feet, she now danced on his body, threatening to
bring death to him as well as to the rest of the world. Finally, however, she
became aware that she was dancing on her husband's body and stopped,

thus saving the universe from the ravages of time's mad dance. Interpreting the story, the attendant commented that Kali's terrible dance is really the dance that destroys evil. All those who come to her for refuge, throwing themselves at her feet, she rescues. She destroys evil for them just as she did for the gods and goddesses when Shiva threw himself at her feet.

Why, if Kali is ultimately a beneficent protector, does she appear in such gruesome and terrifying forms? The Hindu answer is clear: these images help us recognize the presence of evil in life, of fear, terror, despair, suffering, and death. To confront the goddess in her fearsome forms is to confront our own fears of loneliness, terror, and death and to see the suffering present in all existence. Kali refuses to allow us to pretend that everything is really all right, to suppress our fear and hurt. She insists that we face up to the fearful aspects of existence, for fear cannot be conquered until it is recognized. Thus, the aim of Kali is not to terrorize and frighten her devotees, but to face life as it really is—beauty, peace, and joy mixed with ugliness, violence, and sorrow. To those who accept her, coming to her feet in refuge, she gives the strength and courage to conquer fear, allowing them to accept the full richness of life, participating wholeheartedly in its total expression in every moment of existence.

Shiva

Shiva is a paradoxical god. He is simultaneously the lord of death and of creation; the cosmic dancer and the immobile yogi. He is symbolized by the male phallic symbol, the linga, but is also the great ascetic, refusing to have sex even with his wife. In addition to these images, he is also regarded as transcending all polarities, beyond all images.

As the "great god," beyond all polarities, Shiva is not merely the lord of destruction functioning in partnership with Brahma, the lord of creation, and Vishnu, the lord of sustaining life. He is the one Supreme God, performing all of these functions. Furthermore, he provides the grace whereby the impurities that defile the self, appearing as imperfections and defects in the bound self, can be removed.

Shiva can combine the functions of all the other deities because he is the primordial consciousness present in all existence. His being is coterminous with all existence. But he goes beyond this, for he is also the original undifferentiated whole out of which existence is created, transcending all forms and expressions of existence. In his own mysterious being he not only comprises everything that exists, but he also transcends existence. As the great yogi, he guards and protects the undifferentiated wholeness of the uncreated; as the great lord of creation, the dancing Shiva, he is the energy and rhythm that bring forth existence from the womb of *Brahman*.

The fundamental symbol of Shiva, the linga, is the axis of the universe. Extending infinitely beyond the universe, it declares the transcendence of the infinite/finite polarity in Shiva's being. Symbolizing the deep stillness of the absolute prior to creation, the linga simultaneously symbolizes the throbbing potency of the creative power of life, suggesting the reconciliation of the opposition between manifested existence and the unmanifested *Brahman*. That Shiva is both lord of the dance and the great yogi shows that he also overcomes the opposition between immanence and transcendence.

To get a sense of how Shiva combines the functions of world creation, maintenance, and destruction while at the same time transcending these polarities, it is helpful to examine his image as Lord of the Dance (*Nataraja*)—see photo. Dancing within the ring of fire, Shiva embodies the primordial creative energies of existence. The rhythm of his dance and the energy of his movements transform the primordial energy into life. The entire universe is the effect of Shiva's eternal dance, which simultaneously creates and destroys the world in a never-ending process.

In the palm of his upper left hand Shiva holds a tongue of flame, representing the destructive forces that have long been associated with this deity. The flickering flame marks the changes brought about by the destructive forces. In the upper right hand is the drum that furnished the dance's rhythm, the rhythm of creation. It symbolizes the eternal sound vibrating in the ether of space to create the first stirring of revelation and truth, and the first forms of existence. These two polar forces, the creativity embodied in sound and the destruction embodied in fire, complement each other. In their harmonious balance they constitute the continuous creation and destruction that characterizes all existence.

The lower right hand, displayed in the traditional "fear not" gesture, shows that this cosmic dance of creation and destruction is not to be feared. Indeed, the lower left hand points to the upraised left foot which shows that this is really a dance of liberation. His devotees know that by worshipping the raised foot of Shiva they will find refuge and salvation. The other foot is planted firmly on the infant form of the demon of ignorance, showing that ignorance must be stamped out in order to attain the pure wisdom that brings liberation from bondage.

As Shiva dances the world into existence, maintains it, and dances it out of existence, he removes the veil of illusion that misleads us into taking

Shiva as Lord of the Dance. *The Asia Society, New York: Mr. and Mrs. John D. Rockefeller 3rd Collection.*

existence to be the fundamental reality. The movements and symbols of the dance are revealed to be none other than the manifestations of Shiva himself: creation, destruction, maintenance, concealment, and divine favor or liberation. The hand with the drum represents creation, the hand with the flame represents destruction, and the "fear not" gesture represents maintenance. The foot planted on demonic ignorance symbolizes the concealment of reality, and the upraised foot signifies the divine favor which makes liberation possible.

While the energy of the dance immediately captures our attention, when we begin to see the dance as a whole, rather than in terms of its various motions, our attention is drawn to the center of the image. There we see the wonderfully calm face of the Lord, seemingly independent of the dance. This blissfully calm face, and the balanced immobile head, symbolize Shiva's transcendence of space and time and the frenzied dance of existence. The beautiful inward smile suggests the peace of absorption into that deeper reality where all polarities are reconciled in a harmony.

The sacred ring of fire that surrounds the dancer symbolizes both the sacredness of existence and the destruction of ignorance. With the destruction of ignorance comes release from bondage to time and change. Thus, the ring of fire also suggests a purification process whereby the dancer is released from the dance.

Shiva, as lord of the dance, is the embodiment of the total energy of manifested existence in all its forms. But his face, which is the face of the ascetic, embodies the peace and tranquility of self-fulfillment that transcends the dualities of manifested existence. However, since Shiva is both his dancing body and his peaceful face, this image informs us that energy and substance, manifest and unmanifest, transcendent and immanent, are ultimately one and the same reality. In Shiva all polarities are reconciled in a greater unity.

The fundamental pair of opposites reconciled in Shiva is that of created, manifested reality on the one hand, and uncreated, unmanifested reality, on the other. Hinduism tends to see the original, uncreated reality as primary; creation or manifestation is a kind of degeneration of the primordial undifferentiated wholeness, and is therefore relegated to a lower level of reality. If we see Rudra of the Vedas as a kind of proto-Shiva, then there is a very ancient myth that presents Shiva as both the guardian of the ultimate, uncreated reality, and, because he allowed it to degenerate, of created existence.

According to this story, Rudra, the fierce archer, was guarding the original, uncreated reality, protecting it from any efforts to transform it into manifested existence. Suddenly he saw the Father, the Creator, preparing to plant the seed of the uncreated reality into the womb of the mother of existence, so that created existence could issue forth. Rudra let fly an arrow to destroy the father before he could complete the act. But he was too late; the seed of creation had already been planted. Because his arrow, the arrow of time itself, provided the dimension needed for creation to occur, Rudra unwittingly became a cause of the very creation he was trying to prevent. Though originally, as the guardian of the uncreated, he tried to prevent creation from occurring, now that reality had passed over into created form, his task as guardian was to protect the reality embodied in the various forms of existence. Shiva's cosmic dance, as we have seen, destroys old

forms of existence even as it creates the new. In this dual act of destroying and creating he maintains the existence that he allowed to be created. Although originally the guardian of the uncreated, he now becomes the protector of the creation he dances into existence, the lord and protector of all creatures (Pashupati).

Shiva's primary symbol, the linga, reaching from the very womb of created existence to the invisible realm of the primordial, uncreated reality, encompasses both dimensions of his being, the transcendent and the immanent, the uncreated and the created. As the lord of the dance he symbolizes the energies of creation, but as the great yogi engaged in ascetic practice he goes beyond to the undifferentiated consciousness that reaches the primordial, uncreated reality, recalling his function as guardian of the uncreated.

When it became popular, in later tradition, to think of the creative energy of existence as female, as the divine *shakti*, Shiva was frequently visualized with a divine consort, often Parvati or Kali. Here Shiva symbolized the uncreated wholeness of *Brahman* and his inseparable spouse the creative energy of existence. But because Shiva is actually both, he also comes to be portrayed as combining in his own person both the eternal male and the eternal female. As half male and half female (*ardhanaraishvara*) he visibly reconciles the male/female polarities of existence in his own being.

The many myths and images and the innumerable names that belong to Shiva do not even begin to define this great god, however. As the life of all beings and the ground of existence beyond all names and forms, the names and forms that describe him can never define him. The eternal Shiva is always unmanifest and invisible in his highest being.

REVIEW QUESTIONS

1. What are the main differences between the conceptual and religious approaches to the understanding of ultimate reality?
2. How does Vishnu's incarnation as Krishna reveal his essential functions?
3. According to Krishna of Vrindavana, what is the ultimate nature of reality, and how should one approach the ultimate?
4. Why is Kali so gruesome and terrifying—how do her frightful appearances contribute toward salvation?
5. What are the fundamental polarities that are reconciled in Shiva?

FURTHER READING

The Sword and the Flute, by David R. Kinsley (Berkeley: University of California Press, 1977), is a good place to begin one's study of Hindu devotionalism. Focusing on Krishna and Kali, this little book (of 168 pages) brings these deities to life, enabling us to appreciate their influence on Hindu religious life.

The Presence of Śiva, by Stella Kramrisch (Princeton: Princeton University Press, 1981), is a wonderfully rich, scholarly account of the myths, images, and meanings of Shiva. Kramrisch, curator of Indian art at the Philadelphia Museum of Art, is an excellent storyteller. She weaves the many myths of Shiva into a tapestry that displays the vitality of this great god and reveals the significances of his paradoxical nature for understanding not only the Indian tradition, but ourselves as well. The thirty-two plates of Shiva sculptures from Elephanta provide rich materials for visual contemplation.

Love Song of the Dark Lord: Jayadeva's Gitagovinda, edited and translated by Barbara Stoler Miller (New York: Columbia University Press, 1977), is an excellent translation of one of India's greatest devotional poems. Celebrating Krishna as the embodiment of love, the *Gitagovinda* offers an inspiring glimpse into the beauty and power of the way of love as a form of worship. The sixty-page introduction by Stoler Miller to the paperback edition is excellent.

The Divine Hierarchy: Popular Hinduism in Central India, by Lawrence A. Babb (New York: Columbia University Press, 1975), provides a good account of the practice of Hinduism. The last chapter, on the Hindu pantheon, is particularly helpful.

The Bhagavadgītā, translated by Kees W. Bolle (Berkeley: University of California Press, 1979), is an excellent, readable translation of what is sometimes called "The Hindu Bible." It lacks introduction and commentary, but for additional background readers might consult the explanation of the central teachings of the *Gita* in chapter 9 of my book, *The Indian Way* (New York: Macmillan Publishing Co., 1982).

CHAPTER 9

❦❦❦❦❦❦❦❦❦❦❦❦❦❦❦❦❦❦❦❦❦

The Continuing Tradition

THE HINDU PHILOSOPHIES we have examined are not merely relics of ancient thought, but are living traditions. They possess a continuity stretching from their beginnings more than two thousand years ago right up to the present time. Advocates and teachers of each of these different philosophies carry on their activities in India today much as they have over the ages. They study the basic texts and commentaries, enter into debate with each other, and create new interpretations according to their own insights and analyses. In this way they continue the traditions, keeping them alive and fresh.

Throughout the centuries new ideas and ways of thinking have been introduced into India, catalyzing philosophical thinking. As a result, traditional philosophical positions have been interpreted and reinterpreted in a fascinating variety of ways. In modern times the influence of the West has been considerable, thanks primarily to a century of British rule over the subcontinent. This Western influence provoked a vigorous intellectual response by Indian thinkers and a renewal of philosophical activity in the nineteenth and twentieth centuries. This chapter will focus on the thought of three philosophers who typify, each in his own way, the renewal of traditional philosophy in modern India.

Mohandas Gandhi brought together the traditional values of *ahimsa* (non-hurting) and *satya* (truth) as a basis for social and political thought and action, providing a basis for social reform. His philosophy is a renewal of the ancient vision of *dharma* or moral order. It is informed, however, by his understanding of Christianity and modern Western thought and shaped by his involvement in contemporary events. Sarvepalli Radhakrishnan, late President of India, was essentially a Vedantist of the Advaita, or non-dual, School. But he was sensitive to and influenced by Western thinkers, especially Kant and Hegel. Aurobindo Ghose represents a largely traditional *yoga* approach to philosophy, but he incorporates a philosophy of process and progress shaped by his understanding of Western thought.

Gandhi

Gandhi's philosophy cannot be divorced from his life, which was a continuing experiment of putting ideas into practice and developing ideas through practice. Richard Attenborough's 1982 film, *Gandhi*, shows the great leader's determination to put his vision of life into practice, vividly depicting his efforts to transform not only his own life, but the lives of all of India's people. Although many of Gandhi's ideas changed as a result of attempts to put them into practice, his conviction that truth and love are the most powerful forces affecting human life never waivered. Nor did his adherence to the principle of absolute equality of all persons, regardless of religion, race, sex, or birth.

Gandhi saw the moral order of the universe as a fundamental dimension of its reality, a part of the eternal truth, discoverable by participation in the processes of everyday existence. But to discover this truth one must overcome the self-centeredness that separates most of us from the deeper reality grounding our existence. Profound self-awareness and self-transformation are required. Gandhi devoted his life to self-experimentation and practice aimed at discovering truth and cultivating a deep love for others, even for evil-doers. His motto was to fight evil with all his strength, but to love the doer of evil from the bottom of his heart. Thoughts of retaliation, anger, or hatred had to be replaced with love, compassion, and kindness. Undoubtedly, part of Gandhi's greatness lay in his unceasing efforts to put his ideas into practice. His own self-sacrifice, including discarding all of the luxurious trappings of modern civilization, and his rigorous insistence on truth and righteousness probably contributed as much to his influence in the world as did his ideas.

Although Gandhi's philosophy continued to evolve throughout his life, its foundations were provided in early childhood. Born in 1869, he grew up in a pious Hindu family. His mother was especially devout, impressing on him Rama's love and concern for the well-being of his devotees. In addition, listening to conversations between his father and men of Jaina, Muslim, and Zoroastrian religious persuasions taught him something in early life about the universality of religion.

More important, however, were the lessons contained in the two maxims that dominated family and community life in his childhood. The first of these, "There is nothing higher than truth," reflects a wisdom taught already in the *Rig Veda*, three thousand years ago, where the normative functioning of existence (*rita*) is regarded as its truth. The second, "*ahimsa* (non-hurting; love) is the highest virtue," also incorporates moral wisdom that has shaped the Indian tradition for thousands of years. The Jaina community in which Gandhi grew up is noted for its strict adherence to the principle of *ahimsa*, providing an example that made a great impression on young Gandhi.

In his *Autobiography* Gandhi reveals his first object lesson in the power of truth and *ahimsa*. Influenced by older students, Gandhi began experimenting with cigarettes and meat-eating, practices strictly forbidden at home. Even worse, he stole money to buy these forbidden items, creating a deep sense of guilt. Finally, filled with shame and remorse, he confessed the whole thing to his father, quite prepared to suffer any punishment his father might inflict. To his complete surprise, his father neither rebuked nor punished him, but with silent tears, forgave him. Gandhi was so deeply moved that he never again smoked or ate meat. This, he said, was his first real lesson in the power of truthfulness to arouse love, and of love to transform the heart.

The three years (1888–1891) that Gandhi spent in London studying law convinced him of the greatness of Indian culture. Here he encountered both the New Testament and the *Gita*, coming to see their common message, and further, the unity of all religions. What especially impressed him at this time was the universal religious emphasis on love as the greatest power of self-transformation. Both Jesus and Krishna emphasized that pride, greed, and self-centeredness must be renounced to make room for love. Gandhi saw this renunciation as the highest form of religion, devoting his life to its practice.

After a brief and relatively unsuccessful period of legal practice in India, Gandhi went to South Africa. It was during the nearly twenty years Gandhi spent there, working to secure the rights of the "colored" Indian community, that he formulated his basic philosophy of life. Here, the influences of the ancient principles of *dharma* (adherence to righteousness) and *ahimsa* on his childhood and youth were reinforced by his contacts with Christians and Muslims and by his study of major Western writers.

In his *Autobiography* Gandhi tells us that Tolstoy's book, *The Kingdom of God is Within You*, and Ruskin's *Unto This Last* made lasting impressions on him. From Tolstoy he learned to see that Christianity was concerned primarily with infusing life with the power of God, who dwells within all of us in the form of love. This convinced him, as it had Tolstoy, that the Sermon on the Mount represents the essential teachings of Christianity. These teachings, that hatred should be conquered by love, and evil overcome by nonresistance, seemed to Gandhi to echo the Jaina, Buddhist, and Hindu teaching of *ahimsa*, which had inspired India's ethical life for thousands of years.

Ruskin's book impressed Gandhi with the dignity of manual work, and reinforced the *Gita*'s teaching that the highest life is a life of service, helping him to see that the fulfillment of both the individual and society are to be achieved through one's chosen work. Here also, as Ruskin pointed out, lies a natural bond between educated and peasant classes, a bond that needed to be formed to give India unity in its efforts to achieve freedom.

It is interesting that Gandhi's idea of using truthfastness (*satyagraha*) as a means of active, but nonviolent resistance to British rule, was inspired by Thoreau's essay "Civil Disobedience," because Thoreau himself was influenced by the *Gita* and the *Upanishads*. Gandhi was totally convinced that all evils could be conquered by love—on the condition that one adheres firmly to the truth. But to adhere to the truth and apply love to the injustices of the world is an extremely difficult challenge, as Gandhi clearly saw.

According to Gandhi, the reason for our ability to overcome the difficulties of this challenge is that we, along with all other beings, are enveloped by truth, and move according to its power, the power of love. This is implied, he says, by the first mantra of the *Isha Upanishad* (his favorite), which declares that "All this, whatever moves and changes in this changing world is enveloped by the Lord." The Lord is the Creator and Ruler of all existence, and rule of this Divine Ruler is the truth of all existence, the divine law of the universe. As Gandhi interprets this, it means that when we find this truth and live in accord with its rule we can find the perfection of our lives and of our society. This is the basis of the principle of truthfastness (*satyagraha*), for holding fast to the truth expressed in the divine law of existence means acting in accord with one's own nature and purpose, and at the same time acting in accord with the nature and purpose of all other beings.

Although Gandhi recognized that the truth from which all existence issues is present in every being, he also recognized that it is obscured by ignorance and vice. Self-purification, self-sacrifice, and critical reflection are needed to realize this inner truth. One must be constantly vigilant, on guard against the claims of pride and greed made by the self-centered ego.

But vigilance alone is not enough; the active power of love must be allowed to purify and transform the self. For Gandhi, Truth is the God that dwells in all beings, and love is the soul-force by which they move. Through love God, or Truth, is revealed. The word Gandhi used for love was *ahimsa*, which, as we have seen, literally means non-hurting. But he recognized that this negative sense of the word was too narrow to express his meaning, explaining that he was using the term in its broadest sense to refer to a pure and perfect love. This is a love that proceeds from the very depths of one's being and expresses itself in kindness, compassion, and selfless service to others.

This broader sense of *ahimsa* as love underlies Gandhi's abhorrence of violence. Violence is an expression of fear and anger, growing out of weakness, trying to compensate for itself. Love, on the other hand, is strength, growing out of the deepest truth of one's being and the unity of all existence. Violence only calls forth more violence, further weakening the individual and society. Love, however, calls forth love, strengthening both oneself and others. This explains why Gandhi was completely convinced that the truth and love expressed in nonviolent resistance to wrongdoing was bound to succeed.

Radhakrishnan

Sarvepalli Radhakrishnan, the recent president of India, wrote scores of philosophical articles and dozens of philosophical books. By and large, he can be classified as a Vedantin, like Shankara. He agrees with Shankara that the empirical is not the ultimate reality, but he is aware that just as the criteria of logic and experience demand that philosophy admit an ultimate reality, so also do they require inclusion of the empirical and practical. For him there is no inconsistency in a philosopher actively participating in social and political affairs, for these are appearances of *Brahman*, and thus are means to be utilized in the effort to achieve the experience of the ultimate reality.

Recognizing that the experience of ultimate reality—*Atman*-realization —is the goal of human life, and seeing religion as the chief vehicle employed in the human quest for the absolute ground of all reality, Radhakrishnan's main philosophical problem consisted in working out a satisfactory philosophy of religion. The task of philosophy of religion is to develop a theory of the nature of things in the world, selves, and the ultimate ground of things and selves that will explain the interrelations between these three realities. This theory must account for the facts of religious experience and at the same time accommodate reason, for no attempt at explanation which is self-contradictory can be satisfactory. Granted rational consistency, the theory must have its basis in religious experience itself. The experience and statements of religious persons must be explained—not repudiated or ignored—by a philosophy of religion.

Radhakrishnan's view of religion sees theology, dogma, ritual, and various institutions as the external trappings of religion, not its essence. The essence of religion is the attempt to discover the ideal possibilities of human life. This quest is personal and necessarily involves the whole person. Experience which involves merely an aspect of a person, such as feeling, thinking, or volition, is not religious. What distinguishes religious experience from aesthetics, science, philosophy, and morals is that these are guided primarily by feeling, reason, and volition, respectively. Religion includes feeling, reason, and volition, but it goes beyond them to the innermost center of the person to the very source of these aspects of humanity, integrating these faculties and directing them from the wholeness that is their source, using it to transform the life of the person into something complete and whole.

This inner self, which is the very source of the limited aspects and faculties of human nature, is referred to as Spirit. The substance and essence of religion, according to Radhakrishnan, is experience of the life of the Spirit—not just as it is in humans, or as it is in the world, but Spirit as it joins together self and other in a whole that is complete and perfect in itself. Though this experience itself is deeply inner and inexpressible, there are clues to its character, for this experience takes form in the manifestations of spiritual encounter which constitutes the essence of all religious life. As such it is attended by ritual, dogma, interpretation, and the varying institutions which provide forms that allow the expression of contact with the Spirit in an intelligible and understandable way, and which serve to guide other persons to the direct experience of spiritual encounter.

These forms of religion may all change as culture and civilization change. In fact, as the forms of culture and civilization change, the forms of religion *must* change if they are to adequately manifest the immediate experience of spiritual encounter. Radhakrishnan says:

Theory, speculation, dogma, change from time to time as the facts become better understood. *Their value is acquired from their adequacy to experience.* When forms dissolve and the interpretations are doubted, it is a call to get back to the experience itself and reformulate its content in more suitable terms.[1]

Although a philosopher of religion could hardly proceed except by giving primacy to religious experience—that is, by considering the data of religious experience to be the basic material out of which one fashions a theory of religion—to do so is exceedingly complicated because of the great difficulty in describing religious experience. Religious experience is unlike the ordinary experience that provides the foundations for thinking and talking about ourselves and the reality around us. Our ordinary experience presupposes that the something experienced is always distinct from the experiencer; the subject is never the object, and vice versa. A person sees a stone or hears a bird; a person's reason is aware of a certain feeling consequent upon encountering a work of art, or one's feeling is aware of one's reason at work. In these cases we maintain the distinction between subject and object. But in religious experience the whole person is involved: there is nothing outside of the person, so the experience is radically different from ordinary experience. Because of this radical difference the distinctions that are usually made or presupposed between subject and object are left behind. The claim is that in religious experience the subject and object merge, becoming one, and the whole person, rather than just certain faculties, is involved in the experience. But when the subject-object distinction is overcome all ordinary distinctions presupposed by thought are also left behind. Past, present, and future become so many abstractions that have no reality—there is only the *Now*, perfectly dimensionless. And there is no room for various locations in space; there is only the *Here*, without location.

Radhakrishnan explains religious experience as follows:

It is a type of experience which is not clearly differentiated into a subject-object state, an integral, undivided consciousness in which not merely this or that side of man's nature but his whole being seems to find itself. It is a condition of consciousness in which feelings are fused, ideas melt into one another, boundaries broken and ordinary distinctions transcended. Past and present fade away in a sense of timeless being. Consciousness and being are there not different from each other. All being is consciousness and all con-

---

[1] *An Idealist View of Life*, ch. 3 (London: Allen and Unwin, 1929), and reprinted in Sarvepalli Radhakrishnan and Charles A. Moore, eds., *A Source Book in Indian Philosophy* (Princeton: Princeton University Press, 1957), p. 616. Italics added.

sciousness being. Thought and reality coalesce and a creative merging of subject and object results. Life grows conscious of its incredible depths. In this fullness of felt life and freedom, the distinction of the knower and the known disappears. The privacy of the individual self is broken and invaded by a universal self which the individual feels as his own.[2]

Granted this view of religion and religious experience, what kind of theory of selves, things, and ultimate reality will serve to adequately accommodate, in a rationally acceptable way, the facts of religion? If the ultimate reality—*Brahman*—is taken to be alone real it is difficult to see how religion is possible, for the self struggling to realize *Brahman* would have to be regarded as unreal. And without a self struggling to achieve ultimate reality there can be no religion. On the other hand, if selves and *Brahman* are taken to be distinct and different realities, it is difficult to see how the self could ever successfully identify itself with *Brahman*, without self-repudiation or self-annihilation.

Radhakrishnan's solution to this dilemma is to interpret *Brahman* not as static but as dynamic being. *Brahman* is the absolute reality, providing the ground of all existence and giving the universe unity. All things are united in *Brahman* which is the source and ground of all being. As the source and ground of all being *Brahman* is ever active, by its function expressing its substantial nature. It is this functioning of *Brahman*, which is not different from its existence, that manifests itself in the various things and processes that make up the universe of selves and things. Thus, things and selves are not unreal, for they are the expression of *Brahman's* functions. But as expressions of *Brahman* they are not totally distinct and separate from *Brahman* either. This explanation provides for distinctions between individual things and selves, for the functions of *Brahman* are dynamic, ever new. Since no one of *Brahman's* functions (nor aspect of the functioning of *Brahman*) totally exhausts the nature of *Brahman*, any given expression of *Brahman's* function lacks the total reality of *Brahman* wherein all functions and all expressions of those functions are united.

Proceeding with this interpretation of *Brahman*, Radhakrishnan goes on to regard the self as the locus where *Brahman*, as absolute Spirit, and the world, as the functioning of this absolute Spirit, come together, for the person combines Spirit with matter. He makes this point by distinguishing between the empirical or lower self and the higher or spiritual self, which in its purity is one with the absolute Spirit. The essence of the religious quest is now interpreted to be the lower self struggling to return to its source in

[2] *Ibid.*, pp. 617–18.

the higher self. It is the movement toward transformation of self—never the annihilation or repudiation of self—in identification with its source, *Atman-Brahman*.

In explaining the relations between selves and things, and both of these to *Brahman*, Radhakrishnan abandons the static view of reality according to which the world is thought to be made up of a great many independent beings or substances, each attended to by a greater or lesser number of characteristics or qualities. Instead, he views the world as constituted by processes. The structure of reality is not due to the relations qualities have to their substances, but to the inner structure of the activities making up reality. Thus, the world is essentially dynamic, with all of the various processes interconnected. The various processes can be distinguished from each other according to the structure of their functioning. In this way, for example, living "things" can be distinguished from non-living, conscious from nonconscious, etc. They are similar in that they are of the nature of process, being essentially activities, but they differ according to the structure of the activities involved.

To explain the diverse structures found in the processes corresponding to the various gradations of existence, Radhakrishnan postulates unceasing activity of the absolute Spirit. Spirit is the source and ground of all the various grades of existence encountered on the empirical level. But these various distinctions do not imply absolute differences; they merely serve to mark out modes of spiritual activity. Even matter, finally, is spiritual activity. It is merely a different mode of the Spirit than consciousness or life. But regardless of the mode of manifestation, Spirit remains Spirit, and insofar as it is Spirit there is no denial of its reality. The various grades of matter and life are real and are expressions of *Brahman*, the absolute Spirit. But no one mode in itself is the totality of *Brahman*, and no single mode can be equated with the absolute reality.

Against this background, the main purpose of religion is to help a person rise above the limits imposed by matter, life, and consciousness; to realize that the innermost self is identical with the absolute Spirit, completely free from the limitations inherent in identification with simply one particular mode or function of Spirit. This realization is possible only in terms of practical activity; an activity of being rather than knowledge. It is the spiritual realization of Uddalaka's teaching to his son, Shvetaketu, "Thou art that [*Brahman*]," according to Radhakrishnan.

Aurobindo

Sri Aurobindo, the great philosopher-yogi of Pondicherry, gained his initial fame as a leader of a Bengal revolutionary group advocating violent over-throw of British rule. After a brief term of imprisonment for conspiring to overthrow the government, however, he abandoned revolutionary politics in order to devote himself to revolutionizing the life of the Spirit. This led him into explorations of metaphysics and social philosophy. It also led to an intense life-long involvement in yoga and meditation.

Emphasizing the spirituality of human existence, Sri Aurobindo recognized as the great problem of our times the transformation of our present lowly and ignorant condition into the greatness of which we are capable. To this end he worked out a theory of social organization not radically different from the ideals contained in the theories of *purusharthas, varnas,* and *ashramas.* His major works, *The Life Divine,* and *Synthesis of Yoga,* are attempts to show the type of life we can achieve by a total and comprehensive discipline, or *yoga.* The "life divine" is, of course, the life lived in full realization of *Brahman,* and the *yoga* is the means to this life. Sri Aurobindo emphasizes that the *yoga* must be practiced by people in their present condition as a means of changing this condition, for therein lies the secret of the transformation into the Ideal Person.

Aurobindo's conception of the task of philosophy and the nature of reality is indicated in the following statement:

> The problem of thought therefore is to find out the right idea and the right way of harmony; to restate the ancient and eternal spiritual truth of the Self, so that it shall re-embrace, permeate and dominate the mental and physical life; to develop the most profound and vital methods of psychological self-discipline and self-development so that the mental and psychical life of man may express the spiritual life of man through the utmost possible expansion of its own richness, power and complexity; and to seek for the means and motives by which his external life, his society and his institutions may remould themselves progressively in the truth of the spirit and develop towards the utmost possible harmony of individual freedom and social unity.[3]

According to this view, the reality constituted by things and selves is the manifested power of the spirit. Spirit provides the unity of reality, and

---

[3] *Arya,* July 15, 1918, pp. 764–65; reprinted in *A Source Book in Indian Philosophy,* p. 577.

the manifested power of spirit provides the manifoldness of the universe. The various levels of existence—matter, life, mental life, supramental life —are distinguished insofar as the fullness of spirit emerges through these manifestations of its powers.

The main problem for Aurobindo is that of explaining how all the many things experienced—both at the conscious level of the empirical and the rational, and at the supra-conscious level of mystic intuition—came to be, and why they are different. His solution is to explain that the absolute existence which makes it possible for anything whatsoever to exist is itself pure existence, complete and perfect. This existence—*Brahman*—for no reason whatever, simply out of the sheer exuberance of its being, manifests its *maya*, or power, in the manner of creative play. The manifestations of this power constitute the universe of existing things. The universe exists, therefore, as the creative play of pure existence. But it is not simply capricious, for this play is directed by the Being-Consciousness-Joy (*sat-chit-ananda*) that constitutes the absolute Spirit of the universe. The evolution of the universe as a whole and of particular species within the universe is seen as the returning of the manifested powers of *Brahman* to their source. As these powers move toward their source, evolution moves to higher and higher forms of life and consciousness.

According to this explanation, the differences between levels of reality are due to the evolution of Spirit. As the Spirit evolves, higher life-forms come into existence. But this is not the evolution of one *kind* of thing to another *kind* of thing, such as matter becoming Spirit. Rather, it is the evolution of one thing—Spirit—from its many lower forms and manifestations to its higher forms, the aim being to reach the fullness of being, consciousness, and joy that constitutes Spirit.

The usual problems attending evolutionary accounts of existence, the problem of blind matter groping impossibly to evolve beyond itself, into something quite other than itself, and the problem of blind matter being lifted beyond itself by some other reality without any effort on its own part, do not arise for Aurobindo. According to his explanation the lower is ever evolving into the higher, but these are not absolutely different. The higher is making itself felt in the lower, and the lower is struggling to express itself according to the higher laws of the Spirit within, and this is the mutual effort that constitutes the play of *Brahman* manifesting itself through its powers, but always remaining *Brahman*.

Seeing evolution as involving the mutual activity of both the lower and higher forms of Spirit has important consequences for human life, for it means not only that it is possible to evolve to a higher kind of being, but also that we can, at least in part, direct this evolution. The aim of human existence—in its self-consciousness higher than the existence of matter and non-conscious life-forms—is not to remain at its present level, but to transcend itself, moving on to higher levels of existence just as previously lower levels of existence moved up to the level of human existence. This is possible, Aurobindo points out,

> for the evolution proceeded in past by the upsurging, at each critical state, of a concealed power from its evolution in the inconscient, but also by a descent from above, from its own plane, of that power already self-realized in its own higher natural province. . . .[4]

How are human beings to direct their own evolution? Aurobindo's answer is that we must practice self-discipline (*yoga*) that is all-inclusive, not ignoring any part of our being. We must integrate the various aspects and faculties of our being, so that the lower comes under the control and direction of the higher, allowing us to gradually come to live according to the laws of the spirit dwelling within us, at the very center of our being. This requires, among other things, the material and social conditions that will enable people in their present state successfully to reach beyond themselves, elevating their existence until it becomes the "Life Divine."

In his social philosophy, Aurobindo argued that justice and freedom are to be provided for and guaranteed by society as necessary conditions for the higher evolution of humanity. His view of the object of all society is:

> first to provide the conditions of life and growth by which individual Man—not isolated men according to their capacity—and the race through the growth of its individuals, may travel towards its divine perfection. It must be secondly, as mankind generally more and more grows near to some figure of it—for the cycles are many and each cycle has its own figure of the Divine in man—to express in the general life of mankind, the light, the power, the beauty, the harmony, the joy of the Self that has been attained and that pours itself out in a freer and nobler humanity.[5]

---

[4] Sri Aurobindo, *The Life Divine*, p. 859, reprinted in *A Source Book in Indian Philosophy*, p. 604.

[5] Sri Aurobindo, *The Human Cycle* (Pondicherry: Sri Aurobindo Ashram, 1962), pp. 83–84.

REVIEW QUESTIONS

1. How has Indian philosophy renewed itself over the centuries?
2. What are the fundamental principles of Gandhi's philosophy? How do they figure in his lifestyle and his role in Indian life?
3. What impact did the writings of Tolstoy, Ruskin, and Thoreau have on Gandhi?
4. What is Radhakrishnan's view of religion? How does he distinguish between the externals and the essence of religion?
5. How does Aurobindo conceive of the nature of reality and the function of philosophy?

FURTHER READING

Probably the best way to begin your study of Gandhi is to see the 1982 film *Gandhi*, directed by Richard A. Attenborough and distributed by Columbia Pictures. It does an excellent job of showing the unity of thought and action in Gandhi's life, the primacy of *ahimsa* and truthfastness in his thought, and his identity with the poor and suffering people of India.

The Philosophy of Mahatma Gandhi, by Dhirendra Mohan Datta (Madison: University of Wisconsin Press, 1953), is the best book with which to begin. Small and nontechnical, it conveys the essentials of Gandhi's philosophy, whetting the appetite for more detailed studies, such as that by Raghavan N. Iyer in *The Moral and Political Thought of Mahatma Gandhi* (New York: Oxford University Press, 1973). Gandhi's autobiography is available under the title, *The Story of My Experiments With Truth*, in many editions.

The Mind of Light, by Sri Aurobindo, introduction by Robert A. McDermott (New York: E. P. Dutton & Co., 1971), is an excellent, brief (100 pages) introduction to Aurobindo's thought. *The Life Divine*, *The Synthesis of Yoga*, and *The Human Cycle* contain Aurobindo's most significant writings. They are available in various editions, easily obtainable almost anywhere in the world.

Radhakrishnan: Selected Writings on Philosophy, Religion and Culture, edited by Robert McDermott (New York: E. P. Dutton & Co., 1970), is a good introduction to Radhakrishnan's life and thought. For more ambitious readers there is the large volume edited by Paul Arthur Schlipp, *The Philosophy of Sarvepalli Radhakrishnan* (New York: Library of Living Philosophers, 1952). This contains a reply by Radhakrishnan to his critics.

PART TWO

BUDDHIST PHILOSOPHIES

Seated Buddha. *The Asia Society, New York: Mr. and Mrs. John D. Rockefeller 3rd Collection.*

CHAPTER 10

Buddhism and Suffering: Basic Teachings

NO ONE who has lived in the world can be untouched by human suffering. Into every life there has entered injury, illness, misery, anxiety, death, or some other form of unwholesomeness and evil. Human existence is far from perfect. Even the most fortunate, the happiest people in the world have to admit a measure of unhappiness. Most people, in fact, recognize that life is not perfect. Either they simply shrug their shoulders and exclaim, "That is the way life is," or else they set about trying to reduce the imperfections in life. Ordinarily, when the latter attitude is adopted, effort is directed toward reducing poverty by increasing available wealth; reducing illness and premature deaths by extending sanitation or by promoting the practice of medicine; and taking other measures to improve life generally.

But seldom is there a person who carefully and systematically directs attention to the fundamental *causes* of suffering and the ways of eliminating these causes. Gautama Siddhartha, the Buddha, was such a person, and the religious philosophy that issued from his teachings presents a systematic analysis of the nature and causes of suffering and provides a manifold of means for the overcoming of suffering.

Buddhism as a *Way of Wisdom*, taught and practiced for the sake of improving the quality of life by removing the sources of suffering is, in its details, a complicated phenomenon incorporating a great many historical changes. In its essence, however, as taught by the Buddha, it is a relatively simple teaching to grasp. But one must hasten to point out that understanding the outlines of a Way of Wisdom is quite different from following that

Way. Following the Way is difficult. It is, indeed, so difficult that it has not yet been mastered by the discipline and self-control of the majority of humankind. Consequently, it should be kept in mind that there is all the difference in the world between *following* the Way and *talking* about following the Way. To follow the Way there is no substitute for practice. In fact, without practicing the Way, it is unlikely that one will even achieve a satisfactory intellectual understanding of what the Way is. Nevertheless, it is possible to achieve considerable knowledge about Buddhism by studying and analyzing the main features that constitute this Way of life.

The Buddha

According to widely accepted legends concerning the life of the historical Buddha, Gautama received the immediate impetus for meditation and concentration on the problem of suffering by dramatic encounters with sickness, old age, death, and renunciation. His father, the ruler of a prosperous principality, had been told that if his son became acquainted with the evils of the world he would renounce the kingdom and become a great ascetic and teacher of men. Not wanting to lose his son in this way, the father resolved that everything would be done to seclude him from the cruel world. Accordingly the king provided him with all of the wealth and pleasures of life one could want—palaces, young and comely servants, entertainers, a beautiful wife—to protect him from experiencing the suffering of the world. The father was determined that Gautama should remain ignorant of the sorrows that beset humankind.

But one day, when the young Gautama was out riding in his chariot, the young lord saw an old man,

> as bent as a roof gable, decrepit, leaning on a staff, tottering as he walked, afflicted and long past his prime.[1]

Upon seeing him Gautama asked his charioteer why that man was not like other men. The driver informed him that the man was old, but this word Gautama did not understand. He had no experience with old age. The driver explained that this man was nearly finished, he was soon to die. As understanding began to trouble his spirit, the young lord asked,

---

[1] This account of Gautama's encounter with suffering is found in *Digha Nikaya*, XIV. The quotations are taken from Clarence H. Hamilton, ed., *Buddhism: A Religion of Infinite Compassion* (Indianapolis: Bobbs-Merrill, c. 1952), pp. 6–10.

"But then, good charioteer, am I too subject to old age, one who has not got past old age?"

The answer horrified Gautama; and from this time he began to think about the suffering of old age:

"You, my lord, and we too, we all are of a kind to grow old; we have not got past old age."

Many days after this, Gautama was once again setting out for the park, when he encountered "a sick man, suffering and very ill, fallen and weltering in his own water, by some being lifted up, by others being dressed."

Upon seeing this, Gautama asked his charioteer what this man had done that he was not like other men. The driver explained that the man was ill, and that this meant that he was not far from being finished, that he might not recover. Gautama asked again,

"But am I too then, good charioteer, subject to fall ill; have I not got out of the reach of illness?"

The answer that sent him back to his palace meditating on illness was,

"You my lord, and we too, we all are subject to fall ill; we have not got beyond the reach of illness."

Many days later, when Gautama was again driving to the park, he saw "a great concourse of people clad in garments of different colors constructing a funeral pyre. And seeing this, he asked his charioteer, 'Why now are all those people come together in garments of different colors and making that pile?' "

Upon being told that this was because someone had died, Gautama demanded to view the corpse to discover what this thing called "death" was all about. When he had been told about death, he asked, as before,

"But am I too then subject to death, have I not got beyond reach of death? Will neither the *raja*, [king] nor *ranee*, [queen] nor any other of my kin see me more, or shall I again see them?"

And once more the answer was,

"You my lord, and we too, we all are subject to death; we have not passed beyond the reach of death."

· Many days after seeing the dead man, Gautama was once again driving to the park. On the way he saw a shaven-headed man, a recluse, wearing the yellow robe, looking contented and at peace with himself. Upon learning from the driver that this recluse is one who is said to have "gone forth," Gautama was curious to learn what this meant. Approaching the recluse, he asked,

"You, master, what have you done that your head is not as other men's heads, nor your clothes as those of other men?"
"I, my lord, am one who has gone forth."
"What, master, does that mean?"
"It means, my lord, being thorough in the religious life, thorough in the peaceful life, thorough in good actions, thorough in meritorious conduct, thorough in harmlessness, thorough in kindness to all creatures."

Upon hearing this the lord Gautama bade his charioteer return him to his palace, saying,

"But I will even here cut off my hair, and don the yellow robe, and go forth from the house into the homeless state."

Having been thus duly impressed with the *fact* of suffering, Gautama meditated on that *fact*, concentrating on discovering a way to the cessation of all suffering. After years of effort and discipline, including the most severe forms of asceticism, Gautama resolved that neither the extreme of over-indulgence in pleasures nor the extreme of excessive asceticism was conducive to extinguishing suffering. Adopting then a middle path between these extremes, Gautama, self-disciplined and purified, concentrated all of his energies on discovering the causes of suffering. As he concentrated, the causes of suffering were revealed, and Gautama Siddhartha became the Buddha—the Enlightened One. Enlightenment as to the causes and the cessation of suffering were now his.

The Four Noble Truths

The content of this enlightenment constitutes the basic message of Buddhism. This message, in simplest form, consists in the Four Noble Truths and the Noble Eightfold Path. These truths are: (1) There is suffering; (2) Suffering is caused; (3) Suffering can be extinguished by eliminating the causes of suffering; (4) The way to extinguish the causes of suffering is to follow the Middle Way constituted by the Noble Eightfold Path.

This teaching constituted the Buddha's first sermon after his enlightenment, delivered in the Deer Park at Benares. It was the teaching of the Middle Path,

> which leads to insight, which leads to wisdom; which conduces to calm, to knowledge, to perfect enlightenment, to Nibbāna [Nirvāna].

Concerning the First Noble Truth Gautama taught as follows:

> This, monks, is the Noble Truth of Suffering; birth is suffering; decay is suffering; illness is suffering; death is suffering; presence of objects we hate is suffering; separation from objects we love is suffering; not to obtain what we desire is suffering. In brief, the five aggregates which spring from grasping, they are painful.

Explaining the Second Noble Truth, Gautama taught that suffering

> originates in that craving which causes the renewals of becomings, is accompanied by sensual delight, and seeks satisfaction now here, now there; that is to say, craving for pleasures, craving for becoming, craving for not becoming.

Taking up the Third Noble Truth, he explained as follows:

> This, monks, is the Noble Truth concerning the Cessation of Suffering; verily, it is passionless, cessation without remainder of this very craving; the laying aside of, the giving up, the being free from, the harboring no longer of, this craving.

Coming now to the Fourth Noble Truth concerning the Path which leads to the cessation of suffering, he taught:

> It is this Noble Eightfold Path, that is to say, right views, right intent, right speech, right conduct, right means of livelihood, right endeavor, right mindfulness, and right meditation.

Having thus taught the essential truths about the fact of suffering, the Buddha concluded his first sermon by saying:

This Noble Truth concerning Suffering I have understood. Thus, monks, in things which formerly had not been heard of have I obtained insight, knowledge, understanding, wisdom and intuition.[2]

The First Truth, concerned with the existence of suffering, lists seven areas of suffering familiar to everyone. But these seven areas should not be taken as a definition of suffering; they are simply examples of suffering, examples obvious to anyone who has lived in the world. Suffering goes much deeper than those examples. It must be recognized that the pleasures of one person are often the pains of another. And the pains of others are disturbing to one's own contentment. Thus, though it would seem that the wealthy person who has all of the goods of society at his disposal should be happy, this may not be the case. For a truly sensitive human being, the poverty of others may very well be the bitter dressing spoiling the enjoyment of wealth. To be aware that one's pleasures come at another person's expense is not to bring suffering only to the other; it is also to bring suffering to oneself.

But even if one's pleasures are not tied to the sufferings of anyone else, they still are fraught with suffering. The pleasures that one enjoys bring with them an attachment to the objects and activities enjoyed. The anxiety resulting from the possibility of separation from the objects or activities in question is a hidden cancer in the pleasures, and thus a source of suffering.

Another feature of the suffering underlying the various pleasures of life concerns the fact that they are not only self-perpetuating, but that they are self-accelerating. Deriving pleasure from an activity or object does not diminish the drive for that pleasure, but rather serves to strengthen the drive. The more pleasures one achieves the more are sought. This cycle goes on unendingly, catching one up in its increasing tempo, with seemingly no escape. Granted that the achievement of pleasure does not bring complete happiness and contentment, but rather leaves one even more dissatisfied and unhappy, it appears that grasping at the pleasures of life ultimately increases suffering.

This last point is tied in with a basic assumption of Buddhism which holds that the drive for pleasure is too shallow and insignificant to fulfill a person and bring true happiness. In the *Dhammapada* it is said, "One is the path that leads to worldly gain; and quite another that leads to *Nibbana*."[3] If this is the case, then the pleasures that one finds in the world, being

---

[2] The foregoing account is taken from Hamilton, ed., *Buddhism*, p. 29.
[3] *Dhammapada*, V. 75, trans. by Acharya Buddharakhita Thera (Bangalore, India: Buddha Vaccna Trust, 1966).

shallow, are really factors producing unhappiness. In recognition of this, the observation in the *Dhammapada* noted just above is followed by the advice:

> Understanding this, let not the Bhikku, the disciple of the Awakened One, delight in worldly honour but develop detachment instead.[4]

Thus, not only do those seven examples given by the Buddha in his first sermon belong to suffering, but even those examples that would be given of the "good" side of existence are, at bottom, only disguised suffering. The basic illness that is responsible for suffering goes deeper than the examples given; it is the grasping of the aggregates or constituents of self.

The Second Noble Truth is the truth that suffering originates in craving. In one sense, suffering is caused by craving what one cannot have or craving to avoid what cannot be avoided. Thus, craving money when one is poor leads to suffering; craving health when one is ill leads to suffering; craving immortality in the face of the inevitability of death leads to suffering; craving extinction faced with the continuity of the stuff of which life is made leads to suffering, and so on. But there is a deeper sense of craving. This is craving in the sense of a *blind compulsion to be or have a self.*

If the obvious forms of suffering are analyzed it will be seen that there are two basic factors involved. First, there is what might be called the existence of certain objective factors in the world. There is the fact that Jones has no money, that Smith's child just died, or that Singh's leg was cut off. But these objective facts in the world do not of themselves involve suffering. After all, who suffers when a boulder is split in two? Who suffers when a young oak is broken in the wind? Probably no one would ever think of ascribing suffering to the boulder, or the "parent" oak. But probably everyone would attribute suffering to Jones, Smith, and Singh. The difference between these cases is obvious. Trees and boulders do not have selves; hence there is no one to suffer. But Jones, Smith, and Singh have, each of them, a self. And this self is aware of changes in its condition.

This points to the second factor involved in suffering; the existence of a self. There is no suffering until objective factors in the world are related to a self. When these objective factors are related to a self this self may crave them or crave to avoid them. And when what is craved is not obtained there is suffering.

But what is this self which constitutes the second basic factor involved in

[4] *Ibid.*

suffering? And does it make sense to attribute a self to a person? What is this "I" to which reference is made when a person claims, "I have lost my child?" The truth of the origin of suffering is that *it is the craving of a self that gives rise to suffering*. Blindly, a person craves a self that though separate is attached to the factors constituting the person. This craving leads to the invention and projection of a self. This self, being attached to the factors making up a person, suffers when the identification is threatened by changes in the factors to which it is attached, whether these be the factors of that person, other persons, or other objects and activities in the world.

According to Buddhism, analysis of a person reveals the existence of (1) the activities constituting what we call the bodily, or physical, self; (2) activities of sensing; (3) activities of perceiving; (4) impulses to action; and (5) activities of consciousness. But in addition to these five groups of activities nothing more is to be found. The self, as that to which the groups of activities belong, is a fiction, a fiction created by ignorant craving. And it is the craving for this fictitious self that underlies all suffering.

The Third Noble Truth, that suffering can be extinguished, follows upon analysis of the causes of suffering. If selfish craving is the cause of suffering, then the cessation of suffering lies in the extinction of that craving. This is precisely what the Buddha recommended. In fact, the very goal of the Buddhist—*Nirvana*—has the meaning "be blown out." What is blown out —like a lamp—or extinguished, is selfish craving. When selfish craving is extinguished, suffering is pulled up by the root. Thus, the truth of the cessation of suffering is the truth that the extinction of craving will bring about the cessation of suffering.

It is a long way, however, from the recognition of what will bring about the cessation of suffering to the actual accomplishment of that cessation. And the Buddha, good physician that he was, did not stop with an analysis and diagnosis of the malady nor with the recognition of what was required for cure, but he prescribed a method of treatment which would destroy the illness. The prescription constitutes the Fourth Noble Truth, which teaches the famous "Middle Way" of Buddhism.

The Noble Eightfold Path

This Middle Way, which sums up the way of life that characterizes Buddhism as a practical philosophy, is built upon the eight principles constituting the Fourth Noble Truth. These principles are as follows:

1. Right views (*Samma ditthi*)   )
2. Right resolution (*Samma sankappa*))   Wisdom
3. Right speech (*Samma vaca*)   )
4. Right action (*Samma kammanta*)   )   Conduct
5. Right livelihood (*Samma ajiva*)   )
6. Right effort (*Samma vayama*)   )
7. Right mindfulness (*Samma sati*)   )   Mental Discipline
8. Right concentration (*Samma samadhi*))

The various actions of life prompted by and expressing these eight principles should proceed more or less simultaneously, the aim being to achieve a completely integrated life of the highest order. The relationships between actions of life and the principles that underlie these actions can be seen by considering the three axioms of Ethical Conduct, Mental Discipline, and Wisdom, which underlie all principles and actions. The axiom of Ethical Conduct includes right speech, right action, and right livelihood. The axiom of Mental Discipline includes right effort, right mindfulness, and right concentration. The axiom of Wisdom includes right views, and right resolution. The purpose of Ethical Conduct is to check the inflow of additional cravings. Mental Discipline aims at destroying the already present cravings, and Wisdom is prescribed for living a sufferingless existence.

Understanding ourselves and the universe in which we live, action will be based upon a universal love and compassion. Accordingly, Ethical Conduct is based on love and compassion and springs from wisdom, or an enlightened mind. But to achieve wisdom and to cultivate love and compassion, discipline of the self is required. Thus, Ethical Conduct, Discipline, and Wisdom are the three axioms of the Good Life.

Wisdom includes both the correct understanding of things as they are and the resolution to act in accord with this understanding. Having right views consists in seeing things as they are. This includes, on a lower level, intellectual understanding of things. But intellectual knowledge takes place within a system, or network, of concepts and principles which reflect necessarily limited perspectives as underlying assumptions. Accordingly, intellectual knowledge is conditioned by the concepts and principles of the system and its truth is relative to the truth of the system in which it takes place. Consequently, intellectual knowledge is considered a lower kind of understanding than the understanding that results from seeing things just as they are by a direct penetration. This direct seeing is the complete illumination of things just as they are in themselves and not as limited by concepts and labels. It is this direct penetration of things that is properly called

Wisdom. It reveals the relative and conditioned nature of all things and shows suffering to be caused by selfish grasping.

Wisdom reveals the nature of things and the causes of suffering, but does not stop there. It also expresses itself in the resolution to overcome suffering by leaving aside all selfish cravings. This involves the resolve to cultivate a love universal in depth and scope that reveals itself in compassion and non-hurting. Selfish desires, ill-will, hatred, and violence are entirely given up when Wisdom is achieved.

Wisdom cannot be achieved without discipline, and therefore one practices right effort, right mindfulness, and right concentration. Practicing right effort includes (1) preventing evil and unwholesome states of mind from arising, (2) getting rid of such evil and unwholesome states of mind that may already exist, (3) bringing about good and wholesome states of mind, and (4) developing and perfecting good and wholesome states of mind already present.

Right mindfulness consists in being aware of and attentive to one's activities. This includes the activities of (1) the body, (2) sensing and feeling, (3) perceiving, and (4) thinking and consciousness.

To be aware of and attentive to one's activities means understanding what these activities are, how they arise, how they disappear, how they are developed, controlled, gotten rid of, linked together, and what they are in themselves.

Right concentration is essentially a matter of recreating oneself as an enlightened person. Ignorance and enlightenment and suffering and happiness have their root in one's mental activities. It is said in the *Dhammapada*:

> mind precedes all unwholesome states and is their chief; they are all mind-wrought. If with an impure mind a person speaks or acts, misery follows him like the wheel that dogs the foot of the ox. Mind precedes all wholesome states and is their chief; they are all mindwrought. If with a pure mind a person speaks or acts, happiness follows him like his never-departing shadow.[5]

If this is the case, it is entirely plausible to concentrate on purifying one's mental activities as a means of achieving happiness.

Ordinarily four stages of concentration are distinguished. In the first stage one concentrates on getting rid of lust, ill-will, laziness, worry, anxiety, and doubt. These unwholesome mental activities are replaced by feelings of joy and happiness. In the second stage one concentrates on

[5] *Dhammapada*, 1,2.

Wheel of Becoming. *Information Service of India; photograph courtesy of Professor Grace E. Cairns.*

seeing through and getting beyond all mental activities, although retaining an awareness of joy and happiness. In the third stage one goes beyond the mental activity responsible for the feeling of joy, and achieves an equanimity pervaded by happiness. In the fourth and final stage of concentration there is complete equanimity and total awareness, beyond both happiness and unhappiness.

Ethical Conduct is both a reflection of, and a condition for, Wisdom and Discipline. Only a wise person can be good, and only a good person can be wise. And both wisdom and goodness require discipline. Accordingly, one begins and ends with all three simultaneously. To act ethically means to be correct in speech, action, and means of earning a living.

Right speech means generally to avoid all talk that will lead to unhappiness and to use speech to bring about happiness. Its negative application includes: (1) no lying; (2) no slander, or character assassination, or talk that might bring about hatred, jealousy, enmity, or discord among others; (3) no harsh or rude talk, no malicious talk, no impolite or abusive language; and (4) no idle or malicious gossip, or foolish chatter. Its positive application teaches that one should tell the truth, speak in a kindly and friendly way, use language meaningfully and usefully. This includes knowing the time and place for which certain talk is appropriate. This implies that sometimes one should maintain "noble silence."

Right action means avoiding killing or hurting, and precludes stealing, cheating, and immoral sexual activity. Positively, it means that one's actions should aim at promoting peace and happiness for others and respecting the well-being of all living beings.

Right livelihood extends the principle of right action to one's chosen profession throughout one's life. Accordingly, it precludes professions that would harm others, such as trading in firearms, liquors, drugs, poisons, killing, sexual procurement, etc. Only those means of earning a living which promote peace and well-being are in accord with this principle.

It is obvious how the axiom of Ethical Conduct rests upon compassion and love for others. But further, this compassion and love is the natural result of a recognition of the conditionedness and relativity of things. If no things have independent being (*svabhava*), then all are dependent upon each other. But this leaves no foothold for selfishness. Consequently, ignorance and selfishness must be replaced by wisdom and compassion.

REVIEW QUESTIONS

1. What is the significance of the four signs that Gautama saw during his chariot rides outside the palace grounds?
2. What are the Four Noble Truths taught by the Buddha in his first sermon? How are they linked?

3. According to the Second Noble Truth, suffering is caused by craving. What did the Buddha mean by craving, and how does craving cause suffering?
4. What are the components of the Noble Eightfold Path? How are they related to each other?

FURTHER READING

What the Buddha Taught, by Walpola Rahula, 2nd ed. (New York: Grove Press, 1978) is an excellent introduction to Buddhism by a practicing Buddhist monk. The ninety pages of text provide a thorough explanation of the Four Noble Truths, the Noble Eightfold Path, and the practice of mental discipline from a Theravada perspective. The accompanying translations from key scriptures provide the flavor of the Buddha's teachings, as do the seventeen carefully chosen illustrations.

The Buddha in the Robot, by Masahiro Mori (Tokyo: Kosei Publishing Co., 1981; distributed in the United States by Charles Tutle Co., Rutland, Vt.), introduces Buddhism by showing the relevance of its basic teachings to life in a technological age. Mori is one of Japan's leading robotics engineers and also a practicing Buddhist who has a knack for presenting complex ideas in simple ways. The emphases are on interconnectedness, no-self, and creative living, as Mori discusses their relevance for a good life in the present age.

Buddhist Philosophy: An Historical Analysis, by David J. Kalupahana (Honolulu: University of Hawaii Press, 1976), is a clearly written account of the key ideas in early Buddhism and their development in the Theravada and Mahayana traditions. The appendices on metaphysics and on Zen are excellent.

Buddhism: Its Doctrines and Its Methods, by Alexandra David-Neel (New York: Avon Books, Discus edition, 1979), is a lucid description of the essential teachings of Buddhism by a fine scholar who knows how to write for the uninitiated. Although her experience and scholarship are steeped in the Tibetan tradition, she has a remarkable appreciation for both the Theravada and Mahayana traditions. The chapters on karma and interdependent arising are outstanding.

CHAPTER 11

Historical Considerations

THE LAST CHAPTER was concerned with the ethical-religious teachings that constitute the basic core of Buddhism as a way of life, reflecting the main teachings of the historical Buddha. These teachings, aimed at inculcating the discipline and compassion that characterize the life and attitudes of a Buddhist, are not basically different today than they were twenty-five hundred years ago. On the other hand, the philosophies of Buddhism, which reflect the intellectual attempts to systematize the Buddhist way of life and to provide a rational basis for these ethical-religious teachings, have undergone considerable change and development.

The distinction between Buddhism as a way of life and Buddhist philosophies is the distinction between a way of living and the attempted justifications for that way. Thus, though Buddhists through the ages could agree on how to live, they could also disagree on the question of *why* they should live that way. If one is a Buddhist it follows that the Buddhist Way is accepted as the best way of life. But the question of justifying this acceptance is still open. Buddhism is sufficiently tough-minded and empirically inclined to rule out justification of the Middle Way by appeal to the fact that the Buddha said it was superior. In fact, appeal to faith as the only justification of the Middle Way was ruled out by the Buddha himself, as he encouraged his followers to examine the doctrine for themselves. Aside from an appeal to faith one could appeal to the consequences of following the Noble Eightfold Path. If this kind of life provided for goodness and happiness it could hardly be said to be an inferior way of life. But granting this kind of justification, and granting even that in a very important sense the results of a certain kind of life are the only justification for that kind of life, it is possible to raise the question of *why* that kind of life leads one out of suffering and provides peace and contentment. It is this question that serves as a starting point for the *philosophies* of Buddhism. In the different answers to this question the different philosophies of Buddhism are to be found.

By way of providing a basic orientation to the cultural phenomenon of Buddhism and of seeing the historical relations between the religion and the philosophies of Buddhism, this chapter will be devoted to a brief historical account of the development of Buddhism.

Pre-Buddhist India

The philosophical atmosphere of India in which Buddhism took its place in the sixth and fifth centuries B.C. was dominated by three attitudes. First of all there was the attitude that ritual and sacrifice were the principal effective means of securing whatever was desired. This attitude was connected with the belief—probably thousands of years old already by this time—that the creation and functioning of the world was due to, and controlled by, the effects of sacrifices and rites. The second attitude, reflected in the Upanishads, regarded the observable world and the observable self as mere "name and form." What was mere name and form was only temporary and passing, possessing no abiding reality. What was of abiding reality was the unchanging Self and the unchanging Real. This attitude was connected with belief in *Atman* as the abiding inner reality and *Brahman* as the abiding external reality, and with the identity of *Atman* and *Brahman*. The third attitude was skeptical. It was probably associated principally with the denial of the principal beliefs underlying the other two attitudes. Judging by various criticisms of the skeptical philosophy, it would appear that its adherents were the materialists, who denied physical, moral, and sacrificial causality, and who denied the possibility of knowledge.

The skeptical attitude obviously offered no help in the struggle to overcome suffering because it consisted chiefly in denying the possibilities suggested by the other attitudes. The sacrificial and ritualistic attitude was at this time so involved with magic and with the cult and corruption of the priests that it also failed to offer any real hope in the perennial struggle against suffering. While the attitude reflected in the Upanishads was not as obviously helpless as the other two, its philosophical abstractness and the underlying belief in the unchanging nature of the Real made it appear relatively unserviceable as the basis for a way to overcome or lessen suffering. Consequently, when the Buddha appeared teaching the causes of suffering and the way for ending suffering he found a ready acceptance.

Beginnings of Buddhism

Gautama Siddhartha was born about 563 B.C. at Kapilavastu, in what is today Nepal. Shielded by his father from the ugly scenes of suffering to be found all around, and happily married to a beautiful girl, Gautama led the easy pleasure-filled life of a prince of leisure until he was twenty-nine years old. Then, having been exposed to the sufferings of old age, sickness, and death, and having reflected that it would be well to discover some means for overcoming suffering, he left his palaces and family and took up the life of an ascetic. For six years he practiced the most extreme forms of self-discipline and self-denial. All to no avail. Finally, on the brink of death, he determined that the truth of the cause and cessation of suffering was not to be achieved by following the extreme of asceticism. Resolved now to follow a Middle Way between indulgence and asceticism, he soon achieved the enlightenment he was seeking. For the next forty years of his life the Buddha traveled around India teaching the Four Noble Truths and the Noble Eightfold Path. During these years of teaching the Buddha attracted many followers, and the Order of Buddhist Monks was already of good size when he died, in about the year 483 B.C.

The history of Buddhism after the death of the Buddha is a very complicated subject. Its early history can be viewed in terms of the changes in the Order prior to its split into two main movements, the more conservative movement characterized in the literature of the Theravada School, and the more liberal movement known as Mahayana. From that point on, Buddhist history is a matter of changes within each of these movements.[1]

---

[1] It must be noted that historical accounts of Buddhism are, for the most part, tentative because of insufficient evidence. The reader interested in the historical development of Buddhism would do well to turn to E. J. Thomas' *The History of Buddhist Thought*, 2nd ed. (London: Routledge & Kegan Paul, 1951), which very carefully points out the kinds and amounts of evidence available for the various historical claims made. The reader is advised to construe this historical account as no more than "a likely account" of what took place historically.

The Buddhist Councils

The content of early Buddhism was contained not only in the actual teachings of the Buddha about suffering and its cessation, but also in the rules for living developed by the Order of Monks. In fact, it appears that clashes of opinion within the Order over interpretation of disciplinary rules occurred earlier than differences of opinion over the religious-philosophical teachings. Furthermore, these differences of opinion over disciplinary rules were considered more serious than other differences of opinion. So important was the matter of discipline that the early divisions in Buddhism and the formation of different schools were primarily the result of arguments over these matters. This is not surprising, of course, for after all the Buddha was concerned chiefly with getting rid of suffering. And getting rid of suffering is more closely tied up with how one lives than with theoretical teachings. Thus, the first three Buddhist councils were held for the purpose of discussing and resolving differences of opinion concerning interpretations of disciplinary rules.

The first council of Buddhists was held shortly after the death of the Buddha at Rajagaha. This council, attended by five hundred monks, resolved—in the face of a suggestion that since the Master was dead the monks could do as they chose—that the rules were to be kept exactly as the Buddha prescribed, without either addition or deletion.

Probably about a hundred years after the first council there was a second council—the council of Vesali. Again the occasion of the council was a dispute over discipline. But this time it appears that the number of monks wanting a relaxation of the rules was relatively large. It was either at this second council or at the next council, that of Pataliputta, that the first main division took place. This division resulted in the Mahasanghika school being formed. It was followed by a series of further splits, both in the old order and within the Mahasanghika school. This development of differing schools is shown in the diagram on the following page.

Theravada and Mahayana

The exact teachings of each of these various schools, however, is a matter of considerable uncertainty. No doubt, these schools differed from each other on matters both of doctrine and disciplinary rules. But the exact nature of these differences is not known. Partially, the uncertainty in this

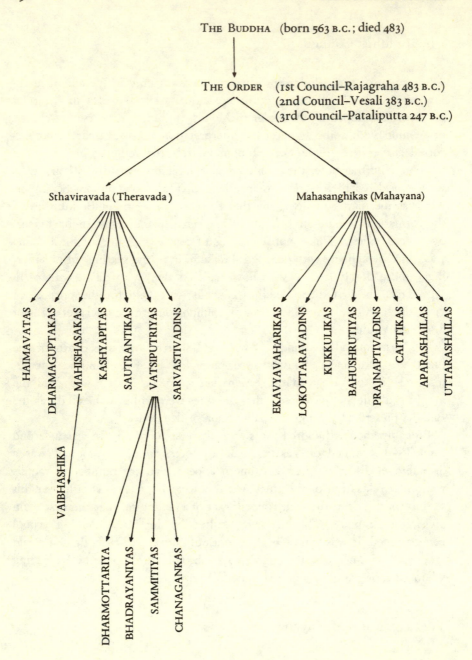

THE BUDDHA (born 563 B.C.; died 483)

THE ORDER (1st Council–Rajagraha 483 B.C.)
(2nd Council–Vesali 383 B.C.)
(3rd Council–Pataliputta 247 B.C.)

Sthaviravada (Theravada)

Mahasanghikas (Mahayana)

HAIMAVATAS

DHARMAGUPTAKAS

MAHISHASAKAS

KASHYAPITAS

SAUTRANTIKAS

VATSIPUTRIYAS

SARVASTIVADINS

EKAVYAVAHARIKAS

LOKOTTARAVADINS

KUKKULIKAS

BAHUSHRUTIYAS

PRAJNAPTIVADINS

CAITTIKAS

APARASHAILAS

UTTARASHAILAS

VAIBHASHIKA

DHARMOTTARIYA

BHADRAYANIYAS

SAMMITIYAS

CHANAGANKAS

HISTORICAL SKETCH OF THE EARLY DEVELOPMENT OF
BUDDHIST SCHOOLS

area is due to the fact that by the fifth century of Buddhism, the major division was not that of these twenty schools, but rather, the division into the Theravada and Mahayana schools, or sects. This was a division along religious lines, the chief differences being concerned with the interpretations of the Buddha's teachings concerning the attaining of *Nirvana.*

In Theravada there was great emphasis on self-discipline and individual achievement. The goal was *arhat*-ship, which symbolized the extinction of the fires of lust and craving in the individual, brought about by his or her own efforts. In Mahayana the goal was to become a *Bodhisattava*—a being whose only concern was with helping others extinguish suffering. The compassion shown by the historical Buddha was emphasized greatly, and as a result there came to be less reliance on individual effort and self-discipline, and more reliance on faith in the Buddha and *Bodhisattavas* who would provide assistance in overcoming suffering. In time these two different emphases in Buddhism came to be supported by different metaphysics. The emphasis on universal salvation represented by the Mahayana ideal of the *Bodhisattava* came to be underwritten by metaphysics of philosophical skepticism and absolutism. The emphasis on individual salvation represented by the Theravada ideal of the *arhat* came to be underwritten by a metaphysics of realistic flux, as formulated in the doctrine of momentariness.

Philosophical Schools

Thus, whereas from the religious perspective, the main division was into Mahayana and Theravada, from the philosophical perspective the division was into philosophies of realism as opposed to philosophies of idealism and absolutism. The philosophies of realism, which tend to be identified with Theravada Buddhism, are represented by the Vaibhashika and Sautrantika schools. The philosophies identified with Mahayana are (1) the "suchness" absolutism of Ashvaghosa, (2) the relativism of the Madhyamika school, and (3) the idealistic absolutism of the Yogacara school.

Before continuing with an historical outline of Buddhist schools of philosophy it must be pointed out that a division of Buddhism into religious and philosophical schools is somewhat arbitrary, and it is necessary to emphasize that the division is possible only from a certain perspective. In this case it is a perspective assumed primarily on the basis of the distinctions ordinarily made between religions and philosophies of the West. Buddhism as the living cultural phenomenon of the Orient is neither philosophy nor religion; nor is it really both religion and philosophy. It is simply Buddhism. The above distinctions do not apply. It might well be said that to look for philosophy in Buddhism is like looking for the tracks of birds in the air. Buddhism is essentially a way of life; it is not a philosophy about life.

But granting this, Buddhism, as a way of life, does rest upon certain views of human nature and the world. The fact that Buddhism presupposes certain philosophical views means that one path to the understanding of Buddhism is through an analysis of these views. However, it is important not to mistake the metaphysical views found in the philosophies of Buddhism for the "Essence of Buddhism." The "Essence of Buddhism" consists in understanding and getting rid of suffering; not in theoretical views of man and the world. But an understanding of the views implicit in Buddhism can lead one to recognize the logical foundations of Buddhism and makes possible a philosophical estimate of these basic foundations.

Probably the earliest of the philosophical schools was the Vaibhashika, as all of the other schools refer to the teachings of this school. The criticisms found in other Buddhist schools as well as in the Hindu schools reveal that the Vaibhashika held that the world is made up of atoms in continuous motion and also that this world can be directly perceived as it exists. But the individual philosophers belonging to this school are unknown.

The Sautrantika school may also be older than the schools belonging to the Mahayana, but the individual philosophers who are known to be connected with this school are contemporary with Madhyamika and Yogacara philosophers. Kumaralabdha, a contemporary of Nagarjuna, probably lived in the second century A.D. Probably he is not the first philosopher of this school, but he is the earliest known to us today. Other philosophers connected with this school are Vasubandhu, who composed the famous *Abhidharmakosha* as a summary of realistic philosophy, probably sometime in the fifth century A.D., and Yasomitra, who wrote a commentary on this work. One of the logicians of this school, Dharmottara, lived in the ninth century A.D.

The Madhyamika and Yogacara philosophies probably developed out of the insights present in the philosophies of Ashvaghosa and the *Lankavatara Sutra*. Ashvaghosa formulated his philosophy of the "Thusness" of reality sometime in the first century A.D. This philosophy emphasized the role of consciousness in knowledge and understanding and pointed to the ultimate unknowability of reality. The *Lankavatara Sutra*, also emphasizing the activity of the mind in experience, is probably earlier than Ashvaghosa.

The Madhyamika school concentrates on the ultimate unknowability of reality by conceptual and perceptual means. It is thus a school of philosophical skepticism. It is not, however, a school of unqualified skepticism, for conceptual reality and conceptual activity are not regarded as the ultimate reality. The earliest and greatest of the Madhyamika philosophers was Nagarjuna, who should probably be placed in the middle of the second century A.D. His pupil, Aryadeva, commented on some of his works. Later philosophers of this school who attracted the attention of other philosophers in India and China were Kumarajiva, who lived in the fourth century A.D., and Buddhapalita and Candrakirti, both of whom flourished around the middle of the sixth century A.D.

The Yogacara school represents many of the tenets of the *Lankavatara Sutra*, as it emphasizes the activity of mind—to the exclusion of everything else, according to its critics. It is the "Mind-only" doctrine of Vasubandhu of this school that attracted the most criticism from philosophers outside of this school. This is the same Vasubandhu who summarized the realistic philosophy of the Sautrantikas. He was converted from Sautrantika to Yogacara by his older brother, Asanga. And even prior to Asanga, there is a philosopher named Maitreyanatha who belonged to this school.

With Dinnaga, a pupil of Vasubandhu, Yogacara philosophy took on an emphasis on logic that brought it closer to the Sautrantika school. Dinnaga, Dharmakirti, and Dharmottara are all logicians who seem to have a philosophy midway between Sautrantika and Yogacara. Sometimes this philosophy is referred to as Svatantra Yogacara. Later Yogacara philosophers are Shantarakshita and Kamashila.

After the ninth century A.D. Buddhist philosophies began to disappear from India. Although Buddhist philosophical activity did not disappear, as Buddhism spread to China and other parts of Asia, there was never again to be the intense and critical philosophical activity in connection with Buddhism that was found during the first thirteen centuries of the Buddhist era in India. Whether it was because of a widespread feeling that the inadequacies of intellect for solving problems about ultimate reality had been so clearly shown by this time that no one wished to devote his or her life to the intellectual activity of philosophizing, or whether it was due to the more practical inclinations of the Oriental mind outside India, is hard to say. But though Buddhism as a way of life was as strong or stronger than ever, the heyday of Buddhist philosophy in India was over by 1000 A.D.

REVIEW QUESTIONS

1. What was the philosophical atmosphere in India in the Buddha's time?
2. What are the two main divisions of Buddhism? What do they have in common? How do they differ?
3. What are the main philosophical schools of Buddhism? How do they differ?
4. How would you characterize the historical development of Buddhism?

FURTHER READING

The book by David J. Kalupahana, *Buddhist Philosophy: An Historical Analysis* (Honolulu: University of Hawaii Press, 1976), referred to at the end of chapter 10 is an excellent place to begin one's historical studies of Buddhism.

Buddhist Thought in India, by Edward Conze (Ann Arbor: University of Michigan Press, 1967), is a very good account of the key ideas as they developed in the various philosophical schools. His treatment of the Madhyamikas is especially good.

A Short History of Buddhism, by Edward Conze (Boston: Unwin Paperbacks, 1982), provides an overview of the development of Buddhism in the compass of 130 pages. Chapter 1 deals with the first five hundred years; chapter 2 with the second five hundred years, tracing the early development of Mahayana and its spread to Central Asia and China; chapter 3 with the third five hundred years; and chapter 4 with the last thousand years.

Buddhist Sects in India, by Nalinaksha Dutt (Calcutta: Firma KLM Private, 1977), is a comprehensive review of the development of the eighteen sects of Indian Buddhists that developed in the early history of Buddhism. Like his other books, *Mahayana Buddhism* and *Early Monastic Buddhism*, this is a work of careful scholarship.

CHAPTER 12

❦❦❦❦❦❦❦❦❦❦❦❦❦❦❦❦❦❦❦❦❦❦❦❦❦❦❦❦❦❦

The Nature of the Self

THE MAIN philosophical implications of the ethical-religious teachings of Buddhism are contained in the doctrines of no-self (*anatta*) and impermanence (*anicca*). Both of these doctrines in turn are underwritten by the principle of dependent origination (*paticca samuppada*), according to which everything that exists is constantly changing and depends on everything else. The chief difference between the doctrines of *anatta* and *anicca* is that the former refers to the non-substantiality of the self, whereas the latter refers to the non-substantiality of things in the world. Both doctrines presuppose the theory of dependent origination.

As Buddhism developed, the principle of dependent origination underwent different interpretations. These different interpretations were then used to underwrite different theories of the non-substantiality of things and the self. The basic Buddhist philosophies can be studied by considering first the theories concerning the self, and then the theories concerning the nature of things in the world. In this chapter different views of the self will be considered.

Basic Principles

The Buddha's prescription for curing the ills of life follows upon his analysis of the causes of these ills. The Noble Eightfold Path was prescribed because it was what was needed to uproot the causes of suffering.

No doubt, the religious genius of the Buddha is what made possible his diagnosis of the causes of suffering and the prescription for its cure. But both the discovery of the causes of suffering and the prescription for its cure are dependent upon the Second Noble Truth—that suffering is caused.

The recognition that suffering is caused reflects an understanding of the relations between events and things in the world. The Buddhist understanding of these relations is reflected in the theory of dependent origination (*paticca samuppada*) which holds, roughly, that whatever is, is dependent upon something else. The formulation of the theory is as follows: (1) If this is, that comes to be; (2) From the arising of this, that arises; (3) If this is not, that does not come to be; (4) From the stopping of this, that stops.

There are several features of this view of dependent origination that need to be noted before applying the theory to an analysis of the self. First, if whatever is, is dependent upon another, then any kind of "straight line" causality is ruled out. There are no independent beings who are responsible for the existence of dependent beings. For example, the theistic notion that one absolutely independent being—God—created the rest of what exists, and that this created universe depends for its existence upon God, makes no sense in the Buddhist view of dependent origination. Rather, whatever creates is also created, and the processes of creating and being created go on simultaneously without beginning or end.

Second, as a consequence of the mutual dependence of all beings, it follows that no beings are solely "other-created," but that all are mutually self-creating. The ongoing processes that make up the universe are co-dependent and mutually influencing. Each aspect of the process shares in the creation and the continuation of the other aspects of the process.

Third, ordinary notions of space and time are ruled out by the Buddhist theory of dependent origination. Ordinary notions of space and time depend upon the location and duration of independent beings. Spatial characteristics are derived from the comparison of the location of one being relative to another. Temporal characteristics are derived by comparing the duration of one being to another. But according to the theory of dependent origination there are no beings independent of each other. There are only ongoing processes of mutually dependent factors. Reality is of the nature of process; *things* are merely abstractions. But ordinary notions of space and time depend upon these abstractions, and hence must also fall into the category of abstractions rather than realities. There are no beings; there are only becomings.

Fourth, adequate definitions are impossible. If the universe is thought to consist of things, relatively complete and independent, it is possible to adequately define the things making up the universe. But when the universe is considered to be of the nature of process, definitions are not possible, for whatever might be defined would belong to past stages of the process and never to the present reality of the process. Furthermore, because of the interrelatedness of everything, the definition of any one thing involves the definition of everything else.

Dependent Origination and the Wheel of Becoming

Avoiding linear notions of time and space, Buddhists ingeniously diagram the endless continuum of processes constituting reality by using the figure of a wheel. The wheel of becoming (*bhavacakra*) represents the major aspects of the continuous processes constituting what we ordinarily call a person. It is essentially an application of the theory of dependent origination to the processes constituting the self, and represents an attempt to exhibit the causes of suffering. The stages of becoming constituting the suffering person are usually represented as in the diagram on the following page.

In the cycle of life depicted by the wheel, suffering (*dukkha*) is symbolized by old age and death. It is not that *dukkha* is thought to consist solely in becoming old and dying, but rather, since these are two of the ills that are especially dreaded, they serve well as representatives of all the ills of life. Now it is asked, Upon what do old age and death depend? The answer is that is upon the arising of birth that there is death, for death follows birth as surely as night follows day. Without birth there would be no death; and birth would not occur if there were no "becoming forces" (*bhava*) available to be born. In turn, the "becoming forces" depend for their existence upon grasping and clinging to life; grasping and clinging could not exist without desire; desires depend upon perception; perception follows upon sense impressions, which would not be possible without the six sense organs. The sense organs, in turn, depend upon the mind and body (*nama-rupa*), but the functioning of mind and body is dependent upon consciousness. And consciousness is dependent upon the impulses to action, for consciousness is clearly an activity, and without an impulse to action there could be no consciousness. All of these phases of the processes and activities constituting the life of the individual can belong to the self only upon the presence of ignorance. And ignorance, in turn, depends upon the preceding factors in the cycle. And so the cycle goes, without beginning

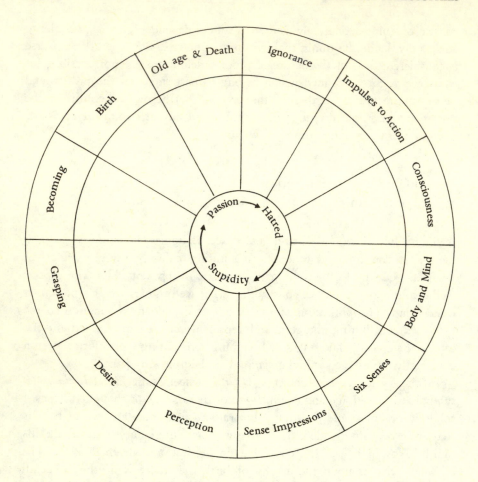

THE WHEEL OF BECOMING (*BHAVACAKRA*)

and without end. Each phase or factor is relentlessly brought about by others, which in turn are brought about by still others; the arising and the falling of the various factors of existence constitutes the unending continuum of process that makes up reality. Human beings are caught up in this cycle, being born, suffering, and dying; being born, suffering, and dying, time after time. Life brings death and death brings life, as these are no more than phases in the eternal process.

Although all of the factors constituting a being are intertwined and interdependent, constituting one ongoing process, the factor of ignorance is usually taken as the root-cause of the processes causing suffering. Accordingly, the wheel of becoming can also be interpreted by starting with suffering and then examining it in forward order. When this is done the reflections are as follows: ignorance makes possible the impulses to action, which make possible consciousness; these factors together make possible the mind and body organism; given the mind and body, use of the six senses is possible, making sense impressions possible. Sense impressions make possible perception, which leads to desire to achieve or avoid what is perceived. Desire opens the way for grasping at and clinging to life in its various aspects, which in turn provides for the forces of becoming, without which there would be no self to be born. And without birth of a self there would be no suffering.

It is customary when commenting upon and explaining the wheel of life to divide the factors into those concerned with the present life, those concerned with the past, and those concerned with the future, so that ignorance and the impulses to action are regarded as the causes from the past, and birth and old age and death are regarded as effects to occur in the future, with the other factors making up the present existence of the individual. But this division into past, present, and future is somewhat misleading. After all, if the self is really of the nature of process, then there are no sharp lines between past, present, and future. Past, present, and future merely proceed from certain arbitrary perspectives which result from emphasizing the *thingness* rather than the process nature of reality. This can easily be seen by considering that what we call a person is no sooner born than he begins dying; the process of aging which culminates in death is going on already at conception. But by the same token, the process of aging and dying is also part of the process of conception and birth. In fact, it might be said that basically this ignorance of process and the consequent cutting of this process into segments—which are regarded as independent of each other—underlie the grasping and clinging that inevitably leads to suffering. It means that the individual is constantly out of tune with reality.

The divisions of past, present, and future result from taking an arbitrary point of view which looks at reality as if it were cut up into distinct and separate pieces or things, rather than seeing it as an integral process. But the division of becoming into the twelve factors represented by the wheel also represents an arbitrary point of view, for in reality there are an unlimited number of factors that could be distinguished in the processes constituting an individual, with no clear lines of demarcation between them. Consequently this list of factors should not be taken as a complete list of the separate factors of reality. Instead, it should be regarded as an attempt to effect a transition from an attitude which cuts up reality and makes possible clinging and grasping, to an attitude which is consonant with the flow of reality. The latter attitude cannot itself be adequately represented conceptually, for the whole conceptual approach rests upon the attitude that reality is of the nature of being rather than process. Concepts can adequately reveal only a static reality. However, they can point to (though not express) a different kind of reality.

Taking care that the picture of reality represented by the wheel of becoming is not taken to be the last word and truth about the subject, there are other traps one must avoid when reflecting on this symbol of the wheel. It would be easy to be misled into thinking that Buddhism is basically nihilistic if one seized a wrong interpretation of the causes of suffering and the way to their removal. If old age and death follow upon being born, and if birth were stopped, then old age and death would be stopped. And isn't this precisely what the Buddha taught? "Locate the factors upon which suffering is dependent and remove them, and this will bring about the elimination of suffering." It is true that the Buddha taught that removal of the causes of suffering will eliminate suffering. But it does not follow from this that he maintained that nonexistence was the way to non-suffering. On the very face of it, the teaching that only nonexistence would lead to non-suffering is absurd, for who could subscribe to this teaching as a way of deliverance? And history reveals that Buddhism has been embraced as a saving teaching by hundreds of thousands of persons for many, many centuries. If the Buddha did not teach nihilism, then what did he teach? Upon the nonexistence of what would there be nonexistence of suffering? To answer this question it is necessary to reflect on the Buddhist notion of what a person is.

Stopping the Wheel of Becoming

Ordinarily when we talk about what a person is, especially when we talk about what we ourselves are, we assume that in addition to the bodily and mental characteristics constituting the individual there is also a self, an "I." Thus we say, "*I* will do that, *I* am doing this," etc. And the claim is made that various things, including our bodies and minds, belong to the person. We say, "It's *his* body." Or, "I'm improving *my* mind." It is this ego-self—this "I"—to whom suffering is attributed, as for example when we say, "It's terrible, the doctor just told me that I am dying of cancer, and this is why I am suffering so." Clearly, if there were no ego-self, or "I," there could be no suffering, for suffering is always the suffering of a self; it always belongs to someone.

What foundation is there for the ordinary belief in the existence of an ego-self? This is the question underlying the Buddhist analysis of the self, undertaken to uproot the conditions upon which suffering depends. It is to the nonexistence of the ego-self that the theory of *anatta* refers, and it is in overcoming attachment to the "I" that release from suffering is found. As the Buddha said,

> Therefore say I that the Tathagata has attained deliverance and is free from attachment, inasmuch as all imaginings, or agitations, or proud thought concerning an Ego or anything pertaining to an Ego, have perished, have faded away, have ceased, have been given up and relinquished.[1]

But surely it is paradoxical for anyone to claim that he or she does not exist. To say "I do not exist" obviously is not to make any claim at all, as the remark negates itself, since a nonexistent being could not make the claim and an existing being would be asserting existence in making the claim. Consequently, the Buddhist claim that the self does not exist could not be a claim that there is no individual existence, that the person is nonexistent.

It seems more reasonable to regard a remark such as "I do not exist," as an attempt to get attention for another claim that is to be made. For instance, it might reasonably be claimed that I do not exist as a substance independent of the processes that constitute me. This is not a claim about my existence *per se*, but a claim about my existence as a "such and such." And these are quite different matters. The Buddhist claim about the nonexistence of the self is a claim about the nonexistence of the self as a being *in addition to*, or *apart from*, the various factors that are ordinarily said to belong to the self. It clearly is not a claim about the nonexistence of the factors that make up the individual person. This is evident from the Buddha's reply to Vacchagotta's question concerning whether the Tathagata had any theories of his own (concerning the nature of the self). His reply was as follows:

> The Tathāgata, O Vaccha, is free from all theories; but this, Vaccha, does the Tathāgata know,—the nature of form, and how form arises, and how form perishes; the nature of sensation, and how sensation arises, and how sensation perishes; the nature of perception, and how perception arises, and how

---

[1] *Majjhima Nikaya, Sutta* 72, in Henry Clarke Warren, *Buddhism in Translations* (New York: Atheneum, 1963), p. 125.

perception perishes; the nature of the pre-dispositions, and how the pre-dispositions arise, and how the pre-dispositions perish; the nature of consciousness, and how consciousness arises, and how consciousness perishes.[2]

This answer reveals that rather than considering various theories of the substantiality of the self, the Buddha took a long hard look at what a person is, and found no extra-mental or extra-physical thing to which the word "self" might refer. Rather, upon analysis it became evident that a person is constituted by a large number of processes. These processes can be grouped together, for the sake of convenience, in the way indicated by the Buddha's answer to Vacchagotta's question. Schematically, this analysis of a person can be represented as follows:

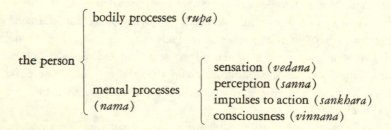

All of the various things that can be said of a person are about one or another of these processes. No person ever engages in any activities that do not belong to one or another of these five groups. But if the analysis of a person does not reveal anything other than these five groups of processes, then what foundation is there for claiming the existence of another component, namely, the self or the "I"? Ordinarily we say that the body, or the habits, or the thoughts of a person *belong* to a self, and thus suggest that there is, in addition to what is owned, also an owner of the processes. It is clear upon analysis, however, that this is simply a way of speaking, and cannot be taken as evidence that there exists a self in addition to the groups that make up a person.

It is now possible to become clearer about exactly what is meant by the theory of *anatta*, which denies the substantiality of the self. The *anatta* theory denies the existence of a self only when the word "self" is taken to refer to some thing in addition to the groups of factors making up a person. The *anatta* theory does not deny the existence of a self when the word "self" is taken to refer to only the five groups of processes constituting the

2 *Ibid.*

person. Thus, it is the view that the self is a substance independent of the processes making up a person that is denied by the doctrine of *anatta*.

With this explanation of the *anatta* theory in mind it is possible to see that the theory of dependent origination applied to the rise and fall of suffering in the wheel of becoming has nothing to do with nihilism. The ignorance that must be destroyed is the ignorance that consists in living as though the self exists over and above the groups of processes. The conviction that there is a substantial self is the root-cause of suffering, for this results in the attitude that underlies and makes possible the attachment of the various processes to a self. It is this ignorance that allows the attachment and thereby makes possible suffering.

It is important to note that the processes in themselves are not capable of suffering; it is only a self that suffers. Because of ignorance, a self is considered to exist and is attached to the groups. And now, when the groups change in relation to the self, there is suffering.

On the other hand, if the ego is not born there can be no attachment to the groups. The groups will continue their flow in conformity with the process nature of reality; there is no stopping this flow, even if one wished to do so. But the ego—the "I"—need not be born; it need not arise. It is from the arising of this ego that suffering arises. And upon stopping that ego from arising, the suffering will stop.

With this in mind, the wheel of becoming can be meditated upon as follows: old age and death come to a self because the self is born; a self is born because there is attachment to the becoming forces; there is attachment to the becoming forces because there is grasping; and there is grasping because there is desiring. Feeling leads to desiring. Feeling is possible because of attachment to the sense impressions; and because there is attachment to the sense organs impressions are received. Attachment to the sense organs follows upon attachment to the mind and body; this in turn follows upon attachment to consciousness, which follows from attachment to impulses to actions, which proceeds from ignorance.

Meditating on the wheel in forward order, reflection reveals that without ignorance there would be no attachment to the impulses to action, no attachment to the processes of consciousness, no attachment to mind and body, to the sense organs, to the sense impressions, to the feelings, to the cravings, to the grasping and clinging, to the becoming forces; and there would then be no ego to be born and no self to grow old and die.

It is important to notice that the various processes would go on without interruption; the removal of ignorance would not alter that. But the processes cause suffering only because of a wrong attitude toward them; an attitude that mistakes them for something other than what they are by cutting up reality and attaching this cut-up reality to a self which in ignorance is thought to exist. It is *attachment* to the groups, and not the groups themselves, that brings about suffering.

The difference between groups of processes and attachment groups is explained by Buddhaghosa (400 A.D.) as follows:

> "Groups" is a general term; while the term "attachment groups" specifies those which are coupled with depravity and attachment.[3]

Then, after indicating his intention to teach the difference between the five groups and the five attachment groups, he goes on to say:

> All form whatsoever . . . belongs to the form-group. All sensations whatsoever, . . . all perception whatsoever, . . . all predispositions [impulses to action] whatsoever, . . . all consciousness whatsoever, ... These, O priests, are called the five groups.

Distinguishing between the groups as such and the groups as attached to an ego he says,

> . . . those groups which are in the grasp of attachment are attachment groups.[4]

Clarifying the distinction between the groups and the attachment groups, Buddhaghosa goes on to say:

> When there is form, O priests, then through attachment to form, through engrossment in form, the persuasion arises, "This is mine; this am I; this is my ego." When there is sensation, . . . when there is perception, . . . where there are predispositions, . . . when there is consciousness, O priests, then through attachment to consciousness, through engrossment in consciousness, the persuasion arises, "This is mine; this am I; this is my ego."[5]

This distinction between the groups of existence and the attachment groups (attachment to the groups of existence) makes clear why the Buddhist teaching that to get rid of suffering the self must be rooted out has nothing to do with nihilism, but has to do only with the destruction of the product of ignorance. The groups of processes constituting existence are not

---

[3] *Visuddhi-Magga*, ch. 14, in Warren, *Buddhism in Translations*, p. 155.
[4] *Ibid.*, pp. 155, 156.
[5] *Ibid.*, p. 157.

to be destroyed. Only the falsely imagined self is to be destroyed. The reason this false self is to be destroyed is that it makes possible the attachment to the groups which underlies all forms of suffering. Without this false ego-self, which is only a creation of ignorance, there would be no looking to the past, bemoaning what has been lost, and no looking forward to the future lamenting over what has not yet come about. Without this ego-self life could be lived in the full richness of the present moment, without distinction, division, or attachment. Consequently, once this ignorance is removed life will be found complete and perfect just as it is.

This realization of the completeness and perfectness of life is beautifully expressed in a remark by a twenty-five-year-old woman by the name of Yaeko Iwasaki, who achieved enlightenment after only five years of discipline and meditation. In a letter to her master, Harada-*Roshi*, dated December 27, 1935, she said:

> You can appreciate how enormously satisfying it is for me to discover at last, through full realization, that just as I am I lack nothing.[6]

The incompleteness and insecurity and the feelings of aloneness and estrangement that characterize the basic anxiety underlying the mental suffering of most people proceed from the activity of the ego attaching itself to various processes, clinging and grasping in a desperate effort to claim existence. Undeniably, the mark of the ego is that it is a struggling-to-be; it is not a being already complete. Nor is it simply an aspect of process. It is a striving-to-be and grasping-to-be which seeks to collect and dominate all of reality. No wonder then that the realization that the ego is unreal, that it is simply the product of ignorance, frees one from the basic causes of suffering. And this is why the doctrine of *anatta* is one of the fundamental principles of Buddhism, for the belief in the reality of a self is incompatible with the extinction of suffering at which Buddhism aims.

Theories of the Non-Self

Despite agreement among Buddhist schools that the doctrine of *anatta* was basic to the Budda's teaching and central to the message of Buddhism, there was considerable controversy concerning precisely what it was that

---

[6] The letter from which this is taken, along with seven other inspiring letters, are contained in Philip Kapleau, *The Three Pillars of Zen* (New York: Harper & Row, 1967), pp. 269-91.

this doctrine of non-self did allow and what it did not allow. Since the doctrine of *anatta* was, at least formally, a negative theory denying a theory of self, and since a variety of theories of the self are possible, it is not surprising that there should be disagreement concerning just which theories of the self the *anatta* doctrine denied, and which theories it did not deny.

Consequently, even though Buddhists agreed that the doctrine of *anatta* was a basic and true teaching of the Buddha, there came to be considerable disagreement over who it was that could be saved by following the Way. The location of the five groups constituting the empirical individual, and the rejection of the supposed existence of a substance in addition to the groups, left open the question of what distinguished one set of five groups from another, and what connection there was between treading the Path and becoming enlightened. The problem presented itself as especially acute to the Buddhist mind, for unless there was a means of distinguishing one set of groups from another, there would be no basis for differentiating between one person to be saved and another. Furthermore, there would be no basis for distinguishing between the ignorant and the enlightened person unless there were some kind of identity or continuity within each set of groups. And if the latter distinction could not be made, it would follow that the Buddha is no different from the ignorant and suffering people to whom he addressed himself. And such a conclusion about the Enlightened One is not acceptable to any Buddhist.

Self Analyzed in Terms of Elements

The earliest systematic reflections about the *dharma*, or teachings of the Buddha, are contained in the third portion of the orthodox collection (Pali canon) of Buddhist works known as the *"Abhidharma* basket." The main concern of the Abhidharma writers was not with the question of whether or not there were substances, or selves. They assumed that existence was not of the nature of substance, but rather consisted in the continuous flow of elements, called by the Abhidharmists, *dharmas*. The problem for the Abhidharmists was one of classifying these *dharmas* and of establishing their interrelations.

The basic Abhidharmist teaching on the nature of the self holds that at the core of individual existence, instead of a permanent and unchanging substance, or soul, there is a stream of continuously flowing discrete elements of sensation, consciousness, feeling, activity impulses, and bodily processes. These continuously moving elements give rise to the appearance of an enduring self. But this appearance is to be disregarded, for the individual is never anything more than these various elements in motion. Over and above these elements, which even though conditioned and transitory, are regarded by the Abhidharmists as ultimately real, there is the element of *Nirvana*, which is held to be unconditioned and non-transitory. *Nirvana* is universally regarded as beyond description and definition, but when, from time to time, philosophers have felt compelled to say something about it, they have called it the indefinable essence of the various conditioned elements in a quiescent condition. The reasoning behind this is readily understandable even if the characterization is unintelligible; the teaching of the Buddha provides for the "quieting" of the elements of existence, and since it is impossible to regard total extinction as any kind of salvation, the philosophers postulated that salvation, or *Nirvana*, must consist in the quiescence of the conditioned elements.

There are numerous lists of the basic elements given in the Abhidharma literature showing the interrelations between them. The lists occasionally disagree with each other, and frequently overlap, but the lists all indicate that the fundamental elements, or *dharmas*, are of the nature of elemental forces rather than elemental substances. Using an analogy, it could be said that the *dharmas* are likened to elemental energy charges rather than to minute bits of solid matter; though devoid of spatial and temporal characteristics themselves, by their motions and combinations they give rise to the compounded elements or processes which can be located spatially and temporally. The individual is simply a combination of these impersonal forces in motion.

Concerning what the self is, the Abhidharma question is, How are the fundamental *dharmas* constituting the individual to be classified? Five groups, or *skandhas*, are taken as basic categories of the empirical self. These categories are then analyzed into constituent components, or *dharmas*. In this way lists such as the following are derived: (1) the group comprising the bodily processes (*rupa*) are constituted by the *dharmas* of ear, eye, nose, tongue, and skin, and the corresponding *dharmas* of color, sound, odor, flavor, and resistance; (2) the group comprising the processes involved in feeling (*vedana*) and, (3) the processes constituting perception, are left undivided at this point, but (4) the processes constituting the conscious and unconscious impulses to action (*sankharas*) are divided in such a way as to reveal the *dharmas* constituting perception and feeling as well. This division is as follows: (A) *constituents of mental activity present in consciousness*: feeling, perception, will, immediate sensation, desire, understanding, memory, attention, inclination, and concentration; (B) *con-*

stituents of virtue: faith, courage, equanimity, modesty, disgust at objectionable things, non-greed, non-hatred, compassion, and mindfulness; (C) *constituents of vice*: dullness, doubt, sloth, carelessness, immodesty, anger, hypocrisy, envy, jealousy, deceit, trickery, hatred, and pride. (5) The group consisting of the activities of consciousness is divided into the elements, or *dharmas*, responsible for the three categories of consciousness: pure, impure, and indeterminate (capable of being either pure or impure). Altogether, these three categories of consciousness include eighty-nine elements, or *dharmas*, when they are associated with the various processes constituting the *sankharas*.

However, the division of the five groups of processes constituting the individual into these *dharmas* is not the end of the story, for all of these *dharmas* are conditioned, or made—that is, they are not independent; they have no existence in their own right, and are dependent for their being upon something else. So the question can be asked, Of what are these *dharmas* made? When this question is taken seriously, the *dharmas* themselves come to be divided into an indefinite (and potentially unlimited) number of components, or moments, which are regarded as the ultimate *dharmas* of existence. Each of these ultimate *dharmas* is by itself without characteristics of mass or duration, but all together they are responsible for the characteristics of things in the world.

This analysis of the self destroys the idea of a permanent and independent self. Nowhere is there found a trace of ego. Only impersonal elements are found, in constant conjunction and process, giving rise to the appearance of an enduring self.

While this Abhidharma doctrine is in conformity with the Buddha's teaching that nowhere is there a self to be found, that all *dharmas* are without self,[7] and that enlightenment requires giving up all attachment to an ego,[8] it offered little assistance in understanding the continuity of the individual. Nor did it provide for an explanation of how the effects of actions of one person could possibly affect that person at a later time; but unless this were possible, the teaching that individual persons could overcome suffering would be wholly irrelevant. Now, it is true that a nominal explanation had been provided for these points in that it was held that the grouping of elements provided individual continuities. These individual continuities served the purpose of explaining the enduring characteristic of the person by providing for endurance without permanence; they also pro-

---

[7] *Dhammapada*, XX. 7, trans. by Acharya Buddharakkhita Thera (Bangalore, India: Buddha Vaccna Trust, 1966).
[8] *Majjhima Nikaya, Sutta* 72.

vided for the distinction of one continuity from another. The difficulty with this view of personal continuities, however, is that there is no reason why the processes should form such continuities. Unless the *dharmas* contain something other than discrete impersonal forces, it is not necessary that these forces should combine into these personal continuities.

The Personalist View

These difficulties with the Abhidharma interpretation of the *anatta* doctrine led Buddhists in the Vatsiputriya, Sammitya, Dharmottariya, Bhadrayaniya, and Chanaganka schools to claim that in addition to the impersonal *dharmas* there was a person (*pudgala*) to be found. These Buddhists, known as Personalists (*Pudgalavadins*), sought an explanation of the *anatta* teaching of the Buddha that would square with the common belief in a self, and at the same time not violate the basic teachings concerning the alleviation of suffering.

The "person" claimed by the Personalists was recognized as something real in its own right that an enlightened person experiences. It is this "person" that accounts for individuation of processes so that individual persons and things can be distinguished from each other. It also makes possible the continuity within one distinct and continuous process, so that the effects of one person's activities accrue to that person and not to another. It is the "person" that provides the element of connection between the ignorant and the enlightened individual. This "person" is the agent of activities, and is responsible for coordinating the activities of the various mental processes involved in knowing and acting.

Even though the addition of the "person" to the impersonal realities catalogued by the Abhidarmists made it possible to stick to familiar and commonsense ways of talking about self and experience, the Personalists could not achieve a satisfactory theory unless they could show how this "person" was related to the impersonal elements. They also had to show that their view was in conformity with the Buddha's no-self teaching. The difficulty involved in establishing both of these points proved insurmountable for the Personalists. To avoid a wrong belief in self, they could not identify the "person" with the groups themselves. Nor could they claim that the "person" was either inside or outside of the groups. If the "person" were to be identified with the groups nothing would be gained, for the "person" would appear and disappear when the groups arise and disappear.

If it is distinguished from the groups, the "person" must be attached in some way to them. But this clearly violates the teaching of non-attachment, which all Buddhists accept.

What remains as a possibility for relationship between the groups and the "person"? According to the Personalists, the relation is one of *correlation,* which they contend cannot be further explained in terms of other relations. The difficulty with this claim is that only one of the correlatives is known, for by their own admission, the "person" is undefinable in every respect. But if one of two elements held to be correlated with each other is completely unknown, there is no basis for establishing either that there is a correlation, or what the correlation is, if it exists. Trying to avoid the difficulty, the Personalists resort to an example: the "person" is like the fire that is correlated with the fuel and the flame; though they are always found together, fire has a reality of itself, evident in its nature as heat; fire is not the same thing as fuel or a series of flames.

The difficulty with examples in general is that while they may illustrate a point, they do not prove the point. The difficulty with this particular example is that it is unclear in itself and consequently does not even serve to illustrate a point. As a result, the Personalist theory, which comes closest of all Buddhist theories of the self to the ordinary commonsense point of view, is really nothing more than a rather dogged insistence that since we ordinarily talk and act as though there were a "person" in addition to the groups of processes constituting the individual, that "person" must exist, even though it is not possible to say what it is or how it is related to the processes.

Self as "Suchness"

Dissatisfaction with the Personalist theory of the self led the Mahayana philosophers to seek other ways of solving the problems of personal continuity and enlightenment without invoking a theory of substances. For Ashvaghosa, the "person," or *pudgala,* of the Personalists came to be replaced by *tathata,* or suchness. For the Madhyamika philosophers it was *shunyata,* or emptiness, that took over the role of *pudgala.* It is important to note here that *suchness* and *emptiness* were not postulated as theories to explain the empirical continuity of an individual. As the Mahayana philosophers saw it, the problem had its roots in the attempt to understand the connection between the empirical individual and the enlightened one, between the ignorant self and the one who had attained *Nirvana* by achieving *Buddhi*. No problem arose in connection with empirical identity and continuity because it was universally accepted that what was empirical was compounded; was unreal; was transitory; was of the nature of *dukkha* (suffering); and was to be eradicated, not explained. But if those persons to whom the Buddha preached were to become enlightened, it must be the case that somehow, somewhere, within the empirical world there must be that which is not of the nature of the compounded and is not inseparable from suffering. It would be this—whatever it is—that would constitute the nature of the enlightened person. The problem presenting itself here is not that of determining the essence of the ignorant empirical self, but that of understanding the essence of the enlightened self—the Buddha-nature itself. The almost impossible difficulty of this problem is compounded by the fact that it is the ignorant self who is trying to understand the enlightened self.

No doubt it was appreciation of the magnitude of the problem created by the ignorant self trying to understand the enlightened self that led the Personalists to say that the "person" is completely undefinable. But as the Mahayana philosophers point out, if this "person" is completely undefinable it ought not to be called a *person*, for a person is something determinate and (at least roughly) describable. If the nature of the enlightened self is beyond the empirical and conceptual it cannot be named by the word "person" or anything else. In recognition of this, Ashvaghosa refers to it as *tathata*—"such as it is." In other words, the enlightened self is just what it is, and since nothing can be said of it as it is in itself, rather than trying to make it something determinate, it is better just to refer to it by using the non-name "suchness."

The Madhyamika philosophers also objected to attaching the name "person," or *pudgala*, to the enlightened self. The non-name they used for the enlightened self was *shunyata*, or emptiness. The clue to what the Madhyamikas were getting at is made obvious by the question that naturally follows a claim that something is empty, i.e., "Empty of what?" What the Madhyamika philosophers were claiming was that the *pudgala postulated by the Personalists* was empty of reality. The argument behind this claim was supported by the position that whatever is determined perceptually and conceptually is of the nature of mind and not of reality. Perceptual and conceptual claims are based upon a cutting up of reality, and thus do not represent reality as it is. Hence these claims are empty of reality. The Personalist claim that there is a *pudgala* over and above the groups of processes is just an empty claim if it is about anything definite. On the other hand, if the *pudgala* claim is not regarded as a claim about anything definite, it is really not a claim about a reality. At best it could be regarded as a claim that since the theory of the groups is based on a cutting up of reality, this theory necessarily fails to establish the existence of the real self. This view would come close to the Madhyamika position, but there is no evidence that the Pudgalavadins ever advanced such a view.

The Madhyamika philosopher's own view about the nature of the enlightened self is really a non-view. Not claiming any views, avoiding clinging to one theory as true and another as false, the Madhyamika understands that any theory of the self will be one-sided and incomplete. The achievement of enlightenment will directly reveal the peace and bliss of *Nirvana*. Thus, though Nagarjuna has theories about other theories, he has no theories about the enlightened self. He knows that concepts cannot capture this reality.

Self as Consciousness

The Yogacarins replace the Personalist's theory of a *pudgala* with the theory of *alaya-vijnana*, or "seed-consciousness." Their claim is that there is an extremely subtle and pervasive consciousness underlying ordinary consciousness, out of which ordinary consciousness evolves and into which it returns. This seed-consciousness provides the continuity between the activities of consciousness required to give continuity to the individual's mental activity. It also provides an answer to the question of the connection between treading the Path and being saved, for the essence of the self is contained in this seed-consciousness, and when everything impure and evil has been removed from this basic consciousness all *dukkha* is automatically eliminated and *Nirvana* is achieved.

That there must be a seed-consciousness can be seen by considering the nature of conscious activity, the Yogacarins argue. Building on the Abhidharma analysis, consciousness, or conscious activity, is reduced to a stream of moments, or points of consciousness. Sometimes this stream runs underground, and sometimes it surfaces, as when we are conscious of things and activities around us. Since consciousness could not come to the fore unless it were present in a latent, or seed form, it must be the case that there is a seed-consciousness. Into this seed-consciousness goes the residue of all past moments of consciousness, and from it comes the basis for the present consciousness.

This theory has the advantage of providing an explanation of *karma* (the retribution of effects of actions to the doer), rebirth (an individual is born and dies many many times), the distinction between one individual and another (different seeds), and the connection between treading the path and becoming enlightened (purification of the seed-consciousness).

The Yogacarins reject the Madhyamika criticism that all *dharmas*—including the *dharmas* of consciousness—are unreal because arrived at conceptually or perceptually by cutting up reality. Their argument is that if consciousness is taken as unreal, then the arguments whereby the Madhyamikas establish the unreality of all *dharmas* would also fall to the ground, since they are conceptual arguments, arising within consciousness. However, rejecting the unreality of all *dharmas* outside of consciousness, the Yogacarins are left without a basis for claiming the existence of other individuals, let alone distinguishing between them. The reason is that if the only reality admitted is that of my own consciousness, then any other existence could be known only insofar as it existed within my own consciousness; whether there existed an objective counterpart to what was found in my consciousness would be forever unknown.

Aside from that difficulty, the Yogacarins are hard pressed to show that their theory of a seed-consciousness is correct. After all, there might be other theories that would also square with ordinary experience. It is one thing to suggest a probable theory of the self and another thing to show either that the theory is correct or that it is superior to every other theory. According to the seed-consciousness theory, ordinary consciousness arises out of, and exists in, a seed-consciousness. But out of what does the seed-consciousness arise? And in what does it exist? If something be postulated in response to these two questions, it appears that seed-consciousness is not the ultimate self, but simply an intermediary stage in the analysis. If, on the other hand, it is claimed that seed-consciousness is eternally existent and exists only in itself, it is difficult to see why the same thing could not be said about ordinary consciousness. A further difficulty is that only from the standpoint of ordinary consciousness can anything be said about the seed-consciousness, and therefore claims about seed-consciousness itself are completely untestable.

The difficulties confronting these various theories of the self reveal some of the problems encountered in trying to provide a philosophically acceptable account of what a person is. It is clear that the Personalist and the Yogacarin views are both difficult to maintain without violating the principle of dependent origination. In addition, they face the various philosophical problems pointed out above. On the other hand, the views of

Ashvaghosa and the Madhyamika philosophers, which provide the chief basis for the practices constituting the Mahayana Buddhist way of life, do not provide a definitive theory of the self. The Madhymika philosophers, being complete relativists, appear to be most closely in accord with the principle of dependent origination. But this very fact prevents them from having any ultimate theory of their own, for they have no ultimates upon which to base such a theory. Even their claim that all views are relative is itself a relative claim.

It would appear that only the Madhyamikas interpreted the principle of dependent origination as applying to all conceivable existence. The realistic philosophers of the Abhidharma took the ultimate moments of existence as fundamental, or absolute, relating all other existence to these fundamental elements. The idealistic philosophers of the Yogacara school regarded the seed-consciousness as fundamental and absolute, relating all other existence to this fundamental reality.

Because they allowed exceptions to the principle of dependent origination both the realistic and the idealistic philosophers had a basis upon which to erect their theories of the self. The Madhyamika philosophers, however, did not interpret the principle in such a way that certain kinds of existence were exceptions, allowing for them to become the absolutes in a philosophical system. The price they paid for refusing to make exceptions is that they were unable to establish any view of their own, for they had no basis for any view. This, however, seemed a relatively small price to pay, for as seen above, the Buddha also professed to have no views of the self.[9] In fact, for a practicing Buddhist, having no views might well represent considerable progress along the Way, for this eliminates the possibility of clinging to purely conceptual entities, and thus marks non-attachment to the ego of ignorance that underlies suffering.

REVIEW QUESTIONS

1. How are Buddhist views of the self related to the theory of dependent origination?
2. How does dependent origination relate to the arising and cessation of suffering?
3. Buddhist analysis of the self reveals five interrelated groups of processes, but no self to which they are attached. What are these five groups? What are the attachment groups?

[9] See above, p. 161.

4. Compare and contrast the Abhidharmist, Personalist, Madhyamika, and Yogacara views of the self. Which do you think comes closest to the Buddha's teachings? Why?

FURTHER READING

Most of the books on different aspects of Buddhism mentioned in previous chapters are also relevant here. Alexandra David-Neel's *Buddhism* is especially good, as is *What the Buddha Taught*, by Walpola Rahula.

Causality: The Central Philosophy of Buddhism, by David J. Kalupahana (Honolulu: University of Hawaii Press, 1975), is an excellent study of dependent origination in its historical development.

Buddhism: The Religion of Analysis, by Nolan Pliny Jacobson (London: Allen and Unwin, 1966), interprets Buddhism as a way of analysis that can provide freedom from the domination of a fictional self or ego. In this the book follows traditional Buddhist understanding. But the author also shows the particular relevance of this way of life for the contemporary world.

Cutting Through Spiritual Materialism, by Chogyam Trungpa (Berkeley: Shambala Publications, 1973), offers both theory and advice on the spiritual life according to Tibetan Buddhism. These lectures are studies in the application of no-self to the transformation of life. Comparisons with other spiritual traditions illuminate many of the author's points.

CHAPTER 13

❧❧❧❧❧❧❧❧❧❧❧❧❧❧❧❧❧❧❧❧❧❧❧❧❧❧❧❧❧❧

The Nature of Reality

An Outline of Different Views of Reality

JUST AS Buddhist theories of the self took shape according to their interpretations of the principle of dependent origination, so also were different
theories of the nature of external reality influenced by this principle. As a
consequence of sharing the common principle of dependent origination,
Buddhist theories of the world and self have certain features in common.
(1) Neither selves nor external things are of the nature of substance. (2)
Both are constituted by processes of elemental forces. (3) Permanence is
not found in either things or selves. (4) Space and time are not determining
characteristics of either things or selves, since space and time are relative to
the processes (which are already relative to each other). Nevertheless,
despite this core of doctrine common to the different schools, there are
many differences among their views of the nature of the external world as a
result of different interpretations of the principle of dependent origination.

The main differences in the teachings concerning the nature of external
things can be summarized in terms of the views of the schools of
Vaibhashika, Sautrantika, Madhyamika, and Yogacara. The first of these
schools, the Vaibhashika, is associated with early, or Theravada, Buddhism.
Its view of the world is that the elements (*dharmas*) constituting the
empirical world are what make up ultimate reality. These elements constitute the basic content of experience, and are directly presented in experience. Since it is held that there are a great number of these ultimate
elements, the Vaibhashika metaphysics can be called pluralistic realism.

The Sautrantika school, though often associated with Theravada

Buddhism, is really a transitional philosophy, bridging the gap between Theravada and Mahayana. At first glance it appears that the Sautrantika view of the world is quite similar to the Vaibhashika view, for both views are pluralistic and realistic. There is an important difference, however, as the Sautrantikas reject the notion that the basic features of ordinary experience constitute the ultimate elements of things. They argue that whatever is experienced depends upon other elements which are not directly experienced. After all, the principle of dependent origination maintains that there are no beings, but only comings-to-be. And these comings-to-be are interdependent; no one of them has an independent reality of its own. But if this is the case, then the fundamental elements of experienced reality must also lack independent reality. Consequently, the Sautrantikas teach that the fundamental elements of reality are not known directly, but lie beyond the contents of experience, giving rise to these contents and being represented by them.

The Madhyamikas give up pluralistic realism completely. Agreeing with the Sautrantikas that a correct interpretation of the principle of dependent origination does not allow the directly experienced "reals" claimed by the Vaibhashikas, they went further and claimed that the fundamental elements, or *dharmas*, claimed by the Sautrantikas were as good as no elements at all. Their argument is that by removing the ultimate elements from the realm of the experiencable, the Sautrantikas had really relegated them to the realm of nothingness. Supposedly the ultimate elements of things claimed by the Sautrantikas were represented by the contents of ordinary experience. But since there is no way of determining whether or not the content of experience represents the fundamental elements of reality, the representationalism of the Sautrantikas is without basis.

The Madhyamikas stressed the relativity of the components of things. Their reasoning is that if whatever is, is dependent upon something else, then it is not possible to postulate some existents (*dharmas*) which exist first and are independent of other existents. The quest for ultimate elements, real in themselves, was a misguided seeking of a mere chimera. It was the result of a failure to penetrate the principle of dependent origination, for it belied a clinging to the erroneous substance view. Stressing the interdependence of elements upon each other and their essential relativity, the Madhyamika philosophers became famous for their theory of *shunyata*. The word *shunyata* means "devoidness," and the theory of *shunyata* holds that all elements are devoid of ultimate reality. That is, there is no existence in and of itself; all existence is interdependent. Whatever exists is relative to, and dependent upon, everything else.

The Yogacarins agreed that pluralistic realism was incompatible with the theory of dependent origination, and that no absolute and ultimate elements of existence could be claimed to exist in the world. The Madhyamikas were, therefore, correct in pointing out the essential relativity and interdependence that characterized all external reality. But the Yogacarins felt they went too far in characterizing *all existence* as relative and therefore unreal (i.e., possessing no independent reality), for if this claim is correct, it follows that the existence of consciousness is also relative and unreal. But, if this were the case, the results of consciousness would also be relative and unreal. Since the Madhyamikas' arguments were the results of conscious activity they would be relative and unreal, and there would be no way to maintain their position. Consequently, the Yogacarins insisted that consciousness must be allowed to exist in its own right; it alone is independently real, and everything else has reality only relative to consciousness.

Here the Yogacarins had come full circle from the Vaibhashika point of view. The Vaibhashikas postulated the basic elements of external reality as absolute, with everything else having reality only relative to those fundamental *dharmas*. The Yogacarins regarded those elements as relative to consciousness, giving consciousness itself the position of the fundamental and absolute reality in the system. This view—that whatever exists, exists only relative to consciousness—is known as idealism.

The basic difference between realism and idealism is that realism takes the reality of external things to be ultimate, and everything else, including consciousness, is relative to external reality. Idealism takes consciousness to be ultimate; everything else, including external things, is real only relative to consciousness. The Madhyamika view—that everything is devoid of reality—differs from both realism and idealism in that it does not regard either consciousness or external reality as ultimate. It is, therefore, a complete relativism, without an absolute. Consciousness and external reality are on the same ontological footing—both are real only in relation to each other.

Pluralistic Realism

According to the interpretation of dependent origination underlying Theravada Buddhism, the processes constituting reality are comprised of an unlimited number of discrete and evanescent elements, or forces, in continuous motion. These elements, or *dharmas*, are the ultimate forces in the universe and are responsible for whatever exists. They exist independently in their own natures and everything else originates in dependence upon these ultimate elements. Though of extremely short duration, they are held to be ultimately real, for they have effects. The effects are the sticks and stones, tables and chairs, etc., that constitute the ordinary world of experience.

The relation between the fundamental *dharmas* and the world of ordinary experience is comparable to the relation between the modern scientific theory of the atomistic components of things and common-sense perception. The common-sense view is that tables and chairs are stable and enduring things, as solid as you like. But the scientist informs us that what is called a table and thought to be a solid and permanent thing is really a collection of various forces and elements in constant motion. This is quite similar to the Buddhist view of *dharmas* as the ultimate constituents of things, for they too hold that the things of common sense turn out to be no more than collections of much more elementary forces in constant motion. For the Buddhist, as for the scientist, this way of looking at things does not mean the repudiation of the common-sense world, nor the denial of any of its objects. The real world is out there, just as real as anybody thinks it to be. But its reality is constituted in a way different than usually imagined. It is, in fact, constituted by combinations of discrete, evanescent elemental forces in constant motion.

In arriving at their metaphysical views the Vaibhashikas and Sautrantikas accepted the reality of the world of ordinary experience, but rejected the imposition of an abstract theory of substance on this reality. Experience is not denied. Whatever is experienced is real, otherwise it could not be experienced. However, a distinction must be made between the reality of what is experienced and the truth of theoretical claims about what causes experience. The data of experience, clothed with the fabric of theory, may be overlooked when attention is focused on the theoretical entities postulated to account for experience. The substance view of reality is a prime example of this. Experience in and of itself never carries with it data of the identity and permanence of things. Identity and permanence, which are essential to a substance view of reality, are imposed on the data of experience as an interpretative framework. It is this framework that the Buddhist wishes to reject, for it is not given in the experience itself. The doctrine of *anicca*, or impermanence, is essentially a denial of the substance view of reality. But to deny the reality of substances in the world is not to deny the reality of the world. It is only a denial of the reality of the world *as substance*, and it leaves every other alternative open. Buddhists claim that reality consists of processes, not substances.

The whole question of what process is, and how processes make up the world of everyday experience, is another matter. But it is clear that the reality of process is not denied. And it is because the reality of process is affirmed that the Vaibhashikas and Sautrantikas earn the name "realist." Furthermore, they are *pluralistic* realists because they hold that the processes constituting reality are made up of a great many discrete and interacting elements.

Existence

The main features of the metaphysics of the Vaibhashikas and Sautrantikas are determined by their rejection of the substance view of reality—a view that was held by many of the Hindu philosophers, especially those belonging to the Nyaya and Vaisheshika Schools. The substance view in metaphysics emphasizes the reality of being over becoming. Unchanging being is taken as fundamental, and change and becoming must be explained in relation to this reality in the best way possible. If it turns out that no theory of change can be found which is compatible with permanence and being, then change must be denied, as even more ancient thinkers of India (and Parmenides of Greece) had argued.

In order to see what metaphysics the Vaibhashikas and Sautrantikas were rejecting, it is necessary to examine the assumptions inherent in the substance view. To assume a substance view of reality is to accept (1) permanence, (2) universality, (3) identity, and (4) unity as the basic characteristics of whatever exists.

(1) Emphasizing permanence consists in stressing the stability and duration of things in the universe. In this view the unchanging rather than the changing features of reality are taken as basic. Changelessness becomes the criterion of the real. The acceptance of permanence as a basic characteristic of existence is often accompanied by accepting the characteristic of identity.

(2) Identity refers to the sameness of things despite apparent changes in them. For example, stressing identity, one would say that though a puppy grows and becomes old, and though in the process every cell is replaced, nevertheless, it is still the same individual animal. Despite the various changes the old dog is identical with the little puppy, except for age. The acceptance of identity is often accompanied by accepting universality.

(3) To regard existence as essentially characterized by universality is to view the differences in existing things as less basic than their similarities.

For example, emphasizing similarities, various animals are lumped together into the category *dog* on the assumption that there is something important about each of them which is the same in all of them despite the differences between, say, a poodle and a St. Bernard. This sameness is the essence of "dogness," and is taken to be the same for all times, in all animals, within a certain range. This essence is a universal, basically independent of space and time. Accepting universality as a basic characteristic of existence, it becomes possible to say that even though there are many different dogs, and even though the species is evolving, *what it is to be a dog* does not change. This "what it is to be a dog" is the universal found in all dogs at all times, and constitutes their essential reality.

(4) The division of existence into distinct things which have a universal nature, which are permanent, and which are identical with themselves over a period of time, is usually accompanied also by accepting the unity of distinct things. For example, one particular thing, say, a dog, is made up of many parts. But though it is made up of many parts, it is still one thing. The assumption of many parts, or aspects, under the heading "one thing" is what is meant by the unity of a thing. Though flesh is not bone, and blood is yet a third thing, and all three of these are different from habits or appetites, and though a dog consists of all of these different things (along with many others), it is commonly assumed that they are all so related to each other that they form one thing, this dog. Sometimes this doctrine of unity is coupled with the doctrines of universality and identity and it is held that the reason why the different parts of an organism are related in such a way that they form one thing is that they all belong to the same underlying thing, namely, the substratum of the dog. On this view the unity, identity, and universality of things is attributed to an unperceived substratum in which the perceivable characteristics of things are thought to inhere.

With the main features of a substance view of existence in mind, it is now possible to discuss the metaphysical views of the Vaibhashikas and Sautrantikas who were, above all else, concerned to deny the substance view. Their main views are just the opposite of permanence, unity, identity, and universality. The opposite of permanence is momentariness. The opposite of unity is conglomeration. The opposite of universality is particularity. And the opposite of identity is discreteness.

In the Buddhist view, all existence is regarded as momentary, being made up of discrete particulars in various conglomerations. This view of existence is common to both Vaibhashikas and Sautrantikas, who also share the following views: (1) The discrete particulars which make up existence are "points instants" of force, or energy. (2) These "point instants" are in constant flux. (3) Arising and ceasing are inherent in existence. (4) The criterion for being real is the ability to have effects: only that can be admitted to be real which produces effects; that which does not produce effects could never be known to be real, for realities are known by their effects. (5) And of course, both of these schools accept the universal Buddhist doctrine that the elements of existence are interrelated according to the principle of dependent origination (*paticca samuppada*), the law of arising and ceasing of elements of existence.

Before going into the arguments used to support the metaphysical views of these two schools, certain differences in their views need to be pointed out. The first difference concerns the duration of existence. The Vaibhashikas hold that the production of the succeeding moment in the sequence of becoming that constitutes reality would be impossible unless each moment existed in the past and the future as well as in the present. Unless it existed in the past it could not be affected by the moment of existence that preceded it most recently in the past. That it exists in the present is obvious. But it must also exist in the future in order to influence the next moment of existence which has not yet arisen. A considerably oversimplified picture of existence in this view would reveal each moment of existence having a small portion of its existence in the past and another small portion in the future, with the bulk of its existence in the present.

The Sautrantikas reject the view that the past and future constitute part of reality. They admit only the present as real on the grounds that (1) *ultimate* moments of existence could not be further divided into past, future, and present moments if they were really ultimate, and (2) the past, by very definition, has passed on and no longer exists. And the future is not yet here; how then, could past and future be regarded as real?

The second difference concerns the nature of the ultimate elements, or moments, of existence. According to the Vaibhashikas these elements are the basic elements of the experienced datum. The most elementary features of the experienced datum constitute the ultimate moments of its existence. The Vaibhashikas did not distinguish between the features of the datum ("object") as it is in itself and the features of the datum as experienced. The Sautrantikas, on the other hand, regarded the ultimate *dharmas*, or elements, as themselves not experiencable. They are outside the realm of time and space, for as constituting the basic components of existence they are therefore the very conditions of space and time, and could not themselves be located in space and time. Thus, on the basis of distinguishing between the datum as perceived and the datum independent of perception, the Sautrantikas viewed the ultimate *dharmas* as the unexperienced and indescribable constituents of the perceived.

The third difference between Vaibhashikas and Sautrantikas concerns ways of knowing. The Vaibhashika is a direct realist, holding that what is, is perceived directly as it really is. Between what exists and what is perceived to exist, there is no difference. Perception conforms exactly to what is to be perceived. The Sautrantika is an indirect or representationalist realist, holding that we do not *directly* perceive things as they are in themselves, but that we perceive them only indirectly by means of certain representations. The data of experience, which are distinguished from the data experienced, are regarded as a means whereby the knower is acquainted with existence. A rough analogy can be made to a photograph. The photo is not reality itself, but it represents reality to us. If the photo is good, the datum photographed is not distorted and is presented as it really is. But nevertheless, the photo is not the reality; it is only a means for representing reality. Similarly, for the Sautrantika, the sensations and percepts of experience are only means for representing reality. Even though these are held to be adequate, in that ordinarily they do not distort reality, still reality is presented only indirectly through these means.

Arguments Against Substance

Turning now to the arguments used by the Vaibhashikas and Sautrantikas to support their metaphysics of flux and momentariness, we find that the overall argument is disjunctive in structure.[1] The basic assumption is that either the substance view of reality is correct, or else the opposite of that view—the flux view—is correct. Consequently, the major effort is directed toward showing the substance view to be untenable.

The arguments used to demolish the substance view of reality are arguments against (1) permanence, (2) identity, (3) unity, and (4) universals.

1. The arguments against permanence assume that the reality of something can be tested by determining whether or not it is a force capable of producing changes. Only that may be admitted to be real which can be known to have effects. The metaphysical support for this assumption is that the quest for

---

[1] The following arguments are formulated historically by the Sautrantikas, but they are essentially the same as the arguments used by the Vaibhashikas. For fuller treatment of these arguments the reader might consult Th. Stcherbatsky, *Buddhist Logic* (Leningrad: Academy of Sciences of the USSR, 1932), vol. 1, pp. 79 ff.

ultimate reality is a quest for the causes that do not produce effects. Epistemologically, this assumption is supported by the fact that knowledge represents a change in the knower, and that nothing could be known which was not capable of producing a change in the knower. Therefore, it would be impossible to have knowledge of a reality which did not produce changes or have effects.

Assuming that action is the test of the real (for no changes can be caused except by bringing about a change), it remains to show that the permanent is not active. This can be done by showing that both terms of the following disjunction are false: either the action of causation is instantaneous and complete, or else it is temporally extended. The action of causation cannot be instantaneous and complete, for then all the effects would be produced at once, and reality would, except for that moment, be static. Furthermore, if the action were instantaneous and complete, the question would arise as to whether or not the permanent exists after the first moment of change—if it does, then it should give rise to the same effects as it did in the first moment, and the same for each succeeding moment. But this is absurd, for it results in an infinity of complete universes. If the permanent continues to exist after the first moment of causation but not as a cause, then apparently it changed from a cause to a non-cause. But the changing is not permanent. Also, that would make the permanent two opposing things at the same time for it would have to be both cause and non-cause. Since it is not possible for a self-contradictory thing to exist, such a reality is not possible.

The alternative to instantaneous and complete causal action is temporally extended causal action. This view is untenable also, for if it were the case that the permanent cause produced first x, then y, and then z, etc., it could be asked whether or not y or z could have been produced while x was being produced. If the answer is affirmative, it would turn out that all the effects were producible at once, and this alternative would be indistinguishable from the first. But if the first cause could not produce effects y, z, etc. at any given time, say when x was being produced, it would be impossible for it to cause them at any later time, for what is not capable of producing a given effect at a given time cannot produce that effect at any other time, except by assuming other causal activity. For example, a barren woman cannot produce a child at this time. And for the same reason she cannot do so, she also cannot produce a child at any other time.

An objection might be made to the Sautrantika argument on the grounds that while time itself does not produce a capability in the cause, nevertheless, time may allow for certain modifications to take place so that causation is possible. For example, sometimes a seed does not cause a plant, but sometimes it does. The reason is that time allows certain modifications in the conditions which enable the seed to cause a plant at one time, though not at another. But this objection begs the whole question of causation. If it is admitted that time itself does not cause things, then it cannot be admitted that time brings about modifications, for modifications are nothing other than changes or effects. Thus some other causality is required, and the same questions arise concerning the possibilities of this causation. Even if it is admitted that certain modifications in the cause are required, the Buddhist argument is successful, for this is an admission that the cause has changed. But if the cause has changed, then there are really two things: the cause prior to change and the cause after change. To admit that the substance changes as it produces effects is to deny permanence and to admit different existences at different moments. And this is in accord with the doctrine of momentariness which the Buddhists wish to support.

2. The arguments against identity proceed by trying to show that the identity of things is illusory. Advocates of a substance view of reality maintain that a thing remains identical with itself over a period of time by assuming that a thing naturally continues to exist unless destroyed or altered by outside and violent forces. But this assumption is false, for unless a thing were naturally subject to change and cessation, nothing could bring about change and cessation with respect to that thing. For example, when forces such as a blow from a stick act upon a jar, the jar is destroyed. But one cannot say that the nature of a jar is to exist identical with itself without change unless acted upon by an outside force. After all, unless arising and ceasing belonged to the jar as part of its nature, nothing could cause or destroy a jar. If destruction was not inherent in the jar blows from sticks would mean nothing; the jar would continue to exist. But the nature of a jar is such that blows from sticks provide the occasion for its cessation. If it were not the blow from the stick then it would be some other occasion that would accompany the destruction of the jar, for the nature of a jar is not such that it can exist identical with itself forever.

The illusory quality of identity is quite clear in the case of the aging of a dog. It clearly is not the case that a dog goes along unchanging for several years, and then, at some precise time, begins to age. The process of aging begins when the puppy is conceived, and by the time it is born it has already aged considerably. Aging is simply change, which is a combination of cessation and arising of elements. The illusion of identity is based on certain arbitrary perspectives. When we fix on certain elements and notice their cessation we lament over the old age, decay, and death inherent in things. When we fix not on that ceasing of elements, but on the arising of elements, we rejoice over birth, life, and youth. But in reality, arising is always accompanied by ceasing, and ceasing is always accompanied by arising. Birth and death are parts of the same process, and it is simply the assumption of a certain attitude toward a part of the process that leads to revulsion and despair on the one hand, and to exultation and rejoicing on the other. The truth is that there is no identity. There is only the continuous arising and ceasing of elements.

3. The argument against unity is based on the impossibility of knowledge of a *whole*. According to the substance view, an object such as a table, though consisting of many parts, is held to be one whole. The Sautrantika argument against this view proceeds by showing that it is not possible to know the whole. For example, it is not possible to see the whole table. Only a small part of the table is seen. And only a small part can be touched, etc. Ordinarily this is explained by saying that it is one part of the whole table that is seen, and that by moving around to various perspectives one can consecutively come to see the whole table. But this explanation will not do, for even at best, all that would be seen would be the various *surfaces* of the table. It would not be possible to see beyond the surface of the table, even though the table is assumed to consist of more than mere surfaces. Even if more than surfaces could be seen, the explanation would not be satisfactory, for the different visual perceptions attained from different perspectives do not of themselves also carry with them the perception that they are of the same whole. It is entirely possible that each different perception is the perception of a different thing. There is nothing in the perception itself to guarantee that it belongs to the same object as other perceptions. Therefore, there is no basis for claiming that there are wholes made up of different parts. All that can be claimed are the perceptions, and since there is no valid basis for connecting these perceptions together into wholes, the supposed "oneness" of things must be illusory. Just as a movie is really no more than consecutive still pictures, so reality is no more than succeeding elements. And just as the consecutive passage of the still pictures gives rise to the appearance of one continuous whole moving picture, so the incessant rise and fall of elements gives rise to the appearance of the unity of whole things. In reality, however, the moments of existence are no more than "point-instants" of force, rising and falling in dependence upon each other.

4. The argument against universals rests on the unknowability of such entities. The identity of one thing with another, such as the sameness of two tables, by virtue of their being tables, depends upon the supposition of a universal—tableness. How can one universal entity exist in many different entities widely separated in space and time, and be totally unaffected by

what happens to the entities in which it exists? Furthermore, if such universals exist, how can they be known? Even the supporters of the substance view admit that perception is of particulars. To explain the perception of universals they assume a kind of double perception, first perceiving the particular, and then perceiving the universal as a sort of timeless, spaceless duplicate of the particular. But there is no evidence of this kind of duplication in perception. Consequently the Sautrantikas take the position that the universals attributed to reality are nothing more than logical constructions placed on a reality that is in every respect particular.

In addition to arguing for their position indirectly, by arguing against the opposite view, the Sautrantikas support their position by arguing that certain problems which arise as a result of trying to interpret reality systematically are more easily solved by taking a flux view of reality. Without doubt, the basic problem for a metaphysician is that of change. If change is admitted it would seem that permanence would also have to be admitted, for a change is always a change of something to something else, as when a green leaf changes into a red leaf. And the something undergoing change—the leaf—does not change, but some of its characteristics appear (red) and disappear (green).

The claim that a permanent reality exists is a difficult position to defend, as seen by the preceding arguments. On the other hand, if change is denied, the whole metaphysics is out of tune with our basic and immediate experience.

In order to maintain that reality is in complete flux, undergoing only change without any vestiges of permanence, the Buddhists obviously cannot think of change as the alteration of a permanent something underlying the various perceivable characteristics of things. In fact, they cannot accept any ordinary notions of causality, for nothing endures long enough to produce an effect. What they substitute for causality is the law of dependent origination, according to which entities and elements *replace one another rather than cause one another*. The law of dependent origination is a law of connectedness between moments, but it is not a law of causal connectedness. If it were a law of causal connectedness one moment in a sequence would be the cause of the next, and it would be necessary to attribute duration to the moments, as some of the Vaibhashikas did. But to attribute duration to the moments is to postulate a kind of permanence.

By replacing the law of causal connectedness with the law of dependent origination, the Buddhists are in a position to explain the appearance of continuity and duration that characterize the common-sense view of reality without giving up the momentariness of existence. There is continuous change without permanence because change is the *replacement* of one moment of existence by another, and not the *causing* of one moment by another. The replacement of moments occurs with a rapidity that looks like continuity and endurance—it is this false appearance that underlies the mistaken claims about permanence and identity. The mental constructions placed on the content of perceptions give rise to apparent unity and universals.

As indicated by these arguments, the Vaibhashikas and Sautrantikas hold a metaphysical position quite different from the substance view. The substantialists hold that reality has more permanence than it appears to have: the Buddhists hold that things do not have the unity that they appear to have. The substantialists hold that there is less change in individuals than appears: the Buddhists hold that there is more. The substantialists hold that there is a greater amount of sameness (universality) in reality than appears: the Buddhists hold that there is less than appears. Thus, the Vaibhashika and the Sautrantika theory of reality is summed up in the view that reality consists of a numberless quantity of spaceless and timeless forces constantly arising and falling in dependence upon each other.

Knowledge

The theories of knowledge underlying the metaphysical views of the Vaibhashikas and the Sautrantikas are quite different. Though they agree that reality can be known as it is in itself, and therefore are classified as realists rather than idealists, they disagree about how reality is known.

Concerning knowledge of reality two main views are possible. According to the first, external objects are known as they exist in themselves; there is no difference between what exists and what is known to exist. According to the other view, all that is ever known is the content of consciousness, and there is no way of showing that the contents of consciousness do or do not correspond to what really exists. This latter view, known as idealism, is rejected by the Vaibhashikas and the Sautrantikas, for they claim it allows no way of distinguishing (1) consciousness itself from the contents of consciousness, or (2) valid from erroneous consciousness.

The view that in knowledge objects are revealed as they exist in themselves has two major variations. The first variety is characterized by the claim that external reality is directly perceived to exist. The second variety is characterized by the claim that external reality is not known directly, but is inferred to exist from perceptual evidence. The first of these two views is held by the Vaibhashikas, who are therefore called *direct* realists, and the second view is held by the Sautrantikas, who are therefore called *indirect* realists, or representationalists.

The Vaibhashikas support their direct realism against the Sautrantika view by arguing that representationalism is an incorrect theory. According to the representationalist view, the ultimate elements of things are never directly perceived, but are inferred to exist, as they are *represented* by the perceptual experience. It is rather as if a person who has never seen Mt. Everest, but has seen photographs of it, can infer the existence of the mountain from the existence of the photos—for if there were no mountain, photographs of it could not possibly exist. In a similar way, even though the blueness present in the visual perception of a blue object is not the same as the blueness in the object itself, nevertheless it is a kind of copy of it, and enables the viewer to infer that there is really an independent blueness existing objectively in reality.

The difficulty with this view is that if nothing is perceived directly there is never any basis for inference. It is one thing to see Mt. Everest and then to see a photo of it and consequently judge the photo to be a good or bad likeness of the mountain. But if one saw nothing but photos, never experiencing a real mountain, it would be impossible to judge whether or not the photos resemble the mountains. In fact, there would be no basis for even conjecturing, let alone knowing, that anything existed other than the photos. If a person were completely unfamiliar with external objects it is not possible that any content of perceptual consciousness could appear as the sign, or representation of an object.

The foundation of the Vaibhashika argument is the claim that inferential knowledge is necessarily a secondary knowledge, for the essential feature of inference is that it proceeds from prior knowledge. Without the prior knowledge there would be no inference. But if all perceptual knowledge is essentially inferential, what would be the source of the required prior knowledge? Since obviously there is no knowledge prior to perceptual knowledge it cannot be the case that perceptual knowledge is inferential, and it must be admitted that at least some perceptual knowledge is direct.

One of the main reasons the Sautrantika reject direct realism is that they think it conflicts with the theory of momentariness. Since moments of existence are without duration it is not possible for objects to be present at the time they are perceived. By the time they are perceived these objects have given place to succeeding objects. What happens in perception, according to the Sautrantikas, is that in its instantenous arising and ceasing, the moment of existence leaves its mark on the perceiving consciousness. This mark is converted, in consciousness, into perception of the object. But by the time this occurs the original object has ceased to be, and has been replaced by another. What happens, consequently, is that from the mark left on the perceiving consciousness the prior existence of the object is inferred. This explanation may be likened to the way we see a star. Since the star is so very far away the light waves from the star may reach us only after the star itself has ceased to exist. Still, even though it was not perceived directly, but only indirectly, through the light it gave off, from the mark (light) left on the mind by the star we can correctly infer that the star did exist.

In addition, the Sautrantikas urged that the Vaibhashika view does not readily allow for perceptual error. If what is perceived is perceived directly as it is, how is error possible? According to the Sautrantika view, a representation may be mistakenly attached to an object and thus result in erroneous knowledge claims. But the Vaibhashika view does not allow such an explanation of error.

Idealism

The Yogacara school denies the existence of reality separate from and independent of consciousness. The basic appeal of this position derives from the difficulty of knowing the existence of a reality outside of consciousness. Since, by definition, whatever is known is known within consciousness, it is not possible to know a reality totally separate from consciousness.

The chief obstacle in the way of accepting this view is the common tendency to suppose that consciousness is always consciousness *of* something. Unless there were objects outside of consciousness there would be nothing for consciousness to be consciousness of, and then there could be no consciousness. Since this latter view is held by the realists, the Yogacarins directed many of their arguments against the Vaibhashika and Sautrantika views of reality.

In the first place, the realist view that there are objects external to consciousness can at best be regarded as a speculative theory designed to answer questions concerning the arising of consciousness and changes in consciousness. It cannot be regarded as a *fact*, for there is no direct evidence for it. It is not possible for anyone to experience an object outside of consciousness, for to experience something means to experience it in consciousness. Consequently, all the purported evidence and proofs for the existence of extra-conscious objects must come from consciousness itself.

But clearly, the existence of objects within consciousness cannot be regarded as proof that objects exist outside of consciousness.

There is no possible direct evidence for the existence of objects different from the objects of consciousness. The Yogacarins argue that this can be seen clearly by considering the example of color. Often a distinction is made between the awareness of the color blue, and the color blue itself. According to the Yogacarins, however, this distinction is without basis, for the color blue is never perceived except in awareness of something blue. And since they are never perceived independently or separately, there is no possibility of assuming that the awareness of the color blue and the color blue itself are anything other than identical with each other. But if they are identical, the distinction between them disappears. And when this happens, the basis for claiming an extra-conscious reality disappears.

A kind of intuitive objection to the conclusion of the foregoing argument maintains that there must be a difference between consciousness of an object and the object itself, because nearly everyone feels that the two can be distinguished. This objection is countered by the Yogacarins with the example of dreaming. Most people dream, and while they are dreaming they assume that the objects of which they are aware have objective existence outside of their dream. Now, just as the assumption within the dream that there are objects existing outside of dreams does nothing to establish the existence of such objects, so the assumption of people in a state of ignorance that objects of consciousness have an objective existence outside of consciousness does nothing to establish the existence of such objects.

Since the realism of the Vaibhashikas and Sautrantikas is not simply a matter of obvious fact, but is a philosophical theory about the nature of the world and knowledge, the Yogacarins could attempt to defend their view of "consciousness only" by demonstrating that realism rests on an untenable basis. To this end arguments were brought forth to show the impossibility of "objective" existence.

If objects exist independently of consciousness they must either be simple wholes, without any parts, or else they must be wholes composed of parts. Objective existence in the sense of a simple whole is ruled out by the nature of knowledge claimed by the realist, who holds that knowledge consists in the revelation of relations. Since there are no relations unless there are parts to be related, there could be no knowledge of simple wholes. And if it is said that it is the simple wholes that are related to each other the difficulty remains, for now all the wholes together are taken as comprising a new whole, in which the simple wholes inhere in their various relations. But this is equivalent to the atomistic view of reality, according to which objects are composed of atoms or parts. And the problem with this view is that the atoms or parts in themselves are unknowable, but are simply postulated to account for the objects of consciousness.

According to the Yogacarins, the chief difficulty in trying to prove the existence of extra-conscious objects is connected with the inseparability of the object from knowledge. There is never the least shred of evidence for the existence of an object except when the object is known. But since the object is known only in consciousness there cannot be any evidence for the existence of objects outside of consciousness.

The Yogacarins reject the argument that the very existence of consciousness constitutes a proof for the existence of independent objects because consciousness is constituted by the activity of relating objects to each other and to a subject. For example, it might be said that in consciousness of a chair the existence of a chair is assumed; otherwise there would be nothing to be related to the self, and there would be no consciousness. Consciousness is always consciousness of something and any proof that there is no "something" is, by the same argument, proof that there is no consciousness. And just as the attempt to prove the nonexistence of consciousness by the exercise of consciousness is absurd, so also the attempt to disprove objects of consciousness is absurd.

According to the Yogacara analysis, though consciousness cannot be denied since it is self-revealing, this does not provide evidence for the existence of objects, for it is the nature of consciousness to be self-existent. That consciousness does not require an object is clear from the example of dreams, where the dream objects are by none admitted as having objective existence, but by all admitted to have existence in consciousness. If this is the case with some instances of consciousness, it proves that consciousness can exist without the assumption of extra-conscious objects. It does not, however, prove that *in fact* consciousness either does, or can, in all cases, exist without the assumption of extra-conscious objects. Granted the impossibility of proving that there are extra-conscious objects and granted the possibility of consciousness without extra-conscious objects, as evident from dreams, the Yogacarins maintain that it is more reasonable to hold that the various objects of consciousness are simply the creations and projections of consciousness. The purported difficulty of accounting for the variety of objects and modes of consciousness disappears upon recognition that consciousness is itself a dynamic unfolding of its own inherent tendencies.

Supported by the foregoing objections to realism, the Yogacara position maintains that consciousness only is real. The distinctions usually made between subject and object, between things and ideas, and between existence and knowledge are really only distinctions within consciousness. They are never distinctions between what is within consciousness and what is outside of consciousness. Consequently, the central theme of this school is that whatever is experienced is mind-wrought.

This position, which is supported by the arguments against realism examined above, is also based upon psychological experience. The arguments against realism are not definitive, for they are relative to those views, and not independently valid. But the direct realization of absolute consciousness as the sole reality stands as irrefutable justification of the Yogacara position. For those who have not achieved such a direct realization there is still the evidence of consciousness in trance. On the assumption that someone who has disciplined and developed the powers of meditation sees deeper into reality than one who has not, the fact that a multitude of varied forms and colors can be directly experienced in meditative states is convincing evidence that objects are really only manifestations of consciousness. For those without even the experience of trance there remains the faith in the reports of the enlightened who have experienced ultimate reality. For others, there are the various arguments against realism, and the various explanations of the nature of consciousness to lend plausibility to the "consciousness-only" view of reality.

In order to show that the realist views are unsatisfactory it is not enough simply to show that the arguments for their positions are unconvincing. It is also necessary to show how the plausibility of the realist view depends upon a wrong interpretation of experience. Basically, this is a matter of showing that the belief in external reality rests upon a misinterpretation of inner experience or consciousness. The misinterpretation rests upon a failure to recognize the nature and functions of consciousness.

The Yogacarins distinguish between various levels of consciousness, all of them dependent upon an absolute consciousness called *alayavijnana,* or "seed-consciousness." By reference to this seed-consciousness it is maintained that consciousness can exist independently, and that the various conscious activities arise from its own potentiality. Furthermore, this consciousness is entirely self-determining and self-revealing. It is this consciousness that creates the objects believed by the ignorant to exist outside of consciousness.

At one level of consciousness there is the awareness of the various objects of the senses, accounting for the six consciousnesses of eye, ear, nose, tongue, touch, and mind. But at another level there is consciousness of these six consciousnesses. This is a kind of self-consciousness which under-

lies the other consciousnesses and gives them unity. These two levels of
consciousness are within the realm of the experiencable. The third level of
consciousness is not experiencable except in ultimate enlightenment. It is
the seed-consciousness, which is the ultimate reality underlying all the other
levels and modes of consciousness. This is not to be confused with what is
experienced in the various modes of consciousness, but is entirely undifferentiated. From this seed-consciousness originate the other activities of
consciousness, and to this seed-consciousness return the effects of those
other functions of consciousness.

The nature of this seed-consciousness cannot be stated literally, for it is
beyond all differentiations and distinctions. As a result, the relations between this fundamental consciousness and ordinary experience are indicated only in similies. For example, in the *Lankavatara Sutra* the following
illustration is given:

> Consciousness, consisting of the *skandhas* [five groups], *dhātus* [elements of
> being], and *āyatanas* [sense fields], which are without a self or of anything of
> the nature of a self, arises from ignorance, *karma*, and craving, and it functions
> through being attached to grasping at things by means of the eye and all the
> organs, and makes the presentations of its store-mind [seed-consciousness] ap-
> pear as bodies and vessels, which are manifestations of its own mind [the
> store-consciousness].[2]

As to be expected, since all reality is regarded as consciousness only, the
ultimate reality is equated with the fundamental consciousness, or seed-
consciousness. As the ultimate reality, it is beyond differentiation and
plurality, so there is no question of its being either one or many.

What then is to be made of the many distinctions ordinarily made, and
assumed by the Four Noble Truths and the Noble Eightfold Path? According to the Yogacarins, a distinction must be made between absolute reality
and absolute truth on the one hand, and relative reality and relative truth on
the other. From the perspective of the unenlightened the relative reality constituting ordinary experience can be conceived of as a manifestation of the
absolute reality, evolving out of the basic seed-consciousness. It is seed-
consciousness itself which is manifested as touch, mental activity, feeling,
perception, and choice. And it is seed-consciousness that manifests itself as
an underlying self-consciousness, thus making possible the heresy of a self.
But all this is only from the standpoint of the unenlightened.

[2] E. J. Thomas, *The History of Buddhist Thought*, 2nd ed. (London: Routledge & Kegan
Paul, 1951), p. 234.

In ignorance the activities proceeding from the seed-consciousness are differentiated from that consciousness and taken to exist in their own right. This gives rise to the error of externality of objects. In ignorance of the truth that both object-consciousness and self-consciousness are nothing other than manifestations of seed-consciousness, the self-consciousness distinguishes itself from object-consciousness and relates itself to object-consciousness as subject is related to object. This is manifested in the constant grasping for objects characterizing the lower levels of consciousness. This grasping, however, is without real basis, for as Vasubandhu points out:

> The various consciousnesses are but transformations. That which discriminates and that which is discriminated are, because of this, both unreal. For this reason, everything is mind only.[3]

What this absolute reality of seed-consciousness is in itself cannot be said, but must be experienced directly. As Vasubandhu says:

> To hold something before oneself, and to say that it is the reality of mind-only, is not the state of mind-only, because it is the result of grasping. But when [the objective world which is] the basis of conditioning as well as the wisdom [which does the conditioning] are both eliminated, the state of mind-only is realized, since the six-sense organs and their objects are no longer present.[4]

Relativism

Whereas the Sautrantikas and Vaibhashikas took the existence of the elements of external objects as the absolute basis for their theory of reality, and the Yogacarins took the existence of fundamental consciousness as the absolute basis for their theory of reality, the Madhyamika philosophers regarded both external reality and consciousness as only relatively real. Because the Madhyamika philosophy recognized nothing in the conceptual realm as ultimately or absolutely real, it came to be known as the philosophy of *shunyata*, or relativism.

No doubt, all of the schools of Buddhism agree that peace and wisdom

---

[3] Sarvepalli Radhakrishnan and Charles A. Moore, eds., *Source Book in Indian Philosophy* (Princeton: Princeton University Press, 1957), p. 336.
[4] *Ibid.*, p. 337.

are not to be found in subtle conceptual theories, but can be realized only by a direct participation in the processes of reality. The Buddha-nature is the ultimate reality, regardless of how conceived, and is the ultimate basis of each person. Consequently, only participation in that Buddha-nature will bring illumination and an end to suffering. In Madhyamika philosophy, however, this attitude comes to be underwritten by a critical analysis of conceptual construction. No philosophical view escapes the criticism of the Madhyamika, and no conceptual absolutes are tolerated. According to Nagarjuna, the principal philosopher of this school, mistaking conceptual absolutes for ultimate reality lies at the heart of man's suffering.

Nagarjuna's philosophical position appears to recognize that the most basic and exciting fact about human beings is their quest to be. This quest to be—the most fundamental of all quests—manifests itself in the activity of creating a world out of the fundamental elements of experience. We see around us only the "other." In our quest to be, we cannot tolerate the other, for the other is not-self; it represents the being that we seek. To make that other—that not-self—part of our self is the challenge. The most obvious effort to convert the other into self occurs in knowledge, where there is a uniting of the other with the self in the act of knowing. In knowledge one can make the other self, for knowledge is a unity of the self and other. The thirst for knowledge is simply one manifestation of the quest to be, for in attempting to satisfy that thirst we attempt to make the world our own, to make it part of our being. In our knowledge we create a world which is part of our own being.

The problem with this procedure is that it is temptingly easy for us to mistake the world we have created in our knowledge, which is merely a world of names and forms, for reality itself. When we succumb to the temptation, we fix on the name and form of self that we have created in our knowledge, as our own self. We identify our own being with this construction of name and form. Then the real self, burdened by the ignorance resulting from mistaking the self and world of name and form for the real self and the real world, gets overlooked in the struggle that ensues between the false self of name and form and the false world of name and form. The resulting bifurcation, which underlies this inauthentic existence in this inauthentic world, is responsible for the disease—the *dukkha*—that Buddhism wishes to overcome.

Distinguishing between reality itself and our views of reality, Nagarjuna attempted to show the dangers inherent in regarding any one view of reality as being absolutely true. Views are conceptual constructions of name and form, and to claim any view as absolutely true is to refuse to recognize the insights of other views, and thus to rule out possible avenues of illumination.

The positive conception of Nagarjuna is that while theories and views are constructions of name and form, and therefore could not be equated with reality itself, these conceptual constructions can point to reality. Therefore a dialectic of views could provide a basis for insights into reality itself, although surely direct participation in reality is a matter beyond all views. Nevertheless, views constitute an invaluable aid to realization, if they are regarded not as absolute and independent, but as relative and complementary.

Historically, it appears that one of Nagarjuna's primary aims was to remove the sources of strife and differences found among the many different schools of Buddhism. This he attempted to do by providing a sufficiently broad base for the teachings of the Buddha. Surely, since each of the schools clung to its own interpretation of the teachings of the Buddha, and since the Buddha clearly taught the need for non-clinging, these schools must be making a mistake. To exhibit the mistake was the job Nagarjuna set for himself. The task consisted in assuming the views (conclusions and arguments) of each Buddhist school of philosophy and showing that ultimately they were self-contradictory. The lesson drawn from the self-defeating views of the various philosophies is that a person should not cling to any one theoretical view, mistaking that view for the complete truth about reality.

The dialectic, which assumed the various conclusions and standpoints of the different philosophical systems and rigorously applied to them the canons of logic and reasoning that were accepted by their supporters, was itself not part of a philosophical system. It did not constitute or rest upon a view of reality. Rather, it was a method. Even as method it had nothing of its own to offer, for the critical analyses constituting the Madhyamika dialectic assume the principles and methods used by the supporters of the various systems. Concept after concept was taken up and shown to contain within it the seeds of its own contradiction; every system examined was shown to be inconsistent within itself. But the dialectic rested on the assumptions of the various systems and not upon assumptions accepted as true by the Madhyamikas. Every system contains certain assumptions which are not, at least within the system, questioned. The Madhyamikas, however, refused to accept any assumptions as undeniably true.

The critical aspect of Madhyamika thought, however, represents only one side of its development within Buddhism. On the other side is found the customary Buddhist emphasis on discipline, meditation, and direct realization. It is through the meditative practices that one can go beyond the emptiness of concepts and systems to the fullness of reality as it is in itself. Reasoning is a conceptual matter and always rests upon assumptions. Even though for their own methodological approach the Madhyamika philosophers do not regard the assumptions of their arguments as true, but only as accepted by their opponents, all the arguments can possibly do is to reveal something about the system in which the assumptions are located. They can never reveal the truth of things as they are in themselves, independent of conceptualization. Consequently, even the dialectic of the Madhyamika is not to be accepted as in itself valid for uncovering the nature of reality. It too must be abandoned at some stage in favor of direct insight and realization.

Thus, even though it is Nagarjuna's view that clinging is the cause of conflict and suffering, and even though his dialectic is aimed at showing the futility of clinging to various conceptions of reality because of the complete relativity of all conceptual systems, still, in consistency with this relativity, he does not cling to relativity either. That is, it is considered just as perverse to regard relativity as the truth about reality as it is to consider any other view as the truth about reality. In fact, Nagarjuna says, "but if people then begin to cling to this very concept of Relativity, they must be called irreclaimable."[5]

Candrakirti, who wrote an extremely subtle commentary upon Nagarjuna's aphorisms, provides a quite unflattering comparison for those who insist on regarding relativity as itself absolute, and thus cling to nonclinging. "It is," he says, "as if somebody said, 'I have nothing to sell you,' and would receive the answer, 'All right, just sell me this—your absence of goods for sale!' "[6]

On the positive side of the Madhyamika philosophy is the insight that through practice in non-clinging and meditation a person can realize directly the fullness of existence. The primary function of philosophy is to lead a person to this realization, clearing away the tangles of conceptual knots and one-sided views that constitute the barrier to a full and direct participation in reality. Both the formulation of systems of philosophy in an attempt to delineate the nature of this reality, and the critical attempts to show the relativity and incompleteness of such systems, are tasks secondary to that of encountering the unconditioned reality itself.

It needs to be emphasized that this underlying conviction of the Madhyamika is not put forth as a philosophical theory. It is a fundamental

[5] *Madhyamika Karika*, XIII, 8, in Th. Stcherbatsky, *The Conception of Buddhist Nirvāna* (The Hague: Mouton & Co., 1965, originally published by the Academy of Sciences of the USSR, Leningrad, 1927), p. 49.
[6] Quoted by Stcherbatsky in *Ibid.*, p. 49.

insight issuing from an experience more basic than logic and reason. Logic and reason, though of considerable usefulness when properly understood and wisely used, are lower and secondary means for the realization of the unconditioned and undivided reality.

When unwisely used, however, logic and reason themselves become barriers to this ultimate realization. The truth of *shunyata* is that no theories or views in themselves are complete and absolutely true. Concepts and systems of concepts are relative to each other. Thus, whatever truth is uncovered within concepts and systems of concepts is always relative to other concepts and other systems, and is at best only partial truth. This is the essential relativity of views that Nagarjuna attempts to demonstrate with his critical dialectic. This is done, however, not for its own sake, nor for the sake of destroying confidence in the ability to achieve a genuine encounter with reality, but for the sake of preparing a person for the higher way, the way of greater wisdom—the *Prajna-paramita*—carrying him or her beyond the limited wisdom of conditioned and relative existence.

According to the Madhyamika, both realists and idealists make the mistake of confusing the conditioned with the unconditioned. Neither takes the middle path between *is* and *is-not*. Exclusive *is* and exclusive *is-not* are both mistakes. Exclusive *is* does not avoid the pitfall of eternalism and exclusive *is-not* does not avoid the pitfall of nihilism. Both views really regard the conditioned and the relative as the unconditioned and the absolute, and this is the basic mistake. The error lies not in recognizing that there is an unconditioned or absolute reality, but in taking what is conditioned and relative to be unconditioned and absolute.

The Madhyamikas also recognize that there is an absolute, an unconditioned reality. But they do not fall into the trap of mistaking the conceptual for the unconditioned. For them the unconditioned is beyond views; i.e., it is the ultimate truth which cannot be grasped conceptually and which can only be realized by direct insight. As Nagarjuna says, "The teachings of the Buddha are based on two truths, the mundane and the ultimate. Those who do not know the distinction between these two truths do not understand the profound meaning in the teaching of the Buddha."[7]

Critical Dialectic

The *Madhyamika Karika* is directed to pointing out the relativism and incompleteness of the various systems and the inadequacies of the concepts

---

[7] *Madhyamika Karika*, XXIV, 8,9.

put forth as elucidations of reality. The method used in the *Karika* involves showing that when the various theories about reality which have been put forth as the ultimate truth about reality are carefully analyzed, according to the very logic of their construction, they are seen to be self-contradictory. The series of reductions to the absurd of the positions examined in the *Karika* should not be taken as establishing any positive view, but only as pointing out the fallacy of mistaking the conditioned and relative for the unconditioned and the absolute.

The first chapter of the *Karika* reveals the structure and the method of the work, and contains the examination of causality which underlies every theory of reality. To appreciate the fundamental importance of the analysis of causality, it must be recognized that every attempt to explain the nature of reality rests upon an assumption about the causal connectedness of reality. Unless a connectedness between events in the world is assumed, there would be no basis for inferences from one observed "fact" to another. And without causal connections, knowledge would, at best, be nothing more than a chaotic collection of observations. Organization of observations presupposes a connectedness between the observations.

The inferences and deductions characteristic of both scientific and philosophical theories of reality are of a logical nature, dependent for their validity upon the nature of the concepts and theories wherein the various relations underwriting the inferences and deductions are given. Ordinarily we assume that even though the inferences and deductions characterizing these theories are logical in nature, nevertheless, they have a foundation in the real world. This is the assumption that there is a correspondence between the connections made in theories about the world and connections within the world itself. This assumption must always remain an assumption, for to attempt to demonstrate its truth would only be to show the logical necessity of a theory or a concept, and would not say anything about reality (except on the chance that reality in fact corresponds to logic).

The important link between the connectedness of concepts and the supposed connectedness of reality itself is constituted by the concept of causality. Various theories of causality are possible, but they all have in common that whatever is or comes to be, is or comes to be in dependence upon something else. The search for causes is essentially the search for the conditions of the world that is experienced. Whenever the conditions upon which something depends for its existence, or coming-to-be, are known, then the conditioned—that which comes to be in dependence upon the conditions—is also known.

The assumption underlying all theories of causality is that experienced reality is not self-existent and self-explanatory. Its existence and its explanation are tied to various more fundamental factors, and these factors must be known in order to have full knowledge of the experienced reality itself. Where did it come from? Why is it shaped like this? How does it do that? etc., are questions asked by one desiring to know a reality being observed. And these are all questions about the conditions and causes of the item in question.

It is the purpose of the first chapter of the *Karika* to show that the assumptions about causality underlying the prevalent theories of reality are shot through with inconsistencies, that these theories are at bottom self-contradictory and untenable. If this can be done, it will have been shown—at least for the theories in question—that philosophical theories do not yield the ultimate truth about reality.

The first aphorism of the first chapter of the *Karika* states, "At nowhere and at no time can entities ever exist by originating out of themselves, from others, from both (self-other), or from the lack of causes."[8]

The claim being made here is that none of the four possible views of causation are tenable. These four views are: (1) whatever originates, originates out of itself; (2) whatever originates, originates out of another; (3) whatever originates, originates both out of itself and out of another; and (4) whatever originates, originates neither out of itself, nor out of another, nor out of a combination of itself and another, nor out of nothing.

As pointed out above, the arguments against each of these views of causality do not rest upon any claims made by the Madhyamika philosopher, but proceed by accepting the principles and conclusions adopted by the supporters of the view being examined. Consequently, the result of the argument is not to advance any independent claim about the nature of reality, but only to point out that the claim in question is untenable.

The first view of causality, that things are self-caused, is rejected on the grounds that identity of the cause and effect does not allow for causality. If things are their own cause, there is no difference between the cause and the effect. But if the cause and the effect are identical, then it does not make sense to talk of causality, for causality is possible only as a relation between two things, one of which is productive of the other. Identity, however, rules out the possibility of all other relations, including the relation of causality, for it precludes real differences and genuine distinctions. Thus, to assume the complete identity of the effect and the cause is to rule out a causal

[8] In Kenneth K. Inada, *Nāgārjuna: Mūlamadhyamakakārikā* (Tokyo: Hokuseido Press, 1970), p. 39.

relation between the supposed cause and the supposed effect. And if the cause and the effect are held to be identical only in certain respects and different in others, the problem still exists; for if they are identical in the aspects relevant to causation, the differences are irrelevant. But if they are different with respect to the aspects involved in causation, there can be no question of self-causation, for the thing as cause is held to be different from the thing as effect, and the view of causation is really one according to which things are caused not by themselves, but by another.

The second view, that things are caused by something other than themselves, is undoubtedly the ordinary view of causation. For example, when the potter is said to be the efficient (or agent) cause of the pot, and the clay is said to be the material cause, the cause is clearly being regarded as something other than the effect. This is the view according to which whenever something new is really produced, it is so because of the productive capacity and activity of other factors which are its causes. It is the view held by the Vaibhashikas and Sautrantikas, who agree that to assume self-causation is nonsensical, on the grounds that it postulates the prior existence of the thing in question and removes the basis of causation altogether by assuming the eternal existence of that thing.

Against this view of causation the Madhyamikas urge that it is the equivalent of claiming that being can be produced by non-being, which is to get something from nothing. If the cause and effect are different, what can the relation between them be? To say that they are related inasmuch as one is cause and one is effect is to beg the whole question, for the question at stake is the *reason* for calling one thing cause and another effect. Thus to say that cause and effect are completely different from each other except insofar as one is said to be cause and the other effect is equivalent to saying that one is cause because it is called cause and the other is effect because it is called effect. But this would make sense only upon the assumption that saying that something is something else makes it that something else!

On the other hand, it has already been argued that to the extent effects preexist in their causes, they are identical with their causes. But the identity of cause and effect destroys the notion of causation, for causation is a relation, and a thing cannot be in relation with itself. Thus, the realist can only argue that the cause and effect are, in all respects relevant to the question of causality, different from each other. But this means that the effect was totally nonexistent before being produced. However, if production is taken to be the manifestation of a certain relation—a causal relation between cause and effect—it would seem that effects could never be produced, for what is nonexistent cannot enter into relation with anything. Consequently, it is not possible for a nonexistent effect to enter into a causal relation with the cause in order to be produced.

If no relation is assumed between effect and cause, it makes no sense to talk of causality, for then anything could be produced by anything else. That is, unless the causation of the sprout by the seed, or the curd by the milk, were due to certain relationships between seeds and sprouts, or milk and curd, there is no reason why gold should not be produced out of milk and sand out of seeds. The point is that the total lack of relationships between cause and effect leads inevitably to the abondonment of causality. And since the preexistence of the effect in the cause also leads to the abandonment of causality as superfluous, Nagarjuna points out that things cannot be caused either by themselves or by others.

The next claim in the aphorism follows directly, for if the claim that things originate out of themselves is untenable, and if the view that they originate out of something else is also untenable, then it follows that things cannot originate out of both themselves and others, for the mere combination of two non-causes does not produce a cause.

The last claim of the aphorism—that things do not originate from lack of causes—makes clear that Nagarjuna is not abandoning the principle of dependent origination in his rejection of these various theories of causality.

The four views just examined represent a "strong" theory of causality according to which the cause represents a real creative power by means of which it produces the effect. The relationship between cause and effect according to this "strong" theory is rooted in this creative power of the cause. There is a weaker theory of causality according to which the relation between cause and effect is one of coordination rather than creative production. This is the view of causality Candrakirti puts into the mouths of the Buddhist realists, when he has them say,

> We are satisfied with establishing the fact that entities, such as sensation, arise in a certain coordination with (other entities), e.g., the organ of vision, etc. (This is all that we mean, when we assert that the existence of an organ of vision, etc. are the conditions under which a visual sensation, etc. can arise.) [9]

According to this view there are certain conditions which are not in themselves causes, as for example, a blue flower. And there are other conditions,

[9] Stcherbatsky, *The Conception of Buddhist Nirvana*, p. 170.

such as the eyes of a person, also in themselves not causes. But when these conditions come together they give rise to a third factor, the sensation of blue. When this third factor arises, the previous conditions, the factors of flower and eye, can be seen to be causes in the sense of conditions of the sensation of blue.

This weaker view of causation, or coordination, is also rejected by the Madhyamika philosophers. The difficulty with this view is that certain factors—the blue flower and the eye—are said to be conditions for the arising of a third factor—the sensation of blue. But if the sensation of blue has not yet arisen, how is it possible that it should have conditions? The eye and the blue flower would be non-conditions. But if the sensation of blue had already arisen, there would be no question of the conditions giving rise to it. So either it must be assumed that the sensation of blue always existed, or it must be assumed it came to exist dependent upon non-conditions. The former is implausible, and the latter makes nonsense out of dependent coordination as an explanation of the arising of new factors.

The only possibility remaining is that though the factors of blue flower and visual perception are not themselves conditions for the production of the sensation of blue, they are the conditions for a concomitance which is a condition for the production of blue. This is the view that it is not the eye or the blue flower, but the concomitance of the two that is the causal condition. But to defend this view it must either be assumed that the concomitance of two things is something other than the simultaneous presence of two conditions and that this simultaneity is itself causally productive, or else that this simultaneity causes the non-conditions of blue flower and the eye to become conditions. But if simultaneity itself were a causal condition, then the concomitance of any factors should be sufficient for the production of a new factor. But the concomitance of a blue flower and an ear does not produce the third factor of a blue sensation. And if mere concomitance is not causally productive, how could it effect the change of non-causes into causes? Candrakirti puts the arguments against regarding concomitance as a causal condition as follows:

This also won't do! Because this concomitant condition, concomitant with something which is not yet a condition, can be considered as a condition only if the other fact is (really) a condition. We are in this case faced by the same difficulty as before. Therefore this explanation cannot be accepted.[10]

---

[10] *Ibid.*, p. 171.

The Constructed World

If the Madhyamika attack on the examined views of causality is successful, and every view of causality is rejected, does it follow that there are no
causes in the world, but only effects? Clearly, that cannot be, for effects are
effects only of causes, and where there are no causes there are no effects.
But if both causes and effects are denied, is not the existence of the world
denied? And is this not one of the pits—the pit of nihilism—to be avoided,
according to the Buddha?

The answer to this question is that it is only upon the assumption that
reality is constituted by effects and causes that a denial of causes and effects
implies a denial of reality. And since no sense can be made of any attempt
to deny reality, it is clear that the implication of the Madhyamika arguments is to deny the assumption that reality is constituted by causes and
effects. Lack of difference between cause and effect may well render the
concepts of cause and effect empty and meaningless. It is a long way,
however, from the emptiness of concepts to the emptiness of reality, and it
is only by identification of concepts with reality that one would take the
emptiness of concepts for the emptiness of reality. And, as we have seen,
Nagarjuna is careful to point out that while things do not originate out of
causes, they do not originate out of non-causes either.

The Madhyamikas distinguished between the world of concepts—a
world of logical construction, a world outlined by philosophical theories of
reality—and reality itself. The latter, as it is in itself, is entirely beyond
views. The former cannot be the ultimate reality for it is shot through with
contradiction and inconsistency. Nevertheless, the world of logical construction is based upon reality itself, even though it misrepresents it as
something other than itself. It is similar to what happens in the mistaking of
a shiny shell for a coin. The thing—the shell—is really there, but in
ignorance the perceiver misrepresents it as a coin. The coin is not real; it
exists only as a construction in the mind of the perceiver. Still, it is not a
construction of nothing, but is based on an existing reality—the shell—
which is not seen for what it really is.

In a similar way, the world in which most people move is the world
they have constructed in their mind. No doubt, there is a reality with which
they come into contact and which provides a basis for the construction of
the world of determinate entities and relations. But usually this reality is
not seen for what it is in itself, but is mistaken for the world of names and
forms which characterize the world constructed by the mind.

The constructed world created through the ignorance of its maker serves
to veil the truth of the reality which underlies it. The essential furniture of
this constructed world consists in (1) gross things, such as tables, chairs,
persons, and trees, (2) the constituent elements of the gross things, and
(3) relational entities.

The gross things, such as tables and chairs, are the collections of perceptions designated by the expressions "chair," "table," etc. For example, curd
is a gross thing constituted by resistance, smell, taste, and touch. Granted
the combination of these entities produced by the mind in contact with
something, there is produced the "thing" to which the name "curd" is
applied. Curd in itself has no independent reality. It is like a forest, having
no reality of itself apart from the individual things (trees) that make it up.
The name "curd" is simply a conventional term applied to a collection of
perceptual items in conjunction with each other. The subtle elements of
existence, which are the constituents of the gross elements of the constructed world, are also conventional entities. When the perceptions of the
mind, such as tables and curd, are subjected to logical analysis it is seen
that they are constituted by simpler elements. The elements that are ultimate in such analysis are taken to be the subtle elements of the world, the
elements taken as ultimately real by the Vaibhashikas and Sautrantikas.
There is no basis, however, for regarding the results of the analysis of the
conventional entities, such as curd, as themselves having any more than a
conventional reality. After all, the name "subtle element" is merely imposed on what is conceived by someone to be the subtlest element constituting his experience. Since it is only by contrast with the "gross" entities that
there can be "subtle" entities, and since the gross entities are seen to be
merely conventional, it follows that the subtle elements, too, are merely
logical constructions of the mind.

The third kind of entities in the constructed world include such things as
length, weight, direction, time, and death, to name just a few. These are
clearly relational entities, since they are derived by relating gross entities to
each other and subtle entities to each other, and by relating the subtle
elements to the gross elements. There is no length without shortness, no
lightness without heaviness, no east without west, etc. The names of the
relational entities are merely references to a comparison of the perceptions
which give rise to the gross things of experience. There is no time except in
the sense of duration of other entities. Death, too, has no being in its own
right, but is simply a name given to a construction based on the comparison
of certain changes to certain other changes.

The world referred to here as "the constructed world" is, of course, the world most of us take to be the real world. It is the world of ordinary things, such as people and cows, the world of the constituents of the ordinary things (such as atoms), and the world of relations between ordinary things and their constituents. But all of this is regarded by the Madhyamika as a world constructed by mind for the reasons just presented. The items in this world are constructed by the mind and analyzed by the mind. Mind is by itself incapable of dealing with anything other than what is mind-made. And what is mind-made is relational, for the nature of mental construction requires that one thing be in relation to another.

Philosophical views, just as all other items created by the mind, are constructions, and are therefore relative. There is no saying, from the perspective of any philosophical view, that what is constructed by the mind is of the nature of reality, or that it represents reality as it is in itself. Nor can it be said that what is of the nature of the mind is unlike reality, that it distorts reality. The distinction between the relative world of mental construction and the ultimate reality of direct insight can only be based on direct insight. As in the case of mistaking the shell for a coin, it is only by seeing the coin for what it is that one can recognize that what had been perceived as a coin was in reality only a shell.

The dialectic, whereby the essential relativity of the mind-constructed world is demonstrated, reveals the non-ultimacy of the various views about this world, shows the conditionedness and dependent character of the entities of this world, and thus paves the way for a going beyond mere views of reality to a direct realization. But it does not, by itself, provide such a realization. Such a realization is necessarily entirely beyond the world of conceptualization.

With the realization of the complete relativity (*shunyata*) of the mundane world of mental construction, all basis for clinging to anything as absolute and ultimate will disappear. All distinctions, including the distinction between *Nirvana* and *samsara* (ordinary existence), will be seen to be only relative. With the abandonment of the ignorance and perverseness which insisted on taking the mind-made world as the ultimate reality, and with a direct participation in reality, it will be realized, as Nagarjuna says, "There is no difference at all between *samsara* and *Nirvana*."[11]

---

[11] *Madhyamika Karika*, XXV, 19.

REVIEW QUESTIONS

1. Four different philosophies of reality are found in the Vaibhashika, Sautrantika, Madhyamika, and Yogacara Schools. What do these philosophies have in common, and how do they differ?
2. What are the basic assumptions inherent in a substance view of reality? How do the Vaibhashikas and Sautrantikas argue against these assumptions?
3. What does it mean to say that Vaibhashikas and Sautrantikas have *realist* theories of knowledge? Explain the differences between Vaibhashika and Sautrantika theories of knowledge, outlining the arguments each uses to defend its position.
4. What is the Yogacara view of reality and knowledge? How do the Yogacarins differ from the Vaibhashikas and Sautrantikas?
5. Contrast the Madhyamika view with both the Yogacarin and the Vaibhashika views. Is the Madhyamika really a "Middle Way" philosophy? Explain your answer.
6. Nagarjuna declares that there is no difference between *samsara* and *nirvana* in his treatise on the Middle Way philosophy called *Madhyamaka Karika*. What does he mean by this, and how does he argue for this view?

FURTHER READING

Buddhist Thought in India, by Edward Conze (Ann Arbor: University of Michigan Press, 1967), is very good on the doctrines of the Vaibhashikas and Sautrantikas and their relation to the Mahayana schools of Madhyamika and Yogacara.

On Knowing Reality: The Tattvārtha Chapter of Asaṅga's Bodhisattvabhūmi, translated, with an introduction, by Janice Dean Willis (New York: Columbia University Press, 1979), is an excellent translation of one of the central Yogacarin texts. The introduction shows the place of this work within the Yogacara and the larger Mahayana tradition, stressing that the key teaching of "mind-only" functions to reveal the emptiness of both an independently real external reality and an independently real mental reality. Her explanations accompanying the translated texts are exceptionally helpful, making it possible for a serious student to read this important primary text even in an introductory course.

The Three Jewels: An Introduction to Modern Buddhism, by Bhikshu Sangharakshita (Garden City: Doubleday & Co., Anchor Books, 1970), contains a clear and concise account of the main Buddhist teachings of the different schools (in part II, pp. 44–141). The author is a Westerner who entered the Buddhist *sangha* (*Sthavira*), and had practiced some twenty years before writing this book.

Nāgārjuna: A Translation of his Mūlamadhyamkakārikā with an Introductory Essay, by Kenneth K. Inada (Tokyo: Hokuseido Press, 1970), is an excellent translation of this basic Madhyamika text. It contains explanatory notes on each chapter and an excellent introductory essay which explains the main features of Nagarjuna's philosophy and relates them to the basic teachings of historical Buddhism.

Nagarjuna's Philosophy, by K. Venkata Ramanan (New York: Samuel Weiser, 1979), is probably the single best book on the philosophy of Nagarjuna, considered by many to be the foremost Buddhist philosopher. Although a scholarly volume, it is clearly written and accessible to the serious beginning student.

The Buddhism of Tibet and the Key to the Middle Way, by Tenzin Gyatso (London: George Allen and Unwin, 1975), is a succinct presentation by the Dalai Lama of Tibetan Buddhism. The second part is concerned with the realization of the undivided nature of reality (emptiness) that constitutes the core of Tibetan Buddhism.

Time, Space, and Knowledge: A New Vision of Reality, by Tarthang Tulku (Emeryville, Ca.: Dharma Publishing, 1977), presents a vision of reality based on the Buddhist teaching of interdependent arising as interpreted within Madhyamika and Tibetan Buddhism. Its aim is to show the unity and fullness of existence at the physical, psychological, and ontological levels. The fluid and unified nature of the fundamental experiential process is emphasized, as Tulku explains how to envision the undivided nature of reality.

CHAPTER 14

êêêêêêêêêêêêêêêêêêêê

Zen Buddhism

Indian and Chinese Roots

ZEN, A UNIQUE FORM of Buddhism emphasizing the practice of seeing directly into the undivided nature of reality known as *zazen*, developed in China some fifteen hundred years ago. Its origins are linked to Bodhidharma, an Indian Buddhist said to have come to China in the fifth century, transmitting the practice of sitting meditation and the teaching of sudden enlightenment. Legend has it that he established the practice of sitting meditation by sitting motionless in meditation ("wall-gazing") for nine years in the Shao-lin-ssu monastery.

According to Zen tradition, Bodhidharma is the first Chinese Master and the twenty-eighth Indian Master, in direct lineage with the historical Buddha. Maintaining the lineage is very important in the Zen tradition. In the first place, it establishes the direct continuity of Zen with the enlightenment and teachings of the historical Buddha. Second, since Zen takes the teachings of experience—rather than of words or texts—to be primary, the authenticity of the enlightenment experience needs to be certified by a qualified person. Since only one who is already enlightened can judge the authenticity of another's enlightenment experience, the transmission of the teaching—through experience—is naturally from master to disciple. Thus, the lineage certifies the authenticity of the teaching from the historical Buddha to the present. Because he was able to certify the enlightenment experience of his disciple Hui-k'o, Bodhidharma could pass down to him the seal of the Buddha-mind, establishing Hui-k'o as the second Chinese Master, thus keeping the lineage with the historical Buddha intact.

Although Zen insists that the true teaching is not transmitted through the scriptures, but directly through experience certified by a person recognized as already having experienced the realization of the true reality, it attaches considerable importance to the fact that the seal of transmission goes back in unbroken lineage to Shakyamuni, the historical Buddha. The *Mumon-kan*, a collection of *koans* (Zen sayings) with Master Mumon's commentary on each that was published in China near the end of the Southern Sung Dynasty (thirteenth century), locates the origins of the Zen practice of wordless transmission of the teaching in an encounter between Shakyamuni (the historical Buddha) and his disciple, Kashyapa. According to the koan, "Long ago when the World-Honored One (Shakyamuni Buddha) was at Mount Grdhrakuta to give a talk, he held up a flower before the assemblage. At this all remained silent. The Venerable Kasho (Kashyapa) alone broke into a smile. The World-Honored One said, "I have the all-pervading True *Dharma*, incomparable *Nirvana*, exquisite teaching of formless form. It does not rely on letters and is transmitted outside scriptures. I now hand it to Maha Kasho [Mahakashyapa]."[1]

Not only does this koan connect Zen practice and enlightenment with the historical Buddha, but it also provides the reason why Zen insists that the fundamental Teaching is transmitted outside of the scriptures, directly through experience. The Buddha himself announced that the Teaching (*dharma*) is "of formless form." That is, it is beyond words and concepts: "It does not rely on letters and is transmitted outside scriptures." True to the spirit of this teaching, Zen has always insisted that the highest truth cannot be put into words. A profound silence, punctuated by a smile or laugh, may reveal the transformation wrought by the enlightenment experience, but no words can describe it.

Although little is known of the historical person, the legendary Bodhidharma is a key figure in the Zen tradition. He symbolizes the emphasis on sitting meditation, sudden enlightenment, and the wisdom beyond words that give Zen its unique character. We have already noted that Bodhidharma is said to have spent nine years in sitting meditation or *zazen*, motionlessly gazing at a wall during this time. The wall at which he gazed during his practice symbolizes the precipitousness of the enlightenment experience in which all constructs placed on experience suddenly fall away, revealing the underlying experiential process in its own undivided nature. This experience, precisely because it goes beyond the dualities of

---

[1] Zenkei Shibayama, *Zen Comments on the Mumonkan.* English translation by Sumiko Kudo (New York: New American Library, Mentor edition, 1975), p. 59.

thought constructs, cannot be grasped or communicated intellectually; only profound silence can express it.

Good works to gain merit and verbal formulations of truth are brushed aside in Bodhidharma's emphasis on direct, experiential knowing. His disdain for the institutional trappings of Buddhism are clearly revealed in a popular Zen account of a conversation with Emperor Wu-ti shortly after Bodhidharma's arrival in China. Wu-ti, a zealous Buddhist, very proud of his accomplishments in fostering the development of Buddhism during his reign, asked Bodhidharma what merit he had gained by building many temples, having many monks initiated, and many scriptures copied. When Bodhidharma replied that all this had gained him no merit whatever, the emperor was dumbfounded. "How could all these wonderful works have gained no merit whatever?" he asked. "Because they are impure motives for merit," replied Bodhidharma. "Like a shadow following a person, they have no reality."

When the emperor asked what does have true merit, what is real, Bodhidharma said, "It is pure knowing, wonderful and perfect, the essence of which is emptiness. Such merit cannot be gained by producing worldly things." Wondering how there could be such knowledge, the emperor asked for the foundation of this sacred truth, but Bodhidharma said simply, "Vast emptiness, nothing sacred." Now, thinking to test Bodhidharma, the emperor asked, "Who now stands before me?" But Bodhidharma would not be tricked into making some final affirmative statement: "I don't know," he replied.[2]

This conversation reveals the typical Zen attitude toward religious merit-seeking and doctrine. No amount of effort in promoting religious institutions contributes to the direct insight into the undivided nature of reality that Zen insists is a necessary condition of holistic living. So Bodhidharma tells the emperor that all of his efforts to support Buddhism have earned him no merit whatsoever. But when the emperor asks for the central truth or doctrine of the wonderful, pure, and perfect knowing at which Zen aims, Bodhidharma says there is no such doctrine, for he knows that this knowing is beyond all concepts and words. Indeed, he tells the emperor that this knowing should not even be called sacred, for this would introduce precisely the kind of dichotomy Zen wants to leave behind. The opposition between "sacred" and "ordinary" bifurcates reality—just like the opposition between "I" and "that," and the opposition between "is" and "is not."

---

[2] For a similar account see H. DuMoulin, *Zen Enlightenment* (New York: John Weatherhill, 1976), p. 40.

These opposites, which are responsible for cutting up reality and distancing it from ourselves, are seen as constructions which we impose on a reality which in itself is undivided. Thus, when the emperor asked who stood before him, Bodhidharma refused to say either that there is someone or that there is no one; he simply shrugged his shoulders, saying, "I don't know."

The emphasis on direct seeing that goes beyond the constructs of experience to the ultimate, undivided reality that Zen associates with Bodhidharma reveals the influence of the Mahayana tradition. The *Perfection of Wisdom* scriptures constituting the core of the Mahayana teachings stress the emptiness of all the constructions we place on the undivided flow of reality. Not only are things and self said to be empty of reality, but even *samsara* and *nirvana* are declared empty. Mistaking these empty constructions for reality itself is the root of the incomplete, fragmented, and meaningless life characterized as *duhkha*, for it underlies all forms of grasping and clinging. But the emptiness of the constructions imposed on the undivided process constituting reality can be seen only when reality is experienced directly, without the meditation of concepts. Only through the meditative experience of emptying oneself of all the constructs of the mind can the undivided wholeness of reality be experienced. This experience of the wholeness of reality, of the non-duality of self and the world, cannot be expressed in words; it cannot be taught. Thus, Bodhidharma's motionless sitting and insistence on wordless teaching are entirely consistent with earlier Mahayana teachings.

These Mahayana teachings were quite congenial to the Chinese mind, for they echoed the fundamental teachings of Taoism, a way of life rooted in the teachings of Lao Tzu, a Chinese sage who lived in the fifth century B.C. Lao Tzu emphasized that the ultimate Way (*Tao*) is beyond all words, itself undivided. It is the source of all things, giving rise to the many distinct things that comprise the world around us, and thus in some sense is present in all things. Yet in its undivided nature it goes beyond the things which arise from it and through which it flows. Lao Tzu regards the *Tao* as the root of all things, nourishing them and giving them life. To live in accord with the *Tao*, he says, is to return to one's roots, to reunite with the Source. But words do not reach the Source; here, at the root of life, is vast and profound stillness.[3]

Taoism also emphasized meditative practices for calming the mind and allowing the spirit to reunite with its source. "Sitting in forgetfulness" was

---

[3] See *Tao Te Ching*, chs. 1-4, in Wing-tsit Chan, *The Way of Lao Tzu* (Indianapolis: Bobbs-Merrill, 1963), pp. 97–106.

a recommended Taoist practice long before Buddhism appeared in China. In chapter six of the *Chuang Tzu*, a Taoist text composed in the fourth century B.C., Yen Hui is pictured in conversation with Confucius, explaining how he sits in forgetfulness: "I cast aside my limbs, detach from both body and mind, and become one with the Great *Tao*. This is called sitting down and forgetting everything."[4] This Taoist yoga is similar in spirit to the meditative practices Buddhism borrowed from the Indian yoga tradition. For all we know, Bodhidharma's motionless sitting in front of the wall owes as much to the Taoist meditative tradition as to the Buddhist. Undoubtedly, the Taoist tradition reinforced key practices and teachings of Mahayana Buddhism, contributing significantly to the development of Zen.

Aims of Zen

Does the Zen mistrust of conceptual thought and words, and its insistence on direct seeing into the undivided nature of self and reality, mean that Zen itself cannot be described? Not at all. If we remember that our descriptions of the reality of Zen are simply descriptions and not Zen itself, there are many useful things that can be said to help us understand this phenomenon. But this distinction is important, for no amount of intellectual understanding will provide the direct seeing into reality at which Zen practice aims. A merely intellectual understanding of Zen is of no more merit than emperor Wu-ti's building of monasteries and ordaining of monks!

In this spirit we should begin by defining Zen as a way of life, rather than as a set of teachings. As a way of life it has certain aims, prescribes various practices, and rests upon an understanding of reality that distinguishes it from other ways of life. Even though, in the last analysis, we may not be able to fully understand Zen without practicing it, if we study its aims, practices, and teachings about reality we will get a good sense of what it is about.

The first thing to note is that as a way of life, Zen is not so much a matter of beliefs, but of doing. What does a person do to follow the Zen way? The core of practice consists in training in the experience of seeing directly into one's complete self in the fullness of the experienced moment without the mediation of intellect. Within the context of Zen experience this attempt at definition suffers the inevitable inadequacies of every attempt to

---

[4] See Wing-tsit Chan, *Source Book in Chinese Philosophy* (Princeton: Princeton University Press, 1963), p. 201.

comprehend things in a merely intellectual way. The reason for this is that the entire activity of conceptualization is inadequate for comprehending things as they really are, because it rests upon the arbitrary and falsifying division of reality into subject and object. Zen emphasizes the integrity and completeness of the present experience wherein there is no distinction between subject and object.

As opposed to the Zen emphasis on the completeness of the present experience, there are other ways of life that insist on living in the past, either wishing to regain the past or to avoid it. There are also ways of life which insist on living in the future. Here the emphasis is on tomorrow. Tomorrow we will change the world by clearing the slums, invading other galaxies, unfreezing and curing yesterday's cancer patients, and so on. From the religious perspective adopted by Christianity, Islam, and Judaism, tomorrow is the big event. Tomorrow will see us, if Divine providence works in our favor, enjoying the kingdom of God.

What this attitude of looking so hard to the future that the present is virtually ignored can do in the economic spheres is well known from our understanding of the Middle Ages in Europe. But what it can do to the emotional and spiritual self is not so well understood. It is possible to get a glimpse of the dangers inherent in this attitude when we see the threats and fears resulting from taking seriously the claim, formulated recently in the West, that God is dead. What the death of God means in the religious sphere is that the source of life and value in the universe has disappeared, for creation and endowing value are the main functions of God. But for those who take seriously the death of God, the belief in God as the source of value and meaning in life must now be seen not only as an illusion—the fulfillment of the wish for a powerful father image—but also as a delusion, for no God exists. But if God, who created the world and bestowed value upon it, no longer exists, then what is the source and guarantee of value in the universe?

The recent answer to this question is that human beings themselves are the source of value in the universe. But notoriously, this has left people with an uneasy feeling. We are too much aware of our own inadequacies to assume the role of God. But at the same time we may be too completely caught up in the presuppositions of God's existence to be satisfied without the fulfillment of God's functions. When human beings rely upon themselves, they must face their own incapacities and inadequacies. The transformation of the world through knowledge is a noble ambition. But the large gaps in our knowledge and understanding rightly leave us with doubts and anxieties about the outcome of the transformation.

The effect of the philosophies of Kant and Hume in the West, and Nagarjuna and Shankara in the East, was to draw attention to the limitations of reason. In this century faith in the power of reason was severely shaken when it was discovered in mathematics—the very darling of reason —that the completeness of mathematical systems could not be attained. And Heisenberg's indeterminacy principle was an unpleasant dose of medicine for those confident that modern physics would completely lay bare the organized structure of the universe. In short, the universe shows no signs of being the completely rational structure in which reason would feel completely at home.

Despite the fact, however, that the inadequacies of reason are being felt at this time, the projections of life still presuppose the older goals of reason —the complete understanding of life and reason through rational means. We have not adjusted well to the inadequacies of reason. We still proceed —though more uneasily of late—as though reason were the adequate guide to a complete and fulfilling life. Thus we continue to see ourselves existing in one moment, but reaping the fullness of that existence in a future moment. But underneath the plans for achievement in the future lies an awareness—sometimes so dim and murky that it passes unnoticed, and sometimes so disturbingly acute that it is frightening—that there is no existence and life except in the present moment. The future moment belongs to the future, which belongs not to life, but to forms of understanding, just as the past belongs to memory.

What Zen does, rather than postponing the complete life to some chimerical moment in the future, is to make the most of the present moment, finding therein the wholeness of self and the completeness of life. It is the quality of experience here and now that assumes paramount importance for the Zen Buddhist.

This Zen aim of discovering the fullness of life in each moment of experience reflects both the Taoist and Mahayana teachings that the ultimate is not separate from the everyday; that ordinary things, when rightly seen, are the supreme reality. Enlightenment does not take us beyond the ordinary things of life, but allows us to experience them in a new light, revealing their profundity. Dogen, regarded by many as Japan's leading Zen philosopher, tells two stories about his experience in China that brought home to him the fact that the real aim of Zen is to live ordinary life fully, rather than to transcend it. Both involve conversations with a *tenzo* monk (the senior monk in charge of cooking).

The first story records a conversation Dogen had with the *tenzo* monk from Ayuwan monastery who had come to buy some Japanese mushrooms from the ship on which Dogen was staying during his first visit to China in April of 1223. Eager to talk to this monk, Dogen hoped to persuade him to remain on ship for the rest of the day, saying

> "I am very glad to have this unexpected chance to meet and chat with you for a while here on board ship. Please allow me to serve you, Zen Master *tenzo*."
>
> "I'm sorry, but without my supervision tomorrow's meals will not go well."
>
> "In such a large monastery as Ayuwan-shan there must be enough other cooking monks to prepare the meals. They can surely get along without a single *tenzo* monk."
>
> "Old as I am, I hold the office of *tenzo*. This is my training during my old age. How can I leave this duty to others? Moreover, I didn't get permission to stay out overnight when I left."
>
> "Venerable sir! Why don't you do *zazen* or study the koan of ancient masters? What is the use of working so hard as a *tenzo* monk?"
>
> On hearing my remarks, he broke into laughter and said, "Good foreigner! You seem to be ignorant of the true training and meaning of Buddhism." In a moment, ashamed and surprised at his remark, I said to him, "What are they?"
>
> "If you understand the true meaning of your question, you will have already realized the true meaning of Buddhism," he answered. At that time, however, I was unable to understand what he meant.[5]

What the *tenzo* monk is telling Dogen is that Zen is life; it is cooking, cleaning, studying, or whatever one is doing at the time. *Zazen* and koan practice are important training, but the real practice of Zen is the daily living of life. Buying mushrooms is *zazen* and talking to Dogen is koan practice for the *tenzo* monk. Walking back to his monastery and preparing the mushrooms is also zen practice for him.

Dogen's second story also involves a *tenzo* monk. After he left ship, Dogen went to the T'ien-t'ung monastery for further training under Master Wu-chi. One day, on his way to visit the Master, Dogen came across an old, bare-headed *tenzo* monk with a bamboo stick in his hand, earnestly drying some mushrooms in front of the Buddha hall. The sun's rays beat down upon him, causing him to perspire profusely. Still he continued to move here and there, drying the mushrooms. Moved by this sight, Dogen drew near him and asked, "What is your Buddhist age?"

[5] Taken from Yuho Yokoi, *Zen Master Dogen* (New York: John Weatherhill, 1981), p. 29.

"Sixty-eight," the *tenzo* monk answered.

"Why don't you make the other cooking monks under your supervision do it?"

"They are not me."

"You are really one with Buddhism, but I wonder why you work so hard in the burning sun."

"When else can I do it but now?"[6]

This story, like the first, emphasizes that Zen and life are not two different things, but that Zen is simply living life in the fullest way possible. But the second story brings out the urgency of living each moment fully. There is no time other than the present moment to live life. The past is gone, retained only as memory. The future is present only as an anticipation. It is in the precious present that life is lived. As the monk asks, "When else can I do it but now?"

The Zen emphasis on the immediacy and completeness of present experience shows up in the underlying principles of Zen practice, in the quality of enlightened life, and in the teachings underlying Zen. Of these three basic features of Zen—practice, enlightenment, and teachings—it is practice that comes first. Enlightenment depends upon practice, and teachings support and are determined by practice and enlightenment. It is fitting, therefore, that we should turn now to a description of the practice of Zen.

Practice

Zazen, the chief discipline of Zen practice, is taken up in order to achieve the optimal conditions for seeing directly into oneself and discovering in the purity of one's own existence the true nature of all existence. This discipline requires assuming complete control and regulation of the hands, feet, legs, arms, trunk, and head. Next, breathing must be regulated so that the activities of the mind can be brought under control. Through a series of special forms of concentration the activities of the mind are brought together, unified and stilled. The emotions and volitions are also brought under control and harmonized with intellect. Having attained the foregoing, it remains to cultivate what is usually called a profound silence in the deepest recesses of one's being.

Why engage in the discipline of *zazen*? The answer is contained in the

[6] *Ibid.*, p. 30.

immediate presuppositions of Zen. Zen presupposes that the ordinary person is caught up in a maze of crisscrossing ideas, theories, reflections, prejudices, feelings and emotions such that every experience is cut up into a variety of segments. These segments are then taken as parts of experience which can be synthesized into a whole. Thus, ordinarily a person does not really experience reality, but only a network of ideas and feelings about reality. These ideas and feelings always stand between the individual and reality, mediating the experience. The aim of *zazen* is to free us from this mediating network, allowing us to enter directly and fully into reality.

There are three basic aims of *zazen*. The first is to increase the powers of concentration by getting rid of all distracting factors and all dualities. Usually the energies of the mind are scattered in many directions, creating a flood of distractions that makes concentration almost impossible. By unifying the mind these distractions can be overcome and the dynamic energy of the mind focused completely on things at hand. Cultivating this power of concentrated consciousness gives one a freedom and equanimity that creates a sense of well-being even as it prepares one for *satori*, or the second aim of *zazen*.

Achieving *satori* is the awakening of enlightenment, or seeing into one's ultimate self and discovering the true nature of reality and the completeness of existence. The enlightenment may come like a flash, but it presupposes intensive training for most people. The *koans*, or problems, that are commonly used in the large sessions in the monasteries and the questions and answers used in the private sessions between master and disciple are famous as devices for triggering enlightenment. For example, the famous Zen master, Dogen, who had been doing *zazen* for many years, had heard his master say on numerous occasions that in order to realize enlightenment body and mind must "fall off." But finally one day when he heard this his mind and body "fell off" and he was enlightened. That is, he had now reached the level of concentration and insight wherein he became empty of the conceptions of mind and body.

Because the enlightenment experience goes beyond the dualities of conceptual thought it cannot be completely described with words. But Zen Masters frequently test their students by asking them about their experiences. In the case of Hui-neng, the sixth Chinese Patriarch, the verse testifying to the depth of his enlightenment has become a Zen classic. Hung-jen, the fifth Patriarch, asked his disciples to compose a poem revealing the extent of their enlightenment. Shen-hsiu, a very bright and learned monk, foremost of all Hung-jen's disciples, wrote the following verse on the temple wall that night:

> The body is the Bodhi tree [enlightenment],
> The mind is like a clear mirror standing.
> Take care to wipe it all the time,
> Allow no grain of dust to cling.

Hui-neng, an uneducated lad who had been relegated to the rice-pounding shed because he could neither read nor write, had Shen-hsiu's verse read to him. Seeing at once that it showed little sign of enlightenment, Hui-neng composed his own verse, asking a temple boy to write it on the wall:

> The Bodhi is not like a tree,
> The clear mirror is nowhere standing
> Fundamentally not one thing exists;
> Where, then, is a grain of dust to cling?[7]

The fifth Patriarch, realizing that it was Hui-neng, not Shen-hsiu, who was enlightened, entrusted him with the line of succession, making him the sixth Patriarch.

Shen-hsiu's verse is regarded as inferior because it fails to recognize the dynamic character of one's true mind. He takes the true mind to be passive; Zen practice is simply a matter of not allowing its purity to be sullied. The grains of dust represent the pollution caused by wrong thoughts, feelings and desires. Meditation aims to prevent this pollution from arising.

Hui-neng's verse is much deeper. The mirror-like mind and the tree-like enlightenment are both repudiated as Hui-neng goes beyond all categories and constructions, declaring that "fundamentally, not one thing exists." The dualistic thinking expressed in Shen-hsiu's verse is left behind here, as Hui-neng intimates that the fullness of ultimate reality cannot be caught in the conceptual net. To the enlightened mind reality is dynamic and whole, not passive and divided. Here is neither dust nor anything to which dust might cling; both dust and the self from which it is to be wiped are seen as the construction of dualistic thinking.

The third aim of *zazen* is to incorporate the complete enlightenment of the total self into all the daily activities. Thus every action and every moment is an action and a moment lived in enlightenment. We have already referred to Dogen's conversations with the two *tenzo* monks, which brings out the identity of zen practice and daily activities of even the most routine

---

[7] DuMoulin, *Zen Enlightenment*, p. 44.

kind. The depth of enlightenment can be gauged by the extent to which it bathes all of life in its radiance. As Dogen says,

> To study the Way is to study the self.
> To study the self is to forget the self.
> To forget the self is to be enlightened by all things.
> To be enlightened by all things is to remove
> the barriers between one's self and others.[8]

In addition to *zazen*, koans are frequently used in Zen practice, though the way in which they are used and the emphasis placed on them varies according to school and master. Koans are statements by Zen masters, often in response to questions about the teachings. In Rinzai they are used as objects of meditation by novice monks, helping them overcome the trap of dualistic thinking. The Soto school also uses koans, but here they are usually studied only in reference to one's own life and practice and not as manifestations of the truth of underlying teachings. This is because Soto, after Dogen, emphasizes the identity of daily life and Zen practice. Thus, life itself is the koan with which one must wrestle; one's ordinary life must be the manifestation of the supreme truth.

Koans serve both to teach and to test the aspirant. Used as a test they reveal whether or not the *zazen* efforts have succeeded in reaching a given level of concentration and enlightenment. As teaching devices, koans represent expressions apt for leading a person beyond the bifurcations of intellect to the direct and immediate participation in the living, whole, and complete reality.

One of the most famous koans is known, by way of the answer, as the *mu-koan*. A monk, in all seriousness, once asked master Joshu, "Has a dog a Buddha-nature?" Joshu replied, immediately, "Mu!" (which literally means "nothing," but is used here as a nonsense word).

Now, what is ordinarily meant by Buddha-nature is that the nature of everything is such that it can become enlightened. This is a common Mahayana teaching, found in many texts. But Joshu refused to say yes. No doubt he would have been right in refusing to answer affirmatively if he had suspected that the monk was thinking that there was some thing called the Buddha-nature, hidden somewhere within beings. Joshu's refusal to answer yes or no was more radical. He saw that the question not only presupposed the conceptions of Buddha-nature and dog, but worse, in asking if a dog

---

[8] Quoted in the frontispiece of Yokoi, *Zen Master Dogen*.

has a Buddha-nature, it presupposes the dichotomy between *is* and *is not*—
between being and non-being. This shows that the question is merely
conceptual, that the questioner has not gotten outside the confines of
intellect. Since it is the aim of Zen to go beyond the limitations of merely
intellectual understanding, Joshu says "Mu!" That is, he said nothing (but
said it immediately!). This is the main point about koans—they have no
intellectual answers. They appear to be problems only upon the assumption
of certain bases and conceptions—all of which should be left behind.

Once a monk asked the master, "What happens to our thought systems
when being and non-being are not distinguished?" In reply, the master
laughed heartily and drank tea. And of course this was the only answer! No
answer to the question would have sufficed, for it would have required
accepting the distinctions making possible the question, in this case the
distinction between being and non-being.

The enlightenment (*satori*) at which Zen aims requires going beyond all
distinctions, including the distinction between *is* and *is not*, upon which all
thought systems rest. Consequently, no definition of enlightenment is possible, except a negative one which points out what it is not. But even this
presupposes *is* and *is not*, and fails to reveal the experience of enlightenment. Short of practicing Zen and achieving some measure of enlightenment, perhaps the only way to get a feeling for the experience of *satori* is
to read the biographies of or talk with people who have achieved *satori*.
What is impressive about these recorded experiences of *satori* is the almost
unanimous reference to the overcoming of distinctions, and the beauty and
perfection of the world just as it is—without any distinctions. For example,
Yaeko Iwasaki, a disciple of Harada-roshi, wrote to him, "You can appreciate how enormously satisfying it is for me to discover at last, through
full realization, that just as I am I lack nothing."[9]

Teachings

Turning to the teachings of Zen, it must be pointed out that the actual
teachings of Zen are primarily teachings connected with the practice of
zazen, koan, and question-and-answer sessions. That is, they are practical
teaching, directed to fostering the way of life that Zen is. Nevertheless,
these questions, as well as the practices to which they are essentially con-

[9] Quoted in Philip Kapleau, *The Three Pillars of Zen* (New York: Harper & Row, 1969),
p. 288.

nected, have certain philosophical presuppositions. These presuppositions can be seen in the Yogacara philosophy.

As the Yogacara philosophy developed it came to regard the empirical world—the world of intellectual consciousness—as the world of *Mind-only*, since what was known thereby was only consciousness. But a reality beyond this was presupposed. It was, of course, beyond reason, but could—by practicing the Noble Eightfold Way—be experienced. Most importantly, to experience this reality would be to put an end to suffering. This ultimate reality is referred to variously as the "pure mind," and "undivided being," and the "Buddha-nature." Buddha-nature, or the pure mind, as the ultimate reality is a basic teaching of Mahayana Buddhism, and underlies the practical aim of becoming one with the all-illumining Buddha-consciousness. To achieve enlightenment is to go beyond seeing everything as mental phenomenon, or of the nature of consciousness, to seeing reality as whole, undivided and without distinction.

This teaching is important for Zen, but the texts containing the teachings about this point are quite confusing, because the expression "mind" is used in different ways. The one sense of mind found in Mahayana is the ordinary view of mind as consciousness engaged in differentiating things. The other notion of mind is called variously *Buddha-nature, the Enlightened mind, Emptiness, No-mind, Mind-only,* and *Suchness.* These expressions all refer to the same reality, which is the very basis of human reality. The discriminating consciousness is merely one expression of this reality. Feelings, emotions, and volitions are other aspects. One could go on indefinitely enumerating aspects of this reality. But the important thing to note is that this enumeration, and every assumption of a perspective which makes possible an aspect is just another activity of discrimination.

So far there is no problem. But the damage is done when this discriminatory activity of the mind presents itself as the ultimate judge of truth—the God's eye point of view which contains all perspectives and all truths. The result is that the perspectives of intellect are taken to be ultimate and absolute when they are only partial and dependent. Dualistic thinking divides reality, isolating the divided aspects, representing them as objects or activities existing independently of each other. Furthermore, when intellect is taken as ultimate the division between subject and object—between *I* and the *that*—is taken as absolute. The result is that we are set apart from the reality in which we live.

Now when the world consisting of the objects of our knowledge is described by saying "all this is mind only," the reference is clearly to the world differentiated by intellect, which means it is indeed the product of consciousness only. But this does not mean that there is nothing other than this consciousness. It means only that the world of which we are intellectually conscious is a world represented from merely one perspective: the perspective of lower discriminatory consciousness, and it should be recognized for what it is—the result of intellectual differentiation. I think it can be seen now that, at least in part, the thrust of the mind-only teaching is to call attention to the fact that we are ignoring the deeper basis of human existence by mistaking one aspect or expression of that basis for the whole reality.

The emphasis in Yogacara Buddhism on the mental nature of the world known in consciousness served to de-emphasize reason as the vehicle for attaining absolute truth and wisdom. When reason was assigned a secondary role, the "thatness" of things achievable by reason also became secondary. Primary now was the "suchness" of things, and the immediate seeing into things just as they are. As a result, the development of techniques for experiencing the suchness of reality assumed greater importance than attempts to define and state what reality is. This resulted in the emphasis on practice so characteristic of Zen.

Ox-Herding: Stages of Practice

Although the enlightenment at which Zen aims comes of itself, suddenly breaking through the veils of construction which hide the true self and reality, disciplined practice is required to clear the way. The ten ox-herding pictures on pages 226–235, with the accompanying commentaries, depict the stages of practice leading to enlightenment. They dramatize the fact that enlightenment reveals the true self, showing it to be the ordinary self doing ordinary things in the most extraordinary way.

The story of the ox and oxherd, separate at first, but united in the realization of the inner unity of all existence, is an old Taoist story, updated and modified by a twelfth century Chinese Zen master to explain the path to enlightenment. The ox symbolizes the ultimate, undivided reality, the Buddha-nature which is the ground of all existence. The oxherd is the self, who initially identifies with the individuated ego, separate from the ox, but who, with progressive enlightenment, comes to realize the fundamental identity with the ultimate reality which transcends all distinctions. When this happens, the oxherd realizes the ultimacy of all existence; there is nothing that is not the Buddha-nature. He now understands the preciousness and profundity of the most ordinary things of life, illuminating ordinary living with his enlightenment.

The first picture shows the oxherd desperately looking everywhere for his lost ox. The second picture shows that he has now caught sight of the tracks of the ox, bringing hope that his ox is not lost forever. In the third picture he actually catches sight of the ox. The fourth picture shows that he has now caught hold of the ox, using the bridle of discipline to control it. This symbolizes the rigorous discipline required of the Zen practitioner. As the fifth picture shows, this discipline brings one into accord with the true nature of reality; now the ox willingly follows the oxherd home. The sixth picture suggests the tranquility and joy that reunion with the source of existence brings; now the oxherd rides on the back of the ox, joyously playing his flute. In the seventh picture the oxherd has realized his identity with the ox; the ox can be forgotten, for it is none other than the true self. The eighth picture tells us that when the duality of self and reality has been overcome not only is reality (the ox) forgotten, but so is the self (the oxherd); the circle symbolizes the all-encompassing emptiness that constitutes the ground of all things. As the ninth picture shows, when self and reality (as constructs) are left behind things are revealed to be just what they are in themselves; streams meander on of themselves and red flowers naturally bloom red. Finally, the tenth picture shows the oxherd entering the town marketplace, doing all of the ordinary things that everyone else does. He does not retreat from the world, but shares his enlightened existence with everyone around him, leading fishmongers and innkeepers in the way of the Buddha and, because of the radiance of his life, even bringing withered trees into bloom.

1. SEEKING THE OX*

The Ox has never really gone astray, so why search for it? Having turned his back on his True-nature, the man cannot see it. Because of his defilements he has lost sight of the Ox. Suddenly he finds himself confronted by a maze of crisscrossing roads. Greed for worldly gain and dread of loss spring up like searing flames, ideas of right and wrong dart out like daggers.

> Desolate through forests and fearful in jungles,
>   he is seeking an Ox which he does not find.
> Up and down dark, nameless, wide-flowing rivers,
>   in deep mountain thickets he treads many bypaths.
> Bone-tired, heart-weary, he carries on his search
>   for this something which he yet cannot find.
> At evening he hears cicadas chirping in the trees.

* The ox-herding pictures were drawn expressly for this book by John Casey. The commentaries and verses of the twelfth-century Chinese zen master, Kuo-an that accompany the pictures are taken from *The Three Pillars of Zen*, compiled and edited by Philip Kapleau. Copyright © 1965 by Philip Kapleau. Copyright © 1980 by The Zen Center. Reprinted by permission of Doubleday & Company, Inc.

2. FINDING THE TRACKS

Through the sutras and teachings he discerns the tracks of the Ox. [He has been informed that just as] different-shaped [golden] vessels are all basically of the same gold, so each and every thing is a manifestation of the Self. But he is unable to distinguish good from evil, truth from falsity. He has not actually entered the gate, but he sees in a tentative way the tracks of the Ox.

> Innumerable footprints has he seen
>   in the forest and along the water's edge.
> Over yonder does he see the trampled grass?
> Even the deepest gorges of the topmost mountains
>   can't hide this Ox's nose which reaches right to heaven.

3. FIRST GLIMPSE OF THE OX

If he will but listen intently to everyday sounds, he will come to realization and at that instant see the very Source. The six senses are no different from this true Source. In every activity the Source is manifestly present. It is analogous to the salt in water or the binder in paint. When the inner vision is properly focused, one comes to realize that that which is seen is identical with the true Source.

> A nightingale warbles on a twig,
>   the sun shines on undulating willows.
> There stands the Ox, where could he hide?
> That splendid head, those stately horns,
>   what artist could portray them?

4. CATCHING THE OX

Today he encountered the Ox, which had long been cavorting in the wild fields, and actually grasped it. For so long a time has it reveled in these surroundings that breaking it of its old habits is not easy. It continues to yearn for sweet-scented grasses, it is still stubborn and unbridled. If he would tame it completely, the man must use his whip.

> He must tightly grasp the rope and not let it go,
>   for the Ox still has unhealthy tendencies.
> Now he charges up to the highlands,
>   now he loiters in a misty ravine.

5. TAMING THE OX

With the rising of one thought another and another are born. Enlightenment brings the realization that such thoughts are not unreal since even
they arise from our True-nature. It is only because delusion still remains
that they are imagined to be unreal. This state of delusion does not originate in the objective world but in our own minds.

> He must hold the nose-rope tight and not allow the Ox to roam,
>   lest off to muddy haunts it should stray.
> Properly tended, it becomes clean and gentle.
> Untethered, it willingly follows its master.

6. RIDING THE OX HOME

The struggle is over, "gain" and "loss" no longer affect him. He hums the rustic tune of the woodsman and plays the simple songs of the village children. Astride the Ox's back, he gazes serenely at the clouds above. His head does not turn [in the direction of temptations]. Try though one may to upset him, he remains undisturbed.

> Riding free as air he buoyantly comes home
> > through evening mists in wide straw-hat and cape.
> Wherever he may go he creates a fresh breeze,
> > while in his heart profound tranquility prevails.
> This Ox requires not a blade of grass.

7. OX FORGOTTEN, SELF ALONE

In the Dharma there is no two-ness. The Ox is his Primal-nature: this he has
now recognized. A trap is no longer needed when a rabbit has been caught,
a net becomes useless when a fish has been snared. Like gold which has
been separated from dross, like the moon which has broken through the
clouds, one ray of luminous Light shines eternally.

> Only on the Ox was he able to come Home,
> But lo, the Ox is now vanished, and alone and serene
>   sits the man.
> The red sun rides high in the sky
>   as he dreams on placidly.
> Yonder beneath the thatched roof
>   his idle whip and idle rope are lying.

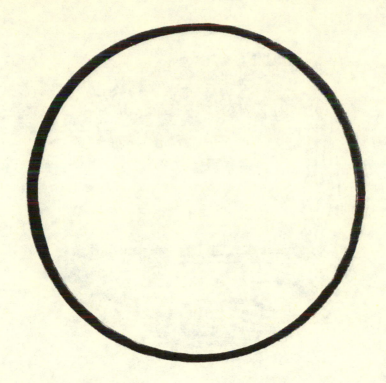

8. BOTH OX AND SELF FORGOTTEN

All delusive feelings have perished and ideas of holiness too have vanished. He lingers not in [the state of "I am a] Buddha," and he passes quickly on through [the stage of "And now I have purged myself of the proud feeling 'I am] not Buddha.'" Even the thousand eyes [of five hundred Buddhas and Patriarchs] can discern in him no specific quality. If hundreds of birds were now to strew flowers about his room, he could not but feel ashamed of himself.

> Whip, rope, Ox, and man alike belong to Emptiness.
> So vast and infinite the azure sky
>   that no concept of any sort can reach it.
> Over a blazing fire a snowflake cannot survive.
> When this state of mind is realized
>   comes at last comprehension
>   of the spirit of the ancient Patriarchs.

9. RETURNING TO THE SOURCE

From the very beginning there has not been so much as a speck of dust [to mar the intrinsic Purity]. He observes the waxing and waning of life in the world while abiding unassertively in a state of unshakable serenity. This [waxing and waning] is no phantom or illusion [but a manifestation of the Source]. Why then is there need to strive for anything? The waters are blue, the mountains are green. Alone with himself, he observes things endlessly changing.

> He has returned to the Origin, come back to the Source,
>   but his steps have been taken in vain.
> It is as though he were now blind and deaf.
> Seated in his hut, he hankers not for things outside.
> Streams meander on of themselves,
>   red flowers naturally bloom red.

10. ENTERING THE MARKET PLACE WITH HELPING HANDS

The gate of his cottage is closed and even the wisest cannot find him. His mental panorama has finally disappeared. He goes his own way, making no attempt to follow the steps of earlier sages. Carrying a gourd, he strolls into the market; leaning on his staff, he returns home. He leads innkeepers and fishmongers in the Way of the Buddha.

> Barechested, barefooted, he comes into the market place.
> Muddied and dust-covered, how broadly he grins!
> Without recourse to mystic powers,
>   withered trees he swiftly brings to bloom.

REVIEW QUESTIONS

1. Explain how Bodhidharma can be associated with the beginnings of Zen.
2. What are the basic aims of Zen?
3. In what does Zen practice consist?
4. What are the important differences between Hui-neng and Shen-hsiu as evidenced in their verses?
5. What philosophical teachings underlie Zen?
6. Explain, picture by picture, how the ox-herding pictures (and commentaries) illustrate the Zen way of enlightenment.

FURTHER READING

Zen Mind, Beginners Mind, by Shunryu Suzuki (New York: John Weatherhill, 1970), conveys the spirit of Zen practice and teaching in a very simple and direct way. It may well be the best place to begin. Suzuki was a Soto Zen master, in the tradition of Dogen, who emphasized that the important thing about Zen is practice. The book consists of talks given to his disciples in California, after *zazen* sessions.

The Three Pillars of Zen, compiled and edited by Philip Kapleau (New York: Harper & Row, 1969), provides a many-faceted look at Zen. Instructions for practice and autobiographical statements describing the achievements of Zen practitioners accompany the explanations of principles underlying Zen. The introductory lectures on Zen training by Yasutani-roshi give a good idea of actual Zen practice.

Zen Enlightenment: Origins and Meanings, by Heinrich Dumoulin (New York: John Weatherhill, 1979), is an outstanding account of the understanding of enlightenment in the history of Zen by a first-rate scholar. I know of no better book on the meaning of enlightenment. Through ample use of Zen literature, always carefully explained, the author achieves a sense of authenticity in this very lively account of a most difficult subject.

Zen Comments on the Mumonkan, by Zenki Shibayama (New York: New American Library, Mentor Books, 1975), is a thirteenth-century collection of the sayings of Zen masters, with the commentary of Master Mumon on each saying, or koan. A widely used manual of Zen training over the centuries, it has been made more accessible to modern readers by the commentary and fine introduction of Shibayama Roshi.

Zen Master Dogen: An Introduction with Selected Writings, by Yuho Yokoi (New York: Weatherhill, 1981), is a good introduction to the thought of one of

Japan's greatest Zen masters. Most of the book consists of translations from Dogen's writings, largely from the *Shobo-Genzo*. The introduction, though brief, is quite helpful.

Zen Action, Zen Person, by Thomas P. Kasulis (Honolulu: University of Hawaii Press, 1981), is a study of the philosophical significance of the core of Zen realization. This is a work of careful scholarship that uses lively examples and concrete illustrations to bring the subject to life. Kasulis uses traditional Japanese concepts to explore the meaning of action and personhood in Zen thought, providing many helpful insights into Japanese culture.

Zen Buddhism: Selected Writings of D. T. Suzuki, edited by William Barret (Garden City: Doubleday & Co., 1956), contains selections from four of Suzuki's earlier works of Zen. The selections trace the development of Zen, exploring its central concepts. Many illuminating comparisons with the West help make this work by the foremost interpreter of Zen to the Western world one of the best bridges to Eastern ways of thinking available.

Zen, by Eugen Herrigel, including *Zen in the Art of Archery* and *The Method of Zen* (New York: McGraw-Hill, 1964), is a fascinating look at Zen through the way of archery. As D. T. Suzuki says in the introduction, "In this wonderful little book, Mr. Herrigel, a German philosopher who came to Japan and took up the practice of archery toward an understanding of Zen, gives an illuminating account of his own experience. Through his expression, the Western reader will find a more familiar manner of dealing with what very often must seem to be a strange and somewhat unapproachable Eastern experience."

CHAPTER 15

Basic Characteristics of Buddhist Culture

THE RELIGIOUS-PHILOSOPHICAL teachings of Buddhism outlined in the preceding pages have left their mark on much of Asian civilization. Buddhism, much more so than most religions, has permeated the cultures with which it has been associated. Consequently, in Sri Lanka, Burma, Cambodia, Thailand, and Laos, where Thervada Buddhism has held sway, and in Tibet, China, Korea, Japan, and Vietnam, where Mahayana Buddhism has been influential, we find rather distinctive Buddhist cultural traits. Prominent among these cultural characteristics are the following: (1) emphasis on human dignity, (2) an attitude of non-attachment, (3) tolerance, (4) a spirit of compassion and non-violence, (5) an inclination to meditation, and (6) a practical orientation.

Human Dignity: In Buddhist cultures human beings have not been subordinated to things and machines. Human beings are regarded as self-creative, capable of determining their fate by their own efforts. What greater dignity can be bestowed upon persons than to recognize that they control their own life and destiny? In theistic religions persons are usually subordinated to God, regarded as something fashioned by God to suit His own aims. In a materialistic culture, on the other hand, humans are often subordinated to nature and external things. But according to the teachings of Buddhism these alternatives represent the projection of, and ensnarement by, our own ignorance. It is entirely up to us whether we will subordinate ourselves to God, nature, or other persons.

Non-Attachment: Because of their conviction that there are no enduring selves or things in the world, Buddhists do not attach themselves either to ego or to things in the world. Recognizing that impermanence is the mark of this world of suffering existence, they refuse to cling to absurd conceptions of permanence. As a result, they are unruffled by change, face the future with equanimity, and do not lament over what has gone by. A spirit of ready acceptance of life marks most Buddhist cultures.

Tolerance: Buddhism is a way of practical realization of the truth of non-suffering attainable by self-discipline and mental purification. It is not based on the commands of jealous gods and is not affected by claims to exclusiveness that grow out of such jealousy. Consequently, it is tolerant both of other religions, and of differing individual interpretations of Buddhist teachings. Despite the many differences found among Buddhists in different countries of the world, they all recognize each other as Buddhists. Furthermore, they do not look upon non-Buddhists as inferior, without a hope of happiness, and for whom salvation is impossible because they live outside the fold of Buddhism. The sickness and suffering that dogs human beings accrues to the individual person, and it is the individual person who must make the Way from suffering to peace and happiness. This recognition lies at the bottom of the respect for individual differences in all spheres of life that is so characteristic of Buddhist cultures.

Non-Violence: In the twenty-five hundred years since its beginnings, Buddhism has spread throughout Asia and has made its way even to the other continents, claiming over four hundred million followers at the present time. During this time no wars have been fought and no blood shed in the propagation of the teaching. Violence is contrary to the teachings and practice of Buddhism. It is a common conviction of Buddhists everywhere that anger and violence are only appeased and removed by kindness and compassion. The compassion demonstrated by Gautama as he traveled around the countryside teaching the causes and cessation of suffering has permeated all of Buddhism, and in Mahayana occupies the central place in the religion, in the form of the *Bodhisattava* ideal. It is a relatively easy thing to say, "Love thine enemies," but a much more difficult thing to do in the face of the enemies' anger, hatred, and violence. Nevertheless, the Buddhist record on this score is excellent, as is seen by the relative lack of war, revolution, or violence in predominantly Buddhist cultures. In this century savage fighting in Southeast Asia has certainly brought a great deal of violence to this part of the world. But even here the Buddhist influence has worked to alleviate much of the violence and suffering that war causes. And we should remember that most of this fighting was precipitated by foreign powers.

Meditation: As a result of the Buddhist emphasis on self-discipline and self-purification, it is common practice for Buddhists everywhere to concentrate on emptying themselves of everything impure and conducive to suffering. The meditative techniques involved in these practices, despite the great variety of forms or degrees, are all essentially a matter of self-cultivation and self-discipline. Their aim is to enable a person to participate directly in reality without the intermediaries of false selves, desires, and ambitions estranging one from reality. The mark of these meditative practices in Buddhist lands is a calm peacefulness that characterizes the majority of the people.

Practical Orientation: Practice in meditation produces an attitude that strikes an observer as very practical and down-to-earth. No doubt, this is due, at least in part, to the Buddhists' ability to immerse themselves in the activity of the present moment. When one is at peace with oneself and not pulled by a thousand desires and nagged by ten thousand doubts, it is possible to freely and completely engage in the activities at hand. For example, a Buddhist does not ordinarily regard eating, working, and playing as simply activities to be gotten over with in order to get on to the "real business of life." Rather, these are counted as the sum and substance of life itself. Consequently, these things are regarded as important, and participation is wholehearted, occupying the total attention of the person. Yet people do not cling to these activities and become long-faced and heavy-hearted when there is not quite enough to eat, or the work is hard.

Learning from the past and planning for the future are, of course, essential for improving the quality of life in all spheres. But learning from the past and planning for the future are themselves activities of the present moment, and should not be confused with living in the past or the future. There can be no real happiness in brooding over the future which has not yet come. Nor can happiness be found in lamenting the past. The Buddhists' recognition of this fact and, in consequence, their relatively complete engagement and immersion in the activities of the immediate present results in an attitude that is extremely practical.

REVIEW QUESTIONS

1. How do Buddhist teachings and practice emphasize the dignity of human beings?
2. How has Buddhism affected Asian culture?

FURTHER READING

Buddhism and Society in Southeast Asia by Donald K. Swearer (Chambersburg, Pa.: Anima Books, 1981), is a combination teacher's guide and introductory text. In just 82 pages the author conveys vividly the relationships between Buddhist doctrine and social life in Southeast Asia. Appendices provide a good annotated bibliography on this subject and a useful critique of audio visual aids to learning about the societal dimensions of Buddhism.

Buddhism and Society: A Great Tradition and its Burmese Vicissitudes (2nd, expanded edition), by Melford E. Spiro (Berkeley: University of California Press, 1982), is the most thorough analysis available of the socio-cultural dimensions of Buddhism in a particular country. The approach is anthropological, the results important for understanding Buddhism as actually practiced.

PART THREE

CHINESE PHILOSOPHIES

Portrait of Confucius. *Courtesy of the Field Museum of Natural History, Chicago.*

CHAPTER 16

Basic Characteristics of Chinese Philosophies

CHINESE CIVILIZATION and culture rest upon a philosophical basis shaped primarily by the principles of Confucianism, Taoism, and Neo-Confucianism. These three philosophies have guided and shaped the lives and institutions of the Chinese people for more than twenty-five hundred years. Stressing the importance of preserving, cultivating, and making great human life, Chinese philosophy has been closely connected with politics and morality and has assumed most of the functions of religion. Consequently, the study of Chinese philosophy is valuable not only because of its intrinsic merit, but also because of the insights into the Chinese mind that it makes possible.

The basic aim of Chinese philosophy has not been primarily that of understanding the world, but that of making people great. Although the various Chinese philosophies share this common aim, they differ considerably as a result of different insights into the source of human greatness. In Taoism, the emphasis is upon becoming great by becoming one with the inner way of the universe. On the other hand, in Confucianism, the emphasis has been upon developing humanity by cultivating human-heartedness and the social virtues. Neo-Confucianism, inspired to some extent by Chinese Buddhism, combines these emphases.

Being great has a double aspect in Chinese thought. First of all, it involves *inner greatness*, which is a magnitude of spirit reflected in the peace and contentment of the individual in his or her completeness. Second, it involves *outer greatness*, which is manifested in the ability to live well practically, dignifying the social context of one's ordinary day-to-day existence. This ideal is called "sageliness within and kingliness without."

This twofold greatness is basic to both Confucianism and Taoism, the philosophies which provide the foundations and inspiration for the later Neo-Confucian philosophy. Lao Tzu says that unless one knows and lives according to the inner laws of the universe, which he calls the "invariables," he ends up in disaster. According to this mystic sage:

> To know the invariables is called enlightenment. He who knows the invariable is liberal. Being liberal, he is without prejudice. Being without prejudice, he is comprehensive. Being comprehensive, he is vast. Being vast, he is with the Truth. Being with the Truth, he will last forever, and will not fail throughout his lifetime. Not to know the invariable and to act blindly is to go to disaster.[1]

For Confucius the most basic thing was to cultivate one's humanness and to regulate all activities in accord with this developed humanness. According to one of the chief texts of Confucianism,

> The ancients who wished to manifest their clear character to the world would first bring order to their states. Those who wished to bring order to their states would first regulate their families. Those who wished to regulate their families would first cultivate their personal lives.[2]

This pervasive aim of becoming great internally and manifesting this greatness externally has tended to make Chinese philosophy inclusive of all aspects of human activity. Philosophy is not divorced from life, and practice is considered inseparable from theory. There have been very few professional philosophers in China. Nearly all of China's great philosophers have held administrative positions in government or have been artists. And the assessment of philosophers in China depends, in the last analysis, upon their moral character. It is not conceivable that a bad person could be a good philosopher, or that a good philosopher could be a bad person. The real test of a philosophy is its ability to transform its advocates into greater persons.

Since greatness of persons is the basic concern, considerations for people come first in China. The human world is primary; the world of things is of

---

[1] *Tao Te Ching*, ch. 16. All references to, and quotations from, this work are taken from *The Way of Lao Tzu*, trans. by Wing-Tsit Chan (Indianapolis: Bobbs-Merrill, 1963).
[2] *The Great Learning* (*Ta-Hsüeh*), in *A Source Book in Chinese Philosophy*, trans. and compiled by Wing-Tsit Chan (Princeton: Princeton University Press, 1963), pp. 86–87.

secondary importance. In Confucianism this characteristic is manifested in the emphasis on social humanism. In Taoism it is evident in the mystical ontological unity of self and the universe.

Emphasis on human greatness leads naturally to emphasis on ethics and the spiritual life. The spirit, rather than the body, is the most important aspect of being human. This spirit must be nourished and cultivated in order that it might develop according to its capacities. And for this development the moral life is a first prerequisite. This is a very obvious characteristic of Confucianism, where there is really no distinction between the moral and the spiritual, and where humans are defined as moral animals. But it is also a characteristic of Taoism, which stresses the quality of life and aims at a higher level of human existence.

Putting greatness into practice led to emphasis on the familial virtues, especially the concept of filial love, which provides the very cornerstone of Chinese morality. The immediate environment surrounding infants in a civilized society is a social structure constituted by the family. Here the child's moral and spiritual character is shaped and molded. Here the beginnings of smallness or greatness are established. Only through great love and respect within the family can greatness be cultivated in persons.

Turning to methodology, it can be seen that the emphasis on inclusiveness of views has been a primary consideration. Rather than seeking truth by excluding various alternative views as false, Chinese thought has tended to look for truth in the combination of partially true views. This leads to a spirit of synthesis and harmony which results in tolerance and sympathy. Persons, practices, and views that are different are to be tolerated and considered sympathetically in order to appreciate their value.

It is characteristic of Chinese philosophy to emphasize complementariness rather than contrariness. Often views and principles are seen to be not only different, but also opposed. But, of course, if they are opposed it is necessary that they have a common basis. In Chinese thought it is this common basis that is emphasized, and the differences are regarded as complementary rather than contrary. The differences are viewed as completing each other, thereby constituting a whole. Instead of thinking, "*A* and *B* are opposed, therefore one must take either *A* or *B*," one thinks, "*A* and *B* are opposed, therefore both are needed for the whole." For example, one does not choose between practice and theory, but chooses *both* theory *and* practice.

This emphasis on complementariness in Chinese philosophy is reflected in a synthetic attitude which sees harmony in apparently conflicting theories and modes of life and fuses them together into a new whole. For example, there are basic differences between Taoism and Confucianism, and Buddhism does not appear to have a great deal in common with either of these philosophies. Yet Buddhism found a welcome home in China, and more than a thousand years ago these three philosophies contributed the materials required for the imposing edifice of Neo-Confucianism. In addition, this synthetic attitude leads to tolerance for the thoughts and actions of others, and promotes sympathy and appreciation for what is different.

This summary of basic characteristics of Chinese philosophy indicates a rich and complete philosophical heritage. The emphasis on the greatness of humanity and the preference for methodological inclusiveness suggest that this tradition should be considered in its own context and in terms of its own merit. It does not fit neatly into European intellectual categories, which have resulted from an emphasis on the greatness of the external world, and a preference for methodological exclusiveness.

REVIEW QUESTIONS

1. What has been the fundamental aim of Chinese philosophy? (What is the meaning of "sageliness within and kingliness without"?)
2. What are the chief characteristics of Chinese thought?

FURTHER READING

Guide to Chinese Philosophy, by Charles Wei-hsun Fu and Wing-tsit Chan (Boston: G. K. Hall & Co., 1978), is the standard bibliography for Chinese philosophy. The annotations are especially helpful for the non-expert, and the table of contents provides a useful survey of the main schools and topics.

The Chinese Mind: Essentials of Chinese Philosophy and Culture, edited by Charles A. Moore (Honolulu: University of Hawaii Press, 1967), consists of papers given at four major East-West Philosophers' Conferences. The introduction, "The Humanistic Chinese Mind," by Moore and the paper by Chan, "Chinese Theory and Practice with Special Reference to Humanism," are especially relevant.

Chinese Thought from Confucius to Mao Tse-tung, by H. G. Creel (copyright © 1953 by H. G. Creel; New York: New American Library, Mentor edition, n.d.) is an extremely lucid account of the main trends in Chinese philosophy. This is a history of Chinese philosophy designed for the non-specialist.

Three Ways of Thought in Ancient China, by Arthur Waley (first published in 1939; Garden City, N.Y.: Doubleday & Co., Anchor edition, n.d.), contains excerpts from Mencius, Chuang Tzu, and Han Fei Tzu arranged and introduced by Waley in a way that gives the feeling of taking part in a lively discussion.

China's Civilization: A Survey of its History, Arts, and Technology, by Arthur Cotterell and David Morgan (New York: Praeger Publishers, 1975), is an excellent introduction to the broad sweep of Chinese civilization. Philosophical ideas are seen in their interrelationship with technologies and the arts. Many excellent illustrations and charts enhance its usefulness as an introductory text.

The Mind of China: The Culture, Customs, and Beliefs of Traditional China, by Ben-Ami Scharfstein. (New York: Basic Books, 1974), is very good on the aesthetic, historical, and literary dimensions of the traditional Chinese way of understanding reality. The book gives the reader a good feeling for how the Chinese mind works.

CHAPTER 17

Historical Perspectives

CHINESE PHILOSOPHY as a critical investigation of human nature and the way of right living has its beginnings in the sayings of Confucius and Lao Tzu. Although this means that Chinese thought prior to around the middle of the sixth century B.C. is pre-philosophical, it does not mean that the philosophies of Confucius and Lao Tzu can be understood without investigating China's pre-philosophical tradition. On the contrary, since both Confucianism and Taoism are critical reactions to earlier theories and practices, it is imperative to have a picture of pre-philosophical China in mind in order to give these philosophies the context required for their understanding.

Pre-Confucian China

Although there is evidence of advanced civilization in China in very ancient times, actual recorded history begins with the Shang dynasty, in the four-teenth century B.C. Available evidence indicates that this was an advanced civilization. For example, art from this period is quite sophisticated, even according to modern standards. This dynasty ended with the invasion by the more primitive Chou people who, according to tradition, established the Chou dynasty in 1122 B.C.

Although more primitive artistically and culturally, the Chou were a powerful and determined people. They conquered huge portions of China by sheer force and might. Not having the means to administer all of the conquered territory as one central state, the Chou delegated administrative power to friendly chiefs and nobles, providing parcels of land in exchange for the friendship and cooperation of these newly endowed landholders. Apparently this feudal system worked quite well during the early Chou period, as each vassal had considerable freedom and power within his own territory, and this seemed well worth the taxes and military conscription owed the king in return for these privileges. Although there is nothing to indicate that the first half of the Chou period was anywhere nearly as advanced as the earlier Shang period, it was a time of relative peace and security within the structure of the new feudal system. And because of this peace it came to be regarded later on as a "golden period" in China's early history.

This peace was relatively short-lived, however. It was only the might of the Chou kings that prevented the vassals and the oppressed serfs from rebelling. As time went on, it was recognized that the kings did not really have the strength to control all of the conquered land, even through the device of feudalism. There came to be greater and greater unrest in the country. Feudal lord turned against feudal lord, and serfs rebelled when they thought the lords sufficiently weak and ineffectual. As neighboring states became weakened by war and strife they were attacked by larger and more remote lords.

By 770 B.C. things had degenerated to the point where a coalition of feudal lords were able to launch a successful attack on the Chou capital in the west. They killed the king and usurped his power. From this date on the Chou kings were puppets controlled by the coalition of feudal lords who happened to be in power at the time. Power was constantly shifting hands, and war and strife were the order of the day during the two centuries immediately prior to Confucius' birth. Violence and intrigue characterized the political scene and expediency took the place of morality. Cheating and trickery provided the basis for the intrigues that functioned in lieu of political government. The costs of these intrigues and the resulting wars are almost unimaginable in terms of poverty, suffering, and death.

Confucianism

It is in the context of this severe crisis crippling China in the centuries immediately preceding the birth of Confucius and Lao Tzu that these philosophers must be viewed. And granted this context, it is not at all surprising that they should both be reformers. For Confucius, born in 551 B.C., it was obvious that the problems of the people stemmed from sovereign power exerted without moral principle and solely for the benefit of sovereign luxury. Small wonder, then, that he urged social reforms that would allow government to be administered for the benefit of all the people. This could be done, he urged, if the members of the government were of the highest personal integrity, understood the needs of the people, and cared as much for the welfare and happiness of the people as they did for themselves.

"Do unto others as you would have done unto you," represents a brilliant and daring principle of reform in the context of the pre-Confucian China just outlined. It is a principle resulting from reflections on the conditions required for an ideal society. The attitude underlying these reflections regards knowing humanity as more important than knowing nature. If people cannot know and regulate themselves, how can they hope to know and control all of nature? Confucius did not look for the basis of human goodness and morality outside of human beings. Within humanity itself is to be found the source and structure of human goodness and happiness. It is this attitude that makes Confucianism a humanism rather than a naturalism.

Confucius lived from 541 to 479 B.C., but some of the ideas of Confucianism are derived from earlier times, while other ideas were not developed until later. According to tradition, Confucius drew inspiration from the Five Classics, and the expression of his thought is contained in the Four Books. The Five Classics are as follows: (1) *Book of Poetry* (*Shih Ching*), a collection of verses from the Chou period; (2) *Book of History* (*Shu Ching*), a collection of records, speeches, and state documents from 2000 to 700 B.C.; (3) *Book of Changes* (*I-Ching*), a set of formulae for explaining nature, widely used for purposes of divination (this work is traditionally attributed to Wen Wang, 1100 B.C.); (4) *Book of Rites* (*Li Chi*), a collection of rules regulating social behavior. This was compiled long after Confucius, but may well represent rules and customs from much earlier times; (5) *Spring and Autumn Annals* (*Ch'un Ch'iu*), a chronicle of events from 722 to 464 B.C.

The Four Books are: (1) *Analects of Confucius* (*Lun Yu*), which are sayings of Confucius to his disciples, collected and edited by them; (2) *The Great Learning* (*Ta Hsueh*), teachings of Confucius containing his suggestions for governing. This work reflects Hsun Tzu's development of Confucius' thought; (3) *Doctrine of the Mean* (*Chung Yung*), teaching attributed to Confucius concerning the regulation of life; (4) *Book of*

Mencius (*Meng Tzu*), an elaboration of some Confucian principles by Mencius, an early commentator of Confucius.

The essence of the Confucian teachings contained in this literature is expressed in the teaching that by developing one's inner humanity a person can become great in personal conduct and private life, as well as in relations with others. When all individuals do this, goodness will abound and happiness will be achieved.

In addition to the development of Confucianism by Mencius (ca. 371–289 B.C.), further elaborations on the teachings of Confucius are found in the *Hsun Tzu*, attributed to Hsun Tzu (ca. 320–238 B.C.). Hsun Tzu emphasized the need for the Confucian virtues by pointing to the evil inherent in human nature. Thus, whereas Mencius emphasized the need to practice the virtues of humanity, righteousness, and filial piety in order to preserve human goodness, Hsun Tzu claimed that they must be practiced to root out the evil inherent in human beings and replace it with goodness.

Taoism

The desperate conditions of the times also provide an explanatory context for the rise of Taoism, which emphasized the need to look beyond the promises and treaties of human beings for a source of peace and contentment. Lao Tzu, born late in the sixth century B.C., urges a simple and harmonious life, a life in which the profit motive is abandoned, cleverness discarded, selfishness eliminated, and desires reduced. In the context of a China in which greed and desire were bringing about nearly unimaginable hardship and suffering, a philosophy emphasizing the need to return to nature's way would understandably find a ready following. Yang Chu's (ca. 440–ca. 366 B.C.) claim that he would not exchange even a single hair for the profits of the entire world makes sense against the background of graft and corruption that resulted from preoccupation with profit. Lao Tzu, who lived earlier than Yang Chu, felt that so long as human actions were motivated by greed and avarice there was no hope for peace and contentment. Consequently he advocated the principle that only those actions which were in accord with Nature should be undertaken.

Taoism, the philosophy of the natural and the simple way initiated by Lao Tzu, received a foundation of metaphysical monism from Chuang Tzu (fourth century B.C.). This philosopher also sharpened the emphasis on the natural way as opposed to the artificial and contrived way of persons. In fact, it was a revival of Chuang Tzu's metaphysical doctrines of naturalism that provided the common meeting ground for Taoism and the Buddhism that developed in China during the fourth and fifth centuries A.D.

Mohism

Although Confucianism and Taoism were to become the most influential of the early philosophies of China, they were by no means the only philosophies of the day. Mohism, which received its main direction from Mo Tzu (468–376 B.C.), shared the Confucian interest in advocating the increased welfare of humanity itself, and also agreed that the measure of human welfare was people rather than Nature or the Spirits. But Mo Tzu felt that the Confucian emphasis on cultivating humanity was too vague and general for actually bringing about an improved human condition. He argued that the way to improve the human condition was to tend to the immediate welfare of the people. The slogan of the school became "promote general welfare and remove evil." The criterion advocated for measuring human happiness was utility. Ultimately, according to Mohism, value was to be measured in terms of benefits to the people. Benefits, in turn, could be measured in terms of increased wealth, population, and contentment.

Although Mo Tzu saw himself in opposition to Confucius, probably thinking of himself as a practical reformer and Confucius as an idealistic dreamer, the long-run effect of his philosophy was to strengthen Confucianism by adding external sanctions and criteria to the internal sanctions and criteria advocated by Confucius. The result was a humanism with a utilitarian flavor and a greater practical emphasis. The special strength of this combination was due to the moral emphasis of Confucianism which served as a corrective to utilitarianism, while utilitarianism added a practicalness to Confucian morality.

School of Names

The School of Names had its early development in the work of Hui Shih (380–305? B.C.) and Kung-sun Lung (b. ca. 380 B.C.). The main interest of philosophers of this school was in the relationship between language and reality. Their motivation appears to have been primarily theoretical, as these logicians were interested in knowledge for its own sake rather than for its utility. This interest in knowledge for its own sake makes the school unique, and caused it to be the source of ridicule by members of the other schools. But despite the opposition between the logicians and the other philosophers of China at this time, the investigation of the relations between words and things and the concern with knowledge for its own sake served as an important antidote to the excessive practicalness of the other philosophers. It served to keep alive an interest in theory, and the studies in the relations between words and things became useful later in both Taoism and Confucianism as they sought a metaphysical basis for their social philosophies.

Yin-Yang

The *Yin-Yang* school, concerned with cosmogony and cosmology, also was influential in the time of early Confucianism and Taoism. Since no individual philosophers connected with this school are known it is not possible to provide specific dates. But most likely this school goes back to late Shang or early Chou times in its beginnings, and continues to be important until long after Confucius.

The beginnings of the *yin-yang* speculation are contained in a natural curiosity about the workings of nature. For an agrarian people living very close to nature and feeling the rhythms of its workings, nothing could be more natural than to speculate about the principles, or "inner workings," of nature's functions. There were two questions implicit in this early curiosity about nature. On the one hand, there was the question about the structure of the universe: What is the organization or plan of the universe? On the other hand, there was the question about the origin of the universe: Where did the universe come from, and how did it originate?

The theory of the Five Agencies is essentially an answer to the question about the structure of the universe. The *yin-yang* theory is essentially an answer to the question of the origin of the universe. According to early versions of the Five Agencies theory, the five powers of the universe that control the functioning of nature are symbolically represented by Wood, Fire, Metal, Water, and Earth. The combinations of these powers determine the workings of the universe. For example, when the power represented by Wood is dominant it is spring. When the power of Fire dominates it is summer. Autumn represents the ascendancy of Metal, and winter results when Water is dominant. In late summer Earth is dominant. The important thing about the Five Agencies theory is that it was an attempt to explain the functions of nature by appeal to inner principles, or powers, which are really the forces responsible for the manifestations of nature.

According to the *yin-yang* theory, the universe came to be as a result of the interactions between the two opposing universal forces of *yin* and *yang*. The existence of the universe is seen to reside in the tensions resulting from the universal force of non-being, or *yin*, and the universal force of being, or *yang*. Whatever is experienced simultaneously has being and lacks being; it comes into being and passes out of being. But this is just to say that it is being pulled between the forces of *yin* and *yang*. The changing world that is experienced—that is characterized as nature—can exist only when there is both being and non-being, for without being there is no coming-into-being, and without non-being there is no passing-out-of-being. Hence *yin*, the negative, and *yang*, the positive, are required as a source of nature.

Both the Five Agencies theory and the *yin-yang* theory were influential in the rise of Neo-Confucianism. In the formulations of various later thinkers these theories underwent metaphysical interpretation and found their place in a general theory of existence.

Legalism

The other early school of considerable importance is that of Legalism. The most important philosopher of this school is Han Fei Tzu (d. 233 B.C.), though the school itself is several hundred years older. The basic presupposition of this school is that people are basically evil, and consequently the authority of laws and the state are required for human welfare. This school is opposed to the Confucian inasmuch as Confucius emphasized morality and goodness over laws and punishment as a means for promoting human happiness, whereas the Legalists advocated law and authority. But the long-term effect of the Legalist emphasis was to add a dimension of legality to morality, making the law a vehicle for morality. In this way the Legalist school added a considerable measure of strength to Confucianism.

Early Medieval Developments

In early medieval times, Hui-nan Tzu (d. 122 B.C.), a relatively late Taoist, developed a cosmology according to which the unfolding of *Tao* produced successively space, the world, the material forces, *yin* and *yang*, and all the things. According to this theory *yin* and *yang* become the principles of production and change among all the things in the world. Tung Chung-shu (176–104 B.C.), a late Confucianist, also referred to the *yin* and *yang* as the principles of things. According to him, all activities are due to the forces of *yin* and *yang*, which manifest themselves through the Five Agencies.

That the Taoist Hui-nan, and the Confucianist Tung Chung-shu, should both make use of the *yin-yang* and Five Agencies theories shows that these philosophies were coming closer together at this time, finding a common ground of explanation. The revitalization of both of these philosophies as a result of their meeting and the resulting cross-fertilization had to wait for many centuries, however, until the catalyst of Buddhism had been introduced. In fact, it was not until around 900 A.D., with the rise of Neo-Confucianism, that the meeting of Confucianism and Taoism prepared by Hui-nan Tzu and Tung Chung-shu bore fruit in the form of a vigorous new philosophy.

Part of the reason for the long delay is due to the fact that Tung Chung-shu was successful in getting Confucianism adopted as the state ideology. This of course meant that Taoism was out of official favor, removing most of the critical challenges required for a vigorous and healthy philosophy. For nearly the next thousand years after being adopted as the state ideology, the philosophy of Confucianism was to see relatively little development, as most of the emphasis was upon putting the philosophy that had already been developed into practice, rather than on developing further the philosophy itself.

Chinese Buddhism

Although Buddhism was introduced into China from India prior to the end of the first century A.D., it remained almost entirely without influence until after the fifth century. All of the different Buddhist schools of philosophy were introduced into China, but only those which could be reconciled with the principles of either Taoism or Confucianism became forces in shaping the Chinese mind. The realistic philosophies of Vaibhashika and Sautrantika which supported Theravada Buddhism failed to take hold in China because of their insistence on the momentary and fleeting character of reality. The idealism of the Yogacara philosophy did not suit the practical emphasis of the Chinese temperament, but thanks to a thousand-year tradition of Taoist yoga, the Yogacara emphasis on meditative practice was well received. Similarly, though the Madhyamika skepticism of ordinary knowledge was too radical for the Chinese, they welcomed its emphasis on the undivided nature of reality, an emphasis which reinforced the traditional vision of the unity of all things.

The Buddhist school of uncompromising idealism, emphasizing the reality of "Consciousness-only," found its counterpart in the Hua-yen school of Chinese Buddhism. But here ideational causation became a universal or total causation, according to which all the elements of reality are perfectly real and reflect each other. The universe is a grand harmony of conscious and unconscious, pure and impure, simple and complex. The Indian disjunction, "either conscious or unconscious," had become the conjunction, "both conscious and unconscious." The Grand Harmony, the harmony of all opposites in the universe, is possible because each of the ultimate elements of which the universe is composed contains within itself all of the differing aspects and tendencies in the world.

The T'ient-t'ai school of Buddhism, which has its beginnings around the beginning of the seventh century A.D., evolved what it called the "Round Doctrine." The school began with the teaching of the non-being of all reality. From this doctrine of the Void, wherein things are held to be unreal, they moved to the position that things have temporary existence. From the temporary existence of things, they moved to the position that things in their temporary existence represent the true state of Being. The "roundness" of the doctrine consists in the fact that these three—the void, the temporary, and the true—constitute the fullness of existence. Ultimately all three are identical.

The other two schools of Chinese Buddhism that flourished are the Pure Land school, which is mainly religious, and the Ch'an (Zen) school. The Ch'an school is really a method of meditation rather than a philosophy, but it is underwritten by the philosophical attitude that through the negation of opposites, reality is affirmed in its true nature. The meditation involves negating both production and extinction; arising and ceasing; annihilation and permanence; and unity and plurality. But this negation is simply an aspect of affirming the presence of the true nature of all things. The enlightenment marked by coming to see all things in their true nature is the aim of the Ch'an meditation.

Neo-Confucianism

The tendency to synthesize opposing features of metaphysical views, so clearly evident in Chinese Buddhism, was the most significant factor in the rise of Neo-Confucianism. Chinese philosophers had tended to be highly critical of Buddhist philosophies ever since their introduction to China. They objected to the emphasis on overcoming suffering and death, which to them seemed little more than selfish escapism. The monastic aspect of Buddhism which involved the renunciation of the family and society seemed wrong-headed, since it was clearly impossible that human beings could ever escape society. They were also critical of the Buddhist emphasis on metaphysics which regarded all things as empty of reality. To regard all things—including food and clothes—as unreal, and yet to depend on them was contradictory, they said. But perhaps the deepest difference between the Chinese philosophers and the Buddhist schools that were introduced to China was the emphasis on social and moral reality as fundamental by the Chinese, as opposed to the consciousness and metaphysical reality emphasized by the Buddhists.

Granted these differences, and the accompanying critical attitude of the Chinese philosophers toward Buddhism, the rise of Neo-Confucianism is not hard to understand. It represents the attempt of the philosophers from the tenth century on to counteract Buddhism with a more comprehensive and superior philosophy. And granted the synthetic tendency of the Chinese philosophers, it is not difficult to predict that the new philosophy would incorporate features of Buddhism along with features of Taoism and Confucianism. Furthermore, granting the preoccupation with social and moral reality that characterized earlier Chinese philosophy, it is not surprising that Confucianism should have the primary role in this reconstruction.

Although the beginnings of Neo-Confucianism can be traced to Han Yu (768–824), it was not until Sung times that a comprehensive and definitive formulation was achieved. It was during the Sung period (960–1279) that the School of Reason of the Ch'eng brothers (Ch'eng Hao, 1032–1085, and Ch'eng Yi, 1033–1108) arose, and the great synthesis of Chu Hsi (1130–1200) was achieved. The School of Mind, which leaned in the direction of idealism, also originated during this period. Its most illustrious philosophers are Lu Chiu-yuan (1139–1193) and Wang Yang-ming (1473–1529). The third phase of the development of Neo-Confucianism is represented by the Empirical school of the Ching period (1644–1911).

The key concept in the Reason school of Neo-Confucianism is that of the Great Ultimate (*T'ai-chi*). This Great Ultimate is the ultimate reality and underlies all existence. It is the reason or principle inherent in all activity and existence. Through activity it generates *yang*. Upon reaching its limit, activity becomes tranquil, and through tranquillity the Great Ultimate generates *yin*. When tranquillity reaches its limit, activity begins, the one producing the other as its opposite.

This reversal of opposites is a notion of Taoism, where it is held that reversal is the way of the Great Way, the Tao of the universe. Through the interaction between *yin* and *yang* the five agencies come into being, the ten thousand things in the universe are produced, and the seasons run their course.

The Great Ultimate, which produces all things and determines their functions, is a combination of stuff (*ch'i*) and principle (*li*). The nature of things is the result of what they are and how they function. The stuff of which they are made is their matter, or *ch'i*, and their function is their principle, or *li*. When *ch'i* and *li* are in harmony, things are in order and there is a grand harmony. Since the Great Ultimate represents a harmony of *ch'i* and *li*, order is the law of the universe. It remained for Chu Hsi to observe that the Great Ultimate is nothing but the principle of ultimate goodness, to transform this pervasive metaphysics into a groundwork for a social and moral philosophy.

The Reason school was dualistic in positing matter (*ch'i*) and reason (*li*) as the ultimate realities. Wang Yang-ming (1472–1529) was monistic in his emphasis, holding that alone reason is ultimately real. He did not deny the reality of external things, but emphasized that it is only through consciousness, or reason, that a person becomes aware of things. Thus mind is the primary reality.

The essential character of mind, according to Wang Yang-ming, is its capacity for love. In its pristine goodness the human mind forms a unity with heaven and earth and consequently the ideal person views all things as one and extends a universal love to all things. This universal love is the basis for all existence and all relationships.

In the Ch'ing period (1644–1911), Wang Yang-ming's idealism came to be tempered with the empiricism of the Empirical school of Tai Chen. Chu Hsi had emphasized the superiority of principle, or reason, over matter. Tai Chen (1723–1777) objected to this emphasis, claiming that neither matter nor principle should be considered superior to the other, since reality is not separated in this way. In reality, there is no separation between principle and matter. In the transformations of matter, principle is manifested, and the orderliness of transformations is due to principle. But there is no transformation without order, and there is no order without transformation. At best these two—matter and principle—are just two different ways of looking at reality.

In the Empirical school, there is a return to the empirical and the particular, a greater concern with the position of the individual in society, and less interest in speculative metaphysics. In this respect, the third phase of Neo-Confucianism is closer to earlier Confucianism.

In summing up the development of philosophy in China it could be said that Confucianism represents the *yang* of Chinese philosophy whereas Taoism represents its *yin*. Philosophy, as everything else, has its *yin* and *yang*, and finds perfection in the Grand Harmony of these two opposing principles. In China it was Neo-Confucianism that sought the harmony of all principles, drawing upon the various earlier philosophies.

REVIEW QUESTIONS

1. How did conditions in pre-Confucian China influence the development of Confucian and Taoist thought?
2. Compare and contrast the Confucian and Taoist philosophies. What are the main differences? How are they similar?
3. What are the theories of the Five Agencies and *yin-yang* about? What do they have in common? How do they differ?
4. Which forms of Buddhism caught on in China? Why these forms and not others?
5. What is Neo-Confucianism? How did it incorporate features of earlier thought? Is the concept of *T'ai-chi* basically Taoist, Buddhist, or Confucian?

FURTHER READING

A Short History of Chinese Philosophy, by Fung Yu-lan (New York: Macmillan Publishing Co., 1960), is an excellent scholarly account of the development of Chinese philosophy, written by one of China's outstanding contemporary philosophers. The *Short History* is a shorter version of the two-volume work by Fung entitled *A History of Chinese Philosophy* (Princeton: Princeton University Press, 1959–60), which is generally acknowledged to be the most comprehensive and authoritative survey of Chinese philosophy available.

A Source Book in Chinese Philosophy, translated and compiled by Wing-tsit Chan (Princeton: Princeton University Press, 1963), contains nearly eight hundred pages of the most important Chinese philosophical texts arranged in a chronological order. The readability of the translations, the choice of materials, and the explanations of difficult passages provided by Professor Chan combine to make this an exceedingly useful aid for the study of Chinese philosophy.

Sources of Chinese Tradition, 2 vols., compiled by William Theodore de Bary, Wing-tsit Chan, and Burton Watson (New York: Columbia University Press, 1964), contains literary, historical, political, and philosophical texts, making it a good source for a broader study of Chinese civilization. The introductions are extremely useful and the translations reliable.

The Chinese View of Life and Creativity in Man and Nature, by Fang Thome H. (Taipei: Linking Publishing Co., 1980), shows how Confucianism, Taoism and Mohism complement and enrich each other. Fang views humanity and nature as a unified whole. Philosophy is seen as a means of discovering and clarifying the underlying unity of existence, with the aim of incorporating this wholeness into every aspect of life. The second book, *Creativity in Man and Nature*, is a lively example of how one contemporary Chinese philosopher (Fang) attempts to practice this kind of philosophy.

CHAPTER 18

Confucianism

Confucius

IT HAS ALREADY been noted that the times of Confucius were marked by political and social disintegration and a widespread breakdown of morality. Granted these conditions, it was natural that Confucius should turn his attention to the reform of society. He was introduced to hard work, suffering, and responsibility at an early age, coming to know from personal experience the poverty, political abuse, and hardship that affected the lives of the ordinary people. No doubt his background aided his understanding of both government and the problems of the ordinary people.

As a young man Confucius accepted a position in the government of his native state of Lu. There he could not only observe the inadequate administration of the kingdom of Lu, but could also, in a small way, do something about this administration by properly carrying out his own duties. This taste of practical politics probably was a factor in his decision to turn his attention to the problems of society. From a background where he could see the misery of the people and the bad administration of the rulers, a person of Confucius' humanistic bent would naturally set himself to thinking about the correction of society.

Recognizing that his times were not all they should be, what was Confucius to do about it? How could the well-being of society be achieved? Confucius' answer to this question is his philosophy, a humanistic social philosophy. It is obvious that if Confucius' philosophy is a social philosophy it is about human beings and their society rather than about nature or knowledge of nature. But what does it mean to say that this is a *humanistic* social philosophy?

The most significant feature of humanism is the conviction that human beings are ultimate. To say that human beings are ultimate has a special meaning, as can be seen by contrasting humanism with naturalism and supernaturalism. According to naturalism it is nature—the non-human world—that is taken as ultimate. Here the principles for human action and life are taken from nature. Humans should act in certain ways because the world is what it is. Discovering how human beings should act is a matter of discovering how nature acts, so that human actions can be in accord with those of nature.

According to supernaturalism, a force or power other than human or natural is taken to be ultimate. A supernatural force is seen as regulating both nature and humans, making them subordinate to this supernatural and superhuman power. The supernatural may be regarded as creating both nature and humanity, as well as determining their behavior. According to this view, discovering how humans should act is a matter of discovering how this supernatural power intended them to act. In a theistic religion this might be seen as a matter of knowing and doing God's will.

Humanism becomes possible when humanity rather than nature or supernature is taken as ultimate. When humanity is taken as ultimate there is nothing superior to human beings as a source of human principles. Here people look to neither nature nor supernature for norms of life and action; rather, they look to their own humanity to find the principles that provide for goodness and happiness. Thus, to call Confucianism a humanism is to note that it is a philosophy that answers the question "How can goodness and happiness be achieved?" by pointing to the principles of action found within humanity itself. The source of these principles is what makes human beings human.

Jen

According to Confucius, what makes human beings uniquely human is *jen*. This is why the Confucian Way is essentially the way of *jen* or human-heartedness. The word "jen" has been translated in many different ways: "virtue," "humanity," "benevolence," "true manhood," "moral character," "love," "human goodness," and "human-heartedness," to name only a few. The English word human-heartedness suggests that *jen* is what makes us human, that it is a matter of feeling as well as thinking, and that it is the foundation for all human relationships. Translating *jen* as human-hearted-ness also reveals the Chinese emphasis on the heart, rather than the mind, as the defining quality of human nature.

In his *Sayings* (*Lun-yu*), Confucius never gives and defends a definition of *jen*. This may reflect his understanding that the way of humanity is highly personal, and lies within each human being and must be realized in one's personal life; to make it an objective characteristic or feature of the world would be a distortion of *jen*. Yet Confucius often talked about *jen* to his followers, trying to help them to realize its meaning in their own lives. For example, when Fan Ch'ih asked what *jen* is, Confucius replied, "It is to love men" (12:22), suggesting that our ability to love constitutes the core of our humanity.[1]

Our ability to love others has important moral implications, however, requiring that *jen* also be thought of in moral terms. Thus, Confucius says

> Wealth and honor are what every man desires. But if they have been obtained in violation of moral principles, they must not be kept. Poverty and humble stations are what every man dislikes. But if they can be avoided only in violation of moral principles, they must not be avoided. If a superior person departs from humanity (*jen*) how can he fulfill that name? A superior man never abandons humanity (*jen*) even for the lapse of a single meal. In moments of haste, he acts according to it. In times of difficulty or confusion, he acts according to it. (4.5)

This statement indicates clearly that *jen* is the ultimate principle of human action. A true human being never departs from the way of *jen*; one who departs from the way of *jen* is not expressing the fullness of humanity. The word translated as "moral principles" in this passage is *Tao* or "way," implying that the right way of human action is not that of satisfying likes and avoiding dislikes, but that of acting in accord with a deeper principle, that of *jen*.

So important is *jen* that life without it is not worth living, according to Confucius. Someone who is wise, a true scholar, would do nothing to injure *jen*. Confucius said, "A resolute scholar and a man of humanity (*jen*) would never seek to live at the expense of injuring humanity (*jen*). He would rather sacrifice his life in order to realize humanity (*jen*)" (15.8).

---

[1] Although the translations use "man" and "men," these terms should be understood in a gender-neutral way, as referring to human beings. Unless otherwise indicated, translations are taken from Wing-tsit Chan, *A Source Book in Chinese Philosophy* (Princeton: Princeton University Press, 1963).

Precisely because *jen* is what makes us truly human, to abandon it is to give up a fully human life. *Jen* is worth sacrificing one's life for; it is the basis of all human value and worth. It is *jen*, ultimately, that makes life worth living.

What does it mean to live according to the way of *jen*? Confucius' followers understood that to live according to *jen* required the development of one's own human-heartedness and the extension of that developed human-heartedness to others. Thus, Tzeng Tzu reminded other followers of Confucius that, "The Way of our Master is none other than conscientiousness (*chung*) and altruism (*shu*)" (4.15). Conscientiousness or *chung* consists in the careful development and manifestation of one's own humanity, while altruism (*shu*) consists in extending *jen* to others. We have here the principle of reciprocity which underlies the famous Golden Rule of Confucius; namely, treat others as you wish to be treated or, "Do not do to others what you do not want them to do to you" (12.2).

Li

Although *jen* is the basis of humanity and therefore the ultimate guide to human action, Confucius recognized that more immediate and concrete guides to action are needed in everyday life. These concrete guides he found in the rules of propriety (*li*) governing customs, ceremonies, and relationships established by human practice over the ages. The best of these practices reflect the concrete embodiment and expression of *jen* in the past, and therefore serve as a guide to its realization in the present. This is why when Yen Yuan asked about *jen*, Confucius said, "To master oneself and return to propriety (*li*) is humanity (*jen*)" (12.1).

Self-mastery in the above quotation refers to the self-development that overcomes selfishness and cultivates the inner qualities of humanity that include sincerity and personal rectitude. That Confucius regards it as the basis of *li* seems clear, for he immediately adds, "If a man (the ruler) can for one day master himself and return to propriety, all under heaven will return to humanity (*jen*). To practice humanity depends on oneself." This suggests that *jen* is the ground of *li*; that what makes *li* a standard of conduct is the fact that it is in accord with *jen*. Customs and regulations not in accord with *jen* are not really *li*, according to Confucius. But the true *li*, those rules of proper action that genuinely embody *jen*, become the means whereby the individual's own humanity can be evoked and developed. They are emphasized by Confucius (who uses the word *li* seventy-five times in the *Sayings*) as the means by which we tame our wild impulses, transforming them into civilized expressions of human nature.

Ceremonial activities, as embodiments of *li*, were very dear to Confucius' heart. It is recorded that one day, after a ceremony, Confucius heaved a great sigh, and upon being asked why he was sighing, replied, "Oh, I was thinking of the Golden Age and regretting that I was not able to have been born in it and to associate with the wise rulers and ministers of the three Dynasties."[2] As Confucius went on to explain that this golden age came about because of the emphasis on *jen* and *li*, he noted that the founders of the Great Dynasties

> were deeply concerned over the principle of *Li*, through which Justice was maintained, general confidence was tested, and errors of malpractice were exposed. An ideal of true manhood, *Jen*, was set up and good manners or courtesy was cultivated, as solid principles for the common people to follow....[3]

The importance Confucius attached to *li* is also seen by his remark that "*Li* is the principle by which the ancient kings embodied the laws of heaven and regulated the expression of human nature. Therefore he who has attained *Li* lives, and he who has lost it, dies."[4]

To understand the importance Confucius attributed to *li* we must examine the meanings this concept had for him and his predecessors. The word "*li*" means many things. It means religion; it means the general principle of the social order; it means the entire body of social, moral, and religious practices taught and rationalized by Confucius. It also means ritual and ceremony. It means a system of well-defined social relationships with definite attitudes toward one another, love in the parents, filial piety in the children, respect in the younger brothers, friendliness in the elder brothers, loyalty among friends, respect for authority among subjects, and benevolence in rulers. It means moral discipline in personal conduct. It means propriety in everything.

Since *li* is of such importance in Confucian philosophy it is appropriate that the concept be explored both from the point of view of its history and from the point of view of its content. The earliest notion of *li* is religious,

---

[2] *Li Chi*, ch. IX, trans. by Lin Yutang, in *The Wisdom of Confucius* (New York: Modern Library, 1938), p. 227.
[3] *Li Chi*, in *The Wisdom of Confucius*, p. 229.
[4] *Ibid.*

where it is concerned with rites for religious performances. It soon came to denote other rituals, such as marriage, and military and government festivals. This sense of *li* coincides with a more or less elaborate set of rules and conventions which demand strict observation in carrying out various activities, mainly religious or social in character.

The second notion of *li* refers to a customary code of social behavior. In this sense *li* is the customary law, or common morality. *Li*, in this sense, takes the place of written law, although it differs from written law in that it is positive rather than negative ("do this," rather than "don't do this"), it does not bring with it automatic punishment, and it generally is assumed to refer to the behavior of the aristocracy rather than ordinary persons.

The third, and extended, meaning of *li* is anything which is proper in the sense that it conforms to the norms of humanity *(jen)*. It is this third sense of *li* that is of most importance for understanding Confucius, although Confucius uses the term "*li*" in all of its meanings. This is not surprising, since the meanings of "*li*" are related. They all refer to acts which are public and ceremonial, acts constituting the important rituals of life. The rituals may be as simple as the exchange of greetings between two people when they meet, or the practice of good table manners, or as complicated as the mourning rites for a deceased relative. Regardless of complexity, however, ritual acts have a ceremonial dimension which emphasizes the social and public character of human action. Ceremony is public in the sense that it involves at least two people in relationship with each other. Furthermore, ceremonial action, because it is out in the open, not private or secret, emphasizes the openness of the participants to each other. It is precisely this open, shared participation in life with other persons who are fundamentally alike in their common human nature that evokes and fosters the development of *jen*. If we think of *jen* as the seed of humanity present in all human beings, we can regard *li* as that which provides the conditions and support needed for this seed to grow and flower.

Hsiao

Because the family constitutes the immediate social environment of the child, Confucius emphasized its importance in developing *jen*. In the family the child learns to respect and love others, first parents, brothers and sisters, and relatives, then, by gradual extension, all humankind. Yu Tzu, a favorite student of Confucius, said, "filial piety *(hsiao)* and brotherly respect are the root of humanity" (1.2).

Hsiao, or filial piety, is the virtue of reverence and respect for family. First of all, parents are revered because life itself is generated from them. In showing reverence for parents it is important to protect the body from harm, since the body is from the parents. Therefore, to protect the body is to honor the parents. But even more, reverence should be shown for parents by doing well and making their name known and respected. If it is not possible to bring honor to the name of one's parents, at least they should not be disgraced. Thus, *hsiao* does not consist merely in giving one's parents physical care, but also in bringing them emotional and spiritual richness. And, equally important, after parents are dead, their unfulfilled aims and purposes should be the aims and purposes of the children. This is even more important than offering sacrifices to the departed spirits of deceased parents.

But *hsiao* is not merely a family virtue. Originating in the family, this virtue influences actions outside the family circle. It becomes, by extension, a moral and social virtue. When children learn respect and reverence for their parents they can have respect and love for their brothers and sisters. And when they have accomplished this, they can respect and love all humankind. And when all actions are directed by love of humankind they are acting according to their humanity, or *jen*. Thus the beginnings of *jen* are found in *hsiao*.

Yi

The other virtue stressed by Confucius as necessary for developing *jen* is *yi*, usually translated as "righteousness." Confucius said, "The superior man regards righteousness (*yi*) as the substance of everything. He practices it according to the principle of propriety (*li*). He brings it forth in modesty. And he carries it to its conclusion in faithfulness. He is indeed a superior man!" (15.17).

Yi informs us of the right way of acting in specific situations so that we will be in accord with *jen*. It is thus both a moral disposition to do what is right, and an ability to recognize what is right, an ability that functions like a kind of moral sense or intuition. Confucius sometimes talks of this ability in terms of a person's character or uprightness. A person of strong moral character who sees a chance to gain thinks first about whether it would be morally right (*yi*) to do so. Such a person is ready to sacrifice his or her own life for someone in danger (14.13).

What is according to *yi* is unconditional and absolute. Some actions must be performed for the sole reason that they are right. A person ought to respect and obey his or her parents because it is morally right and obligatory to do so, and for no other reason. Other actions may be performed for the sake of something valuable they bring about, for the sake of profit. These are to be contrasted with actions performed according to *yi*, which are performed only because they are right, and not because of what they produce. A person who acts for the sake of *yi*, because that action is the right thing to do, is not far from *jen*. To practice *jen* is to act out of a love and respect for humanity for no other reason than that it is the right, or human, way to act.

Li, hsiao, and *yi* are the characteristics of the superior person, the person whose humanity is developed and who is morally cultivated and aware. This superior person is the opposite of the small, or inferior, person who is morally uncultivated, who acts on instinct and for profit.

It is the conviction of Confucius that the cultivation of *jen* through *li, hsiao*, and *yi* will lead to a personal embodiment of virtue, resulting in a well-ordered society. There is no sharp distinction here between ethics and politics. If people are true to themselves, having good faith or sincerity, then they will embody the various virtues. And if every person does this, good government and a happy social order will be assured.

Governing by Virtue

The idea of government by virtue, or goodness, rather than by law, may sound rather strange to Western ears, but government by virtue is exactly what Confucius was hoping to achieve. Before questioning this utopia, the various relations between the virtues embodied in the *jen* way need to be examined.

The most comprehensive statement of the Confucian philosophy is contained in the *Great Learning*. There, after observing that true greatness consists in manifesting the great virtues, loving the people, and achieving the highest good, eight ethical-political items are enunciated as means of achieving greatness. The text reads as follows:

> The ancients who wished to preserve the fresh or clear character of the people of the world would first set about ordering their national life. Those who wished to order their national life, would first set about regulating their family life. Those who wished to regulate their family life would set about cultivating their personal life. Those who wished to cultivate their personal

lives would first set about setting their hearts right. Those who wished to set their hearts right would first set about making their wills sincere. Those who wished to make their wills sincere would first set about achieving true knowledge. The achieving of true knowledge depends upon the investigation of things. When things are investigated, then true knowledge is achieved; when true knowledge is achieved then the will becomes sincere; when the will is sincere, then the heart is set right; when the heart is set right, then the personal life is cultivated; when the personal life is cultivated, then the family life is regulated; when the family life is regulated, then the national life is orderly, and when the national life is orderly, then there is peace in this world.[5]

The last statement in this quotation—"When the national life is orderly, then there is peace in the world"—is an expression, maybe utopian, of what most people would expect from government. Peace within a particular nation and peace among neighboring nations depends upon a great many factors, such as enough to eat for all people, a place to sleep, security against disease, self-expression, etc., all of which may be reduced to the factors of material and spiritual sufficiency. Sufficient material wealth and ample means and opportunity for spiritual development and expression (art, education, religion, etc.) are necessary (though they may not be sufficient) conditions of peace. A pervasive morality may also be needed to regulate competition and to prevent strife and conflict.

It is to be seen, therefore, that the task given to government by Confucius is gigantic, because so utopian. According to him, it is the business of government to insure that material and spiritual sufficiency exist and that people act morally in order that peace be achieved. Granted that this is a very nice ideal, isn't it terribly impractical? After all, how can the government take care of all the material needs, to say nothing of the spiritual needs, of every individual? Is not morality a matter for individuals rather than the province of government?

Besides pointing to the fact that the goal of government for Confucius was very high, such questions point to different ways of thinking about government. One way takes the attitude that the obvious means to material and spiritual plenty, if provision of these is regarded as the function of government, are the passing of laws, the raising of taxes, the building of schools, churches, museums, and the regulation of production and labor so that enough will be produced and each person will get his or her share of the production. Putting this into action would, of course, require great

[5] *The Great Learning* (*Ta Hsueh*), trans. by Lin Yutang, in *The Wisdom of Confucius*, p. 139.

bureaus with much paper shuffling, and hordes of government workers.

However, in the Confucian ideal state the main functions of government are carried out at a local rather than national level, in the communities and the families. The national governor is something of an overseer. The actual government is effected not really by government workers, but by individuals observing their proper relations to other individuals. When proper relations exist between all persons in society the aim of government will have been achieved.

Obviously, the Confucian concept of government is that of a moral system. When all individuals act morally in all of their relations with other persons there will be no social problems. This is why Confucius can say that to achieve world peace it is necessary and sufficient to set right one's heart, cultivate one's personal life, and regulate family life properly. When these three things are done *jen* will be developed and morality and goodness will prevail.

The quotation on page 271, concerning the way to world peace, reflects the idea that education (the investigation of things) is a basic element of Confucian social philosophy. Confucianism emphasizes a certain philosophy of education, which stresses that the most important goal is to come to know humanity. It is necessary to know both what humanity is and what things are, so that life may be ordered in a way conducive to human welfare, making the best use of things in the world. Confucius says, "The principles of the higher education consist in preserving man's clear character, in giving new life to the people and in dwelling (or resting) in perfection, or the ultimate good."[6] Only through education will people come to know themselves and the world. Without this knowledge it is very difficult to order life so that it will be in harmony with things of the world; only when life is in harmony with the world is there peace and happiness.

According to Confucius, "true knowledge" ensues when the root, or basis, of things is known. An example of what it is to have true knowledge is afforded by Confucius when he says, "In presiding over lawsuits I am as good as anyone. The thing is we should make it our aim that there not be any lawsuits at all. . . ."[7] In other words, one should remove the evil by removing the causes of the evil. Knowing the basic causes is primary in the rectification of malfunctions. So, if one has true knowledge, i.e., knowledge of the basic causes of crime, then it may be possible to do away with crime itself, thereby eliminating lawsuits.

[6] *Ibid.*
[7] *Ibid.*, p. 143.

The most important knowledge, however, is self-knowledge rather than knowledge about external things such as social conditions and institutions. "Having knowledge" is above all knowing who and what one is, and this means knowing the principles upon which one acts. Accordingly, true knowledge is obtained only when there is self-knowledge, for in Confucianism it is always the moral and social self that is taken as ultimate.

When it is said that the will becomes sincere when there is knowledge, the reference is to self-knowledge, and the point is that one who has self-knowledge will not deceive himself about the motives and principles of his actions. Thus it is said, "What is meant by making the will sincere is that one should not deceive himself."[8] People should not try to deceive themselves that if they do something in private no one will know and therefore it is all right. The wrong action will be known to the one who commits it immediately, and soon the effects will be known to others as well. Corruptness of private character does not remain purely private—a person does not live in isolation—but affects, and is affected by, the whole community of human beings.

When someone is upset by worries and cares, or is overcome with passions, his or her heart is disturbed. This person is hardly in a position to make fair and just decisions concerning any matters, personal or public. When, on the other hand, "the heart is set right," one avoids the excesses and defects that affect one's ability to make good decisions. That is why Confucius says, "The cultivation of the personal life depends on setting one's heart right." With the proper attitude toward life a person will remain calm even in joy and sorrow and will be able to live a good personal life.

If parents have cultivated their personal lives they can have a family in which the proper relationships exist. By the example of their own lives, parents can demonstrate the way of *jen* to their children. When the family follows the way of *jen*, there will be harmony in the home. And if there is harmony in every home, then there is harmony in the whole country.

This emphasis on proper familial relationships is one of the most important ideas of Confucius and is worthy of some elaboration. Suppose children are born into a family where love and goodness abound. These children will grow up seeing parents loving and respecting each other and will have a model on which to develop their own sense of respect and love. Here the children see their parents respecting other adults, the various offices and officials of government, morality and law. Not only is it possible for the

[8] *Ibid.*, p. 144.

parents to rule properly in this family, but respect and obedience are natural to the children.

Psychologists report that the first five years of human life are the most important for establishing basic attitudes and behavior patterns. This being so, what better way of insuring respect for law, government, and people than by good education of the child in these early years? Since ordinarily these first five years or so are spent in the home, basic education must take place in the home. There is no question here of educating or not educating small children. Education will take place, based mainly on imitation of a model, and the question is whether the education will be good or bad. This, in turn, becomes a question of whether or not the parents provide proper models for their children.

Suppose that children, maybe unwanted in the first place, are born into a family where little love or respect is shown one parent by the other, and where fighting is part of the daily fare. Suppose that also the parents show no respect for anyone or anything else. What will children learn in this home? Where will they learn to respect themselves, other people and the institutions of society? Statistics offered by sociologists suggest that this kind of family situation produces criminals, or at best, maladjusted adults.

It is hard to think of anything more important for good government and peace than proper family relationships, where this means the kind of familial relationships that enable children to grow up with respect and love for other people and a sense of propriety in human relationships. A nation is essentially a family, where the good of the individual is inseparably linked to the good of the whole community. By the same token, the good of the community is the good of many individuals. Since government is ultimately for the sake of the individual, and it is the individual who benefits or suffers from government, it would seem only natural to study means and ways of government from the point of view of the individuals concerned. Put in other words, the study of government ought to start with human beings, not institutions. This is precisely what Confucius is doing. He begins with people in their fundamental relationships with other people. And where is the best place to begin with people? Begin with the beginning! A person begins in a family where he or she is born. If education is the key to a good society, education must begin in the family when the person is born. The family is the basic stable unit of society, and traditionally the most influential unit.

With the individual and the family viewed in this way, it is easy to understand why Confucius stressed the virtue of *hsiao*, and regarded it as basic to all the virtues. Nothing can be more important than that a child should develop the proper attitudes to the rest of the family. By developing respect and love for parents and brothers and sisters, and from them learning respect for other people, the child develops self-respect as well as respect for others.

It is now easy to see that Confucius' analysis of social development is relevant to our own times. What is uncommon is the role that goodness is expected to play in government. Goodness, for many people today, is something for philosophers to talk about, or a subject for religion. Government based on goodness or virtue is almost unthinkable; yet this is what Confucius was suggesting, and what Mencius, a follower of Confucius, taught even more clearly. It is important to see how Confucius, in all seriousness, could suggest as a basis for government that which today seems, at first glance at least, completely impractical and impossible.

It is not so much that Confucius had a different view of the nature of human beings than is commonly held today, but rather that Confucius had quite a different idea concerning the aims of education and government than we have today. While Confucius nowhere explicitly affirms that human nature is basically good, still, it is implicit in his view of government and education, and it is explicitly stated by Mencius.

Many people today also hold that human beings are basically good, and need only develop this goodness. Others hold a Hobbesian view, taking people to be basically selfish and demanding, using other people to serve their own ends. It makes little difference which of these views is held—in either case it will be claimed that moral goodness is an impossible basis for government. The need to develop laws and to punish infractions will always be one of government's most basic tasks. If people are good it may be easier to carry out the laws, in the sense of enforcing them, but it will never make law unnecessary; this is the modern attitude.

There is an important reason for this attitude in our times. Today, in the Western world, whether people are regarded as basically good or basically evil, the purpose of education is regarded as the mastery of a skill or trade that may enable one to obtain sufficient material goods. Young people are urged to go to college so they can get a good job; once enrolled at a university or college they are advised how best to prepare themselves for the professional labor market. This points to a fundmaental difference between our contemporary philosophy of education and the Confucian view of education as the development of moral character. Confucius tells us that "the only way for the superior man to civilize the people and establish good social customs is through education. A piece of jade cannot become an object of art without chiselling, and a man cannot come to know the moral law without education."[9]

If, without enforced positive law (in the relevant sense), there is to be peace and well-being, it is necessary that everyone act appropriately, or practice the virtue of *li*. To act appropriately one must respect and care for others, or practice the virtue of *jen*, and this respect is learned early through respect for the parents, or by practicing the virtue of *hsiao*. This will produce a true moral self, a "real human being." Thus, if the true moral self is to be realized there must be education at all levels. Each individual must take seriously the responsibility for guiding those whom he or she influences. When the true moral self is achieved the person is in harmony with all things and there is peace and fulfillment.

In explaining how the development of *jen* permeates society a modern scholar summarizes Confucius' conviction that

> to be kept stable, society must have leaders who can be trusted; that the only leaders to be trusted are men of character; that character is to be developed through education acquired both from others and through self-discipline; that no man is a safe leader who goes to extremes; that the right cultivation of his own character must be the chief concern of every leader; that no parent, teacher, or public officer has the right to take lightly his responsibilities for guiding, through percept, rules and example, the conduct of those who are under him.[10]

The Confucian philosophy outlined so far probably represents primarily the thought of Confucius, though it is extremely difficult to keep separate and distinct the various streams of thought contributing to Confucianism. There is no doubt that the realism of Hsun Tzu and the idealism of Mencius were influential in the development of Confucius' thought into Confucianism. While Confucius emphasized *jen* and regarded *li*, *yi*, and *hsiao* as necessary for a well-developed and regulated individual and for a well-ordered society, he did not attend to the question of *why* we should practice these virtues. He simply assumed that if we wanted to be happy we *should* act this way. Mencius and Hsun Tzu, on the other hand, were very much concerned with the question of *why* we should live in accord with *jen*, practicing *yi* and *hsiao*. Mencius held that it was because of the original

[9] *Book of Rites* (*Li Chi*), trans. by Lin Yutang, in *The Wisdom of Confucius*, p. 241.
[10] D. Willard Lyons, as quoted by Clarence Burton Day, in *The Philosophers of China* (New York: Citadel Press, 1962), p. 43.

goodness of human nature that we should practice the virtues stressed by Confucius. Hsun Tzu, on the other hand, took the view that it was because of the original evilness of human nature that we should practice these virtues.

Mencius

Mencius agreed with Confucius that *jen* is basic, that it is the source and foundation of all goodness and virtue. And he also agreed with Confucius that *li*, or rules for proper behavior, were required for the development and manifestation of *jen*. In addition, *hsiao* was recognized to be the beginning point for goodness. But Mencius gave a more important role to *yi* than did Confucius. It is *yi*, or righteousness, that above all else contains the key to the development and cultivation of *jen* according to Mencius.

The reason for the emphasis on *yi* is due to a recognition by Mencius of the distinction between goodness and rightness. *Jen* refers to the goodness that is basic to human nature. But *yi* refers to the rightness of human actions. The need for the distinction is due to the fact that although all people possess *jen*, not all people act in the right way.

For Mencius, who claimed that *jen* was an actual beginning of goodness present in each person, the problem was to explain the presence of evil in the world. If evil is due to wrong actions, it becomes necessary to distinguish between the rightness of actions and the goodness of human nature. Despite the presence of goodness it is possible for human beings to act in a wrong way and thus bring about evil in the world. Because this is so, it is necessary to emphasize *yi*, the correctness of action, in order to rid the world of evil. Of course, Mencius did not hold that the distinction between *yi* and *jen* means that they are totally different and do not meet. Rather, he held that if *jen* is completely developed, *yi* will naturally follow. And if all actions are in accord with *yi*, *jen* will come to be developed. But because it is easier and more successful to begin the development of human nature with the correction of the actions, Mencius emphasizes *yi*.

The two most significant points of difference between Confucius and Mencius are their views about human nature, and the relation between goodness and rightness. Confucius claimed that people have a *potential* for goodness, and Mencius claimed that they possess an *actual goodness* as part of their nature. Confucius regarded goodness and rightness as the same, but Mencius distinguished between them.

Mencius did not simply state that people possess an innate goodness, but presented arguments for this view. The first argument runs as follows: (1) All human beings are alike by nature; (2) the sage, who is good by nature, is a person; (3) therefore all human beings are good by nature.

According to the second argument, the goodness of human beings is evident in the virtues of *jen, yi, li,* and *chih* (moral wisdom). All human beings possess the beginnings of these virtues as can be seen by the universality of the basic feelings that constitute the beginning for them. Compassion is the beginning of *jen*. Any person would have compassion for a child about to fall into a well, and would attempt to save the child. Shamefulness is the root of *yi*. Any person who robs another person and thereby causes the death of that person will feel shame and try to make retribution. Reverence is the beginning of *li*. The universality of this beginning can be seen in the fact that all children have a natural reverence for their parents, and in the presence of superiors all people feel their own shortcomings and are modest and reverent. If one were to simply throw the body of a parent in a ditch instead of burying it, and later were to come and see the birds and beasts preying on it, a natural reverence would cause one to hurry and bury the body. The knowledge of right and wrong is the root of the virtue *chih*. Since every person draws his or her ideas about the rightness and wrongness of actions from reflections in his or her own mind, it follows that these innate ideas of right and wrong must be found in every person.

The conclusion of these arguments is that human beings are innately moral. Because of this innate goodness, they know right and wrong, have compassion, reverence, and modesty, and know shame. This means they can distinguish between right and wrong, possessing the basis of moral judgment and character.

But if this innate goodness of human beings is granted, how is one to account for the presence of evil in the world? According to Mencius, evil in the world has three sources. First, evil is due to external circumstances. Although people are by nature good, still their nature is distorted by the externals of life. Society and culture are responsible for the presence of wrong actions and evil in the world. Second, evil is due to the abandonment of self: people abandon their innate goodness. Rather than allowing their nature to manifest itself in goodness, they forsake this goodness and determine to do evil. Third, evil is due to a failure to nourish the feelings and the senses. That is, though the intentions are good, one is incapable of doing the right things because of a lack of knowledge with which to make the correct decision.

If one accepts Mencius' arguments for the innate goodness of human nature and agrees with his explanation of the source of evil in the world, it follows that people should live according to *jen*, *yi*, and *li* because through acting correctly one's humanity is developed, and human behavior will become well regulated. Furthermore, to regulate one's actions by *li* is to live according to the innate goodness that is basic to human nature. In brief, one should practice the Confucian way because it is the way of fulfilling human nature.

Hsun Tzu

The views of Hsun Tzu on this point are diametrically opposed to those of Mencius. According to Hsun Tzu, human nature is originally evil. It is through social institutions and culture that people become good. Human beings not only lack the beginnings of the four virtues claimed by Mencius, but actually possess the beginnings of evil in their inherent desire for profit and pleasures. Yet it is possible for every person to become a Sage, for what every person does possess is intelligence, and through the employment of intelligence goodness is brought about, according to Hsun Tzu. Mencius said that human beings are born good; Hsun Tzu says that they are born evil. Mencius said that society and culture bring about evil; Hsun Tzu says that society and culture bring about goodness. Whereas Mencius says that anyone can become a Sage because of his or her innate goodness, Hsun Tzu says that anyone can become a Sage because of his or her innate intelligence and educability.

The problem for Hsun Tzu is to show how it is that if human beings are born evil they can become good. He argues that goodness comes about as the result of social organization and culture. Social organization and culture come as the result of (1) the drive to live better, and (2) the need to overcome other creatures. The arguments are that (1) people cannot provide the goods needed to live, let alone to live well, except through the cooperation of other persons, and (2) people cannot make themselves secure from the various creatures and forces of nature without mutual cooperation.

Since it is clear, for these two reasons, that people require social organization, the question is this: How does social organization bring about goodness? Hsun Tzu's answer is that social organization requires rules of conduct, and following these rules brings about goodness. His theory is that people are born with desires, some of which are ordinarily unsatisfied. When desires remain unsatisfied people strive for their satisfaction. And when many persons are striving for the satisfaction of their conflicting desires without rules or limits, there is contention and strife which brings about disorder. This is harmful to everyone. Accordingly, the early kings established rules of conduct regulating the activities involved in attempting to satisfy desires: in this way the various rules required for social living came about. By this line of reasoning, moral goodness is brought about as a result of the regulation of human conduct required for social living.

Hsun Tzu also argues for the creation of goodness through the employment of intelligence. He observes that it is not the absence of fur or feathers on this two-legged creature that distinguishes humans from other animals, rather it is their ability to make distinctions. Human intelligence is displayed in the making of social distinctions. Since it is the making of social distinctions and the resulting social relationships regulated by *li* that distinguish human beings from the birds and the beasts, people ought to act according to *li* in order to preserve and manifest their nature.

Both lines of argument given by Hsun Tzu emphasize that goodness is the result of human creation, either through the employment of intelligence or through the making of distinctions in the social sphere. He differs from Confucius in distinguishing between goodness and intelligence and in stressing the actual evil present in nature.

Through their attempts to support the social philosophy of Confucius by providing an answer to the question, Why regulate life by *li*, and, why develop *jen* by practicing *yi*? Hsun Tzu and Mencius strengthened the philosophy considerably. What happened historically was that neither of these philosophers was rejected in the favor of the other, but rather, both the idealism of Mencius and the realism of Hsun Tzu were added to the philosophy of Confucius, thus rounding out the philosophy of Confucianism. From Mencius was taken the emphasis on determining the correctness of action as a means to the development of humanity. From Hsun Tzu was taken the emphasis on following rules of behavior for developing human nature. By adopting both views, Confucianism endorsed respect for internal sanctions, using the internal feelings as guides to behavior, and external sanctions, using social rules as guides to behavior. This is roughly equivalent to employing both the internal criteria of conscience and the external criterion of law to determine how one should live. Of course, conscience tended to have priority in the Confucian way because only those social rules that conformed to *jen* were part of the moral way.

Even though Confucianism, as a result of the influence of various other schools and the contributions of Mencius and Hsun Tzu, had various external criteria available for determining the correctness of actions, it continued to be the case that the primary stress was on the humanity that each person possessed. A person knows what to do here and now because all people have within them a measure for determining whether or not to do something, because everyone possesses *jen*, or humanity. All that is required is that the Golden Rule be applied. If you would not like something done to you, then do not do it to anyone else. It is probably this humanistic measure of goodness that constitutes the timeless essence of Confucianism. Confucianism as a thoroughgoing humanism with respect to the conduct of life and society is something not merely of historical, antiquarian interest. Rather, it is a permanent social spirit that will exist as long as people have respect for themselves and other people—as long as human beings are truly human.

REVIEW QUESTIONS

1. Confucianism has been described as a thoroughgoing humanism. What does this mean? How does humanism differ from naturalism or supernaturalism?
2. What is *jen?* What is the importance of *jen* in Confucianism?
3. Distinguish between *li*, *hsiao*, and *yi*. How are these virtues related to the way of *jen?*
4. Confucius has been described as advocating government by morality, rather than government by laws and punishments. Do you agree with this description? How would you argue for this claim?
5. How does Mencius argue for his view that human beings are inherently good?
6. According to Hsun Tzu, how does goodness come about?

FURTHER READING

Confucius and the Chinese Way, by H. G. Creel (New York: Harper & Row, 1960, first published in 1949 by John Day Co.), is still, thirty-five years after it was first published, one of the best books available to begin one's study of Confucius. After a brief introduction, providing the background against which Confucius' teachings need to be considered, Creel divides the rest of the book almost equally between an account of Confucius and his thought and the Confucianism that has shaped Chinese thought for the last 2,500 years.

Centrality and Commonality: An Essay on Chung Yung, by Tu Wei-ming (Honolulu: University of Hawaii Press, 1976), is an extremely helpful interpretation of the *Doctrine of the Mean*, which is the most important Confucian text after the *Sayings*. Tu Wei-ming brings out the connections between morality and politics and between humanity and society in a way that demonstrates the organic unity of the Confucian vision.

The Wisdom of Confucius, edited and translated by Lin Yutang (New York: Random House, Modern Library, c. 1938), is a good collection of translated texts from the Confucian corpus. The introduction and Lin Yutang's notes are helpful. Although most of the classical texts are not given in their entirety, the portions included here give a balanced account of the central Confucian teachings.

Confucius—The Secular as Sacred, by Herbert Fingarette (New York: Harper & Row, 1972), is a very rich philosophical interpretation of ceremony and ritual (*li*) in the thought of Confucius. *Li* is taken to be the ceremonial or ritual means by which the potential of humanity (*jen*) is shaped into its highest expression in the superior person. How *li* does this is the topic of this wonderful little (84 pages) book, which has become a modern classic of Confucian interpretation.

A Short History of Confucian Philosophy, by Liu Wu-chi (New York: Dell Publishing Co., 1955), is exactly what its title says it is, a history of Confucianism from its beginnings to the present. The chapters on Mencius and Hsun Tzu are particularly good, showing how these thinkers shaped Confucius' own thought into the patterns that were to dominate Chinese thought and life right up to the present time. A brief concluding chapter takes a look at the Maoist challenge to Confucian thought.

CHAPTER 19

≋≋≋≋≋≋≋≋≋≋≋≋≋≋≋≋≋≋≋≋≋≋≋≋≋≋≋≋

Taoism: The Natural Way of Freedom

TAOISM, IN CONTRAST to Confucianism, seeks its principles and rules for human life not within humanity, but within nature. Consequently, instead of emphasizing human society, this philosophy emphasizes the metaphysical foundations of nature.

The story of Taoism can be told in two installments. The first part of the story deals with the philosophy developed in the classical work known as *The Treatise on the Way and its Power* (*Tao Te Ching*). This is traditionally regarded as the philosophy of Lao Tzu. The second part of the story is concerned with the Taoism of Chuang Tzu, who drew out the epistemological and mystical implications of this philosophy.

Lao Tzu

Taoism, just as Confucianism, has its beginnings in a philosophical protest against the conditions of the times. The times of Lao Tzu were approximately the times of Confucius, and Lao Tzu's charges that poverty and starvation were caused by bad rulers, that greed and avarice resulted in wars and killings, and that desires for wealth, power, and glory were bringing about the destruction of society, reveal that his philosophy is inspired by a concern with the deplorable social conditions of the times. However, despite having this inspiration in common, the two philosophies developed in quite different and even opposing ways. Whereas Confucianism stressed the moral goodness of human beings as the key to happiness, the Taoists stressed the harmony and perfection of nature. The Taoist attitude is that the contrivances and artifacts of human beings lead to evil and unhappiness. To find peace and contentment, humans must follow the Way, or *Tao*, of the universe, and achieve a oneness with this *Tao*.

In Confucianism the complex and well-developed life is taken to be the ideal. Lao Tzu, however, considered the ideal life to be simple and harmonious. A simple life is one which is plain, wherein profit is ignored, cleverness abandoned, selfishness minimized, and desires reduced. This last feature of the simple life serves well to contrast Lao Tzu and Confucius. Confucius advocated rites and music so that the desires and emotions might be developed and regulated, for therein lay the development of *jen*, or humanity. To Lao Tzu, efforts to develop and regulate the desires and emotions seemed artificial, tending to interfere with the harmony of nature. Rather than organize and regulate things to achieve perfection, Lao Tzu would let things work to their perfection naturally. This means supporting all things in their natural state, allowing them to transform spontaneously. In this way no action is needed, no regulations required, and yet everything is done and all things are regulated. It is not the case that the contrast between Confucius and Lao Tzu is that between action and inaction, or doing and non-doing. Rather, it is between holding that human beings are the measure and source of all things, and holding that nature is the measure and source of all things.

In Confucianism human beings and nature are differentiated, and goodness and well-being are considered to proceed from what belongs to humanity rather than nature. Taoism sees humanity and nature as a unity and does not differentiate between the two. According to this philosophy, the basis of humanity is not of our own making, but is contained in the being and the function of the totality of the universe. Consequently, in its critical and negative aspects, Taoism analyzes the deficiencies and evils confronting human society and concludes that they stem primarily from a wrong view of humanity and the universe.

Constructively, Taoism offers a view of the universe and man as a unity. Human knowledge transcends the limits of percepts and concepts. It is direct and immediate, not being dependent upon a false duality between the knowing subject and the known object. The principles that should guide life and regulate the actions of human beings are the principles that regulate nature. Life is lived well only when people are completely in tune with the whole universe and their actions are the action of the universe flowing through them. The institutions of society are regulated by allowing them to be what they are naturally; society, too, must be in tune with the universe.

The task of philosophy is to lead humans to a unity with the universe by illuminating its *Tao*, or Way. The word *Tao* refers to a path or a way, and in Taoism it means the source and principle of the functioning of whatever exists. When the *Tao* of humanity and the *Tao* of the universe are one, human beings will realize their infinite nature. Then peace and harmony will reign.

The ethical and social teachings of Taoism represent a constructive attempt to preserve and make great human life. To preserve life is to protect it from threats to its very existence. Making life great assumes the preservation of life and consists in improving its quality. It is above all else the attempt to provide a *Tao*, or Way, to a completely satisfying and fulfilled life that motivates the Taoist philosopher. Lao Tzu's teachings concerning the *Tao* of human life in society can be summed up in the following nine principles:

1. People generally act to fulfill their desires.
2. The result of many individuals attempting to satisfy their desires is competition and conflict.
3. In order to provide peace and harmony among individuals struggling to satisfy their desires, standards of human rightness and morality are devised.
4. Obviously the erection of moral standards does not solve the problem, for competition and conflict remain. Rules are broken and new rules are devised to protect the old rules. But new rules and old rules are broken and desires remain unsatisfied while wrongdoing and evil are fostered.
5. Since devising moral standards does not solve the problem, the solution lies in giving up moral standards.
6. However, standards can be abandoned only when desires as sources of action are given up.
7. Actions arising out of desires can be given up only when people adopt the "easy way" of action.
8. The "easy way" of action presupposes being in tune with the universe and acting in accord with the universal *Tao*.
9. Regulation of society and government of the people should be according to the easy and natural way and should foster the natural way in the people.

In attempting to rectify the evils present in his society Lao Tzu recognized the necessity of understanding the basic causes of these evils. For this it is important to know the sources and guides of human actions. As he turned his attention to these matters it appeared obvious to Lao Tzu that the choices and actions of most people proceed from their desires, and are guided by the satisfaction of these desires. Accordingly, the most basic regulatory principle of action is the fulfillment of desires.

Now if people act in order to fulfill their desires, and if different persons desire the same things, then, when there aren't enough goods to go around, there will be competing and conflicting actions. It is, of course, notoriously the case that people are never able to satisfy all of their desires and that they often desire the same things. Consequently, they compete with each other and conflicts arise. When competition is unregulated and conflicts are settled through the use of power and force, the whole fabric of society is threatened. Therefore, to regulate competition and reduce conflicts moral rules are introduced as guides to human behavior.

The primary function of moral rules and social institutions is to regulate the actions of the people in order to provide for a maximum satisfaction of desires for everyone. Lao Tzu has no quarrel with the aims of morality; rather, he questions the possibility of achieving this aim through the regulation of competition and conflict. Observing that when the great *Tao* prevailed there was no strife and competition, he remarks, "When the Great *Tao* declined, the doctrines of humanity and righteousness arose."[1] The doctrines of humanity (*jen*) and righteousness (*yi*) are the basis of the Confucian morality, and have as their object the satisfactory ordering of all human actions and social institutions. Lao Tzu's remark, however, reveals that he considers morality an inadequate solution, for it comes about only as a result of the decline of the great Way of nature.

Undoubtedly, Lao Tzu saw the failure of Confucian morality to achieve ideal social conditions as a sign of the inadequacy of the moral approach. Morality does not attack the problem at its root. By allowing desires to function as legitimate sources of human action, morality could not remove competition and strife. The best it could do was to regulate the competition and reduce the strife. But this simply complicates the matter of satisfying desires in accord with the moral rules, and leads to rule breaking, thereby bringing about immorality. It does not remove the competition and does not

---

[1] *Tao Te Ching*, ch. 18, trans. by Wing-tsit Chan, in *The Way of Lao Tzu* (Indianapolis: Bobbs-Merrill, 1963). Hereafter references to this work will be cited, by chapter, in the text.

provide for the complete satisfaction of desires. Hence Lao Tzu said, "Therefore when *Tao* is lost, only then does the doctrine of virtue arise. When virtue is lost, only then does the doctrine of humanity arise" (ch. 38).

Since morality is incapable of providing for peace and happiness, it should be regarded as an unsuccessful solution to the problem of achieving the ideal society and abandoned in favor of a different solution. But morality cannot be abandoned without changing the conditions which inevitably lead to the regulation of action by moral rules. These conditions, a world of competition and strife where the powerful subdue the weak at their pleasure, are the result of acting for the sake of satisfying desires. Since acting to satisfy desires brings about the conditions requiring morality, morality cannot be abandoned until desires as a source of actions are abandoned. The reason why acting out of desires leads to evil is that it is contrary to the Way, for the great *Tao* is always without desires. The good is accomplished not by action driven by desire, but by inaction inspired by the simplicity of *Tao*, according to Lao Tzu. He says, "Simplicity, which has no name, is free of desires. Being free of desires it is tranquil. And the world will be at peace of its own accord" (ch. 37).

Advocating giving up desires as sources of action, the important question for Lao Tzu is, How then should people act? His answer, in brief, is that people should adopt the "easy way" of *Tao*, not inflicting their desires upon nature, but following nature's principles. With regard to society, he advocates a government of the people which is in accord with the easy and natural way of *Tao*, and which fosters the natural way in the lives of the people.

The Tao and Its Manifestations

To understand this answer of Lao Tzu, it is necessary to turn to his conception of *Tao* and its manifestations, *te*. Prior to Lao Tzu the principles of *yin* and *yang* were known. They were regarded as opposites, and all of the things in the world were considered to be the production of the interaction between *yin* and *yang*. But *yin* and *yang*, opposed as light and dark, cold and warm, being and non-being, etc., being opposite, could not of their own nature either produce themselves or interact with each other. A third something providing a basis and a context for the interaction of *yin* and *yang* was required. The great contribution of Lao Tzu was his recognition of *Tao* as the source of both being and non-being—of *yin* and *yang*—and the function of *Tao* as the basis for the interaction of *yin* and *yang*.

As the absolutely first principle of existence, *Tao* is completely without characteristics. It is itself uncharacterized, being the very source and condition of all characteristics. In this sense it is non-being. But it is not simply nothing, for it is the source of everything. It is prior to all the existing things, giving them life and function, constituting the oneness underlying all the diversity and multiplicity of the world. Lao Tzu says, "The *Tao* that can be told of is not the eternal *Tao*; the name that can be named is not the eternal name. The Nameless is the origin of Heaven and Earth; the named is the mother of all things" (ch. 1).

The reason *Tao* cannot be named is that it is without divisions, distinctions, or characteristics. It is unified, like an uncarved block, being without change, knowing neither beginning nor end. But if *Tao* cannot be named, what is named by "Tao"? Lao Tzu's point in saying that the *Tao* is beyond all names is that the fundamental source and principle cannot be named, for it is the very source of names and descriptions. Consequently, "Tao" is a non-name; it does not refer to any one thing. Rather it points to that which enables things to be what they are; it is that which gives them existence and allows them to pass into non-existence. When it is said that *Tao* is the source of all being, and non-being, the word *Tao* functions very much like the word "that" when it is said "the 'that' from which being and non-being proceed."

The importance of *Tao* lies in the recognition that there is something which is prior and anterior to the various particular things that exist in the world, something which gives unity to all the existing things and which determines the very existence and function of everything. What that something is cannot, of course, be said, for whatever can be talked about is limited and determined, whereas it cannot be said that the source is limited and determined, for it is the very condition of limits and determinations.

Although what *Tao* is cannot be said, but can only be pointed to, a feeling for what *Tao* is can be achieved by considering the functioning of *Tao*. Strictly speaking the function (*te*) of *Tao* cannot be stated, but since *Tao* supports all things in their natural state, its function can be seen, at least partially, by looking to nature. The *Tao* is manifested in the workings of nature, for what individual things possess of *Tao* is the *te*, or function, of *Tao*. *Tao*, as a source, provides for the very existence of things, but the function of *Tao* provides for their distinctness.

Examining the workings of things in their natural conditions, Lao Tzu observes that no-action (*wu-wei*) is what they inherit from *Tao* as their function. He says, "*Tao* invariably takes no action, and yet there is nothing left undone" (ch. 37). What he means by "taking no action" is not straining and contriving to accomplish, but letting things be accomplished in a natural and spontaneous way. Thus, immediately after the remark quoted above he says, "If kings and barons can keep it, all things will transform spontaneously" (ch. 37). The reference here is to *Tao*. If the ruler will keep to the way of *Tao*, government will proceed in a natural and spontaneous way. There will be no need for harsh laws, conscriptions, punishment, and wars.

Lao Tzu's advice to the rulers is that they should govern as little as possible, keeping to the natural way, letting people go their own way. He suggests that the people are difficult to rule because the ruler does too many things. What the ruler should keep in mind is that "ruling a big country is like cooking a small fish." In cooking a small fish one must take care not to handle it too roughly for too much handling will spoil it. In ruling a country care must be taken not to push the people around, forcing them to rebel. When the people are satisfied there will be no rebellion or wars. Therefore the easy way of governing is to give the people what they want and make government conform to the will of the people rather than trying to force the people to conform to the will of the government.

When Lao Tzu suggests that the ruler should know the mystic *Tao*, and in his ruling emulate the function of *Tao*, he has in mind that the perfection of all things lies in expressing the *Tao* they possess. The job of the ruler is to let the *Tao* operate freely, rather than trying to resist and change its function. What *Tao* is, and how it functions, is revealed in the fourth chapter of the *Tao Te Ching*, where Lao Tzu says:

> *Tao* is empty (like a bowl).
> It may be used but its capacity is never exhausted.
> It is bottomless, perhaps the ancestor of all things.
> It blunts its sharpness.
> It unties its tangles.
> It softens its light.
> It becomes one with the dusty world.
> Deep and still, it appears to exist forever.

To say *Tao* is empty is to note that it is without characteristics; it is empty of all particularity, for it is the possibility and source of all particularity. Even though it is empty of particular things it is the most useful of all things. Just as the most useful thing about a house is its emptiness—its space—so the most useful thing about *Tao* is its emptiness of characteristics, for this means it has infinite capacity. Thus the emptiness of *Tao* is synonymous with its being the infinite source of all things.

The functioning of *Tao* is eternal and recurrent, producing all things and directing their activities. Comparing the functioning of *Tao* to blunting sharpness, untying tangles, and softening light draws attention to reversal as the movement of the *Tao*. The lesson the Taoists drew from nature is that when a thing reaches one extreme, it reverses and returns to the other extreme. Thus, the advice is given that to assist the ruler with *Tao* one does not use force and violence, for this would bring about a reversal (ch. 30). When it gets very cold, reversal sets in and it begins to get warm. When it gets very warm, reversal again sets in and it begins to get cold. This is the way of nature as seen in the passing of the seasons. In similar fashion, when a person becomes extremely proud and conceited, disgrace and humility will follow. To know the reversals that constitute the functioning of *Tao* and to adapt oneself to these movements is the way to peace and contentment. Just as one does not dress lightly in winter and suffer in the cold, and does not dress warmly in the summer and suffer in the heat, but dresses warmly in the winter and enjoys the cold, and dresses lightly in the summer and enjoys the warm weather, so one should not resist the natural way, but should act in accord with the Way of the Great *Tao* in all things.

To recognize that *Tao* becomes one with the dusty world is to understand that *Tao* is not transcendental, but immanent. That is, *Tao* does not remain aloof from the world, directing it from afar, but functions through the world, and is indistinguishable from the functioning of the world. *Tao* is not to be found aside from life, but within life in the world.

A ruler who knows the *Tao* and its *te* knows how to stay out of the way of the people and serve them without intruding. Thus, Lao Tzu says that the people "are difficult to rule because the ruler does too many things" (ch. 25). In accord with the function of *Tao*, Lao Tzu says, "Administer the empire by engaging in no activity." Supporting this advice, he notes that "the more taboos and prohibitions there are in the world, the poorer the people will be," and, "the more laws and orders are made prominent, the more thieves and robbers there will be" (ch. 57).

By giving up desires and letting the *Tao* enter and pervade oneself, life will rise above the distinctions of good and evil. All activity will proceed from *Tao*, the very source of existence, and humanity will be one with the world. This is the solution Lao Tzu brought to the problem of evil and unhappiness in human life. It is a solution that depends ultimately upon achieving a unity with the great inner principle of reality, and is, therefore, basically mystical.

Chuang Tzu

Although the positive foundations of Taoism are mystical, there are good reasons for seriously considering this way of life, as Chuang Tzu points out. Chuang Tzu (ca. 369–286 B.C.) developed a philosophy not basically different from Lao Tzu's though he does develop further the concepts of the total spontaneity of nature, the incessant activity of things, and the underlying unity of all existence. He emphasized that ultimate freedom is achieved through identifying with the *Tao* of reality. Chuang Tzu also provided arguments for rejecting other ways of life and accepting the Taoist Way.

The philosophy of Chuang Tzu is based on the conviction that true happiness is dependent upon transcending the world of ordinary experience and cognition and identifying oneself with the infinity of the universe. This conviction appears quite clearly in his description of the person who has achieved complete happiness. Of the happy person, the true sage, Chuang Tzu says, "Suppose there is one who chariots upon the normality of the universe, rides upon the transformation of the six elements, and thus makes excursions into the infinite, what has he to depend upon? Therefore it is said that the Perfect Man has no self; the Spiritual Man has no achievement; the Sage has no name."[2]

This remark is intended to suggest that the ordinary cognitive scheme wherein one distinguishes between self and other, between doing and not doing, and between names (words) and realities (things) is inadequate. It is claimed to be inadequate because of its limitations; its finiteness. Consequently, in the *Book of Chuang Tzu* it is suggested that the finite point of view (the ordinary cognitive point of view, which is dependent upon perception and conception) should be exchanged for an "infinite," or "transcendent," point of view. This infinite point of view is regarded as becoming one with *Tao*, the essence (normality) of the universe.

Not infrequently the aspects of his philosophy just referred to are regarded as evidence that Chuang Tzu was a Chinese mystic. Being so labeled, Chuang Tzu could be dismissed from further philosophical consider-

---

[2] As quoted in Fung Yu-Lan, *History of Chinese Philosophy*, trans. by Derk Bodde (Princeton: Princeton University Press, 1952), vol. 1, p. 243.

ation. But such dismissal is unfortunate, for Chuang Tzu does not merely suggest that the finite point of view should be exchanged for the infinite. He argues, quite ingeniously, for the acceptance of the infinite point of view by trying to show that the finite point of view (the ordinary cognitive scheme) is inadequate.

The arguments against accepting the ordinary cognitive scheme, which constitute Chuang Tzu's arguments for an infinite point of view, can be classified as (1) the argument from the relativity of distinctions, (2) the argument from the complementariness of opposites, (3) the argument from perspectives, and (4) the argument from general skepticism.

1. The first argument, the argument from the relativity of distinctions, claims that judgments about values and matters of taste are subjective and therefore relative. A particular sauce may be sour to A's taste, but sweet to B's taste. Thinking about the relativity of distinctions may be good for X, and bad for Y. This relativity is taken to hold for all distinctions. Chuang Tzu says, "Let us take, for instance, a large beam and a small beam, or an ugly woman and Hsi-shih [famous beauty of ancient China], or generosity, strangeness, deceit, and abnormality. The Tao identifies them all as one."[3] He also says "There is nothing in the world greater than the tip of a hair that grows in autumn, while Mount T'ai is small. No one lives a longer life than a child who dies in infancy, but P'eng-tsu (who lived many hundred years) died prematurely. The universe and I exist together, and all things and I are one."[4]

The basic reason for regarding all distinctions as relative is that the characteristics attributed to things or events in the making of distinctions are generated by the mind, which is regarded as independent of the so-called characteristics of things generated by it. Chuang Tzu says, "A road becomes so when people walk on it, and things become so-and-so [to people] because people call them so-and-so. How have they become so? They have become so because people say they are so. How have they become not so? They have become not so because [people say] they are not so."[5] The argument from the relativity of distinctions is intended to prove the triviality of knowledge. If the possibility of knowing what is good, or big, or sweet is claimed, and it can be shown that the concepts of good, big, and sweet are relative, it follows that the knowledge claimed is relative, and therefore can be regarded as trivial.

---

[3] In Wing-tsit Chan, trans. and compiler, *A Source Book in Chinese Philosophy* (Princeton: Princeton University Press, 1963), p. 184.
[4] *Ibid.*, p. 186.
[5] *Ibid.*, pp. 183–84. (Brackets are Chan's.)

This argument is directed primarily against the Confucianists and Mohists, both of whom claimed they had genuine knowledge of right and wrong, but who disagreed on nearly every point. Chuang Tzu says, "There have arisen the controversies between the Confucianists and the Mohists, each school regarding as right what the other regards as wrong. . . ."[6] The Mohists were pragmatists, accepting practice as the criterion of knowledge. Their view was that knowledge is possible, for in the main, people live in such a way as to avoid a lot of unpleasantness. Now, since on pragmatic or utilitarian grounds the rightness and wrongness of actions is determined by the amounts of pleasantness and unpleasantness respectively, right and wrong can be known simply by looking to the pleasantness and unpleasantness brought about by actions. The Confucianists, on the other hand, maintained that knowledge of right and wrong proceeded immediately and intuitively from an internal moral sense.

Chuang Tzu uses the argument from relativity to show that pleasantness and unpleasantness are relative concepts, and though people appear to get on well in this life, this may be a mere appearance and not the case at all. Furthermore, it is not clear how practice can serve as a criterion of knowledge, and it may be possible that there is no way of knowing whether or not practice is an adequate criterion of knowledge, for practice itself is relative. For the Confucianist, the problem lies in showing that the moral sense, which is supposed to provide knowledge of right and wrong, is any less relative than any of the other senses.

Both the Confucianist and the Mohist would agree, though for different reasons, that we can have genuine knowledge of the fact that it is wrong to kill. Employing the relativity argument of Chuang Tzu, however, it can be seen that this is not absolute knowledge, but only relative knowledge. From another perspective it might turn out to be mistaken opinion. Suppose it is claimed that it is wrong to kill. Now if a man is starving and the only way to escape death is to kill a hare, all would agree that it is right to kill the hare. But someone might suggest that though in need it is right to kill animals, it is always wrong to kill a man. If, however, the only way to prevent the death of his wife and family is for a man to kill the attacker, it would again be conceded that in this special case it would be right for a man to kill, but only because of the special circumstances. Somewhere along the line it could be suggested, by someone using Chuang Tzu's argument, that there can never be any real knowledge of the wrongness of an action such as killing, because right and wrong are purely relative.

[6] *Ibid.*, p. 182.

Everything depends on who is doing the killing, who the considering, and what the circumstances are. There can be no absolute right and wrong because rightness and wrongness are relative to the circumstances of the actions in question. But this means that there is no real knowledge of right and wrong.

Of course, it might be argued against Chuang Tzu that if all knowledge is purely relative, then so is this knowledge; namely, the knowledge that all knowledge is relative. But Chuang's suggestion is that because of the relativity of knowledge you could never really know that that knowledge is relative. It will not do to return the compliment by claiming that he can never really know whether that, or any knowledge, either is or is not trivial, because the point of Chuang Tzu's argument from skepticism is precisely this: to maintain the impossibility of certain, indubitable knowledge.

Chuang Tzu's position is clear. If it is certitude of knowledge that is doubted, indubitable knowledge is impossible without begging the question. And there seems no way, other than by knowing, of ascertaining that there is indubitable knowledge. Thus, Chuang Tzu's argument, on these grounds at least, is unanswerable.

2. The second argument, from the complementariness of opposites, suggests that any concept logically implies its negation, and that without its negation, or opposite, a concept could not exist. The argument is intended to show that affirmation and negation are simply different ways of looking at the same thing. If A is A, then A is not not-A. Or, the negation of A is the affirmation of not-A. In a similar way, right and wrong are the same thing looked at differently. If A is right, then A is not wrong. If there were no right, there would be no wrong (and vice versa). For if A is right, then A is not wrong, implying a wrong that A is not, and in virtue of which A is, or can be, right. In other words, what is involves what is not, and opposites, from this point of view, turn out to be complementary. Chuang Tzu says, "Nevertheless, when there is life there is death, and when there is death there is life. When there is possibility, there is impossibility, and when there is impossibility there is possibility. Because of the right, there is the wrong, and because of the wrong there is the right."[7] He also says. "There is nothing that is not the 'that' and there is nothing that is not the 'this'. Therefore I say that the 'that' is produced by the 'this' and the 'this' is also caused by the 'that'."[8]

Chuang Tzu appears to be thinking in terms of pairs of correlative terms.

[7] *Ibid.*, p. 183.
[8] *Ibid.*, p. 182.

For example, if there were no concept of up, there could be none of down, and the same holds true for left and right, right and wrong, self and other, etc. For such pairs of concepts, the existence of one presupposes the other and the removal of one is the removal of the other. It might be objected that it is by no means clear that all concepts can function only as correlatives. In fact, if one avoids adjectival concepts and concentrates on substantive concepts, it is by no means clear that a concept is possible only if it is opposed by another concept. By what concepts need the concepts *man*, *house*, *dog*, etc. be opposed in order that they can function as concepts?

According to Chuang Tzu's argument, however, even a concept such as *dog* involves, at least implicitly, the concept of *not-dog*, for if there were no concept of *not-dog*, the concept of *dog* could not be used discriminately. That is, it would be impossible to decide what to call and what not to call a dog. And not being able to properly use a concept in a discriminatory fashion would be sufficient evidence for claiming that a person did not have the concept at all. But a necessary condition of using a concept properly is being able to discriminate between what the concept refers to and what it does not. Thus, in terms of the present example, having the concept *dog* involves knowing what is not-dog, or of having the concept of *not-dog*. The same line of reasoning can be used with any substantive concept, for having a concept of anything presupposes an ability to discriminate between that to which the concept refers and that to which it does not, and this involves knowing what the concept is not. In this way it is seen that a concept of something is always relative to what that something is not. Thus, Chuang Tzu says, "the 'this' is also the 'that'," and, "when 'this' and 'that' have no opposites, there is the very axis of *Tao*."[9]

The question could be asked, Which is the essential feature of knowledge, the not-dog or the dog? According to Chuang Tzu, the answer is neither, since both are necessary. Coupled with the argument from skepticism, this argument implies neither that there is no real knowledge nor that real knowledge is impossible, but that we can never know (i.e., be certain) either what this or that knowledge really consists in, or whether or not we really have knowledge.

3. The third argument, the argument from perspectives, presupposes the previous two arguments. It is obvious that the same thing appears different to different people if their perspectives are different. Or, the same thing appears different to me if I change my perspective. If my organs of sensing

[9] *Ibid.*, p. 183.

were different, no doubt I would perceive things differently. The point of this is that the same thing has many appearances, depending upon the perceiver. Which of the appearances is the correct or true appearance? Is what the worm or the cat perceives the same as what a person perceives? Is what is perceived now the same as what was perceived a minute ago?

Chuang Tzu's point is that these questions cannot be answered. Each thing is just what it is and not something else, and what it is independent of how it appears to anything or anyone. It is contained in itself, in its own perspective, and the only way to get at it is, is to transcend our own perspective and view the other as a totality, from its own perspective. The claim is that everything in the world is a self-sufficient unit with a perspective of its own. Everything has a view of itself and has a function. From its own point of view everything is a totality. But if everything is a totality from its own point of view and no other, then it appears that morality and knowledge are purely relative. And if everything is looked at from its own point of view, right and wrong disappear. This is exactly what Chuang Tzu recommends: obtain the transcendent point of view from which everything is seen in its proper perspective, from its own point of view. Then there will be unity with the universe; there will be enlightenment; the *Tao* will be found in everything. According to Chuang Tzu, "Things do not know that they are the 'that' of other things; they only know what they themselves know."[10] And, "Only the intelligent knows how to identify all things as one."[11] The point is illustrated with the butterfly story:

Once I, Chuang Chou, dreamed that I was a butterfly and was happy as a butterfly. I was conscious that I was quite pleased with myself, but I did not know that I was Chou. Suddenly I awoke, and there I was, visibly Chou. I do not know whether it was Chou dreaming that he was a butterfly or the butterfly dreaming it was Chou.[12]

Going further, Chuang Tzu advises giving up a particular perspective and adopting a universal perspective:

We say this is right or wrong, and is so or is not so. If the right is really right, then the fact that it is different from the wrong leaves no room for argument. Forget the passage of time (life and death) and forget the distinction of right

10 *Ibid.*, p. 182.
11 *Ibid.*, p. 184.
12 *Ibid.*, p. 190.

and wrong. Relax in the realm of the infinite and thus abide in the realm of the infinite.[13]

Here the point of the argument is that we can never really know what a thing is in itself. To make this point, the argument *assumes* a transcendent point of view, for by its own premises, ordinary experience could never show anything about things as they are in themselves, as totalities with their own perspectives. Only by assuming a transcendent point of view can it be known that there are things in themselves, locked within their own perspectives and not accessible to ordinary means of knowledge. To assume a point of view is not the same thing as to argue for a point of view. The argument for a transcendent point of view depends on showing that the ordinary cognitive point of view leads to skepticism, and because of this the argument from skepticism is relevant at this point.

4. Chuang Tzu's fourth argument, the argument from skepticism, advances the claim that the question, Is that really so? can never be answered. Suppose, for example, it is claimed that X is red. The retort is, "But how can it be shown to be *really* red?" The difficulty in proving that the claim is true is that the claim cannot be compared with what is actually the case, because any claim about what is actually the case would be subject to the same doubts as the original claim. What is needed is a standard to judge the first standard, a standard to judge the second standard, etc., *ad infinitum*. But it appears that choosing even a third standard is impossible, for if A and B have opposite views, a standard acceptable to A would be unacceptable to B, and a standard acceptable to B would be unacceptable to A. And if the standard is acceptable to no one, it is of no use. Therefore it would seem impossible to defend the claim that X is really red.

On one occasion Chuang Tzu presented the skeptical argument in the form of the following question: "How can it be known that what I call knowing is not really not knowing and what I call not knowing is not really knowing?"[14] On another occasion he presented the argument in the form of a different question: "For knowledge depends on something to be correct, but what it depends on is uncertain and changeable. How do we know that what I call nature is not really man and what I call man is not really nature?"[15]

This skepticism is pushed even further in the following statement:

[13] *Ibid.*
[14] *Ibid.*, p. 187.
[15] *Ibid.*, p. 191.

Suppose we make a statement. We don't know whether it belongs to one category or another. Whether one or the other, if we put them in one, then one is not different from the other. However, let me explain. There was a beginning. There was a time before that beginning. And there was a time before the time which was before that beginning. There was being. There was non-being. There was a time that was before that non-being, and there was a time before the time that was before that non-being. Suddenly there is being and non-being, but I don't know which of being and non-being is really being or really non-being. I have just said something, but I don't know if what I have said really says something or says nothing.[16]

Chuang Tzu, in suggesting that it is impossible to know whether what is called man is really man or whether it is really nature, or that it is impossible to tell whether it is Chuang Tzu dreaming he is a butterfly or a butterfly dreaming it is Chuang Tzu, is obviously assuming the skeptic's role. Taking the butterfly example, it can be seen that Chuang Tzu's problem is that of ascertaining whether he was dreaming or being dreamed. Chuang Tzu can find no indubitable criteria that can be used to distinguish between being awake and dreaming, and no indubitable criteria to distinguish being dreamed from dreaming. Hence he cannot be sure that he does not exist merely as a character in a butterfly's dream.

The obvious answer to this kind of skepticism is that the doubts expressed make sense only within a certain cognitive scheme, in this case a cognitive scheme wherein individuals such as Chuang Tzu and butterflies can be identified and differentiated. When Chuang Tzu goes on to use this cognitive scheme to reject this identification and differentiation he is rejecting the very conditions in terms of which it makes sense to question such identification and differentiation. In this way he rejects the grounds which make possible the first doubt and which are needed to make sense of his skepticism. For unless Chuang Tzu could accept "Once I, Chuang Tzu, dreamed I was a butterfly" he could not go on to doubt whether he dreamed or was dreamed.

Though the above answer may be sufficient to refute skepticism generally, it will not refute Chuang Tzu's position. To see this, recall that Chuang Tzu is arguing for a transcendent point of view. His arguments are negative, in the sense that they are aimed at refuting a finite point of view. Suppose for a moment that Chuang Tzu's only argument is the skeptical one, and that the above argument adequately refutes the skeptical argument.

Has Chuang Tzu been refuted by the above argument? Not at all. In fact,

[16] *Ibid.*, pp. 185–86.

his position has been strengthened. The reason for this is that Chuang Tzu is arguing that the ordinary cognitive framework is inadequate, and that a new cognitive framework, a universal cognitive framework, must be adopted in order to escape the limitations of the limited cognitive scheme ordinarily employed. It is for this reason that the fact that though thorough-going skepticism is self-contradictory in terms of a conceptual framework which is limited in the relevant ways (e.g., a conceptual framework that is essentially spatial-temporal), this is not an argument for the rejection of thorough-going skepticism, but is an argument for rejecting the limited cognitive scheme.

Does recognition of the limitations of ordinary cognitive schemes and adoption of a transcendent perspective mean rejecting the ordinary and mundane world? The answer is no, for to interpret Lao Tzu and Chuang Tzu in this way is to ignore their concern with social rectification, the concern inspiring their philosophies. Kuo Hsiang, a later commentator on Chuang Tzu, puts the matter as follows:

> To cry as people cry is a manifestation of the mundane world. To identify life and death, forget joy and sorrow, and be able to sing in the presence of the corpse is the perfection of the transcendental world . . .

He then goes on to point out that the true sage, the person who is fully able to transcend the mundane world, finds happiness in the mundane world. He says,

> There has never been a person who has roamed over the transcendental world to the utmost and yet was not silently in harmony with the mundane world, nor has there been anyone who was silently in harmony with the mundane world and yet did not roam over the transcendental world. Therefore the sage always roams in the transcendental world in order to enlarge the mundane world. By having no deliberate mind of his own, he is in accord with things.[17]

In the sage the transcendental and the mundane meet, for here the *tao* of human beings is identical with the *Tao* of the universe. Chuang Tzu puts it this way:

> With the sage, his life is the working of Heaven, his death the transformation of things. In stillness, he and the *yin* share a single Virtue; in motion, he and the *yang* share a single flow. He is not the bearer of good fortune, nor the

[17] *Ibid.*, p. 330.

initiator of bad fortune. Roused by something outside himself, only then does he respond; pressed, only then does he move; finding he has no choice, only then does he rise up. He discards knowledge and purpose and follows along with the reasonableness of Heaven. Therefore he incurs no disaster from Heaven, no entanglement from things, no opposition from man, no blame from the spirits.[18]

REVIEW QUESTIONS

1. Contrast the philosophies of Taoism and Confucianism. How are they similar? How are they different?
2. What does Lao Tzu mean when he says, "Therefore when *Tao* is lost, only then does the doctrine of virtue arise. When virtue is lost, only then does the doctrine of humanity arise"? Is this a criticism of the Confucian way? If so, on what grounds?
3. What is the *Tao* to which Lao Tzu refers? How does it function?
4. Chuang Tzu's philosophy is concerned primarily with freedom. What is the relation between human conventions and freedom according to his philosophy?
5. How does Chuang Tzu argue against the ordinary or conventional cognitive scheme? Identify and describe each of the four arguments he employs.
6. Do Taoists reject the ordinary or mundane world in favor of a transcendent world of infinite freedom? Argue for your answer, citing Lao Tzu and Chuang Tzu where relevant.

FURTHER READING

The Way of Lao Tzu (Tao-te Ching), translated, with introductory essays, comments, and notes, by Wing-tsit Chan (Indianapolis: Bobbs-Merrill, Library of Liberal Arts, 1963), is still the standard English translation of this classic text. The translation of the eighty-one paragraph-length chapters is elegant and simple, with discussion of subtleties of meaning and debates among scholars provided in notes following each chapter. Chan's introductory essays as well as his comments on each chapter of the text itself are extremely helpful.

Tao: A New Way of Thinking. A Translation of the Tao Te Ching, with an Introduction and Commentaries, by Chang Chung-yuan (New York: Harper & Row, 1975), is of special interest to students of comparative thought. Chang's

---

[18] *The Complete Works of Chuang Tzu*, translated by Burton Watson (New York: Columbia University Press, 1968), p. 168.

comments relate Taoist thought to a whole range of Western and Eastern thinkers, with a special focus on Heidegger's philosophy. Chang's *Creativity and Taoism* (New York: Harper & Row, 1970), is also a rich study of comparative thought, focusing on aesthetic experience through a study of art and poetry, East and West.

The Complete Works of Chuang Tzu, translated by Burton Watson (New York: Columbia University Press, 1968), remains the standard English translation of the *Chuang Tzu*. The introduction is brief, but very helpful in orienting the reader to the spirit of the text, one of the great literary, as well as philosophical, classics of the Chinese tradition. The text is sheer delight, with a skillful combination of playful humor and profundity, engaging the reader in Chuang Tzu's own task of examining the whole range of human and social conventions.

Chuang Tzu: World Philosopher at Play, by Kuang-ming Wu (New York: Crossroad Publishing; and Chico, Ca.: Scholars Press, 1982), explores the relevance of Chuang Tzu's thought and style for today's world. The serious playfulness of Chuang Tzu is examined from a variety of perspectives, encouraging the reader to live and think with a similar serious playfulness.

Temple on a Mountain Ledge. *The Asia Society, New York: Mr. and Mrs. John D. Rockefeller 3rd Collection.*

CHAPTER 20

Neo-Confucianism: The Grand Harmony

Challenges to Confucianism

THE THIRD MAJOR indigenous philosophical movement in China is that of Neo-Confucianism. This philosophy represents a harmonizing of the underlying principles of Confucianism and Taoism, inspired, at least in part, by the influence of Chinese Buddhism. The introduction and development of Buddhism in China provided a strong catalyst in the philosophical milieu during China's middle ages. But Neo-Confucianism also is indebted to developments in Neo-Taoism, the School of Names, and the metaphysical developments in the *Yin-Yang* Interactionist School. Without all of these elements it is unlikely that the Ch'eng brothers and Chu Hsi could have reinterpreted the principles and concepts of Confucianism in such a way as to include and coordinate the apparently conflicting principles of the other schools of philosophy in China.

In 221 B.C. the state of Ch'in succeeded in subduing all of the states of China: for the first time China was a unified country. Despite the Confucian teachings that government should proceed according to moral principles, and the Taoist teachings that government should leave the people alone as much as possible, not interfering in the lives of the people except when necessary for their own well-being, the unification of China came about as the result of military power and economic control. However, this event, though brought about by means contrary to both philosophies, did not refute either Taoism or Confucianism. In fact, in the long term it tended to confirm them both, for the excessive regulation of the people coupled with the harshness of the rule and lack of concern for moral qualities led to rebellion against the Ch'in dynasty, and by 206 B.C., just fifteen years later, the Han dynasty controlled the country. The Han dynasty lasted for more than four hundred years, its longevity being due, at least in part, to its attempts to provide for political unity and to construct a new social order along the lines of the Confucian philosophy.

Early in the Han dynasty, primarily through the efforts of Tung Chung-Shu (179–104 B.C.), Confucianism was adopted as the national philosophy of China. This was possible because of the close relation between politics and philosophy in China which permitted the foundation of a civil service examination system designed by Tung Chung-Shu to be based on the Confucian texts. In addition to this, Tung Chung-Shu helped found the Imperial University, where the Confucian texts were the basis of all education. Although these programs secured the continuation of Confucianism it did not preserve the Confucianism of Confucius and Mencius in its purity, for Tung Chung-Shu had interpreted the Confucian texts in the light of his systematization and amplification of the *yin-yang* and the Five Agencies theories, into which he had incorporated certain aspects of Taoism.

One of the effects of adopting Confucianism as the state philosophy was that the challenges of other philosophical perspectives and positions was muted. Confucianism, without these challenges, became conservative. The main effort of Confucian scholars was to put into practice this philosophy rather than develop it further philosophically. A philosophy cannot remain static, however. If it is not subjected to criticism and analysis it fails to develop. Consequently, since the other schools of philosophy were without official support, they never became sufficiently influential to attract the kind of intellectual attention they needed for fuller development, and Confucianism was deprived of the challenges needed for its vigorous development. Thus, there was little indigenous philosophical development in China from around the beginning of the Christian era until the beginnings of Neo-Confucianism.

During this same period, however, Buddhism was introduced into China, and became quite influential. In fact, all of the Neo-Confucian philosophers took considerable pains to discuss the weaknesses of Buddhism in an attempt to decrease the influence of Buddhism and increase the importance and influence of Confucianism. Part of the reason for the growth and development of Buddhism in China was that all of the different schools of Buddhism were brought to China and there was, therefore, the stimulation of mutual criticism right from the beginning. In addition, Buddhism represented a systematic explanation of the world and human life in which practical living was defined by reference to theoretical principles, such as the nature of causality, the nature of Buddhahood, and the nature of consciousness or the mind.

Indigenous philosophies of China had not managed to combine systematic theoretical completeness with detailed prescriptions for living. In Taoism the base was sufficiently broad, but the philosophy remained too abstract to be practical. In Confucianism there was a wealth of detailed rules for the guidance of life, but insufficient theoretical foundation for these prescriptions. By contrast, therefore, Buddhism immediately appeared attractive, and won sufficient attention from Chinese scholars and intellectuals to ensure translation not only into the Chinese language, but also into Chinese philosophical concepts and practice. It turned out that many of the Buddhist schools were too theoretical in their emphasis to catch on in China, and the Buddhist philosophies that did take hold underwent modifications that increased their concern with morality and politics, giving them a more practical bent.

But despite the extent to which schools such as the Hua-yen, Chen-yen, T'ien-t'ai, Ch'an, and Ching't'u became modified by the Chinese scholars responsible for their development, they continued to be regarded as foreign and extraneous philosophies. Among the Confucian scholars there was an increasing concern to replace these foreign philosophies with something having roots in China's ancient past. Since Confucianism was still officially the state philosophy, and the civil service and university systems were based on this philosophy, it is natural that it should be regarded as the basis from which a philosophy could be derived which might prove superior to the Buddhist philosophies. In this way Buddhism proved the critical catalyst in Confucian studies that produced Neo-Confucianism.

Neo-Confucianism begins with an attempt to find a metaphysical explanation of the universe that is as comprehensive as the Buddhist one. But the new metaphysics must be completely affirmative, being built upon the supremacy of individual persons and particular things. Also it must emphasize the moral features of the universe, providing for the achievement of moral goodness among the people. With this metaphysical accomplishment, the ethical and social philosophies of Confucianism could be recast, putting them upon this new basis. In effect, this new basis would allow for a synthesis of Taoist, Buddhist, and Confucian principles and tendencies, and give expression to the practical philosophies of Taoism and Confucianism. Buddhism was very influential in China from around 800 A.D. to 1200 A.D. After that period, however, from about the beginning of the thirteenth century, when Neo-Confucianism came into its own, Buddhism was on the decline, and the next seven hundred years of Chinese philosophical history are clearly Neo-Confucianist.

Chou Tun-i

It was Chou Tun-i (1017–1073) who was directly responsible for laying the foundations of Neo-Confucianism. He was born at a time when the ascendancy of Buddhist philosophies in China was viewed by government officials as a threat to the social organization of the country. These officials feared that the negative attitude of the Buddhists toward life in the world and their preference for retreating from active social life into monasteries would undermine the ancient forms of Chinese social organization.[1]

Ou-yang Hsiu (1007–1072 A.D.), for example, tried to cast this concern into a program by suggesting that Buddhism could be opposed by displaying the indigenous philosophies of China, showing them to be superior to Buddhist philosophies. The difficulty of achieving what Ou-yang Hsiu proposed was due largely to the fact that the various Buddhist philosophies could boast a complete philosophy of life wherein practical considerations rested upon solid metaphysical principles. The Chinese philosophies, on the other hand, were not systematically complete. Chinese philosophers had tended to be concerned with things at hand and did not concern themselves with the elegance of theoretical systems. Consequently, though they had maxims and rules for living, they were not in a position to justify these rules and maxims by appeal to a comprehensive philosophy.

The problem, therefore, in opposing Buddhism was that of having to construct a systematic philosophy of human nature and the world which would be completely life-affirming, emphasizing the importance of particular things and individual persons.

Han Yü (768–824), who planted the seeds of Neo-Confucianism, was expressing a prevalent criticism of his day when he said, "But now the followers of Lao-tzu and the Buddha who talk about rectification of the mind ignore this world and their native land and reduce the normal duties required by heaven to nothingness. Following the ideas of Lao-tzu, a son does not have to consider his father as a father, nor does a man have to

---

[1] The point here is not that the Buddhist philosophies are life-negating and unconcerned with practical social matters, but that they were so regarded by the Chinese officials in question.

regard the king as a king. He does not even have to discharge his duties as a subject."[2]

Han Yü went beyond mere criticism, however, and urged a return to Confucius. As he saw it, this meant a return to an all-pervasive love as the common basis for all human activity. This universal love proceeds from basic human nature, for it represents what is basic to all people. In addition to love, human nature is constituted by propriety, sincerity, righteousness, and wisdom.

Three grades of persons can be distinguished on the basis of how these five virtues constituting human nature are practiced. If one of these—*jen*— is the ruling virtue and if the other four are also practiced the person is superior. If no one of these is perfected and they are practiced only sometimes and in impure form the person belongs to the medium grade. When *jen* is rejected and actions are not in accord with the other four the person is inferior. This system of three grades, usually acknowledged to be an original contribution of Han Yü, emphasizes the priority he gave to the moral principles of Confucianism.

Han Yü's objections were primarily due to the excessive interest in metaphysical speculation in Taoism and Buddhism, at the expense of practical things. Therefore he argued that the *Tao* (Way) of life consists in loving the people and observing proper human relationships. This concern for practical things and the belief that Confucianism was fully the equal of Buddhism and Taoism is also clearly evident in Li Ao, a pupil of Han Yü. Li Ao says, "Everybody has joined the schools of Lao-tzu, the Buddha, Chuang-tzu and Lieh-tzu. They all believe that the Confucianist scholars were not learned enough to know about nature and the heavenly order, but that they themselves are. Before those who raise this hue and cry I do my best to demonstrate the opposite."[3]

In his attempt to demonstrate the adequacy of Confucianism, Li Ao argued that human nature is originally good, but failure to control and quiet the feelings, or emotions, leads to corruption. The Confucian virtues are required to regulate the feelings. But apparently he did not distinguish clearly between the Confucian virtues and the Buddhist (*ch'an*) way of overcoming desires and cravings, for when he was asked how man can return to the original goodness of his nature, he replied, "As long as there is no deliberating and no thinking, one's emotions are not in action. When

---

[2] Carsun Chang, *The Development of Neo-Confucian Thought* (New Haven: College and University Press, 1963), p. 96.
[3] *Ibid.*, p. 109.

emotions are checked one has the right way of thinking. Right thinking means no deliberating and thinking. In the *I-Ching* it is said: 'Where evil thoughts are cleared, truth will be kept.' "[4]

Although Han Yü and Li Ao did not succeed in their attempts to revive Confucianism as a powerful rival of Buddhism, they did pave the way for the first attempt to provide a theoretical basis for Confucianism by Chou Tun-i.

By bringing together and reinterpreting concepts from a variety of philosophies, Chou Tun-i managed to construct a metaphysical basis broad enough for all existence. The notions of *yin* and *yang*, as negative and positive concepts of reality respectively, were familiar to Chou Tun-i. The idea that these two principles were not absolutely first was also familiar to him, for the Taoists had argued that *Tao* was prior to all things, and was the source of being and non-being, or *yang* and *yin*. The difficulty with the Taoist notion, however, was that *Tao* itself was regarded as non-being, and therefore the whole philosophy tended to have a negative character. But if the source of the principles of *yin* and *yang* were positive instead of negative it could be a basis for a philosophical explanation which could emphasize the ultimacy of the particular, while at the same time having a principle for explaining the particular. This is precisely what Chou Tun-i achieved by regarding the Great Ultimate (*T'ai-chi*) as the source of all things, productive of *yin* and *yang*. In turn, the interactions between *yin* and *yang* produce the Five Agencies of Water, Fire, Wood, Metal, and Earth. By further interaction, all of the rest of reality is produced.

Describing the production of *yin* and *yang* from the Great Ultimate, Chou Tun-i says, "The Great Ultimate through movement generates *yang*. When its activity reaches its limit, it becomes tranquil. Through tranquillity the Great Ultimate generates *yin*."[5] His explanation of how the *yin* and the *yang* are produced from the Great Ultimate leans heavily on the Taoist notion of "reversal as the movement of the *Tao*." According to the Taoists, reality is the manifestation of the reversing of *Tao*, as it goes from one extreme back to the other. Thus, he goes on to say, "When tranquillity reaches its limit, activity begins. So movement and tranquillity alternate and become the root of each other, giving rise to the distinction of *yin* and *yang*, and the two modes are thus established" (p. 463).

Having thus provided a basis for the principles of *yin* and *yang* in the

[4] *Ibid.*, p. 110.
[5] As translated by Wing-tsit Chan in *A Source Book in Chinese Philosophy* (Princeton: Princeton University Press, 1963), p. 463. Hereafter, references to this work will be cited in the text, by page number.

Great Ultimate, Chou Tun-i explains that through the interaction of these two principles and their resulting mutual transformation the powers or principles of particular things came to be produced. He says, "By the transformation of *yang* and its union with *yin*, the Five Agencies of Water, Fire, Wood, Metal, and Earth arise" (p. 463). These Five Agencies are taken to be the material principles of things. For example, as principle of direction, Wood is east; as principle of the seasons, Wood is spring; as principle of the body, it is liver; and as principle of color, it is blue. Because these Five Agencies are not conceived of as things, but as principles, they can be considered to be the common basis of all things.

Given the Great Ultimate, the principles of *yin* and *yang*, and the principles of the material agencies of the universe, it remains to explain how these can act on the nonexistent to bring it into existence. Chou Tun-i explains this as follows:

> When the reality of the non-ultimate [non-existent] and the essence of *yin*, *yang*, and the Five Agents come into mysterious union, integration ensues. *Ch'ien* (heaven) constitutes the male element, and *K'un* (earth) constitutes the female element. The interaction of these two material forces engenders and transforms the myriad things. The myriad things produce and reproduce, resulting in unending transformation. (p. 463)

The model for production is the symbolic male and the symbolic female, for male and female are readily understood as principles which by their union bring into existence what was previously nonexistent. The union between the nonexistent and the principles of *yin* and *yang* and the Five Agencies is said to be mysterious, for it is not clear how what exists can be related to what does not exist. Yet if some relation were not possible how could the nonexistent be brought into existence? The particular things that are brought into existence through this mysterious union possess their own modes for reproduction, and consequently there is the ceaseless productive activity of things.

In this part of his explanation of the Great Ultimate, Chou Tun-i has managed to give a metaphysical picture of the origin of things, tracing them to the Great Ultimate. To complete his explanation he needs to show how human beings fit into this picture. This he does in the following words:

> It is man alone who receives (the material forces) in their highest excellence, and therefore he is most intelligent. His physical form appears, and his spirit develops consciousness. The five moral principles of his nature (humanity or

jen, righteousness, propriety, wisdom and faithfulness) are aroused by, and react to, the external world and engage in activity; good and evil are distinguished; and human affairs take place. (p. 463)

The point of this description of the place of humanity in the total order of the universe is that the principle of the Sage, or perfect person, is one with the principle of the Great Ultimate, and therefore human beings, in their perfection, form a harmony with the universe. The beginnings of sagehood are received from the Great Ultimate, just as are the beginnings of everything else that exists. In human beings these beginnings are the moral principles of humanity (*jen*), righteousness, propriety, wisdom, and faithfulness. To become a Sage and be in harmony with the universe one must be true to these moral principles. This is what Chou Tun-i means when he says that *Ch'eng* is the foundation of the Sage, for *Ch'eng* (faithfulness, or sincerity) means being true to one's nature.

In this way the moral principles advocated by Confucius are put on a metaphysical foundation by Chou Tun-i. The reason a person must act in accord with the fundamental moral principles is that these constitute one's fundamental nature as produced by the Great Ultimate.

Philosophy of Principle:
The Ch'eng Brothers

Although Neo-Confucianism received its foundation from Chou Tun-i, it was two brothers, Ch'eng Hao (1032–1085) and Ch'eng I (1033–1107), who gave Neo-Confucianism its enduring structure. This they accomplished by making principle (*li*) the basis for their philosophy. Building upon the work of Chou Tun-i, who had been their teacher for one year, the Ch'eng brothers replaced the concept of the Great Ultimate—which impressed them as being too abstract and excessively Taoistic—with principle.

The main philosophical reason for the substitution was to put the perfection of human nature on a secure basis. Chou Tun-i was concerned primarily with a metaphysics of reality, and found in the concept of the Great Ultimate the key to the overarching unity of things. The Great Ultimate was too abstract, however, to provide a foundation for a practical philosophy of morality, the chief concern of Ch'eng Hao and Ch'eng I.

The Ch'eng brothers could concentrate almost exclusively upon the philosophy of human action because Chou Tun-i had already provided an explanation for the metaphysical unity of reality. Concentrating on explaining how human nature could be perfected so that every person could become a sage, and so that all persons could live harmoniously together, the Ch'eng brothers realized the need to have a first principle that is operative in every thing, person, and action. This principle must be more than simply a source from which everything proceeds. It must also function as the law of being inherent in every being, giving it existence and directing its function.

Because the principle from which all things originate is the same as the principle inherent in particular things (the difference being only one of manifestation or embodiment), all things form a unity with respect to principle. When principle is realized and exhibited in all actions, the perfect harmony will be achieved. Ch'eng I says, "That which is inherent in things is principle," and:

> Principle in the world is one. Although there are many roads in the world, the destination is the same, and although there are a hundred deliberations, the result is one. Although things involve many manifestations and events go through infinite variation, when they are united by the one, there cannot be any contradiction. (p. 571)

Ch'eng Hao, discussing principle as the unifying factor in reality, says, "The reason why it is said that all things form one body is that all have this principle, simply because they all have come from it" (p. 533). He also says, "There is only one principle in the world" (p. 534).

These remarks by the Ch'eng brothers reveal that they regarded principle both as a source of things and as the directive force within things. That is, although principle is regarded as one, the source of all, it is also regarded as many, for it is inherent in all of the many things that have proceeded from the source. How can principle be both one and many? To answer this question it is necessary to understand both the concept of principle generally, and the specific concept of principle that the Ch'eng brothers used.

According to the Ch'eng brothers, for anything to be produced it is necessary that there be both material force (*ch'i*) and principle (*li*). Material force is the dynamic "stuff" of which things are composed, a kind of primordial matter-energy. Principle is the organization of material force that shapes it into specific things, giving them their unique form and function. It is obvious that different things are different; apples are not trees and trees are not people. To what is the difference due? The Ch'engs' answer is that it is due to form and function. Apples do not function or behave the way trees or people do. They do not have the same colors, odors, sounds, flavors, etc. The reason they appear different in color, odor, sound, taste, and shape is because of their different principles. If this is the case, it is clear that the general concept of principle is that of *the reason why something is just what it is rather than something else.* Since there are differences between things, and since these differences can be explained, it follows that there are reasons for the differences, and reasons are possible because things are distinguished according to their principles. That is, in the last analysis, the reasons for distinguishing between any two things consist in identifying the principles of those things; the reasons reveal the principles.

The Ch'eng brothers extended this notion of principle to the totality of what exists. Everything that exists—heaven and earth and "the ten thousand things"—exists due to principle. That is, there is a reason for the existence of things. Furthermore, this principle of the universe is not really different from the principle in any particular thing, for the particular thing exists only as a manifestation of the supreme principle. Things are distinguished according to the *embodiment* of principle, not according to principle as such. What makes a particular thing what it is, is the principle embodied and manifested in a certain way in material force.

It would appear, therefore, that principle in the philosophy of the Ch'eng brothers referred to the reason, or law, operating within things which gives the universe its order. The importance, therefore, of making principle the basis of their philosophy is that it provided them with an ordered universe. Thus, the order in society that issues from the ordering and rectification of the individual was held to have a foundation in the very structure of the universe. This concept gave to Neo-Confucianism the metaphysical basis for its social philosophy that it had been lacking.

With a general understanding of the concept of principle, and the function it served in the philosophy of the Ch'eng brothers, it is possible to turn to the writing of Ch'eng Hao and Ch'eng I for a more detailed analysis of principle, and the application of principle to practical human affairs.

Once someone asked Ch'eng I if in investigating things in order to gain understanding which would allow one to become a Sage, a person should be concerned with internal things, such as feelings and thoughts, or with external things, such as natural happenings. He replied, "It does not matter. All that is before our eyes is nothing but things, and all things have their principles. For example, from that by which fire is hot or water is cold to the relations between ruler and minister, and father and son, are all principle" (p. 568).

This makes clear that the principle of a thing is regarded as the source of that thing's essential activity, for the essential activity of fire is to produce heat, and that which makes fire hot is principle. But it is also clear that it is not the multiplicity of detail that is to be investigated, but only the principles operating through the detailed manifestations of things. Thus, in answer to the question, "If one investigates only one thing, does he understand only one thing or does he understand the various principles?" the answer is, "We must seek to understand all. However, even Yen Tzu [a wise man referred to in the *Analects* of Confucius] could only understand ten points when he heard one. When one finally understands principle, even millions of things can be understood" (pp. 568–69).

Obviously, millions of things in their details could not be understood, so the meaning is that millions of things could be understood in terms of their basic principle. For example, when the correct relation between father and son is understood the relations between fathers and sons in millions of particular cases are understood. When once the love a mother has for a newborn child is understood, then the love of millions of mothers for their newborn is understood even without investigating the particular cases. The reason is that one knows the principle involved. This is why Ch'eng I says, "All things under heaven can be understood in the light of their principle. As there are things, there must be specific principles" (p. 563).

On another occasion he said, "A thing is an event. If the principles underlying the event are investigated to the utmost, then all principles will be understood" (p. 552). It would appear, therefore, that the principles of specific things, or specific kinds of things—*qua* principle—are the same, although with respect to their embodiment and manifestation in material force they differ. For example, the principle of a dog is different than the principle of a person. If this were not the case one could not distinguish between the two. But this difference is due to the embodiment of principle in the particularizing material force, and does not proceed from the nature of principle as such. By analogy, in comparing pieces of china one might notice that cups differ from saucers. It might be suggested that this is due to their different principles. But both cup and saucer are the same insofar as they are constituted by the kind of stuff called bone. It must be admitted that the bone embodied in the cup and the saucer is not different in the two cases. Likewise, it could be said that the great principle participating in the ten thousand things is not different in each case, though the embodiment is different.

The questions that arise from this analysis are: (1) What is the nature of the principle that is responsible for the substance and the function of the universe? (2) How is the principle of the universe related to human beings? and (3) Is mind different from this principle, or one with it? The answers to these questions are revealed in the practical philosophy advocated by the Ch'engs.

According to Ch'eng Hao, "The student must first of all understand the nature of *jen*. The man of *jen* forms one body with all things without any differentiation. Rightness, propriety, wisdom, and faithfulness are all (expressions) of *jen*" (p. 523). The reason the student must first understand *jen* is that *jen* is principle. In other words, the nature of principle in humans is *jen*. But since principle is the same in nature as it is in humans, the cultivation of *jen* is at the same time the establishing of a unity with all things. As Ch'eng Hao points out, "There is no difference between Nature and man" (p. 538). Thus, to know *jen* is to know principle, and to know principle is to know (in a way) all things and to be in harmony ("form one body") with all things.

Ch'eng I points out that knowing *jen* is not a matter of having information about it, but of having experienced this principle. He explained this point as follows:

> True knowledge and ordinary knowledge are different. I once saw a farmer who had been wounded by a tiger. When someone said that the tiger was hurting people, everyone was startled. But in his facial expression the farmer reacted differently from the rest. Even a young boy knows that tigers can hurt people, but his is not true knowledge. It is true knowledge only when it is like the farmer's. Therefore when men know evil and still do it, this also is not true knowledge. If it were, they would surely not do it. (p. 551)

So, when Ch'eng Hao says that the student must first of all understand *jen*, he is really saying that he must first of all cultivate his own humanity, living according to the principle of *jen*. This, of course, is the most important and most difficult of all tasks, for it is the task of becoming a Sage.

Ch'eng I notes that in the school of Confucius there were three thousand pupils, but only one—Yen Tzu—was praised as loving to learn. The reason Yen Tzu was singled out is that he alone concentrated wholeheartedly on learning the way of becoming a Sage. Becoming a Sage is the highest goal, for the Sage represents the perfect person, and in a philosophy where the reality of the person is regarded as the highest reality, the perfection of a person represents perfection of the ultimate reality.

But is it possible for a person to learn to become a Sage? Ch'eng I answers this question in the affirmative.

> From the essence of life accumulated in Heaven and Earth, man receives the Five Agents (Water, Fire, Wood, Metal, and Earth) in their highest excel-

lence. His original nature is pure and tranquil. Before it is aroused, the five moral principles of his nature called humanity, righteousness, propriety, wisdom, and faithfulness, are complete. As his physical form appears, it comes into contact with external things and is aroused from within. As it is aroused from within, the seven feelings, called pleasure, anger, sorrow, joy, love, hate, and desire, ensue. As feeling becomes strong and increasingly reckless, his nature becomes damaged. (p. 548)

Having thus postulated the original goodness and purity of man and having attributed the evil in man to a disturbance of this original goodness due to uncontrolled feelings, it is possible to suggest that one can learn to become a Sage by learning to control the feelings and thereby return to the original principle in its purity. Accordingly, Ch'eng I said, "The way to learn is none other than rectifying one's mind and nourishing one's nature. When one abides by the mean and correctness and becomes sincere, he is a Sage" (p. 548).

These statements reveal that for the Ch'eng brothers principle is the inner law of a thing's nature which is received from the inner law of the universe. Human beings also receive the law of their being from the inner law of the universe, and therefore are in union with the universe with respect to principle. Since mind refers to the original essence of humanity, it turns out that mind is identical with principle. To be human is to be moral, and since morality issues from *jen*, it follows that human nature is *jen*. Since this is the original principle of our being, to realize perfection, we must be true to this principle (practice *ch'eng*, or sincerity) and cultivate it. For this the virtues of propriety, wisdom, and righteousness are also needed.

Chu Hsi

The problem of how *jen* (humanity) can be cultivated and perfected is the central problem for all Neo-Confucianists. The chief obstacle to be overcome in solving this problem is that of the relation between good and evil. Chu Hsi's importance in the Chinese mind (he is considered to be in the same league with Confucius and Mencius) is due primarily to his ability to reinterpret and synthesize the philosophies of earlier Neo-Confucian thinkers, constructing a complete systematic philosophy in which he reconciled the presence of evil with the basic goodness of human nature. This he was able to do along the lines suggested by Confucius and Mencius by incorporating the metaphysical philosophies of earlier Neo-Confucian philosophers, enabling him to achieve a systematic completeness that Confucius and Mencius lacked, while providing a more detailed practical philosophy than his Neo-Confucian predecessors had managed.

For both Confucianists and Neo-Confucianists the central concern of philosophy was the cultivation of *jen*, rectification of the basic human relationships, and development of the constant virtues. The five basic relations between persons are those between (1) ruler and subject, (2) father and son, (3) husband and wife, (4) elder and younger children, and (5) friends. The constant virtues are righteousness, propriety, sincerity, and wisdom. The three activities of philosophy, cultivation, rectification, and development, are all the same essentially, for when the relations are rectified and the virtues developed, *jen* will be cultivated. And when *jen* is cultivated, the virtues will be developed and the relations will be rectified. And when these three are accomplished, evil will be removed and peace and goodness will reign supreme in the world.

The chief difficulty this philosophy encountered was that of explaining the sources of good and evil and the relations between them. The difficulty was felt already prior to Mencius, who attempted to resolve the problem by claiming that human nature is essentially good, but is corrupted by society and culture. Hsun Tzu, on the other hand, tried to resolve the problem by arguing that human nature is essentially evil, but through education and culture this evil can be rooted out and replaced with goodness. Neither of these theories proved satisfactory, however, for if human nature is essentially good, as Mencius would have it, then how can society and culture, which proceed from human beings, be evil and corrupting? On the other hand, if human nature is essentially evil, as Hsun Tzu would have it, how can what proceeds from human nature—in the form of culture and education—be good?

During the centuries following the Mencius–Hsun Tzu controversy it was generally agreed by Confucianists that human nature is basically good, but no satisfactory theoretical support for this position was worked out. Han Yu, a pioneering figure in the Neo-Confucian movement, suggested that human nature was of three kinds, good, bad, and good and bad mixed. But there was no satisfactory explanation of how human nature could be all three simultaneously. Consequently, the need for a philosophical theory of the nature of good and evil continued to be keenly felt by the Neo-Confucianists, for without it their emphasis on the removal of evil by the cultivation of *jen* would be unsupported.

Chang Tsai made a significant step forward when he distinguished between essential human nature and physical nature. But since he failed to establish a satisfactory relationship between the two his theory was deficient. The Ch'eng brothers also made an important contribution to the problem with their theory that principle and human nature were identical. But it was left for Chu Hsi to show how basic human nature was identical with the supreme principle of the universe, and that it was therefore of the nature of pure goodness, while secondary human nature, created by the association of principle with material stuff (*ch'i*) was impure and the source of evil. According to this explanation the source of goodness was basic human nature. But a person is a concrete being with body and feelings, as well as mind. It is the embodiment of human nature that gives rise to evil, for from the feelings come those passions that obscure the original goodness, that deviate from *jen*, the supreme principle of humanity.

Distinguishing between principle in itself and principle as embodied in concrete things, Chu Hsi says: "What exists before physical form is the one principle harmonious and undifferentiated, and is invariably good. What exists after physical form, however, is confused and mixed, and good and evil are thereby differentiated" (p. 597). This statement is the key to Chu Hsi's solution to the problem of how the presence of evil can be reconciled with goodness. The distinction he makes is between the goodness of principle and the evil-producing material stuff of which particular things are composed. In humans, as in all things, principle combines with material stuff, and therefore goodness is mixed with evil. But fundamental human nature is identical with principle, which is of the nature of *jen*; the material stuff constitutes a secondary nature. Since *jen* is basic, the removal of evil depends upon the cultivation and development of *jen* over the secondary nature.

This distinction between basic and secondary natures on the basis of the distinction between principle and material stuff requires a general theory of the nature and source of things as an explanatory context. According to Chu Hsi, all things are the result of a combination of material stuff (*ch'i*) and principle (*li*). He says, "Man and things are all endowed with the principle of the universe as their nature, and receive the material force of the universe as their physical form . . ." (p. 620). That there is principle is obvious from the fact that things are what they are rather than something else. That people are different from dogs is due to different principles.

However, differences in principles are not merely differences in principles but also involve differences in matter. Nothing whatsoever is found that does not involve both principle and material stuff, and the manifestation of principle is regulated by the material stuff while at the same time principle determines the material stuff. When Chu Hsi was asked for evidence that there is principle in material force he replied, "For example, there is order in the complicated interfusion of the *yin* and *yang* and of the Five Agents. Principle is there. If material force does not consolidate and integrate, principle would have nothing to attach itself to" (p. 635).

In explanation of what principle and material stuff are, and how they are related Chu Hsi said:

> Throughout the universe there are both principle and material force. Principle refers to the Way, which exists before physical form [and is without it] and is the course from which all things are produced. Material force refers to material objects, which exist after physical form [and is with it]; it is the instrument by which things are produced. Therefore in the production of man and things, they must be endowed with principle before they have their nature, and they must be endowed with material force before they have physical form. (p. 636)

It would appear from this explanation that principle is prior to material stuff in two senses, for principle is the essential reason for the being of something, and principle is also the knowable characteristic of a thing. Thus principle is first in the order of being and in the order of knowledge. But despite this priority, it remains the case that nothing exists except through the combination of principle and material stuff.

Still, the things that exist have a source from which they receive their natures, and for Chu Hsi's explanation to be complete he must relate principle and material stuff—as the twin determinants of things—to their source. This he accomplishes by integrating Chou Tun-i's concept of the Great Ultimate into his system. His view is that "The Great Ultimate is nothing other than principle" (p. 638). In other words, principle is the ultimate source of all things. As such it gives a unity—a unity of principle—to the manifoldness of reality and serves to integrate all of reality into a harmonious whole. In Chu Hsi the Great Ultimate is regarded as "the principle of heaven and earth and the myriad things."

> With respect to the myriad things, there is the Great Ultimate in each and every one of them. Before heaven and earth existed, there was assuredly this principle. It is the principle that "through movement generates the *yang*." It is also this principle that "through tranquillity generates the *yin*." (p. 638)

And, of course, through the activity of *yin* and *yang* the Five Agents came about and by their power produced the ten thousand things that make up the concrete reality surrounding us. Thus, Chu Hsi has provided for a systematic explanation of the origination and nature of things through his discovery of principle and material stuff and the relation between them.

Applying this explanation to the problem of evil in human nature Chu Hsi said, "The Great Ultimate is simply the principle of the highest good. Each and every person has in him the Great Ultimate and each and every thing has in it the Great Ultimate" (p. 640). The importance of this view is connected with the priority of principle over material stuff. Because principle is more fundamental than material stuff, the goodness of human nature is basic.

Because humans possess the Great Ultimate it follows that *jen* is the basic nature of humanity. Chu Hsi shows this by pointing to the two essential relationships involved. First, after identifying mind with the basic nature of man, he says, "The principle of the mind is the Great Ultimate" (p. 628). Second, he says, "*Jen* is man's mind" (p. 594). These two statements together mean that the Great Ultimate is identical to *jen*. Chu Hsi supports this view in his treatise on *jen*:

In the production of man and things, they receive the mind of Heaven and Earth as their mind. Therefore, with reference to the character of the mind, although it embraces and penetrates all and leaves nothing to be desired, nevertheless, one word will cover all of it, namely, *jen* (humanity). (pp. 593–94)

Granted that *jen* is basic—"the principle originally inherent in man's mind"—the question of greatest importance is how to realize *jen* (p. 633). According to Chu Hsi's philosophy, there are two equally important practices essential to the realization of *jen*. On the one hand, since *jen* is already there as the basic nature, one must concentrate on preserving one's true nature. On the other hand, a person's nature is learned and realized through its function: understanding the function of anything depends upon empirical investigation to discover the nature of principle.

The mind embraces all principles and all principles are complete in this single entity, the mind. If one is not able to preserve the mind, he will be unable to investigate principle to the utmost. If he is unable to investigate principle to the utmost, he will be unable to exert his mind to the utmost. (p. 606)

The twin doctrines of preservation (of goodness) and investigation (of principle) rest upon the distinction between substance and function. Substance refers to what something is, and function refers to how something operates. The distinction itself goes back as far as Lao Tzu, who distinguished between *Tao* (the substance) and *te* (the function of *Tao*), but in Chu Hsi the distinction is applied to principle. Thus human basic nature, or principle—the character of mind—as substance is *jen*. But the function of the human mind is love. In other words, the function of humanity is love. Love, as the function of *jen*, comprises the other virtues and is the basis for the proper human relations. Chu Hsi puts the matter as follows:

> The moral qualities of the mind of Heaven and Earth are four: origination, flourish, advantages, and firmness. . . . Therefore in the mind of man there are also four moral qualities—namely *jen*, righteousness, propriety, and wisdom—and *jen* embraces them all. In their emanation and function, they constitute the feeling of love, respect, being right, and discrimination between being right and wrong—and the feeling of commiseration pervades them all. (p. 594)

The nature of something provides for its function, and its function expresses its nature. Therefore *jen* provides for the function of humanity, namely, acting in accord with the moral qualities, and functioning in accord with the moral qualities is the expression of *jen*.

> If we can truly practice love and preserve it, then we have in it the spring of all virtues and the root of all good deeds. This is why in the teachings of the Confucian school, the student is always urged to exert anxious and unceasing effort in the pursuit of *jen*. (p. 594)

This, then, is the foundation Chu Hsi provides for the practical philosophy of Neo-Confucianism which can be summed up in his own words as follows: "To be sincere, empty of self, courteous and calm is the foundation of the practice of love . . . To love others as we love ourselves is to perfect love."[6]

Wang Yang-ming

The distinction between principle and material force enabled Chu Hsi to recognize both the reality of the mind and the reality of things external to the mind. In philosophical terminology, he was rationalistic to the extent he

---

[6] As quoted by Clarence Burton Day in *The Philosophers of China* (New York: The Citadel Press, 1962), p. 209.

emphasized principle, but empiricistic to the extent that he emphasized the investigation of things. He was idealistic to the extent that he emphasized the Great Ultimate as both the basic nature of all things and the essence of mind, but he also insisted that without material force to embody principle there could be nothing.

After Chu Hsi, however, developments in the School of Principle through the work of Lu Hsiang-shan and his pupils led to the identification of principle with mind. Wang Yang-ming (1472–1529), the most brilliant representative of Neo-Confucian idealism, said "there are neither principles nor things outside the mind" (p. 673). This philosophy is quite sharply opposed to Chu Hsi's, for only when a distinction is made between what belongs to mind and what is outside of mind can the investigation of things be emphasized as the key to the cultivation of *jen*. Investigation of things is one of the two pillars upon which Chu Hsi's philosophy rests. The other pillar—preservation of the original mind—was perfectly acceptable to Wang Yang-ming, but it was not emphasized by Chu Hsi's followers.

Among the reasons for the ascendancy of Wang Yang-ming's idealism during the Ming dynasty (1368–1644), two stand out. First, from 1313 on, Chu Hsi's interpretation of the Confucian classics enjoyed the status of being the official state philosophy in China. In addition to discouraging other philosophies, this meant that the civil service examinations were based on his interpretations. As so often happens, the security attending such entrenchment led to the decline of Chu Hsi's philosophy. Without the need to establish itself against other strong systems of thought there came to be increasing attempts to consolidate and refine translations and definitions, and there was too little attention given to reexamination and rethinking of basic principles and arguments. Since Chu Hsi's interpretation of Confucianism had, as Wing-tsit Chan, the foremost Chinese scholar in America, points out, "degenerated into trifling with what Wang [Yang-ming] called 'fragmentary and isolated details and broken pieces'" (p. 654) it did not provide an adequate basis for assisting the people in forming a satisfactory philosophy of life. Consequently, there was a ready reception for a fresh and vigorous philosophy such as Wang Yang-ming proposed.

Second, following Chu Hsi's emphasis upon investigation of things, but slighting his emphasis on preserving the original mind of man, his followers got further and further away from the moral emphasis that was the distinguishing characteristic of Confucian thought. When Wang Yang-ming turned his attention almost exclusively to moral matters it was greeted as a welcome return to the central concern of philosophy.

Wang Yang-ming's philosophy is characterized by its preoccupation with moral values. It rests upon the principles of the all-inclusive character of the mind and the unity of knowledge and action. These two principles give rise to the doctrine of the extension of the innate knowledge of the good (*chih liang-chih*). These features of his philosophy are all reflected in the following statement:

> The learning of the great man consists entirely in getting rid of the obscuration of selfish desires in order by his own efforts to make manifest his clear character, so as to restore the condition of forming one body with Heaven, Earth, and the myriad things, a condition that is originally so, that is all. It is not that outside of the original substance something can be added. (p. 660)

There is here no appeal to the investigation of things as an essential part of learning or cultivating *jen*. Knowledge is not distinguished from action, for true knowledge is action that proceeds from the love that constitutes the basis of humanity. In Wang Yang-ming's words, "Knowledge is the beginning of action and action is the completion of knowledge. Learning to be a Sage involves only one effort. Knowledge and action should not be separated" (p. 674).

The basis for the unification of knowledge and action is Wang Yang-ming's emphasis on will or choice rather than reason or knowledge. Intellectual or discursive knowledge of the kind characteristic of the sciences can, of course, be separated from choice and morality. But practical knowledge of the value of things has no significance apart from the activity of choosing and acting. When doing is regarded as more fundamental than knowing, then the kind of knowledge required for making choices becomes more important than theoretical knowledge. Furthermore, a person's choices are revealed in the action taken and this shows the combinations of knowledge and action. This is why Wang Yang-ming can claim that the learning of the Sage consists in getting rid of selfishness and in manifesting good character. The general point involved here is that action is more basic than knowledge and all knowledge is for the sake of action. In the language of classical philosophy, this means that Will is higher than Reason.

Wang Yang-ming's philosophy is most clearly revealed in his interpretation of the *Great Learning (Ta Hsueh)*, a classical Confucian text that served as an inspiration to many of the Neo-Confucian philosophers. The text of the *Great Learning* consists in a statement and explanation of "three major chords" and "eight minor wires." The three major chords are (1) manisfestation of the clear character, (2) loving the people, and (3) abiding in the highest good. Asked about manifesting the clear character, Wang

Yang-ming replied, "The great man regards Heaven and Earth and the myriad things as one body. He regards the world as one family and the country as one person. As to those who make a cleavage between objects and distinguish between the self and others, they are small men" (p. 659).

The thinking behind this claim is that all things really form integral parts of one whole, just as the children and the mother and the father really are one family. In the family it is the bond of familial love that proceeds from human-ness of the individual person that creates the unity of one family. In the world it is the bond of great love proceeding from the *jen* of the universe that creates a unity. In the "great man" the *jen* of the universe is identified with the *jen* of the individual and there is a unity of all things ("forming one body").

When he was asked why the learning of the Sage consists in loving the people, Wang Yang-ming replied, "Manifesting the clear character consists in loving the people, and loving the people is the way to manifest the clear character. Therefore, only when I love my father, the fathers of others, and the fathers of all men can my humanity really form one body with my father, the fathers of others, and the fathers of all men" (p. 660). The explanation behind this is that by "clear character" is meant the original purity and goodness of basic human nature or mind.

According to Wang Yang-ming, this original goodness consists in love— a pervasive and universal love which both forms and proceeds from the basic principles of all things. When things are in accord with this love they are perfected. When people are in accord with this love they too are perfected. This can be seen in the fact that when the clear character of love is manifested then the constant virtues are perfected and the human relations are rectified. Thus, Wang Yang-ming goes on to say that when his humanity forms one body with the fathers of all men, then the clear character of filial piety will be manifested. And when his humanity forms one body with the brothers of all men, then the clear character of brotherly love will be manifested. And in sum,

> Everything from ruler, minister, husband, wife, and friends to mountains, rivers, spiritual beings, birds, animals, and plants should be truly loved in order to realize my humanity that forms one body with them, and then my clear character will be completely manifested, and I will really form one body with Heaven, Earth and the myriad things. (p. 661)

When he was asked why the learning of the Sage consists in abiding in the highest good, Wang Yang-ming replied,

The highest good is the ultimate principle of manifesting character and loving people. The nature endowed in us by Heaven is pure and perfect. The fact
that it is intelligent, clear, and not beclouded is evidence of the emanation
and revelation of the highest good. It is the original substance of the clear
character which is called innate knowledge of the good. (p. 661)

All things are present in *jen*, which is the basis of human nature. Therefore to realize perfection people must cultivate this basic nature. But
nothing external is required for this task, since this nature is pure and
perfect of itself. To know the good is to do the good, and knowledge of the
good is already contained in human basic nature as *jen*. Therefore, what is
required is the extension of this innate knowledge of the good into all
spheres of action. As Wang Yang-ming puts it, "This is what is meant by
'manifesting the clear character throughout the empire.' This is what is
meant by 'regulation of the family,' 'ordering the state,' and 'bringing peace
to the world.' This is what is meant by 'full development of one's nature'"
(p. 661).

Tai Chen

Neo-Confucian philosophy through Wang Yang-ming had emphasized the
principles of things over their material constitution and elevated the
"fundamental mind" over the feelings. In the seventeenth and eighteenth
centuries there was a reaction against this rationalism and idealism, and the
empirical came to be emphasized more and more, both in the studies of
human nature and in the studies of things. An objective study of things
characterized by detailed and analytical investigations of things came to be
regarded as the path to truth, and the feelings of persons exhibited in day-to-
day living came to be regarded as the real source of human actions. According to Tai Chen (1723–1777), generally accepted as the greatest of the
empiricistic Neo-Confucian philosophers, "A thing is an affair or event.
When we talk about an event, we do not go beyond daily affairs such as
drinking and eating. To neglect these and talk about principle is not what
the ancient sages and worthies meant by principle" (p. 713).

This remark clearly indicates the empiricist's impatience with metaphysical speculation and idealistic introspection. Tai Chen was concerned with
the principles that could be discovered empirically in things, feelings, and
actions; abstractions were useless. It is not the case that Tai Chen rejected
the concepts and principles of earlier philosophers of the Sung period, but

rather that he reinterpreted them in such a way that the concrete and particular were not overlooked. This, of course, gave a balance to Neo-Confucianism, bringing the metaphysics down to an empirically verifiable level. This was, by the same token, a paving of the way for the empirical sciences of physics and psychology which were to come later. In fact, much of Tai Chen's work is often regarded as scientific rather than philosophical because of his minute investigation of particular things.

The emphasis during this later period of Neo-Confucianism continued to be on human nature, however, which continued to be regarded as the source of morality. Consequently, the primary objects of investigation continued to be the actions of human beings, and the categories used in this investigation were primarily moral. This means that instead of classifying and investigating the relations between the components of external things, human actions and relations between persons were classified and investigated. When external things are investigated it is important, for example, to know what neutrons, protons, and electrons are, and how they are related to each other. But when morality is being investigated the virtues of humanity, righteousness, sincerity, propriety, and a wisdom must be known, and the relations between these virtues in terms of the principal relations between persons must be investigated.

Throughout the earlier Confucian tradition human beings as moral agents and society as a moral institution were regarded as the primary objects to be known. In the Neo-Confucian tradition there was an attempt to provide metaphysical support for this view that held morality to be the subject of ultimate concern. To Tai Chen it appeared that some of the Neo-Confucianists had allowed the metaphysics of morality to become the subject of primary importance. This he was concerned to rectify, for clearly the moral relations between persons and the moral virtues are of primary concern, and the metaphysics of morality is secondary.

REVIEW QUESTIONS

1. How did Chinese Buddhism and Taoism influence the development of Neo-Confucianism?
2. How did Chou Tun-i's concept of the Great Ultimate (*T'ai-chi*) provide a basis for Neo-Confucianism? In your answer, explain how this concept incorporated features of Taoist, *Yin-yang*, and Five Agencies thinking, and how it furthered the Confucian interest in morality.
3. What is the Ch'eng brothers' concept of principle? How does it differ from

Chou Tun-i's concept of the Great Ultimate? What does it mean to say "The man of *jen* forms one body with all things without any differentiation"?

4. What is Chu Hsi's solution to the problem of the relation between good and evil? Is his theory of the priority of principle (*li*) over material stuff (*ch'i*) sound? Does it support his distinction between basic and secondary human nature?

5. How does Wang Yang-ming explain "manifestation of the clear character," "loving the people," and "abiding in the highest good"?

FURTHER READING

Neo-Confucian Orthodoxy and the Learning of Mind-and-Heart, by William Theodore de Bary (New York: Columbia University Press, 1981), is the single best source for an in-depth study of Neo-Confucianism. The historical period emphasized is thirteenth and fourteenth century China, the formative period of Neo-Confucianism. The philosophical emphasis, as indicated in the title, is *hsin-hsueh*, "the learning of mind-and-heart." In explaining this deep and comprehensive moral vision, de Bary rethinks the whole issue of Neo-Confucianism Orthodoxy, correcting many early interpretations.

The Development of Neo-Confucian Thought, by Carsun Chang (New Haven: College and University Press, 1963), has long been the standard survey of Neo-Confucian philosophy. Although partially superseded by de Bary's *Neo-Confucian Orthodoxy and the Learning of Mind-and-Heart*, Chang's book remains a valuable source. It reveals the great influence of Buddhism on Confucian thought and shows the vitality and creative development of China's dominant philosophy over the last 2,500 years. The generous excerpts from Neo-Confucian thinkers allow the reader to encounter these philosophers on their own terms.

Instructions for Practical Living and Other Neo-Confucian Writings by Wang Yang-ming, translated, with notes, by Wing-tsit Chan (New York: Columbia University Press, 1963), contains the major writings of Wang in an excellent translation. The introduction and notes are extremely useful, enabling the reader to get to the heart of Wang Yang-ming's philosophy. *Instructions for Practical Living* brings out Wang's concern for everyday living and concrete action, giving us a sense of the persuasiveness of his dynamic idealism.

Self and Society in Ming Thought, by William Theodore de Bary and the Conference on Ming Thought (New York: Columbia University Press, 1970), provides an in-depth view of the intellectual temper of Ming times (1368–1644). The first half of the book contains essays devoted primarily to Neo-Confucian philosophy, including an outstanding essay by de Bary entitled "Individualism and Humanitarianism in Late Ming Thought." The remainder of the book helps us see Neo-Confucianism in its larger context, including the interaction between Taoist, Buddhist, and Confucian thought.

The Liberal Tradition in China, by William Theodore de Bary (New York: Columbia University Press, 1983), focuses on the lasting significance of Neo-Confucian thought, emphasizing its contemporary relevance. Uses and control of political power, education, moral cultivation, and humanitarian individualism are among the topics de Bary concentrates on in this splendid effort to provide an historical perspective from which to evaluate Chinese thought and practice of the last three decades.

Chinese Buddhism: Aspects of Interaction and Reinterpretation, by W. Pachow (Lanham, Md.: University Press of America, 1980), is a collection of essays on Chinese Buddhism from an historical perspective. They deal both with the interaction of Buddhism with Taoism and Confucianism, and with the reinterpretation of Indian Buddhism in China.

CHAPTER 21

Recent Chinese Thought

DURING THE LAST century and a half Chinese thought has been concerned with establishing an appropriate basis for modernization. The Opium War (1840–1842), in which the British decisively defeated China, marks a watershed in the history of Chinese thought. Invasion and conquest by Western countries during the early nineteenth century forced Chinese thinkers to reevaluate the very basis of their civilization and culture. What is wrong with our traditions, they asked, that allows these foreign powers to conquer and rule us with such ease? The answer was not at all clear. Some thought it was because the ancient traditions had become corrupt and needed to be restored. Others argued that the attitude of looking to the past for solutions to contemporary problems was itself the root of the problem. Some of these thinkers urged turning to the West, borrowing the modes of thought and practice that had enabled the West to achieve world ascendancy. For these thinkers, the crucial question was whether the science and technology of the West could be borrowed and grafted to traditional Chinese culture, retaining the substance of Chinese culture but enabling it to function in the modern world on par with the West, or whether a much broader program of westernization was required to make China a modern nation.

The debate over whether China's modernization should be based on its own traditions or whether it should be based on Western traditions stimulated a critical reassessment of traditional thought and opened the door to Western studies. In this chapter we will look at five representative thinkers who carried on this debate, influencing the shape and direction of China's twentieth-century development.

K'ang Yu-wei

K'ang Yu-wei is probably best known as leader of the Hundred Days' Reform of 1898. In 1895, after Japan defeated China in the first Sino-Japanese War, K'ang organized young intellectuals from eighteen provinces to protest the peace treaty with Japan. Urging the Emperor to engage in reform rather than acceding to Japanese demands, K'ang met with initial success, persuading the Emperor to issue a series of edicts calling for far-reaching reforms in 1898. Opposition to the reforms by the Empress Dowager led to their abandonment after some three months, however, and K'ang had to flee the country. When he returned, in 1912, he found himself playing the role of a political conservative, opposing the democratic policies of Sun Yat-sen. In 1918 he advocated adopting Confucianism as the state religion, and three years later took part in an unsuccessful attempt to restore the deposed Hsuan-t'ung emperor. Although his whole life was spent trying to put Confucian principles into action, he began as a revolutionary thinker, but eventually ended up trying to restore the old ways.

The basis for K'ang's reform efforts was provided by a philosophy of historical progress and a vision of humanity as bound together by a universal love, a basis shaped by his education in both traditional and Western thought. His early education focused on Confucianism, Buddhism, and Taoism. At about the age of twenty-two, however, he began reading Western authors, becoming interested in the ideas of progress, reform, and ideal societies, ideas that fueled his ambition to reform Chinese society and that led him to search for parallels in traditional Chinese thought. When the parallels could not be found, he invented them, as when he reinterpreted Tung Chung-shu's cyclical theory of the three ages as a progressive theory of social evolution, or when he presented Confucius as an evolutionary thinker interested only in transforming the past.

K'ang's theory of historical progress is presented in his commentary on Confucius, in which he claims not only that Confucius actually wrote the *Spring and Autumn Annals*, but that he did so in order to advance his own progressive or evolutionary view of history. Chinese scholars have traditionally regarded the *Annals* as the work of earlier historians. K'ang even goes so far as to suggest that Confucius made up the historical reforms attributed to the legendary Sages Yao and Shun of the third millennium, so that he would have precedents for his own reforms. Because Confucius lived in the First Age, the Age of Disorder, it was necessary for him to invent the precedents of the legendary reforms of the ancient sages to persuade the people to change. Only then could they enter on the way to the Second Age, the Age of Rising Peace, and eventually reach the Third Age, the Age of Great Peace. K'ang says,

> Confucius was born in the Age of Disorder. Now that communications have extended throughout the great earth and important changes have taken place in Europe and America, the world has entered upon the Age of Rising Peace. Later, when all groups through the great earth, far and near, big and small, are like one, when nations will cease to exist, when racial distinctions are no longer made, and when customs are unified, all will be one and the Age of Great Peace will have come. Confucius knew all this in advance.[1]

K'ang's view of Confucius as a reformer provided him with a model for his own ambition to reform Chinese society. His progressive view of history, attributed, as we have seen, to Confucius, inspired confidence in the eventual success of reform efforts. In addition, K'ang needed a philosophical view of human nature and society as a basis for reform. This he also found in Confucius, particularly in the Confucian view expressed by Mencius, that true humanity cannot bear the sufferings of others, and therefore acts to alleviate their suffering. The human sharing that constitutes the essence of love begins between parents and children, but because it is a universal feature of human nature, with careful nurture it can be extended to all people. Indeed, in the Age of Great Unity, this love will be extended to all creatures as a benevolent kindness.

Building on the principle that "the mind that cannot bear to see the suffering of others is humanity (jen)," K'ang goes on to say that "the word jen consists of one part meaning man and another part meaning many. It means that the way of men is to live together. It connotes attraction. It is the power of love. It is really electrical energy."[2] Seeking support for his vision of progressive humanization through reform and nurture, K'ang invokes the authority of Confucius, saying,

> Confucius instituted the scheme of Three Ages. In the Age of Disorder, humanity cannot be extended far and therefore people are merely affectionate to

---

[1] As translated by Wing-tsit Chan, in *A Source Book in Chinese Philosophy* (Princeton: Princeton University Press, 1963), p. 726.
[2] *Ibid.*, p. 735.

their parents. In the Age of Rising Peace, humanity is extended to one's kind and therefore people are humane to all people. In the Age of Great Peace, all creatures form a unity and therefore people feel love for all creatures as well.[3]

The Age of Great Peace is the inspiration for K'ang's vision of a utopian world, a world he calls the Age of Great Unity. Here divisions between classes of people, between nations, between races, and between the sexes will be overcome so that all human beings may experience the unity of a single family. Drawing upon Buddhist, Taoist, and Western, as well as Confucian thought, K'ang articulated the fullest utopian vision ever produced by a Chinese author. It was regarded as so radical that it was not published until 1936, eight years after K'ang's death. Even Mao Tse-tung found this vision of democratic communism attractive, although he criticized K'ang for failing to see the kind of revolutionary struggle needed to actually achieve such a society.[4]

Chang Tung-sun

In the last decade of the nineteenth century and the first three decades of the twentieth, Western philosophy became very popular in China. Famous philosophers like John Dewey and Bertrand Russell were invited to lecture. Others, like Bergson and Whitehead, became the focus of special journals and clubs. Most of the classical and modern philosophers were translated into Chinese, becoming the subject of intensive study. In the 1920s and 1930s it appeared that the philosophy departments in Chinese universities were likely to become branch offices of the large philosophy departments in Europe and America. Although this never happened—primarily because of the simultaneous revival of traditional thought in various reflective and self-critical forms on the one hand, and the influence of Marxist thought on the other—this surge of interest in the West has had a lasting impact on the development of modern China.

Chang Tung-sun (1886–1962), a largely self-educated philosopher, was one of the most influential interpreters of Western thought. Wing-tsit Chan says of him, "the one who has assimilated the most of Western thought, established the most comprehensive and well-coordinated system, and has

---

[3] *Ibid.*, pp. 734–35.
[4] See *Selected Works of Mao Tsetung*, vol. V (Peking: Foreign Language Press, 1977), pp. 329–32.

exerted the greatest influence among the Western-oriented Chinese philosophers, however, is indisputably Chang Tung-sun."[5]

Chung's influence was due partially to his wide reading and deep understanding of Western philosophers. He translated many Western texts into Chinese, including works of Plato, Kant, and Bergson. His theory of knowledge, though based largely on Kant, reflects also the influence of Russell, Dewey, and C. I. Lewis. More important, his philosophy goes beyond the dualisms of modern Western thought, insisting on the unity of knowledge and action and the unity of substance and function. This enabled him to overcome the Kantian problems arising from the opposition between knowing and willing and between the unknowable structure of things in themselves and the imposed structure of cognitive process. His many books work out the details of his unique synthesis of modern and traditional insights into the nature of the human mind and social processes, which he combined with his understanding of modern logic and epistemology.

Although Chang's early interest was primarily in metaphysics and theory of knowledge, as he matured he became more interested in society and culture. The combination of these interests led him to develop a theory of knowledge which stressed the role of social interests and feelings in the knowing process. This, in turn, brought him closer to Marxist philosophy—to which he had been strongly opposed in the mid 1930s. Indeed, his emphasis on concepts as products of social processes led him to see the necessity of a thoroughgoing social revolution in China. This, in turn, led him to move further to the left, as he joined first the Progressive Party, then the State Socialist Party, and, after the war, the Democratic League. In 1949 he became a member of the Central Committee of the People's Government.

According to Chang, people claim the truth of an idea when it meets their fundamental social needs. He suggests that people accepted the truth of God's existence for centuries because doing so gave them a sense of social unity, overcoming the forces of fragmentation inherent in their concrete social relations. As he says in his 1946 book, *Knowledge and Culture*, "For when society needs a centripetal force stronger than the centrifugal force, some theory or idea must arise to hold the people together so that they feel in their own minds that it is the truth. . . ."[6] On the other hand, when people feel a need for change or revolution greater than their need for

[5] Wing-tsit Chan, *A Source Book in Chinese Philosophy*, p. 744.
[6] *Ibid.*, pp. 749–50.

unity or cohesiveness, they will emphasize the truth of freedom or individuality or the class nature of society, ideas that inherently reflect social conflict. Thus, according to Chang, the most profound truths accepted by a people do not reflect the physical or metaphysical nature of reality, but only their own most strongly felt social needs. As he says,

> What we have been talking about does not concern society as such but to show how social conditions are reflected in ideas so readers may realize that while ideas seem on the surface to be independent and represent laws of logic or the structure of the universe that we talk about, actually they are secretly controlled by social needs. . . .[7]

Hsiung Shih-li

Hsiung Shih-li (1885–1968) reflects the Chinese effort to find a basis for modernization in traditional thought. His philosophy may be broadly characterized as Neo-Confucian, a creative interpretation of the idealist wing of Neo-Confucian thought, very much in the spirit of Wang Yang-ming. But it also draws heavily upon the *Book of Changes*, and the Buddhist Consciousness-Only school. Modern scholars tend to regard him as the most original Neo-Confucian philosopher of recent times, and his work has had considerable influence on contemporary studies in traditional thought.

Hsiung, like most young intellectuals in China at the turn of the century, began his studies with a strong interest in Western science and politics, seeking a way to modernize China as quickly as possible. For a number of reasons, including his conviction that the new China must be based on traditional culture if it was to endure, he soon turned his attention to more traditional studies. Initially he was interested in Buddhism, and studied the philosophy of Consciousness-Only, tracing it back to its Indian roots. Eventually he found the dualisms inherent in the Indian Buddhist schools uncongenial to his sense of the unity of humanity and nature. The *Book of Changes*, which not only emphasized the deep unity of existence, but also the process nature of reality, now became the focus of his study.

Subsequently, as he turned his attention to the philosophy of humanity (*jen*) in Wang Yang-ming, he found that the concept of "Original Mind" or "Buddha Nature of all Things" in Buddhism provided a solid metaphysical basis for the universal human nature stressed by Wang. The emphasis on

---

[7] *Ibid.*, p. 750.

eternal and constant transformation stressed in the *Book of Changes* enabled him to see human nature in terms of process rather than substance, providing a basis for a dialectic of change leading to greater and greater perfection and harmony. In this way Hsiung was able to develop a philosophical basis for a modern and progressive China based on traditional thought which he was able to present as an alternative to the Marxist-Leninist thought stressed by Mao Tse-tung.

As Professor of Philosophy at Peking University, Hsiung first worked out the philosophy circulated privately in 1932 and published in 1944 as *The New Doctrine of Consciousness-Only*. In this work he developed three central and interrelated ideas. First, the very nature of existence, which Hsiung calls "original substance," is that of constant change; unceasing production and reproduction characterizes reality at its very core. Second, the dynamic of change is provided by what he calls the "opening" and "closing" of the perpetually changing primordial reality. "Opening" is the tendency of reality to maintain and preserve itself. This tendency is observable in people's efforts to be their own masters, free of external domination. "Closing" is the tendency to integration and manifestation found in specific things. Third, the primordial reality and its manifestations, substance and function, are not actually separate. Ultimately they are simply different aspects of the same process, with opening and closing seen as simply different phases of the same process.

Concerning the first idea, Hsiung says, "Thus if we say that original substance is that which can transform, or call it perpetual transformation, we must realize that perpetual transformation is formless and is subtle in its movement. This movement is continuous without cease."[8] He is concerned here to make clear that ultimate reality or original substance is not a particular thing, but the inner dynamic inherent in all things, that in virtue of which all things change. He emphasizes this again when he says, "We must realize that original substance has neither physical form nor character, is not physically obstructed by anything, is absolute, whole, pure, strong, and vigorous."[9]

In explaining the concept of closing, the tendency of change to direct itself toward the production of something new, to consolidate beginnings into an integrated act of being, Hsiung continues,

However, in the functioning of the original substance to become many manifestations, it is inevitable that there is what we called closing. This closing

[8] *Ibid.*, p. 765.
[9] *Ibid.*, p. 766.

possesses a tendency to become physical forms and concrete stuff. In other words, through the processes of closing individual concrete things obtain their physical form. As perpetual transformation manifests itself as a tendency to close, it almost has to be completely materialized as if it were not going to preserve its own nature.[10]

Closing, however, is simply one aspect of the larger process of transformation. When this whole process is analytically broken down, the closing force can be seen more clearly. But this analysis also reveals an opposing kind of force, which works to open reality to its own primordial nature. Thus Hsiung goes on to say,

However, as the tendency to close arises, there is another tendency arising simultaneously. It rises with perpetual transformation as the basis. It is firm, self-sufficient, and would not change itself to a process of closing. That is to say, this tendency operates in the midst of closing but is its own master, thus showing its absolute firmness, and causes the process of closing to follow its own operations. This tendency—strong, vigorous and not materialized—is called opening. . . .[11]

Opening and closing, like *yin* and *yang* in traditional thought, represent the dynamic function of reality, the active polarities of ceaseless transformation. These tendencies account for the simultaneous coming into existence and passing out of existence that characterizes the life of everything that exists. When life is harmonized with the transforming activity of opening and closing it is whole and strong; otherwise it is fragmented and weak. Thus, to find the way of human and social progress it is necessary to understand the processes of opening and closing that control the functioning of all existence.

After the war, with the establishment of the People's Republic, Hsiung retired in Shanghai, where he continued to think and write for almost two decades. Here he produced his most clearly Neo-Confucian work, published in 1956 as *An Inquiry on Confucianism*, and also the *Development of the Philosophy of Change* (*Ch'ien-k'-un-yen*), published in 1961, a work he regarded as superseding *The New Doctrine of Consciousness-Only*.

In his *Inquiry Into Confucianism* Hsiung stresses the unity of substance and function. Explaining that substance means what is there originally, the ultimate reality, and that function means the universal operation of this

[10] *Ibid.*
[11] *Ibid.*

ultimate reality, Hsiung goes on to explain how they are identical, yet different. He offers the analogy of the water and waves making up the ocean, pointing out that the water is one, but the waves are many. The waves, comparable to the function of the water, are distinguishable from each other and from the deeper stillness of the ocean. Yet all are just water, the original substance. Applying the analogy, he says,

> Therefore we say that the universal operation of the original substance is its great functioning. By functioning is meant putting substance into functioning, and by substance is meant the true character of function. Therefore substance and function are basically one. However, although they are one, yet in the final analysis they cannot but be different, for in universal operation there are physical forms which are fathomable, whereas the original substance of the universal operation has no physical form, is most hidden and subtle, and is difficult to know.[12]

In Part II of this work Hsiung constructs a dialogue to clarify his position on the unity of substance and function. The questioner, agreeing that the central teaching of the *Book of Changes* is that substance is at the same time function, and function is at the same time substance, goes on to ask: Does this mean that the "ten thousand things" (all the concrete existences) are simply the functioning of original substance, or does it mean they are the products of this functioning? Hsiung answers, ". . . The ten thousand things and the great functioning cannot be separated." He goes on to say that if production means something new and different coming into existence (as when a mother produces a son), then the ten thousand things cannot be thought of as products, for they are not separate from the great functioning of the original substance. Insisting that things and function are not ultimately different, he continues, "Put differently, the concrete self-nature of the ten thousand things consists in the great functioning which operates unceasingly and in a very lively and dynamic manner. Can they and the great functioning be said to be two?"[13]

Now the questioner objects, claiming that by this doctrine Hsiung has ruled out the distinctness of concrete things; ultimately everything is the same, the great functioning of the original substance. He says, "If the ten thousand things and the great functioning are one, then the ten thousand things will lose their own selves. Why is this the case? The reason is that if

[12] *Ibid.*, p. 769.
[13] *Ibid.*, p. 771.

the ten thousand things are merely traces of transformations, how can they possess evidently independent selves?"[14]

Hsiung replies strongly, insisting that the continuously changing processes we call the ten thousand things are not outside of or separate from the great function of the original substance, but are constitutive of the universal functioning of substance. That is, the great functioning is not something in addition to the functioning of concrete things. Coming back to the analogy of ocean waves and water, he says,

> The many waves are also traces and forms. Do you think that the water is outside the waves? Or take, for example, a torrent bursting violently, with thousands and thousands of white drops lashing up and down. These white drops are also traces and forms. Do you think that they are outside the torrent? Please think it over. The ten thousand things manifest themselves and seem to be individual objects, but really their self-nature consists in the great functioning operating without cease.[15]

Applying this theory of change which insists on the identity of substance and function to concrete human and social affairs, Hsiung advocates a communally organized society. He argues that the implication of the Confucian emphasis on developing "sageliness within and kingliness without" is to overcome the self-centeredness that sets individuals and groups at odds with each other, and to establish the practice of treating all equally, using one's own developed humanity as a guide. The Confucian principle "Treat all fathers as one's own father and treat all sons as one's own son," if put into practice, would eliminate ruling and servile classes, replacing them with a humanitarian based communalism. Because of Hsiung's insistence on principle (*li*), however, the dialectic underlying this communalism is different from the Marxist materialistic dialectic. Hsiung's social philosophy, like that of Confucius and Wang Yang-ming, is solidly rooted in humanity (*jen*). The ultimate key to social progress and human development is not economic transformation, but moral development. Only with the development of one's inner humanity and its outer expression can effective economic and political transformation take place.

[14] *Ibid.*
[15] *Ibid.*, p. 772.

Fung Yu-lan

Fung Yu-lan (1895–) is well known in the West for his classic two-volume *History of Chinese Philosophy* and *The Spirit of Chinese Philosophy*. He is an international figure, graduated from Peking and Columbia universities, who has taught at the universities of Hawaii and Pennsylvania. After the establishment of the People's Republic, Fung, a professor at Peking University, participated enthusiastically in Maoist efforts at political and ideological reform, engaging in self-criticism to root out his own bourgeois ideas and to set a good example to other Chinese intellectuals. Eventually he became an ardent supporter of Mao Tse-tung thought and China's leading critic of Confucius during the anti-Confucian campaign during the early 1970s. At this time he was an intellectual consultant to Mao's wife, Chiang Ch'ing, and her friends, the group that later came to be called the "gang of four." Shortly after Mao's death in 1976, Chiang and her group fell from power and were publicly disgraced, a disgrace in which Fung shared, bringing to a humiliating close a brilliant philosophical career.

Fung's philosophical development can be traced through a series of stages, marking his journey from traditional to radical Maoist thought. During the first stage, which ended with his return to China after getting his Ph.D. from Columbia in 1923, Fung was sympathetic to the traditional Confucian philosophy and engaged in serious studies of pragmatism in an effort to find a modern philosophical formulation of the insights and wisdom of the Confucian tradition.

The fruition of this first stage is found in his early writings, which mark the second stage. Here he attempted to mediate the controversy between those who wanted to reject the tradition in favor of modern science and those who argued that a traditional metaphysical basis was required for the adoption of Western science and technology. Fung's approach was to apply the pragmatic philosophy he had studied at Columbia to this issue, arguing that both scientific truth and human morality are derived from, and tested by action. His book, *Philosophy of Life*, is the expression of this second stage of his development, where he is developing a comparative East-West perspective on philosophy.

In his third stage Fung turned to a global study of Chinese philosophy, producing the widely acclaimed two-volume *History of Chinese Philosophy*. While this work is a mainly traditionalist interpretation of Chinese philosophy, it is modern insofar as it attempts to locate the social influences on the development of metaphysical ideas. Although Fung was to later reject this work because it did not adequately reflect the influence of material conditions on traditional thought, it is a work of solid scholarship which continues to be influential.

The fourth stage of Fung's development is represented by a highly original philosophical system set out in a series of six books, of which *The New Rational Philosophy* (*Hsin li-hsueh*) is central. This system is the most original and most discussed philosophical work of this century, according to Professor Wing-tsit Chan.[16]

Taking the philosophy of the Ch'eng brothers and Chu Hsi as his basis, Fung reconstructs Neo-Confucian philosophy in a fundamental and sweeping way. Distinguishing sharply between philosophy and science, he construes philosophical concepts as purely logical or formal, having no specific content or material existence. Science, on the other hand, deals with actual existence, studying the structures embodied in matter. Because there are things, there are both principles or formal structures and matter or specific contents. Philosophy is concerned with principles or the logical nature of things, and science is concerned with matter or the actual material existence of things. In this way philosophy provides the basis for science, but science is required to provide knowledge of the actual world.

To explain the movement by which principle and material force interact Fung brings in the concept of *Tao*. As the dynamic way of all things, *Tao* is the very process by which principle is embodied in actual things through its interaction with material force. Fung uses this concept to explain the universe as process, as incessant change and continuous renewal. Inspired by the *Book of Changes* and modern process philosophy, Fung sees becoming rather than being as the fundamental nature of reality.

But Fung does not ignore being. Recognizing that the unceasing movement of the Tao is responsible for the continuous production and reproduction of things, he employs the concept of the Great Whole to refer to the totality of things. But this totality is neither static nor a mere plurality. It is a dynamic interpenetration of things wherein all things are identical. Here Fung incorporates the Buddhist insight that because of the mutual interdependency of all things the whole universe is present in each particular thing, and no particular thing exists except in relation to everything else. To explain the relation between Tao and the Great Whole, Fung asks, "Why have Tao in addition to the Great Whole or the universe? Our answer is

16 *Ibid.*, p. 751.

that when we talk about the Great Whole or the universe, we speak from the aspect of tranquillity of all things, whereas when we talk about Tao, we speak from the aspect of activity of all things."[17]

The interpenetration of principle and material force and the ultimate identity of Tao and the Great Whole provide a basis for the identity of sageliness within and kingliness without that Fung champions in *The Spirit of Chinese Philosophy*. Here he stresses that precisely because the absolute (Great Whole) is present in the concrete things and actual processes of everyday living, the aim of life must be to achieve perfection within everyday practice. Perfection cannot be achieved through detachment from or abandonment of the actual world of experience. Rather, this world and this self must be transformed through regular practice of the highest ideal within the ordinary affairs of life.

With the establishment of the People's Republic in 1948, Fung entered into a fifth stage of his philosophical development. Turning to serious study of Marxism-Leninism and the thought of Mao Tse-tung, he searched for a way to apply philosophy to the task of transforming Chinese society. His goal now was to go beyond the idealism and abstract ideas of his earlier work in order to improve the lives of the people. In making this transition, Fung distinguished between the abstract and the concrete meaning of philosophical ideas, emphasizing the importance of the concrete for improving the lives of the people, but insisting also that without considering the abstract meaning one could not see the whole picture.

In a major Chinese conference on philosophy in 1957 Fung said,

> In the past I have paid attention almost entirely to the abstract meaning of some of these [philosophical] premises. This, of course, is wrong. Only in the last several years have we paid attention to their concrete meaning. . . . But their abstract meaning should also be taken into consideration. To neglect it would be to miss the total picture. . . .[18]

Later, in the spirit of mutual self-criticism that dominated the conference, Fung added,

> What we have to continue is essentially the materialistic thought in the history of Chinese philosophy, the type of thought that is for the people, scientific, and progressive. I did not particularly mention this because I thought it was a

[17] *Ibid.*, p. 759.
[18] *Ibid.*, p. 778.

matter of course. That shows that I believed in continuing anything abstract whether it was idealistic or materialistic.

This clearly shows Fung struggling to revolutionize his own thought, trying to overcome what he now perceived to be the idealistic errors of his earlier thought. Through mutual self-criticism he was able to see that earlier categories and habits of thought were still dominant. This led him to append still another "confessional" statement to his earlier remarks: "What I said in my article is incomplete and my presentation of the problem is also incorrect."[19]

In his practice of self-criticism, Fung now began to rewrite his *History of Chinese Philosophy*. But when the Cultural Revolution began in 1966 he decided that the first two volumes of his *New History of Chinese Philosophy* were still written from a largely idealistic and abstract perspective. Thoroughly committed now to Marxist and Maoist thought, Fung decided to rewrite the entire *History* from a Maoist-Marxist perspective, using the ideology of the Cultural Revolution as a guideline, a project on which he is still working.

Mao Tse-tung

The thought of Mao Tse-tung (1894–1976) has dominated philosophy in contemporary China. Mao was influenced greatly by Marx and Lenin, but his philosophy is frequently in tune with the principles and attitudes of traditional Chinese philosophies. After his death, as China adopted a more conciliatory posture toward both the West and traditional thought, Mao's philosophy has undergone extensive criticism. But it continues to be used as a guide to a creative interpretation of experience harmonizing Marxist and traditional thought.

Mao's most important philosophical work is probably his lecture delivered in 1937 entitled "On Practice." In this lecture he explained the relation between theory and practice, showing how theory originates in practice and returns to practice for its justification and fulfillment. This approach to the relation between theory and practice grew out of Mao's practice in reconciling the differences among the people as leader of the revolutionary forces. It is not a theory worked out for its own sake, but for the practical purpose of establishing the Great Harmony—the age-old Chinese utopia.

---

[19] *Ibid.*, p. 779.

To see the practical aims presupposed by Mao's theory of the relation between practice and theory it is helpful to consider the address commemorating the twenty-eighth anniversary of the Communist Party of China. In that address Mao outlined the aims of Communist practices in China as follows: "When classes disappear, all instruments of class struggle —parties and the state machinery—will lose their function, cease to be necessary, therefore will gradually wither away and end their historical mission; and humanity will move to a higher stage."[20] The concluding phrase—"human society will move to a higher stage"—reveals Mao's concern for the human condition. Of course, improving the human condition has always been the foremost consideration among Chinese philosophers. It was the hope of the Confucians and Neo-Confucians that when *jen* was made to prevail the Great Harmony would be achieved. That Mao sees the aim of Communist practice to be the achievement of the Great Harmony is clear from his remark that the Party's function is that of ". . . working hard to create the conditions in which classes, state power, and political parties will die out very naturally and mankind will enter the realm of the Great Harmony."[21]

To achieve the Great Harmony, Mao considered it necessary to understand the conditions which regulate the growth and development of humanity and the world, so that the natural processes of growth and development can be assisted in arriving at their final goal. Probably the most important principle to be understood in this connection is that "all processes have a beginning and an end; all processes transform themselves into their opposites. The stability of all processes is relative, but the mutuality manifested in the transformation of one process into another is absolute."[22] No doubt, this principle is the central feature of the dialectic of Marxism, but it also restates the Taoist principle that "reversal is the way of Tao," and that "all things have their opposites." It is a restatement of the Neo-Confucian explanation of the source and structure of all things that has its initial expression in Chou Tun-i's concept of the Great Ultimate, which generates all things through the interaction of the opposites *yin* and *yang*. Mao is quite aware that he is here well within the mainstream of traditional Chinese thought, for he remarks in the same paragraph, "We Chinese often say, 'Things opposed to each other complement each other.' "[23]

---

[20] *Mao Tse-tung: An Anthology of His Writings*, edited with an introduction by Ann Freemantle (New York: New American Library, 1962), p. 184.
[21] *Ibid.*, p. 185.
[22] *Ibid.*, p. 237.
[23] *Ibid.*, p. 238.

According to the dialectical relation between knowing and doing that Mao presents in his lecture "On Practice," knowing begins with practice, moves to the stage of theory, and is completed in doing. Theory represents the halfway house of knowing. Taking seriously the principle that the great dialectic of nature is "reversal of opposites," and holding that the dialectic of any particular thing is also according to this principle, Mao is concerned with the opposites of theory and practice. His concern, of course, is with the successful democratic socialization of the People's Republic. This process, like any other process, proceeds according to its inner dialectic, and for the sake of successful practice Mao is concerned to understand the dialectical relation between practice and theory, for these are the two primary opposites in the Communist program.

This problem—the relation between knowing and doing—has nearly always been of central concern to Chinese philosophers. Mao's solution to the problem is in agreement with traditional solutions, for he holds that knowing and doing form a unity. His theory of knowledge maintains that "human knowledge cannot be separated the least bit from practice, and repudiates all incorrect theories which deny the importance of practice or separate knowledge from practice. . . ."[24] Verification of knowledge is had only when the anticipated results are achieved in the process of social practice. The principle is that "if man wants to achieve success in his work, that is, to achieve the anticipated results, he must make his thoughts correspond to the laws of the objective world surrounding him; if they do not correspond, he will fail in practice."[25]

In attempting to show the plausibility of the claim that social practice is the only criterion of truth, Mao argues that all knowledge has its beginnings in practice, in the activity of changing the world. "If you want to know the taste of a pear you must change the pear by eating it yourself."[26] This is the first stage in acquiring knowledge, the stage of perception. The next step consists in "making a rearrangement or a reconstruction; this belongs to the stage of conception, judgment, and inference."[27] Conception, judgment, and inference constitute rational, as opposed to merely perceptual knowledge, and as such provide for theories about the things perceived. But the acquisition of knowledge does not stop here. Just as perceptual knowledge leads to rational knowledge and is incomplete without it, so rational knowledge remains incomplete until it is applied in practice. As Mao points out,

[24] *Ibid.*, p. 203.
[25] *Ibid.*, pp. 201, 202.
[26] *Ibid.*, p. 205.
[27] *Ibid.*, p. 207.

"What Marxist philosophy regards as the most important problem does not lie in understanding the laws of the objective world, thereby becoming capable of explaining it, but in actively changing the world by applying the knowledge of its objective laws."[28]

Knowledge is nothing but meaningless words and empty ideas until it gets embodied in experience. Only in the changing of the person and the changing of the reality encountered in practical activity does knowledge become real. From practice comes theory, and from theory practice proceeds. But theory and practice are not two different things. They are simply the dialectical opposites of one process—living in the world. The advance of knowledge is dialectically coupled to the advance of practice. The development of democratic socialism in China can ignore neither theory nor practice, but must combine them if the cause is to advance. Mao urged that ". . . the development of things should be regarded as their internal and necessary self-movement, that a thing in its movement and the things around it should be regarded as interconnected and interacting upon each other. The basic cause of development of things does not lie outside but inside them, in their internal contradictions."[29]

This is remarkably similar to the Neo-Confucian theory that through the interaction of the opposed principles of *li* and *ch'i* individual things develop and grow, and the universe as a whole is a cosmic dynamic structure of *li* and *ch'i*. The universe as a whole—as the Great Ultimate—functions through the opposites of *yin* and *yang*. The universe is a unity of all things and human beings participate in this unity. This unity is regarded as dynamic rather than static, being of the nature of process. The process is constituted by the relative processes of particular things. This metaphysical conception of the universe is described by Mao as follows: ". . . In the absolute, total process of the development of the universe, the development of each concrete process is relative; hence in the great stream of absolute truth, man's knowledge of the concrete process at any given stage of development is only relatively true. The sum total of innumerable relative truths is the absolute truth."[30]

It would appear, therefore, that in his metaphysics and epistemology Mao carried forward the traditional attitude which sees a unity in particular things and which sees knowledge as inseparable from practice. Consequently, his philosophy also places the traditional emphasis on the unification of humanity through improved practical living.

---

[28] *Ibid.*, p. 209.
[29] *Ibid.*, p. 216.
[30] *Ibid.*, p. 212.

REVIEW QUESTIONS

1. What was the debate about China's modernization, and how did it influence recent Chinese philosophy?
2. What is the basis for K'ang Yu-wei's reform efforts?
3. Explain what Chang Tung-sun means when he says ". . . ideas . . . are secretly controlled by social needs."
4. What are the three central ideas worked out in Hsiung Hsi-li's *New Doctrine of Consciousness-Only?*
5. How does Fung Yu-lan view the relation between science and metaphysics in his *New Rational Philosophy?* Compare his view of the relation between substance and function with that of Hsiung Hsi-li.
6. According to Mao Tse-tung, what is the relationship between knowledge and practice? Is this a Marxist view or a traditional view?

FURTHER READING

China's Struggle to Modernize, second edition, by Michael Gasster (New York: Alfred A. Knopf, 1982), is a comprehensive and relatively brief introduction to twentieth-century China. The focus is on the tension between the simultaneous effort to modernize and to retain a traditional cultural identity. The roots of modern change are traced to interaction with the West and reinterpretation of traditional thought.

Mao Tse-tung's Theory of Dialectic, by Francis Y. K. Soo (Dordrecht, The Netherlands: D. Reidel Publishing Co., 1981), is a careful examination of Mao's understanding of the dialectical nature of reality. Using crosscultural analysis, Soo argues that Mao's understanding is fully as much Chinese as it is Marxist. He does a good job of showing how the theory of dialectic is the basis of Maoist thought.

A Source Book in Chinese Philosophy, translated and compiled by Wing-tsit Chan (Princeton: Princeton University Press, 1969), has separate chapters on each of the thinkers covered in this chapter. The concluding chapter, "Chinese Philosophy in Communist China," includes reports from the 1957 Conference on Philosophy.

Sources of Chinese Tradition, volume II, compiled by William Theodore de Bary, et al. (New York: Columbia University Press, 1964), is devoted entirely to modern China. Beginning with the opening of China to the West, successive chapters trace the dialectic of China's modernization up to 1960. The introductions are excellent and the sources illuminating, making this an excellent place to begin. The book goes well with Gasster's *China's Struggle to Modernize*.

Glossary of Oriental Words

In order to facilitate pronunciation of Oriental terms and names a phonetic spelling has been provided as a guide. No indications have been provided for accenting syllables because according to native grammarians Sanskrit and related languages place equal emphasis on each syllable. However, since in practice pronunciation without accenting a particular syllable is extremely difficult, the rule generally adopted by modern grammarians and linguists is to accent the last syllable containing a long vowel.

The glossary is organized so that the first column gives the term or name as it appears in the text. The next column provides the usual scholarly transliteration wherever this differs from the form given in the first column. In cases where Sanskrit and Pali terms are sometimes used interchangeably the correct transliterations for both languages are given. The letter *P* next to a word indicates that it is the Pali form; the letter *S* next to a word indicates that it is the Sanskrit form. The third column gives a phonetic pronunciation of the name or term. The fourth column provides information about the items in the first column.

WORD AS IT APPEARS IN THE TEXT	SCHOLARLY TRANSLITERATION	PHONETIC PRONUNCIATION	EXPLANATION
Abhidharma		ah bee dar mah	Collections of advanced reflections on *dharma*
Abhidhar-makosha	*Abhidharmakośa*	ah bee dar mah ko shah	A systematic treatment of Abhidharma philosophy from the Sarvāstivādin viewpoint by Vasubandhu
Agni		ugh nee	Vedic fire god
Aham Brahman Asi		ah hum brah mun us ee	"I am Brahman"
Ahamkara	Ahaṁkāra	ah hum kah rrah	In Sāṁkhya, the principle of individuation. (Lit. "I-maker.")
Ahimsa	Ahiṁsā	ah him sah	Non-hurting
Alaya-Vijnana	Ālaya-Vijñāna	ah lye ah vih gnyah nah	Source of consciousness
Anatta		ah not ah	No permanent self
Anicca		ah nee chah	Impermanence of all existence
Aparashailas	Aparaśailas	ah pah rah shy lus	A Mahāyāna school of thought
Aranyaka	Āraṇyaka	ah rahn yah kah	A portion of the Veda containing reflections on sacrifice
Arhat		are hot	In Theravāda Buddhism, a person enobled by becoming perfect
Arjuna		are joo nah	Leader of the Pāṇḍavas to whom Kṛṣṇa conveys the teachings of the *Gītā*
Artha		are tah	Means of life
Artha Shastra	*Artha Śāstra*	are tah sha strah	Treatise on politics by Kauṭilya.
Aryadeva	Āryadeva	are yah day vah	Mādhyamika philosopher who was a pupil of Nāgārjuna

WORD AS IT APPEARS IN THE TEXT	SCHOLARLY TRANSLITERATION	PHONETIC PRONUNCIATION	EXPLANATION
Asatkaryavada	Asatkāryavāda	ah sot kar yah vah dah	The theory that a cause brings some new being into existence
Ashrama	Āśrama	ahsh rah mah	A stage in life; a place to "do one's thing"
Ashvaghosa	Aśvaghosa	ahsh vah gho shah	Buddhist philosopher who emphasized the "thusness" of all existents
Ashvapti Kaikeya	Aśvapti Kaikeya	ush vup tee kye kay ah	A much respected sage referred to in the *Chāndogya Upaniṣad*
Atharva Veda		ah tarh vah vay dah	The fourth Veda, representing ancient popular Indian religion
Atman	Ātman	aht mun	The innermost self
Aurobindo	Aurobindo Ghose	oro been dough	Twentieth-century Indian philosopher who championed the spiritual nature of man and the world
Ayatana	Āyatana	i ah tah nah	Basis of sensation
Badarayana	Bādarāyaṇa	bah dah rah yah nah	Author of the *Vedānta Sūtra*
Bahushrutiyas	Bahuśrutīyas	bah hoo shroo tee yahs	An early Mahāyāna school
Bhadrayaniyas	Bhadrāyaṇīyas	bha drrah yah nee yahs	One of the Sthaviravādin schools, most likely an offshoot from the Vātīputrīyas
Bhashya	Bhāṣya	bhosh yah	Commentary on a text
Bhaskara	Bhāskara	bhosh kah rah	Ninth-century Vedānta philosopher
Bhava		bah vah	Becoming
Bhavacakra		bah vah chock rah	Wheel of becoming
Bhikku		bhih koo	Buddhist monk
Bhishma	Bhīṣma	beesh mah	One of the heroes of the *Mahābhārata*

WORD AS IT APPEARS IN THE TEXT	SCHOLARLY TRANSLITERATION	PHONETIC PRONUNCIATION	EXPLANATION
Bodhisattva		boh dhee sah twa	An enlightened and compassionate being
Brahmacarya		brrah mah cha rree yah	Student stage of life
Brahman		brrah mun	The ultimate reality
Brahmana	Brāhmaṇa	brrah muh nah	A member of the priestly class; the ritual portion of the Veda
Brihadaranyaka	Bṛhadāraṇayaka Upaniṣad	brrih had dah rahn yah kah oo pah nee shod	One of the oldest Upaniṣads
Buddha		boo dhah	Enlightened; honorific title given Gautama
Budila Ashvatarashvi	Buḍila Aśvatarāśvi	boo dill ah ahsh vah tah rahsh vee	One of the five householders who sought Self-Knowledge from Aśvapti Kaikeya in the Chāndogya
Buddhaghosa		boo dha gho shah	Buddhist philosopher of the Theravāda tradition, fourth century A.D.
Buddhi		boo dhe	Enlightenment
Caittikas		chye tih kahs	One of the early Mahāyāna schools
Candrakirti	Candrakīrti	chan drrah keer tee	A Mādhyamika philosopher, sixth century A.D.
Carvaka	Cārvāka	char vah kah	A materialistic and skeptical Indian philosophy
Ch'an	Ch'an	chaan	The Chinese school of Buddhism which in Japan came to be known as Zen
Chanagankas		cha nah gahnk us	A Theravāda school, most likely a branch of the Vātsīputrīya school
Chandogya Upanishad	Chāndogya Upaniṣad	chun dogh yah	One of the earliest Upaniṣads

WORD AS IT APPEARS IN THE TEXT	SCHOLARLY TRANSLITERATION	PHONETIC PRONUNCIATION	EXPLANATION
Chang tsai		jung tzie	Neo-Confucian philosopher of the eleventh century A.D.
Chang tung-sun		jung doong soon	Twentieth-century Chinese philosopher
Ch'eng		jheng	Sincerity
Ch'eng hao		jheng how	Eleventh-century Neo-Confucian philosopher
Ch'eng I		jheng ee	Eleventh-century Neo-Confucian Philosopher
Chen-yen		jhen yen	Chinese Buddhist school
Ch'i		jhee	Material force; concrete thing
Chih		chee	Moral Wisdom
Chih liang-chih		chee lang chee	Doctrine of the extension of the innate knowledge of good
Ch'in		chin	The Chinese state from which the name "China" derived
Ching-t'u		jing too	Pure Land school of Buddhism
Chou Tun-i		chou toon ee	A pioneer of Neo-Confucianism (1017–1073)
Chuang Tzu		jwung dzuh	Taoist philosopher of the third or fourth century B.C.
Chu Hsi		jhoo she	A major Neo-Confucian philosopher (1130–1200)
Ch'un Ch'iu		choon chew	Spring and Autumn
Ch'ung Yung		jhoong yoong	Doctrine of the Mean
Citta		chih tah	Mind-stuff
Darshana	Darśana	dahr sha nah	Vision
Dharma		dhahr mah	Righteousness; duty as determined by righteousness

WORD AS IT APPEARS IN THE TEXT	SCHOLARLY TRANSLITERATION	PHONETIC PRONUNCIATION	EXPLANATION
Dharma Shastra	Dharma Śāstra	dhahr mah sha strah	Treatise on dharma
Dharma-guptakas		dharh mah goop tah kahs	A school of Theravāda Buddhism
Dharmakirti	Dharmakīrti	dhar mah keer tee	A Buddhist logician of the sixth century
Dharmottara		dharh moh tah rah	Ninth-century Buddhist logician of the Sautrāntika school
Dharmottariyas		dharh moh tah rree yahs	A school of Theravāda Buddhism
Dhatu	Dhātu	dah too	Element of existence
Dinnaga	Diṅnāga	dingh nah gah	A Buddhist logician, pupil of Vasubandhu
Dukkha		doo kah	Suffering, unwholesomeness
Ekavyava-harikas	Ekavyava-hārikas	eh kah veeah vah ha rree kahs	A Mahāyāna Buddhist school
Fung-yu-lan		foong you lon	Twentieth-century Chinese philosopher
Gaudapada	Gauḍapāda	gwad ah pah dah	Early Vedāntic philosopher
Gautama Siddhartha	Gautama Siddhārtha	go tom ah sid darh tah	The founder of Buddhism
Grihastha	Gṛhastha	grrih hah stah	Householder stage
Gunas	Gunas	goo nahs	In Sāṁkhya, the material constituents of things
Guru		goo roo	Spiritual teacher
Haimavatas		hye mah vah tahs	Early school of Theravāda Buddhism
Han fei tzu		hun fay dzuh	Early Chinese philosopher identified with the Legalist school
Han yu	Han yü	hun yewh	One of the earliest Neo-Confucianists (768–824)
Harada-roshi		hah rah dah row she	Twentieth-century Japanese Zen master
Hetu		hay too	Reason (for something)
Hsi-shih		she she	Legendary beauty of ancient China

WORD AS IT APPEARS IN THE TEXT	SCHOLARLY TRANSLITERATION	PHONETIC PRONUNCIATION	EXPLANATION
Hsiung shih-li		shoong she lee	Twentieth-century Chinese philosopher (b. 1885)
Hsiao		showe	Familial love
Hsun tzu	Hsün tzu	shoon dzuh	Naturalistic Confucian philsopher (third century B.C.)
Hua-yen		whah yen	School of Chinese Buddhism
Hui Shih		hoo she	Chinese logician, fourth century B.C.
I-ching		ee jhing	Book of Changes
Indra		in drrah	Vedic god of the heavens
Indradyumna Bhallaveya	Indradyumna Bhāllaveya	in drrahd youm nah bhah lah vay ah	In the *Chāndogya*, a householder seeking Self-knowledge
Ishvara Krishna	Īśvara kṛṣṇa	eesh vah rah krish nah	Sāṁkhya philosopher, author of the *Sāṁkhya Kārikā*
Jana Sharkarakshya	Jana Śārkarākṣya	john ah shar kah rahks yah	In the *Chāndogya*, a householder seeking Self-knowledge
Jati	Jāti	jah tee	Birth; class determined by birth
jen		wren	Humanness of a person
joshu		jah shoo	Buddhist monk to whom the mu-koan is attributed
Kama	Kāma	comma	Pleasure
Kama shastra	Kāma Śāstra	comma shah strah	A treatise on the pleasures of love
Kamashila	Kamaśila	comma she la	A Yogācāra philosopher, probably eighth century
Kanada	Kaṇāda	kah nah dah	Vaiśeṣika philosopher, author of the *Vaiśeṣika Sutra*, probably third century B.C.
Kapilavastu		kah pih lah vus too	Birth place of the Buddha

WORD AS IT APPEARS IN THE TEXT	SCHOLARLY TRANSLITERATION	PHONETIC PRONUNCIATION	EXPLANATION
Karma		car mah	Action; effect of action
Kashyapitas	Kāśyapītas	kahsh yah pee tahs	School of Theravāda Buddhism
Katha Upanishad	*Kaṭha Upaniṣad*	Kah tah oo pah nih shod	One of the older Upaniṣads
Kena Upanishad	*Kena Upaniṣad*	kay nah oo pah nih shod	One of the older Upaniṣads
Koan		cone	Problem set for a Zen pupil
Krishna	Kṛṣṇa	krrish nah	An incarnation of the ultimate reality, Arjuna's teacher in the *Bhagavad Gītā*
Kshatriya	Kṣatriya	kshot ree yah	Class of the protectors of society
Kukkulikas		koo koo lih kahs	An early school of Mahāyāna
Kumarajiva	Kumārajīva	koo mah rah jee vah	Mādhyamika philosopher, probably fourth century
K'un		koon	Earth; hexagram representing earth
Kung-sun Lung		koong soon loong	Chinese logician, fourth century, B.C.
Kuo Hsiang		Kwo shang	Third century Neo-Taoist philosopher
Lankavatara	Lankāvatāra	lahnk ah vah tah rah	The *Lankāvatāra Sūtra* is one of the very early Mahāyāna texts.
Lao Tzu		lao dzuh	Early Taoist philosopher, probably fifth century B.C.
Li		lee	Principle
Li Ao		lee ow	Eighth century philosopher instrumental in reviving Confucianism
Li Chi		lee chee	Book of Rites
Lokottaravadins	Lokottaravādins	loh koh tah rah vah dins	Early Mahāyāna school
Lu		loo	Native state of Confucius

WORD AS IT APPEARS IN THE TEXT	SCHOLARLY TRANSLITERATION	PHONETIC PRONUNCIATION	EXPLANATION
Lu Chiu-yuan	Lu Chiu-yüan	loo choo yoon	Neo-Confucian philosopher (1139–1193)
Lun Yu	*Lun Yü*	loon you	Analects or sayings of Confucius
Madhva		mudh vah	Dualistic Vedānta philosopher
Madhyamika	Mādhyamika	mah dhyah mee kah	Relativistic school of Buddhist philosophy
Madhyamika Karika	*Mādhyamika Kārikā*	mah dhyah mee kah kah ree kah	One of the main critical works of Nāgarjuna
Mahabharata	*Mahābhārata*	mah ha bha rah tah	One of two main long epics of India
Mahasanghika	Mahāsanghika	mah ha sangh hee kah	The large group of Buddhist monks who split off from the rest of the order in the third century B.C.
Mahat		mah hot	"The great one"
Mahayana	Mahāyāna	mah ha yah nah	One of the two main groups of Buddhists
Mahishasakas	Mahīśāsakas	mah hee shah sah kahs	An early school of Theravāda Buddhism
Manu		mun ooh	Indian social philosopher, probably fourth century B.C.
Mao Tse-tung		Mao dzuh doong	Chinese communist leader
Mencius		muhn shoos	Idealistic Confucian philosopher, fourth century B.C.
Mimamsa	Mīmāṁsā	mee mahm sah	Ritualistic school of Vedānta
Ming		ming	Destiny
Mohism		mo izm	Utilitarian school of philosophy named after Mo Tzu
Moksa	Mokṣa	moke shah	Liberation
Mo Tzu		mo dzuh	Utilitarian Chinese philosopher of the late fifth century B.C.
Mu-koan		moo kone	One of Joshu's famous answerless Zen questions

WORD AS IT APPEARS IN THE TEXT	SCHOLARLY TRANSLITERATION	PHONETIC PRONUNCIATION	EXPLANATION
Mundaka Upanishad	*Muṇḍaka Upaniṣad*	moon dah kah ooh pah nih shad	One of the early Upaniṣads
Nagarjuna	Nāgārjuna	nah gar joo nah	Mādhyamika philosopher, second century
Nama-rupa	Nāma-rūpa	nah mah roo pah	Mind-body complex
Nastika	Nāstika	nah stee kah	Unorthodox schools of Indian thought
Nibbana	Nibbāna (S. Nirvāṇa)	nee bah nah	The Buddhist goal of sufferingless existence
Nyaya	Nyāya	nyah yah	Indian school of logic
Paksha	Pakṣa	pahkh shah	Minor term of a syllogism
Panchatantra	*Pañcatantra*	pah cha tahn trah	Collection of Indian fables and stories
Paravidya		pah rah vih dhyah	Higher wisdom
Pataliputta	Pāṭaliputta	pah tah lih puh tah	Place of the third Buddhist council
Patanjali	Patañjali	pah tahn jah lee	Author of the *Yoga Sūtras*
Paticca Samuppada	Paṭicca Samuppāda (S. Pratītya Samutpāda)	pah tee cha sah moo pah dah	Dependent origination
P'eng-tsu		peng dzuh	Legendary Chinese Methusala
Pracinasala Aupamanyava	Prācīnaśāla Aupamanyava	prra chih na shah lah oh pah mah nyah vah	In the *Chāndogya*, one of the Householders seeking Self-knowledge
Prajapati	Prajāpati	prah jah pah tee	Hindu Lord of Creation
Prajnaptivadins	Prajñaptivādins	prah gnyahp tee vah dins	Early school of Mahāyāna
Prakriti	Prakṛti	prah krrih tee	In Sāṁkhya, the source of the material universe
Pudgala	(P. Puggala)	puhd gah lah	Substratum of personality
Purusha	Puruṣa	puh roo shah	In Sāṁkhya, the source of spirituality
Purushartha	Puruṣārtha	puh roo sharh tah	Aim in life

WORD AS IT APPEARS IN THE TEXT	SCHOLARLY TRANSLITERATION	PHONETIC PRONUNCIATION	EXPLANATION
Radhakrishnan		rah dah krrish nun	Twentieth-century Indian scholar, philosopher, statesman
Raja	Rāja	rah jah	King
Rajagaha	Rājagha	rah jah gah hah	Place of the first Buddhist council
Rajas		rah jus	The active element in existence
Rama	Rāma	rah mah	Main hero of the *Rāmayāṇa*
Ramanuja	Rāmānuja	rah mah noo jah	Theistic Vedāntic philosopher of the eleventh century
Ramayana	*Rāmāyana*	rah mah yah nah	One of India's two major epics
Ranee	Rāni	rah nee	Queen
Rigveda	*Ṛgveda*	rrig vay duh	One of the four Vedas making up the ancient Indian vedic literature
Sadhya	Sādhya	sahd yah	Major term of a syllogism
Sama Veda	*Sāma Veda*	sahm vay duh	One of the four Vedas making up the ancient India vedic literature
Samhita	Saṁhīta	sahm hee tah	Portion of the Veda containing hymns of praise and speculation
Samkhya Karika	*Sāṁkhya Kārikā*	sahm khyah kah ree kah	A basic Sāṁkhya text by Īśvara Kṛṣṇa
Sammitiyas	Sāṁmitīyas	sahm ih tee yahs	A Theravāda school, probably an off-shoot of the Vātsīputrīyas
Samnyasa	Saṁnyāsa	sahm nyah sah	Stage in life devoted to complete spiritual realization
Samsara	Saṁsāra	sahm sah rah	Round of births and deaths
Sankhara	Sankhāra (S. Saṁskāra)	sahn kah rah	Impulses to action
Sanna	Saññā	sah nah	Perception

WORD AS IT APPEARS IN THE TEXT	SCHOLARLY TRANSLITERATION	PHONETIC PRONUNCIATION	EXPLANATION
Sarvastivadins	Sarvāstivādins	sahr vah stee vah dins	Realistic Buddhist philosophers, including Vaibhāṣikas and Sautrāntikas
Satkaryavada	Satkāryavāda	saht car yah vah dah	Theory that effects pre-exist in their causes
Satori		sah tory	Zen enlightenment
Sattva		Saht twa	One of the three guṇas constituting all material things
Satyayajna Paulishi	Satyayajña Pauluṣi	soh yah yah gnyah paw loo she	In the *Chāndogya*, one of the householders seeking Self-knowledge
Sauntrantikas	Sautrāntikas	saw trahn tee kahs	A critical school of Buddhist realists
Shabda	Śabda	shahb dah	Word; testimony
Shamkara	Śaṁkara	shum kah rah	Non-dualistic Vedāntic philosopher, eighth century
Shandilya	Śāṇḍīlya	shahn deal yah	Indian sage referred to in the Upaniṣads
Shantarakshita	Śāntarakṣita	sah tah rahk she tah	A later Yogācāra philosopher
Shatapatha Brahmana	*Śatapatha Brāhmaṇa*	shah tah pah tah brrah mun ah	Vedic text explaining the significance of various religious practices
Shih Ching	*Shih Ching*	she jhing	Book of Poetry, one of the Five Classics
Shudra	Śūdra	shoo drrah	Laboring class
Shunya	Śūnya	shoon yah	Empty
Shunyata	Śūnyatā	shoon yah tah	Emptiness
Shurya	Śurya	shoo ree yah	Indian sun god
Shvetaketu	Śvetaketu	shveh tah kay too	In the *Chāndogya*, the recipient of the famous "tat tvam asi" teaching
Sthaviravada	Sthaviravāda	shtah vee rah vah dah	"Teachings of the Elders." The early followers of the Buddha

WORD AS IT APPEARS IN THE TEXT	SCHOLARLY TRANSLITERATION	PHONETIC PRONUNCIATION	EXPLANATION
Sung		soong	Chinese dynasty (960–1279)
Sutra	Sūtra	soo trrah	aphorism or collection of aphorisms
Svatantra		Swa tahn trrah	A Buddhist school midway between Sauntrāntika and Yogācāra
Svabhava	Svabhāva	swah bah vah	Independent existence
Ta Hsueh	*Ta Hsüeh*	dah sheeh	Great Learning
Tai-chen		dye jhen	Chinese empirical philosopher of the eighteenth century
Tai-chi		dye jhee	Great ultimate
Taittiriya Upanishad	*Taittīriya Upaniṣad*	tye tee ree yah oo pah nee shod	One of the early Upaniṣads
Tamas		tom us	One of the three guṇas making up all things
Tathagata	Tathāgata	tah taah gah tah	"Thus gone." Honorific title of Gautama Siddhārtha
Tao		dow	The way of ultimate reality
Tao Te Ching		dow day jhing	Basic text of Taoism, attributed to Lao Tzu
Tathata	Tathāta	tah taah tah	The "thusness" of things
Tat Tvam Asi		tut twum us ee	"Thou art That"
Te		day	Virtue; power
Theravada	Theravāda	tehr rah vaah dah	The more conservative branch of Buddhism
T'ien-t'ai		dee en die	School of Chinese Buddhism
Tung Chung-shu		doong choong shoo	Confucian philospher responsible for making Confucianism the state ideology (second century)

WORD AS IT APPEARS IN THE TEXT	SCHOLARLY TRANSLITERATION	PHONETIC PRONUNCIATION	EXPLANATION
Turiya	Turīya	too ree yah	The fourth stage of consciousness wherein the real Self is discovered
Uddalaka Aruni	Uddālaka Āruṇi	oo dah lah kah ah roo nee	The sage in the *Chāndogya* who teaches his son "tat tvam asi"
Upanishads	Upaniṣads	oo pah nee shods	The concluding portion of the Vedas, containing reflections about ultimate reality
Upanishat	Upaniṣat	oo pah nee shot	Secret; the secret about ultimate reality
Uttarashailas	Uttaraśailas	oo tah rah shy lus	An early school of Mahāyāna
Vacchagotta		vah cha go tah	Man who questioned the Buddha about the nature of the self
Vaibhashika	Vaibhāṣika	vy bah she kah	School of Buddhists who are direct realists
Vaisheshika	Vaiśeṣika	vy shesh ee kah	Hindu system of philosophy that is realistic and pluralistic
Vallabha		vah lah bah	Fifteenth-century Vedantic philosopher
Vanaprastha	Vānaprastha	vaah nah prrah stah	Third stage in life according to the āśrama theory
Varna	Varṇa	vahr nah	Class
Vasubandhu		vahs oo bahn dhoo	Sautrāntika and Yogācāra philosopher of the fifth century
Vatsiputriyas	Vātsīputrīyas	vaht see put rree yahs	Early school of Theravāda Buddhism
Vatsyayana	Vātsyayāna	vaaht see ah yaah nah	Author of the *Kāma Sūtra*
Vayu	Vāyu	vaah yoo	Ancient Indian god of the wind
Vedana	Vedanā	vay dah nah	Sensation or feeling

WORD AS IT APPEARS IN THE TEXT	SCHOLARLY TRANSLITERATION	PHONETIC PRONUNCIATION	EXPLANATION
Vedanta	Vedānta	vay daahn tah	The system of philosophy with its basis in the Upaniṣads
Vesali	Vesālī	veh saah lee	Place of the second Buddhist council
Vinnana	Viññāna (S. Vijñāna)	vih naah nah	Consciousness
Virocana		vee row cha nah	A chief demon in Hindu mythology
Wang Yang-ming		wang yang ming	Idealistic Neo-Confucian philosopher (1472–1529)
Wu-wei		woo way	No artificial action
Yajnavalkya	Yājñavalkya	yaah gnyah vul khyah	Famous sage in ancient India
Yajur Veda		yah joor vay dah	One of the four Vedas or sacred texts of Hinduism
Yamuna	Yāmuna	yaah moo nah	Theistic Vedāntic philosopher of the tenth century
Yang		yang	Active principle of the universe
Yang Chu		yang choo	Early Taoist philosopher who emphasized self-preservation
Yashomitra	Yaśomitra	yah show mih trah	A Sautrāntika philosopher of the sixth century
Yi		yee	Righteousness
Yin		yin	Passive principle of the universe
Yin-yang		yin-yang	Theory of the interaction between yin and yang as a cause of all things
Yoga		yoh guh	Discipline
Yogacara	Yogācāra	yoh guh cha rah	Idealist school of Buddhism
Zazen		za zen	Zen discipline
Zen		zen	Form of Buddhism developed and practiced in China, Korea, and Japan

Index